| DATE DUE | | | |
|---|---|---|---|
| | | | |
| | | | |
| | | | |
| | | | |
| | | | |
| | | | |
| | | | |
| | | | |
| | | | |
| | | | |
| | | | |
| | | | |
| | | | |

Drawing by Elbert L. Nelson

WILLIAM SWAIM

# WILLIAM SWAIM
## FIGHTING EDITOR
*The Story of O. Henry's Grandfather*

by

ETHEL STEPHENS ARNETT

*These are perilous times; and a responsibility,
awful as the tomb and extensive as eternity, hangs
over every man who shall take upon himself the
management of a newspaper.* — William Swaim.

GREENSBORO, NORTH CAROLINA
Piedmont Press
1963

# ACKNOWLEDGMENT

For assistance without which this book could not have been written, very special thanks are due:

To the late Nellie Rowe Jones, former Librarian of the Greensboro Public Library, who followed with perceptive interest my work on William Swaim whom she introduced to me through material published in the *Greensboro Patriot* in 1866, and discovered by her well-nigh a century later;

To Josephine Hege, Associate Professor of History at the Woman's College of the University of North Carolina, who as a consultant and painstaking critic read this work, chapter by chapter, with great discrimination, making excellent suggestions for effective organization of material and clarity of composition, thus improving the writing in style and perspective;

To Dr. Albert S. Keister, Professor Emeritus and former Head of the Department of Economics at the Woman's College of the University of North Carolina, who read the completed manuscript and gave it the benefit of his sound judgment;

To Dr. Sidney Swaim Robins, grandnephew of William Swaim and onetime Head of the Department of Philosophy, St. Lawrence University, who read the book as a representative of the family and as a constructive literary critic;

To Dr. Elmer L. Puryear, Professor of History at Greensboro College, who with particular thought toward historical background, read the manuscript in its final draft and made helpful suggestions;

To Anne McKaughan Farrell, former President of The Art Shop, Inc., in Greensboro, whose technical knowledge of photography and interest in books made her assistance with the illustrations and criticism of this writing unusually valuable;

To the late Fielding L. Fry, business man and former Mayor of the City of Greensboro, and to Andrew Joyner, Jr., lawyer and one-time editor of the *Greensboro Patriot,* who read the manuscript and offered their advice on its content;

To Joshua E. Murrow, lifetime resident and reliable historian of Centre Community, who in private interviews furnished much of the material in Chapter I;

To Lorene J. Ballinger, Chief Index Clerk of the Guilford County Register of Deeds, and Iola Lowdermilk, Assistant Index Clerk of the Guilford County Register of Deeds, who helped me with official records and other primary sources of information;

To Hope Hubbard and Dorothy Hubbard Kearns, second cousins of William Sydney Porter and residents of William Swaim's vicinity, who traveled with me to every spot Swaim is known to have frequented and aided in many other ways to facilitate the writing of this book;

To the staff members of the Greensboro Public Library, the Library of the Woman's College of the University of North Carolina, the Library of Duke University, the Library of the University of North Carolina, the Library of Guilford College, the North Carolina State Library, the North Carolina State Department of Archives and History, the Library of Congress, for their interest and co-operation: especially to Olivia Burwell, Librarian, and Irene Hester, Reference Librarian, the Greensboro Public Library, for giving attention to my frequent requests; to Sue Vernon Williams, Reference Librarian, Woman's College of the University of North Carolina, and to Treva W. Mathis, Assistant Librarian, Guilford College Library, for assistance beyond the call of duty; to Emerson Ford, Assistant Librarian, Library of Duke University, for arranging for me to have in Greensboro the use of odd numbers of the *Greensborough Patriot,* 1826-1836; and to Josephine M. Tharpe, Reference Librarian, Cornell University Library, for making available to me microfilm copies of *The Genius of Universal Emancipation* for the period when William Swaim was its assistant editor; and

To Lillian Jones Carter, who typed the manuscript in its final draft, making suggestions as to facts and structure.

Needless to say, for unlimited permission to use the extant issues of the *Greensborough Patriot,* my deep gratitude goes to Carl O.

Jeffress, General Manager of the Greensboro News Company, which owns the title of the *Greensboro Patriot*.

In the search for data and in the writing of this book, many persons have given generously of their time and knowledge. These contributors, though far too numerous to name, will forever be the recipients of my sincere gratitude.

ETHEL STEPHENS ARNETT

Greensboro, 1963

To My Children:

Georgia Anna Arnett Bonds
Dorothy Stephens Arnett Dixon

# ILLUSTRATIONS

# CONTENTS

# I

## CENTRE COMMUNITY

*"On a clear, cold morning in March, 1828, as the newly-risen sun was brilliantly reflected from the tin-roofs and glittering spires of the Monumental city [Baltimore], a steamboat from Norfolk rode proudly into the bay and up to the wharf. Among the passengers, who descended from it, was a young man, apparently about twenty-five years of age, of middle size and of erect and symmetrical person. This was William Swaim, [a] poor but gifted and ambitious student, . . . now in the pride of strong and buoyant young manhood. His appearance was strikingly handsome. His hair was very black; his beard thick and heavy, but always closely shaven; his forehead, broad, and full in the upper portion, so much so as to make the region of the brow appear flat; his eyebrows, thick and dark; his jaws, square and firmly set; his nose slightly* retrousse, *just enough to give piquancy to that feature and to the whole countenance; his mouth, large, with full under lip; his chin, broad and square, with a dimple in the middle; his eyes dark and, when in conversation, absolutely sparkling with fun, or glowing with the emotion of the moment. As he looked around, nothing save strange scenes and strange faces met him. Truly, he was alone, and the weight of anxiety began to depress his heart. But his heart was rallied by that encouraging Roman sentiment* per angusta ad augusta. *Difficulties were obliged to be encountered and overcome in the path to usefulness and eminence. — From this philosophizing, he took hope and set his face forward toward the heart of the city."*[1]

1

The young man thus described by Will L. Scott was William Swaim, on his way to learn the art of printing. He was taking the first step toward becoming a newspaper editor. Archibald Henderson in his *North Carolina, The Old North State and the New*, called William Swaim a "fiery crusader for freedom and humanity."[2] Other writers have called him talented, intelligent, witty, humorous, sarcastic, and satiric. His contemporaries called him "Friend Swaim," "independent editor," "friend of the people," "libeler," "slanderer," and even "editor of a corrupt sheet," depending upon their reaction to his ideas.[3] Swaim was owner and editor of the *Greensborough Patriot* from May, 1829, through December, 1835,[4] a time in American history when issues were very serious, and feelings ran high. Because his life was short, and the times turbulent, personal records of this young man are very few. From the extant issues of his own newspaper, however, he emerges clearly a man of character, conviction, and courage.

William Swaim was born on December 16, 1802, in Centre Community, a largely Quaker agricultural area in the southern part of Guilford County, North Carolina. Here his forefathers had put down their roots as pioneers. He represented the fourth generation which had pried a livelihood from Guilford soil—a livelihood that had been dependent upon thrift and ingenuity, but that had had its compensations in neighborhood interests. These Swaims were not Quakers; their names do not appear in William Wade Hinshaw's North Carolina volume of *Encyclopedia of American Quaker Genealogy*, nor in other Quaker records,[5] but they were an integral part of this community.

As early as 1740 Centre Community had been settled by the Hocketts, Dicks, Osbornes, Beasons, Bayles, and other Friends from Pennsylvania. In the later years of 1771 to 1775 a group of Nantucket Islanders—the Macys, Gardners, Worths, Coffins, Folgers, and others—had moved in, bringing new blood, new ideas, and a spirit of daring. For years upon years they had been whalers, but when that industry was no longer sufficient to support a rapidly growing population, many of them turned southward, using their whaling ships to convey them to Charleston, South Carolina. There they sold their seagoing vessels and bought oxcarts, by which they transported themselves to Centre. Still later the Stanleys, Reynoldses, and other Friends came down from Pennsylvania.[6] Meanwhile the Swaim family and some others who were not Quakers had become established in the same locality. Here in Centre Community, Marmaduke and Sarah Fanning (Fannon) Swaim, William's parents, "set up housekeeping" when they were married in 1798.[7] And although they were good neighbors, like the other inhabitants of Centre, their household through necessity became a self-sustaining institution.

Swaim found encouragement in remembering that he was from a rural community of people who became effective members of society through their own hard efforts. It was a rather promising group, that little nucleus around Centre, during the first quarter of the nineteenth century when Swaim was growing up. William Adams, who was a member of North Carolina's House of Commons in 1821 and later became the first Constable of Greensboro, North Carolina, and his son Peter, who became a notable financier and statesman; Jonathan Parker, who was five times elected to the State House of Commons and eighteen times to the State Senate; James Neely and William Dickey who also served as state representatives; and Statesman Dr. David Worth[8] and his Quaker family composed of his wife and ten living children, all lived in the same locality at the same time as William Swaim. In fact, William Swaim was born one month after Jonathan Worth was born on November 18, 1802; and about two and a half years before Ruth Worth was born on June 3, 1805.[9] So William Swaim, who was to become the maternal grandfather of William Sydney Porter (O. Henry), was from childhood a close friend of the David Worths' oldest living son Jonathan, who was to become governor of North Carolina in 1865-1866, and of Jonathan's sister Ruth, who was to become the paternal grandmother of O. Henry. These three people whose names are now written on the pages of history shared a typical rural existence in the South of the early nineteenth century—an

3

existence at times as prosaic as brogan shoes and at times as colorful as a Piedmont countryside.

When Swaim's family first came to North Carolina, the land from Salisbury to Danville was especially inviting. In order to insure good hunting, the Indians, who had originally claimed the area, had kept much of it burned off in order to afford wide open stretches for growing food for birds and wild beasts; consequently when the white men arrived, they found the country (except along the streams) either prairie or young forests.[10] Its rolling hills, plains, and dales; its cool spring water, brooks, and rivers; and its new woodlands, all were attractive to pioneer settlers. From the beginning the wooded areas were decorated with native dogwood and redbud; the air was full of the clean scent of young pines; and the clearings were edged with hickories, chestnuts, willows, oaks and lacy leafed poplars. Underneath or alongside the trees in season were bluets, violets, anemones, lobelias, asters, goldenrod, and many other flowering specimens, making a gaily colored design upon the surrounding earth. Indeed, during the early days of Guilford (1771) and the adjoining region, it has been said that the variety of wild flowers and wooded growth was exceeded no where else in the world.[11]

Centre settlement was not far from the Quaker community of New Garden, later Guilford College, and the physical appearance of the two localities was so similar that J. Hector St. John DeCrevecoeur's description of New Garden in his *Letters from an American Farmer* was equally applicable to Centre. He wrote: "No spot on earth can be more beautiful; it is composed of gentle hills, of easy declivities, excellent lowlands, accompanied by different brooks which traverse the settlement. I never saw soil that rewards men so easily for their labours and disbursements. . . . It is perhaps the most pleasing, the most bewitching country which the continent affords. . . . The only drawback is that the softness of the climate and easy results from labour lead to too much idleness and effeminacy."[12]

4

As soon as the first white inhabitants of this section were settled, they built two-story houses, for they had large families to rear. William Swaim's parents had eight children, and their dwelling was called the "Mansion House."[13] As was customary in the early days, homes were located near streams in order to have an ample water supply. It was about fifty years before the settlers did much digging of wells. Several of the houses of Centre Community were built alongside Polecat Creek, as was the William Worth House (1810) in which William Swaim's grandson William Sydney Porter was born on September 11, 1862.[14] Old-timers loved to recount how the wind rustling the canebreaks along the stream and wolves howling in the thickets kept them company at night.

They did not know all about Polecat Creek when they built so conveniently near, but in time they learned. Its unpretentious water zigzagged over the land as though it were planned to accommodate the people. Heavy rains, however, would sometimes so swell the creek beyond its bounds that it flooded farms and dwellings. It is said that a resident of the Jonathan Parker house once returned in the dead of night from a business trip to Salisbury only to find himself completely blocked from his family; and that when his loud call awakened his wife from a deep sleep, she stepped from her high four-poster bed and landed in several feet of water.

Practically all families were landowners and their homes were located on their farms. The homesite carried not only a dwelling, but it also became the pivot for various industrial enterprises connected with home and farm. In addition to their agricultural pursuits the people were constantly experimenting with other ideas. In their spare time some became wagon makers, tanners, potters, millwrights, furniture makers, spinning wheel manufacturers, and makers of other useful articles. By the time young Swaim came along, Centre was possessed of capable industrial talents, and citizens were discussing the great need for ways to market their wares.

This was, indeed, a question they needed to discuss, for during the entire first half of the nineteenth century Guilford's transportation facilities to markets were a positive handicap. There were southward dirt roads to Fayetteville and Wilmington in North Carolina, and to Charleston in South Carolina; and northward to Richmond, Petersburg, and Norfolk in Virginia, and to Philadelphia in Pennsylvania. Sometimes Centre farmers would take wagonloads of such saleable items as they had to these market places where they could be exchanged for sugar, salt, and other articles which were not produced on the home farm. Such sales in the main, however, were for subsistence rather than for large profits, for getting barter goods to trade centers often cost as much as producing them. There were freight wagons that passed up and down these highways, collecting marketable produce and in turn distributing such things as the people were able to buy, but their rates were so high that they usually consumed the little profit the farmers might anticipate.

When William Swaim was only a child, some of the more thoughtful citizens were considering how these conditions could be changed. Judge Archibald D. Murphey, a citizen of the general area who knew the conditions well, had put his finger on the basic trouble while he was state senator (1812-1818). It was he who with prophetic insight first advocated better transportation in North Carolina as indispensable to economic development. He even submitted a plan to the General Assembly of North Carolina for a state-wide system of connecting roads, canals, and rivers which would enable the people of the entire state to sell their produce and buy their supplies through North Carolina market towns instead of trading outside the state.[15]

In speaking of such times, inhabitants of Centre in the 1960's told how those who had lived before them, using the trees along Deep River as their guide, had followed the prairie ridges along the stream until they came with their produce to Cross Creek, North Carolina. This route was particularly used for transporting tobacco. The men would pack the tobacco in handmade hogsheads to which had been added shafts; then by hitching horses to the shafts to pull the hogsheads, they rolled them along the grassy elevations to market, where they sold both the tobacco and the wood in the hogsheads in exchange for salt.[16] Such methods of trade were well-known to the Swaims.

Vehicles for travel were also in their early stages of development during Swaim's childhood. Travel for any distance was made by stagecoach (first intercity service in America was inaugurated in 1756) or by wagon. Although the approach of a stagecoach drawn by four or six spirited horses might have aroused as thrilling excitement then as it does in motion pictures of the twentieth century, for actual travelers of that day this method of transportation lost some of its glamour when the passengers had to get out of the coach and help push it through deep-rutted, muddy roads in order to reach their destinations. Sulkies and gigs were often used for private transportation, but they belonged mostly to public men and there were not enough of them to afford much relief to the transportation problem. In the main horseback riding and plain walking were the most commonly used methods of getting around. William Swaim had his own saddle horse to take him wherever he wanted to go, but so far as is known his travels as a youth were limited to his environs and a yearly trek to court in Greensboro, his county seat town.[17]

Communication was equally difficult. The usual means of transferring messages or giving out information was by word of mouth, or through occasional letters carried by stagecoach for a set fee payable by the addressee. During Swaim's boyhood and youth Centre got its mail through near-by Jamestown.[18] This post office distributed subscriptions to newspapers and periodicals which provided some intelligence, but the news was days, perhaps weeks or months old by the time it reached the readers. Sometimes lawyers, traveling from court to court, would carry important documents to their destinations. Nor was this condition in Piedmont North Carolina unusual. Communication all over the nation was about the same.

Although transportation and communication were very real problems and often the subject of conversation, necessarily the first

7

thought in the minds of all in the community was food. The land would grow any product known to the area in the twentieth century, but the wise planter budgeted his land to his needs. There was little market for surplus foods, and extra farm products could in the main for many years be used only for barter. There was very little money in circulation, and from the time Swaim could talk he probably heard his parents figuring on how to get hold of enough specie to pay their taxes. Therefore few edibles were purchased.

Fortunately native food supplies were plentiful. The streams abounded in fresh fish, such as bream, bass, trout, catfish, and suckers. Quail, doves, ruffed grouse, and wild turkeys in great droves were game birds for the hunters' taking. Centre lore is enhanced by old-timers' tales of the way they hunted when they had a yen for turkey meat. They learned the birds' habits of roosting on certain dead trees; and late in the afternoon hunters would conceal themselves in grass or pea vines, which grew as high as a man on horseback, and wait for the turkeys to perch upon the bare limbs. It then became real sport for those expert marksmen to shoot down the fowl of their choice.[19] Squirrel, deer, bear, rabbit, and opossum also provided a variety of meat for the country table. And during the spring and summer wild strawberries, dewberries, blackberries, plums, and grapes dotted the countryside.

Thanks to an early settler of Guilford County, if the seasons were good, home-grown foods were usually ample. This settler, Ann Jessop by name, who had gone back to England on a visit, returned to North Carolina in 1792 and brought with her seeds of many different kinds of garden vegetables such as squash, cabbage, collards, mustard greens, turnips, peas, beans, and many others. She also brought from England cuttings from fine grapevines which were easily rooted, and apple tree sprigs which were used for grafting. The apple trees which grew from graftings later produced a splendid assortment of fruit in the region. Miss Jessop employed one Abijah Pinson to look after her fruit culture, and he did a magnificent job of blending and improving the apples which provided many of the favorites still grown one hundred and fifty years later— the pippin, russet, horse apple, and others.[20] Sheep, goats, hogs, cattle, and poultry were also a part of every thriving homestead. And corn, wheat, barley, and oats yielded a sufficient return to supply most needs.

The barns were sometimes too small to hold the sheaves of grain, and the extra yield was stacked in the fields, for threshing machines did not come into general use before 1860. When flour was needed for family consumption, a wagonload of sheaves would first be taken to a threshing floor where grain was beaten out and cleaned. The resourceful settlers made this threshing contrivance, usually one to a community, by boring holes in the floor of an upstairs room so as to afford an outlet through which the grain might fall. Onto this punctured floor the sheaves were scattered and trained horses were then driven around and around the room in a circular motion until they trampled the grain from the straw. As it was thus separated the grain was collected as it fell below. It was winnowed from the chaff, and was then made into flour. Although the mills would grind corn into meal, they were not at first conditioned to grind flour, for it came through too pasty. Flour, therefore, had to be made by the use of a mortar and pestle. Because of this difficult method, for many years wheat bread was limited to Sunday breakfasts. With improved milling facilities, however, flour became a daily blessing for every table.[21]

The cooking of food during Swaim's childhood still followed the pattern of the pioneer. Most vegetables were prepared in pots and skillets by open fireplaces; however, breads, pies, and roasts, especially in the summer time, were baked in Dutch ovens built of brick or stone in the yard. Whether the bread was baked inside or outside the house, the housewife had to make her own yeast—a process which required forethought and care, for it had to be brewed at least twelve hours in advance of breadmaking. To mix and raise the dough called for additional skill and finesse. Breadmaking alone in Swaim's day was no small undertaking when considered in view of its consumption by predominantly large families whose members worked hard at manual labor.

The early Centre folk preserved their perishable foods expertly, for they made their own "deep freezes." This was accomplished by digging a pit about fifteen feet deep, fitting it with steps and heavy doors, and covering it with a steep-pitched gabled roof which almost touched the ground. Then in the coldest winter months when water was frozen deep on ponds along the streams, the men of the household would cut ice in large blocks and store it in sawdust at the bottom of the pit. There it would remain frozen until winter came again; and perishable foods stored in this icy cavern stayed almost as fresh as if housed in an electric refrigerator.[22] Such a place intrigued imaginative children, and they turned the roofs into fine slides, but parents were plagued with the horror of a child getting shut in behind the heavy doors.

In connection with food, Centre Community's special celebration, unique in the South, was called the "Festival of the Dogs," and was annually observed until the 1860's. The Quaker settlers from Nantucket Island had brought the tradition with them to Centre. Being daring men of the sea, some Nantucket whaling voyagers at one time had plowed through the icy waters of the Arctic Ocean and to their cargo of whale oil had added a pack of Husky dogs. The return voyage to their island had been so long delayed by fierce winds and storms that food had given out and the hardy sailors had been faced with only two alternatives, to eat their dogs and live, or to save their dogs and die. Naturally, they had eaten the dogs and returned safely home. So grateful were they for their preservation that they established a yearly feast in honor of their saviors; and as a part of their festive board each year dog meat was served in memory of the distressing experience. During the passing of time, as DeCrevecouer predicted in 1782, some of the people became more delicate as to their stomachs, and robust men have been known to lose a hearty meal when informed that they had eaten dead dog. Gradually the celebration evolved into a general picnic day. William Swaim thus became a part of the tradition which was observed for almost a century. It was an occasion at Centre which citizens of the mid-twentieth century remembered not only as relatively recent history, but as a memorial to a solemn and courageous voyage.[23]

By the early nineteenth century, however, conditions had greatly changed in Centre Community. William Swaim was becoming concerned because so much of the once fertile soil had been dissipated. The people were being brought face to face with the questions of erosion, worn-out ground, and consequently less yield of fine foods. And worse still was the fact that many of the most promising young people were moving away in search of greener pastures.[24]

Not only did the inhabitants, during the first hundred years of Centre, turn to the land for most of their food, but they also grew materials for and made their own clothing. Each homestead usually had its own sheep, and the farmers took great pride in fine breeds, such as the Merino, to provide warm woolen garments for winter. Sheep culture required year round attention. In the spring when the breeding season was on, great care had to be taken with the lambs; the older sheep had to be sheared; and since herds were free to roam all over the land, they all had to be branded with their owners' marks. These sheep gathered their own food in spring and summer, but it was most essential for owners to see that they were well-provided with salt during the entire year. In fall and winter, after frost had killed the green foliage, the animals had to be corralled for feeding from barns, and for protection against deep snows and hungry wolves.

As soon as the children were old enough to do small tasks they were trained to help with these first stages in the production of cloth. They loved and happily cared for the baby lambs; and they found pleasure in watching these soft looking creatures as they followed their leader on the hillside. But they were terrified at the sound of a lone wolf's cry.

Indeed, wolves furnished the entire community with horror

11

and excitement, for they brought damage and death among a herd of sheep. When one of the sly animals sneaked into the settlement, news was spread from house to house with a penetrating terror. Such an alarm was not unfamiliar to William Swaim, for it was a part of the natural life around him; but he could take comfort in the fact that every family which owned sheep had a sheep dog especially trained for guarding the herd.

After the sheep were tended and sheared by the men, it then became the responsibility of the women to card the wool and spin it into yarn, to weave yarn into cloth, and to fashion cloth into garments. Cards, spinning wheels, and looms were indispensable tools of the trade and were to be found in connection with every well-ordered household. The women took pride in directing their shuttles to new designs off the old home loom; and they thought nothing of tailoring in expert fashion a suit for their menfolk. Before her marriage to Sidney Porter in 1824, Ruth Worth, O. Henry's grandmother, was said to have been a fine weaver. O. Henry's grandfather, William Swaim, undoubtedly wore hand-made suits most of his life. And O. Henry's great-grandmother, Mrs. David Worth, when she was eighty-two years of age, wove the material which her son Jonathan had made into a suit for his inauguration as Governor of North Carolina in 1865.[25]

Cotton was quite as essential as wool. It was grown in the fields around Centre; and after its fibers had been hand-carded and hand-spun into yarn, they too were woven into fabrics for warm weather wear and various other household uses. Cotton fields could be planted with no dread of boll weevils, but the fibers had to be picked from the bolls by hand and the seeds picked from the fibers by the fingers before the cotton gin came into general use in this locality after 1793. It is interesting to have a description of this process in the words of William Swaim's mother, Mrs. Sarah Fanning Swaim: "In gathering round the winter fire a practice in [our] family was to place cotton upon the hearth before the fire, to make it easy to to pick the seeds out. The children gathered round to work. According to the competency of the child an amount was apportioned to each [for every member of the family was supposed to pick his shoe full of cotton seed before he went to bed]. A candlestick was then set before the fire, with a candle placed thereon. The mother and grown-ups were employed sewing, knitting, etc., while the father read aloud from the family Bible for all to hear. As the system of [our] work called for it, the flax wheel was brought forward. The flax was spun, woven and made into clothes for summer wear. In early spring it was common for the men, out hunting before daybreak, to hear the humming of the little flax wheels as they passed the residences."[26]

Flax has been spoken of in the same breath with cotton in Centre accounts, but flax was used more extensively than cotton before the invention of the cotton gin. From seeds to garments it presented a tedious production. Not only were the preparation of the soil, the planting, and the tending exacting, but the preparation for weaving called for pulling, rippling, retting, drying, rolling, and scutching. Only flax growers would probably be familiar with such terms, but it may be said in truth that none of these processes were as smooth as fine linen. The industrious people of Centre, however, never measured the long hours of labor against possibilities, opportunities, and needs. Fortunately, they were aided in this tedious flax culture by flax journeymen who were specialists in the field and who for wages traveled from farm to farm to help with the different steps between pulling and weaving.[27]

Silk cultivation also had some attention in Guilford.[28] The native groves of mulberry trees and the rapid growth of imported mulberry trees encouraged a few inhabitants of the area to try their hands at this fine textile. So much hope did silk culture promise in this country that the United States government issued free instructions for any who would pursue it; and for a while both the weaving of silk cloth and the manufacture of raw silk thread furnished products that could be sold for money rather than being used for barter. And silk also furnished a good conversation piece for many old-timers who did not want their womenfolk to dress so fine that they would get out of hand. Perhaps that is why, as

13

promising as the production of silk seemed to be, it became a special interest of some, rather than the general practice of all.

Centre, being predominantly a Quaker settlement, placed great emphasis on religion. At first the white inhabitants of that area attended the meetings of New Garden twenty miles away in one direction, and of Cane Creek twenty miles away in another direction. They thought nothing of riding horseback or walking twenty miles twice a week to services. In going to the two meetings they soon wore down deep paths which were later used for roadbeds. In 1757, five of the first settlers — William Hockett, Peter Dick, John Bail, Isaac Beason, and Matthew Osborne — organized their own meeting and called it Centre because it was halfway between New Garden and Cane Creek. Then and thereafter, Centre Meeting more than any other interest bound the community together. At first the new organization met in private homes, but by the time of William Swaim the members had erected their second house of worship.[29] Although Swaim was not an enrolled member of the Society of Friends, he shared many of their experiences, benefited from their philosophy, and absorbed much of their knowledge.

The site for the meetinghouse and graveyard was carefully selected. It was situated on the top of a gently rising knoll; and members of the congregation as they stood about the grounds and visited together could look up across rolling hills for miles; or, casting their eyes downward, they could view the long slope to Polecat Creek with its border of ancient trees.*

Residents of this section all knew each other intimately for a radius of ten to twenty miles; and it is believed that William Swaim knew all the members of Centre Meeting and from them received

*Edward R. Murrow, formerly of Columbia Broadcasting System, recipient of two dozen or more major awards for distinguished service in journalism, radio, and television around the mid-twentieth century, and since 1961 Head of the United States Information Agency, was born on this hillside in sight of Centre Meetinghouse. In fact he was born in the old house of Jonathan Parker of legislative fame. The Parker residence, standing in its original location one hundred and fifty-odd years, was occupied in 1963 by Joshua E. Murrow, foster uncle and second cousin of Edward R. Murrow.

both directly and indirectly the benefit of their influence. Although the membership did not at first include persons of great material wealth, nor of fine cultural bearings, its roll did include men and women who expressed progressive views on politics, education, agriculture, transportation, and other subjects which might contribute to the future development of the country.[30]

As was customary in the Society of Friends, next to religion in importance was education. When William Swaim, Jonathan and Ruth Worth, and Peter Adams were born there were no public schools in North Carolina, nor were there any for about forty years yet to come. Judge Archibald D. Murphey reported to the state legislature in 1816-1817 the needs for educational facilities throughout the state; and he pounded away with unprecedented vigor and intelligence for the establishment of a state-supported school system. It was 1839, however, before such provision was made; and it was not until the 1850's that public schools began to have satisfactory development. During Swaim's youth, therefore, primary education was obtained through the well-known old field schools which were irregularly held in various communities for two or three months each year by means of private subscriptions. Centre, which was above the average in this respect, had at least three such institutions in its different sections, and Swaim occasionally attended one of them.[31] These schools did little more than teach the primary steps of reading, writing, and arithmetic, the females being excused from the latter, for "it was never dreamed that women would ever so far depart from the sphere of kitchen ethics" as to have any use for figures.[32] As can readily be seen the level of educational attainment remained very low. The Quakers continued to emphasize the importance of learning, but they were too poor to promote a culturally polished society. Friends in England sent Bibles and other books from time to time, but even that gesture was not enough to leaven the predominating lump of ignorance.

There were some other efforts which had their influence in a wider distribution of knowledge. During the summer months

Sunday Schools were established in Guilford after 1820, and Swaim who was by that time a young man took a great interest in them. It seems strange that as concerned as they were with religious and educational improvement, older adults took no interest in Sabbath learning as such. Because of that indifference, Sunday Schools in the county were of short duration.[33] There were also private boarding schools of about high school level at near-by Jamestown and Greensboro; but so far as is known, Jonathan Worth and his brother Milton were the only Centre contemporaries of Swaim ever to attend them. Swaim kept a *Diary* in which he positively expressed his feelings on other subjects, but excerpts from it do not show that he had any desire to attend an academy or to acquire a formal education.[34] He wanted knowledge and he developed a highly sensitive social conscience, but apparently he preferred to manage his own education.

In Swaim's day there were many things about Centre Community that were definitely in its favor — the beauty of its natural setting, the spirit of friendliness among its people, the inhabitants' devotion to religion and education, and the upright honesty of the majority of its residents — yet it was a human society and, like most other human groups, it had its degrading practices as well as its admirable features.

The questionable actions of society in Centre came to the foreground more readily, it seems, at times of play. Although recreational facilities were few, early settlers were very ingenious in finding ways to make life interesting. A common sport was the challenge to remove with one shot both eyes of a turkey tied eighty yards away. Gander pulling was frequently described in the old records as an amusement. Someone would suspend from the limb of a tree a tough old gander with its neck well saturated with grease and soft soap. Then mounted contestants while riding at full speed would try to pull the fowl's head off as they passed. Horseback riding, shooting matches, hunting, and fishing were also choice forms of entertainment for the men. Whatever the play, it was not unusual to find betting, heavy drinking, and even fighting at the meets.[35]

Although the majority did not indulge to excess in such practices, Swaim "had the blunt honesty and manly nerve to record [in his *Diary*] this vice of his, ... that the youth of his country, if it ever came to their sight, might learn hence a great moral lesson and never be seduced from the paths of virtue and sobriety by the alluring brandishments of the spirit, which sparkles in the wine-cup and the toddy-bowl."[36]

The heyday of Swaim's youth, however, did not pass without taking a blight from the immorality of the times. Before he was eighteen his early habits of sobriety and morality were much encroached upon by certain vices of the newly settled country.[37] Much of the everyday work of homemaking and farming was turned into pleasuable diversions when everybody worked together; but the occasions more often than not had a side line of corruption. Reflecting upon these neighborhood meetings, Swaim wrote in his *Diary*, "Indeed I did not escape the contagion with which the atmosphere of such society is contaminated. The corn-shuckings, the house-raisings and the log-rollings, to which my situation in life frequently called me, exerted a very deleterious influence over my morals. This influence grew, not out of the nature of these necessary neighborhood parties, but out of the manner in which they were conducted. A jug of brandy or whiskey, at these collections, was generally deemed an indispensable requisite. Many of the people, who were for the most part temperate, would think it nothing amiss to get, what is usually called *tipsy* or *fuddled*, at these gatherings; and to make the boys all drunk was the height of sport. This being the case, habits, not of drunkenness, but of intemperance, gradually fastened upon me, which operated very seriously against my advancement in the acquisition of knowledge."[38]

A specific example of such a gathering was one called to move Jonathan Parker's barn. The home place of Parker, who was twenty-three times elected to the North Carolina legislature, was bought by "Jotty" Hodgin. Hodgin decided that Parker had placed the

17

barn too close to the house, and he, Hodgin, invited his neighbors to help him place it about one hundred yards higher up on the hillside. He marked out a spot ten steps in the direction he wanted the barn to roll and placed there a five-gallon keg of brandy. The men started in a rush for it, but "Jotty" stopped them with the announcement that they were to partake of it only after the barn had been moved to that point. In short order the barn traveled the ten steps and the movers were rewarded with swigs of inspiration served from the keg with a gourd. After several successive "steppings" and installments of inspirational elixir the barn was firmly anchored to the slanting earth, where it was much steadier than the males who had placed it there.[39]

This lack of moral restraint in Centre Community was no exception to the condition which prevailed generally over the country. The demoralizing effects of war following the American and French Revolutions plus the philosophical free thinking of the late eighteenth century were very evident in the laxities among the people. Particularly were the young untrained minds easily influenced to participate in pranks and mild annoyances for the excitement they afforded. In the main such offenses about Centre were of no grave consequences, but there occurred in 1808 a genuine "American Tragedy." Although the crime was thought to have stemmed from a lack of discipline and the general waywardness of the times, it was more than an adolescent prank: it was a premeditated murder which startled the country for miles thereabouts. And it also inspired a tragic "ballit" which has rung in the hills of southern Guilford and Randolph Counties for a century and a half.[40]

William Swaim was only six years old when it happened, but there is no doubt that he heard the story throughout his lifetime, for it occurred in the family of one of his most intimate associates, William Adams; and he must have heard the ballad based upon the incident.

Adams, an honest and warmhearted gentleman, had invited Naomi Wise, a young orphan girl, to come and live in his house.

Not very far away on the slope between Centre Meetinghouse and Polecat Creek lived Richard Lewis, son of David Lewis, who also lived in the vicinity and had a considerable family of boys. Both father and sons were completely ruthless, priding themselves on killing neighbors' cattle, stealing from fish traps, saying and doing well-nigh whatever they pleased. The officials, however, dared not cross them, for they shot to kill. Jonathan Lewis, son of Richard and grandson of David, had definite Lewis traits. Nevertheless, he was often in the hospitable home of the Adamses; and when Naomi Wise had grown into womanhood, he fell in love with her. Jonathan was said to have been as handsome as Naomi was beautiful; and despite his family's reputation she decided to marry him. But Jonathan's mother had another idea: he was to improve his social and financial standing by wooing Hettie Elliott, sister of his employer, Benjamin Elliott, in Asheboro, North Carolina. The idea appealed to Jonathan, but Miss Elliott was coy and would not immediately yield to his wooing. Meanwhile, a rumor spread that Naomi was pregnant. Jonathan, blinded by ambition, deliberately planned to destroy Naomi. He therefore suggested to her that they elope, and she consented. They arranged to meet at the Adams' spring where Lewis took her on his horse beside him. Instead of going to the magistrate's office as Naomi expected, Lewis took her directly to the middle of Deep River. Ignoring her plea for mercy, he grasped her throat, tied her dress over her head, and then held her under the water with his foot until she was drowned and he was frightened away by the glare of approaching torches. (The Davises who lived near-by had heard unearthly screams and had come to investigate.)

Lewis remained at large for a day or two until he was arrested and placed in the Asheboro jail. He soon broke jail, however, and disappeared. The tragedy might have been forgotten but for the "ballit" of "Omi Wise" which was soon being sung in every neighborhood thereabouts. Then there was the tradition that there was a little song as soft as the singing of angels which could be heard around the falls of Deep River in the dusk of evening. In 1815, when it was learned that Jonathan Lewis and his family were living in Ohio, he was arrested, brought back, tried, and acquitted in the Guilford County Court for lack of evidence. A few years later when he was dying he confessed the crime in detail to his father.

By that time the scene of the tragedy had been named Naomi Falls. Over half a century later Naomi Manufacturing Company was erected and Naomi Village grew up as a place with tragic charm, romance, and sorrowing sighs in its history. President Braxton Craven, who from 1842 to 1882 was head of the institution that became Duke University, in 1874 recorded the story of the crime under the pen name of Charlie Vernon. His version was published in the *Greensboro Patriot* and subsequently had private printings in Winston-Salem and Weldon, North Carolina. In 1944 it was republished along with Randolph County sketches; and thus over the years the dreadful tragedy has been remembered.

Swaim undoubtedly recalled this incident when he delivered his ideas on how to deal with juvenile delinquency, which he called waywardness among young people. Without hesitation he blamed parents for such a situation. It appears that he had not yet reached his twentieth birthday when he lamented that fathers and mothers did not consider the development of their children more seriously; and entered in his *Diary* this youthful, but sage paragraph: "A great and prevailing fault is to be found with most parents in neglecting to introduce their children properly into good society, and in bringing them to act their part discreetly and well upon the broad theatre of a vicious and depraved world. Some are so deplorably negligent of this important concern, that they give their children up to the dominion of their own wills, and leave them to any direction that the warm and capricious passions of youth may give them; and others are so insupportably severe in their discipline, that they engender in their bosoms an everlasting hate for parental advice or control, and thus defeat the purpose of their severity."[41]

In hopeful contrast to the rowdies, among Swaim's friends at Centre the Worth family stands out as a fine example of progressive leadership. David Worth and his wife, the former Eunice Gardner, were married in 1798, the same year in which Swaim's parents were married. In time the Worths became the parents of twelve children, and despite the absence of documentary evidence, it is believed that this family exerted a great influence over young Swaim during his formative years.

David Worth was a man of many parts. First of all he was a family man — a devoted husband and father who looked toward more long range provisions than daily bread and who provided the best available education for his children. He took his living from his farm, but he had no desire to accumulate wealth beyond his actual needs. He supported progressive legislation and three times put aside his local responsibilities to sit in the halls of the General Assembly of North Carolina. He did not own slaves, but instead hired Negroes as free laborers while he worked for the abolition of slavery. He kept well-informed on the situation of the country, and particularly on the condition of his own state which badly needed to take inventory of itself and to raise its standard among other states of the Union. And in addition to being a public-spirited citizen, he was a physician of no mean reputation.[42]

It is probably as a "country doctor" that David Worth lengthened his shadow, for from accessible records it appears that he established the first general hospital in North Carolina. His two oldest children had died in infancy, he believed, because there was no physician available. So grieved was he at this loss that he studied medicine in Philadelphia and became a practicing physician in his vicinity. Dr. Worth served an area which is said to have extended as far north as Virginia, and as far south as lower Randolph County; and he covered this radius by horseback or in a two-wheeled vehicle. So much was he in demand that people are reported to have brought the sick in wagons or otherwise for as much as fifty miles in order to have the benefit of his services. His house and near-by small office could not accommodate all who came. Sometimes the sick were left lying in wagon beds or on the yard. Greatly moved by such scenes, Dr. Worth built near his house a row of cabins in which he housed his patients as comfortably as the times permitted. Here he had them cared for by his hired servants under his personal supervision.[43]

Dr. Worth's wife Eunice had studied right along with him and she became his able assistant. Although Dr. David Worth is credited with having built the first general hospital in North Carolina, it should be remembered that Dr. Eunice Worth was his first intern and his lifetime co-worker.[44] Thus, quietly and mercifully giving aid to the suffering whenever and wherever aid was needed, these two noble souls were taking the initial step of social consciousness in the field of medicine in their state.

Another influence which contributed to Swaim's development, a condition which attracted universal attention, was that of slavery; for it became the deep concern of Centre Community. Already the subject had a long history. The philosophy of the Declaration of Independence with its emphasis upon the "inalienable rights" of all men was still fresh in the minds of the people, and undoubtedly moved an increasing number to hold conscientious scruples against slavery. Although the United States Constitution carried regulations regarding the system, leading statesmen such as George Washington, Thomas Jefferson, Patrick Henry, James Madison, and others, had seen its weaknesses and had expressed at the time their opinions in favor of its gradual abolition.[45] Church denominations of the early ante-bellum period had also frowned upon slaveholding. The Great Revival of the late 1700's and the early 1800's had greatly increased the number of church members and had brought three fourths of them in North Carolina to mild antislavery views.[46] There were also professional men and political leaders who expressed their views in opposition to the system. For example, Henry Clay, who had become more and more influential on the national scene after his appointment to Congress in 1806, had presided over the first organization meeting of the American Colonization Society in Washington in 1816. This organization had as its objective, besides manumission, the removal and settlement of Negroes in other lands. Clay later had served as its president, and over the years had held to his antislavery position.[47] By the 1820's the northern states had found slavery uneconomical and had completely abolished the slave labor system.[48]

Somewhat earlier, the Quakers had renounced slavery in 1774-1776, and a group of them had undertaken active steps toward the emancipation of Negroes in North Carolina. They had organized in Guilford and Randolph Counties some local Manumission Societies; and these organizations elected delegates who came together on July 19, 1816, at Centre Meetinghouse and formed the General Association of the Manumission Society of North Carolina, with Moses Swaim, William's cousin, as president. Since *Manumission*—the liberation of a slave—was the key word, the purpose of the organization was to promote for the Negroes better social conditions—to seek educational advantages for them, to establish fair legislation in their behalf, to condition them generally to act as free men and women, and finally to bring about gradual emancipation of the colored race. "Some plan of gradual manumission was the theme of general discussion at that day, but none of the advocates spoke or seemed to think of immediate and unconditional emancipation."[49]

The society was open to all interested parties. Quite a number of slaveholders joined, but as it turned out many of them favored both emancipation and colonization. They considered free Negroes a disturbing element among slaves, and they contended that if slaves were freed they must be sent to Africa or elsewhere—that expatriation must be made a condition of their liberty. Many of the members, however, were opposed to making colonization a condition of freedom. They believed the idea to be an odious plan of the slaveholders to open a drain by which they might get rid of free Negroes and thus remain in more secure possession of their slave property. These members had no objection to free Negroes going to other parts of the world of their own will, but to compel them to go as a condition of freedom was something

23

to which they were conscientiously opposed and against which they strongly contended.[50]

The Manumission Society of North Carolina consequently maintained as its dominant interest the gradual abolition of slavery; and its principles and its progress were made known to the public. Then in his teens, William Swaim therefore had an opportunity to observe and evaluate the Manumission Society's ideas and movements. The first four branches of the organization were at Centre, New Garden, Deep River, and Carraway, all in or near Guilford County. Nor were the Quakers alone in this work, for the Methodists, Baptists, and Presbyterians were also active leaders in the undertaking. According to the minutes of the body, by 1825 there were twenty-eight branches in North Carolina to send delegates to the General Association.[51] Antislavery leader Benjamin Lundy in 1827 wrote that there were one hundred thirty abolition societies in the United States—one hundred six of which were in slave states—fifty in North Carolina.[52]

In December of 1824, William Swaim attended his first meeting of the Manumission Society at Centre Meetinghouse and joined the antislavery crusade.[53] Of his reaction at that time he wrote in his *Diary* as follows: "I joined the society and entered heartily into the principles entertained and propagated by it. Slavery is one of the greatest curses that God, in his wrath, ever permitted to visit the Southern country.—And besides this, it is morally wrong for one man to exact the labor and sweat of another without his consent."[54] In a letter to a friend, Leonard P. McPhail, Swaim later wrote that " *The majesty of the people* has been eloquently compared by Judge Blackstone to a *sleeping* lion. Let him once be awakened from his long protracted slumbers, and he will shake his terrific mane and accompany the motion with a roar that will hurl nabob power from its base in dreadful prostration—he will shake the fetters from the limbs of injured innocence and elevate the man to the dignity of his nature.' "[55]

During the years following 1824 when Swaim first joined the Manumission Society there continued much activity in the organization. Representatives from participating branches met in general conventions, at which time they heard addresses by conscientious antislavery leaders; sent petitions to the state legislature and to Congress, asking for better laws for slaves; received reports from female auxiliaries which were praised for their good work; and made efforts to get more publicity in the newspapers. *The Patriot,* which was edited and published (1826-1829) by T. Early Strange in Greensboro, gave some notice to the meetings, but Joseph Gales, editor of the *Raleigh Register,* at first refused to publish anything about the movement. Other newspapers of the state were inclined to Gales' point of view. The minutes (1825) of the meetings substantiate this point by saying "Some of the printing presses of the State have published extracts from the papers favorable to Emancipation, but we know of none of the Editors who appear earnestly engaged in promoting it."[56] In fact, the General Association had so much difficulty in getting materials printed that it seriously considered establishing a printing press of its own, but it never did.

Notwithstanding this situation, the movement was making its principles felt. In the 1820's there developed a prevailing sentiment, especially in North Carolina, that the slave system was not established in "reason and right and that it ought to be eradicated and destroyed, root and branch."[57] Swaim's Quaker community served as the spearhead in a movement which for a while made notable advancement toward the abolition of slavery in North Carolina. Manumission societies which had their beginning in Guilford and Randolph Counties soon spread to other counties of the state. Whereas at first they had been unable to get newspapers to publish their proceedings and addresses, in time they got more attention, and yet, so far as is known, this procedure excited no wrath and kindled no resentment in the minds of slaveholders.[58] Many who supported the movement were men who had elevated positions in society and wielded a wide and potent influence in public affairs in the counties and in the state legislature.

In addition to the manumission societies in North Carolina, there were also branches of the American Colonization Society.

At first the branches in Guilford were patronized by a large group of highly respectable and intelligent persons, but its narrow philanthropy did not satisfy the hearts and minds of the people of the Manumission Society for a great while. "Perhaps the *impracticability* of such a *scheme* readily presented itself to their extremely practical minds."[59]  But what is more to the point, the Centre branch, through a personal experience, became disillusioned about the colonization organization. It came about in this way. According to William B. Hockett, grandfather of Joshua E. Murrow who contributed this information, two groups of free Negroes were scheduled to be transported to other lands under the direction of the Colonization Society; and they were loaded onto two boats at Wilmington, North Carolina. It was later learned that one boat went to Haiti, but the other one went to New Orleans and there the Negroes were sold back into slavery. When news of the dishonest deal reached Centre, the move for colonization was dropped then and there.

William Swaim was not a member of the Colonization Society, but soon after he joined the General Association of the Manumission Society of North Carolina he was made secretary of that organization, a position which he held for six years.[60] And this position became the medium through which he did some of his greatest work.

Pioneer settlements, transportation, communication, food, clothing, religion, education, recreation, medicine, slavery, and politics—these were some of the things the people of Centre Community talked about as, in the cold of winter, they sat around a blazing fire until it burned to embers, or discussed on rainy summer days when they could not tend the fields, or occasionally debated when they came together at public meeting places. These were the conditions under which William Swaim lived and grew to manhood.

# II

## A REFORMER IN THE MAKING

*"While other members of the family were folded in the embraces of slumber, I employed myself in learning to read."*[1]

William Swaim had vivid memories of his great-grandfather Michael Swaim, his grandfather William Swaim, I, and his father Marmaduke Swaim.[2] To be sure, these forebears had not distinguished themselves in any unusual way, but they were his own family. He was very reserved concerning his kinsfolk, in fact he rarely mentioned them; but when he did mention any of them, he did so with great respect and tenderness.[3]

Michael Swaim, when a mere youth, had emigrated from New Jersey to Piedmont North Carolina during its very earliest days of settlement.[4] Some of his relatives had already established their home in this region, and from them young Michael had probably learned of the opportunities the area offered.[5] As a permanent settler, with the expectation of earning his living by tilling the soil, a little before or around the middle of the eighteenth century he therefore joined his kinsmen in the undeveloped heart of North Carolina. He soon purchased a tract of land, took unto himself a wife, and established his own homestead in the wilds of what later became southern Guilford County.[6]

In time Michael Swaim became the father of many children who, following their father's example, cleared broad fields, cultivated the soil, and likewise reared large families in the environment

27

of Centre Community.   Among the sons of Michael was William, I, the father of Marmaduke.[7]

Marmaduke Swaim was born on April 2, 1771, the month and the year in which Guilford County was created. In the years of his boyhood and youth, social conditions in the Piedmont were crude and the opportunities for even a meager education were few. Young Marmaduke grew into a man of vigorous intellect, but he was quite limited in scholarship, unpolished in his manners, and coarse in his conversation. He was, nevertheless, to become an able business man, well-established in his real and personal estate, and one of the largest landowners in Guilford County.[8]   In 1798, at the age of twenty-seven, Marmaduke married Sarah Fannon or Fanning, born on November 18, 1776. This fine and enterprising but unlearned young couple became the parents of William Swaim, II, whose love of learning and liberal ideas led him to the editorship of a newspaper.

The history of Sarah Fanning's family had been one of dire tragedy until she met and married Marmaduke Swaim. The story undoubtedly both grieved and fascinated her son William, for she lived to tell it over and over to her children, her grandchildren, and her great-grandchildren.[9]

Around the 1730's her grandmother Peggy[10] ———, when a young girl, was innocently taking a walk near her home along the rugged seacoast of Scotland; and strolling leisurely amidst its natural beauty and enchantment, she wandered out of sight of her home.  With no warning whatsoever, she was suddenly kidnaped by complete strangers, was forced on board a vessel, and was transported to America where as an indentured servant she was sold at public auction. Kinless, friendless, moneyless, she was afterwards forced to pay the iniquitous debt of her captors to her purchaser "by the sweat of her youthful brow."[11]

The story of the kidnaped Scotch lassie is well-known to some of the older descendants of Marmaduke and Sarah Swaim. As is the case with most of the records of this family, the details are scant.

For example, specific facts are not known concerning the exact spot on Scotland's coast where she was stolen, the name of the ship which brought her to America, and the identification of her purchaser. The name Peggy ———, however, is known.[12] It seems likely that she, like Flora Macdonald, may have landed in Wilmington, North Carolina, and made her way up the Cape Fear River since later records of her are found in Anson County.

When Peggy reached young womanhood she became acquainted with Thomas Fanning who formed a serious attachment for her; and she warmly reciprocated his feelings. Eventually they were married and settled in Anson County, North Carolina.[13]

The only child of Thomas and Peggy Fanning, William Swaim's great-grandparents, was a son whom they named Thomas Fanning, Jr.[14] Both the father and the son were intensely concerned about the development of their country, and they became leaders in the Regulator movement which in the middle and late 1760's was organized for the purpose of setting up fair, just, and democratic government in Piedmont North Carolina.[15]

The Regulators, as they called themselves, had real cause for their actions. In 1765 William Tryon had become governor of the Province of North Carolina, and some of the officers of the crown under him—the clerks of the several courts, the recorders of deeds, the entry takers, the surveyors, the lawyers, and the petty officers —had been demanding twice or three times the legal fees; and the people were bitterly complaining about the situation. In addition to these unlawful collections, Governor Tryon had promoted a poll tax to cover the cost of an elegant governmental palace at New Bern—said to have been the finest "government house" in all English America—and the people of the western counties vehemently resented that move. Such a tax forced the poorest to pay as much as the richest, which seemed all out of proportion to the new settlers of the Piedmont who could not compete in wealth with the long established aristocracy of the eastern section of the state. Moreover, money was so scarce that these western people found it difficult to secure enough to pay the taxes which were already assessed. And when the exorbitant extras were added, the spirits of the newly settled Piedmont were aroused to action, and they announced that they would pay their just taxes, but no more. By 1767 the situation had become so bad in Anson County that the people pledged themselves not to pay any taxes at all for that year.[16]

The Regulators had reported in detail to the state officials the unfair treatment that was being practiced upon them, and in 1768 both Thomas and Thomas Fanning, Jr., had signed their names to an "Address from the Inhabitants in Anson County. To His Excellency Governor Tryon"[17] in an effort to bring a just application of the law. Governor Tryon, backed by his Council and the legislature, advised the smaller officials to stop taking unauthorized fees; but to no avail. After having endured several years of illegal collections and unsatisfactory dealings with the governor and those in authority with him, by 1770 the Regulators had concluded that they could secure no justice from colonial officials. The Fannings remained active in the movement while Regulators vigorously attacked the presiding officers of a court and took over court matters themselves. In 1771 they even came to blows with Governor Tryon and his army and fought the Battle of Alamance— fought for reforms which did not come to pass until after the American Revolutionary War, and after the revision of the state constitution in 1835. When the Regulator movement was put down by the forces of the king, the Fannings along with other Regulators returned to their homes and farms. But not for long in the case of Thomas Fanning, Jr., for within four or five years he was called to serve as a Patriot in the American Revolution.[18]

In the meantime he had married Katharine ———, and from this union there were three children—Peggy, William, and Sarah.[19] As the young father left his little family, he had high hopes of American Independence—of himself defending freedom which was to be preserved through the establishment of a democratic government. In such a spirit he was willing to give his life for this cause during the American Revolutionary War.

Naturally it was not easy for young Thomas Fanning, Jr., to leave his wife and children. The uncertainty through which he had just passed as a Regulator, however, was enough to impress upon him the importance of trying to establish more stable conditions under which they should live. Evidently the man took a bold stand for all measures of freedom, for in 1770 he had signed, with other inhabitants of Anson County, another petition to the Governor, Council, and General Assembly of North Carolina, asking that a court be established at Campbellton (later Fayetteville) for Anson, Orange, and Cumberland Counties.[20] Now that a call had come for him actually to fight in defense of his country, he departed for American army headquarters.

Nothing is known of his participation in battle. In fact, as was the case of other soldiers, his name does not appear in the Roster of the American Revolution. His family records, however, have more definite information concerning him. He was captured and held as a prisoner by the Tories, who showed him no mercy. He and other captives were shut up in a pen and were "fed on a little corn" as if they had been swine. Just how long he was subjected to such humiliating treatment is not known, but at the end of the war "he was turned out of the pen" and was allowed to start home to his loved ones.[21]

The homeward trek was one filled with unspeakable tragedy. While living in the pen, or soon thereafter, Thomas, Jr., had developed an acute diarrhea, perhaps from malnutrition, perhaps from unsanitary conditions. Because of his illness his health had deteriorated until his weakened condition made it difficult for him to stand. But thoughts of home buoyed his determination and he kept going, much of the time crawling on his hands and knees. After days of such tedious efforts, he reached the house of friends on the Uwharrie River. At this point he was compelled to stop. Since there were no doctors in that part of the county at that time, it was up to his host and hostess to do what they could. They suggested that he drink poplar bark tea, perhaps an "old wives'" or maybe an Indian remedy for such an illness. Consumed with

31

eagerness to recover from his malady, distraught with anxiety to get home to his wife and children, Thomas, Jr., resolved to bring about the quickest possible cure for his sickness. He reasoned that the larger the dosage of the suggested remedy, the quicker the cure, and he therefore drank poplar bark tea in such great quantities that the result was fatal.[22]

It seemed enough that his young daughter, Sarah Fanning, then about five years of age, should have lost her father because of the Revolutionary War; but for her tragedy was heaped upon tragedy. Her widowed mother married a man by the name of Vickory who made a virtual Cinderella of Sarah. There is no record as to whether Vickory was a widower with children by a former wife, or whether they were his and Katharine's children whom he favored over Sarah; but it is a matter of record that he made a veritable slave of this young girl. He was not only partial to his own children, but he allowed them to be very disagreeable in their relations with Sarah. And as she grew older he compelled her to work all day and most of the night. In her reminiscences of the past she recounted that many were the nights when she spun flax all night except for an hour or two when she slept with her head on a tanned sheep skin which she had thrown down on the floor.[23]

With this family background of almost half a century of continous unhappiness, plus her own miserable girlhood, Sarah at last found happiness with Marmaduke Swaim, whom she married at the age of twenty-two. Like him, she had grown up in the environment of an undeveloped rural community, and hence these two who would become the parents of William Swaim were congenially matched. The young couple settled in Centre Community, ten to twelve miles south of Greensboro, North Carolina.[24]

Even though the conditions of Sarah's girlhood and young womanhood were almost as trying as those of her grandmother Peggy, Sarah through the assignments meted out to her had acquired the arts of an industrious homemaker. With her husband she arose each morning when the cock crew, winter and summer, several hours before the rising of the sun. In warm weather the call to arise was more welcome, for the air was cool and invigorating and the earth was promising in its bath of midnight dew. On winter mornings, however, the house was as cold as ice itself. It had gone all night without fire, except for a smoldering log covered over with ashes to hold it dormant until morning, for matches had not yet been invented. As new fuel was added, and with tedious coaxing, flames would begin faintly to flicker. The fire had to burn for a while before there was enough heat to bake bread over its live coals and to fry "fat back" for breakfast. This interval provided time for feeding the animals on the farm, milking the cows, and throwing the morning rations to the hungry chickens. The Swaims usually ate breakfast by firelight and Marmaduke was on his way to the fields by daybreak.

As children came along it was the accepted custom in households of the vicinity for the oldest son, as soon as he was large enough, to kindle the morning fires, and this was probably one of William Swaim's earliest tasks. Thereafter he helped his father with the work of the farm—cultivating fields, building fences, harvesting crops, and caring for the farm animals.[25] Meanwhile his sisters were taught to sweep the house and yard with brooms made of small bundles of sedge securely tied together; and they were instructed to make the beds properly. All the covers were ripped from their anchorage and thoroughly shaken; the combination straw and corn shucks mattress, which rested on ropes laced to the bed railing, was loosened up; the feather bed was punched into fluffiness and smoothed down to a remarkable evenness; and then the coverings were replaced. They must learn this well for future use in order that the beds would always be neat, for no fastidious housewife would allow the beds to be sat upon or disarrayed in any way during the daytime. Sometimes the daughters also assisted with the lighter work of the farm, such as dropping seeds at planting season, hoeing, and picking cotton; but woman's sphere in the main was restricted to keeping the house, cooking, washing, ironing, weaving, and sewing cloth into garments for the family.

33

Whatever were the different assignments in the Swaim family, there is evidence that they were performed cheerfully. Marmaduke Swaim died at the age of fifty-seven, but his wife Sarah's life span lengthened to around ninety years. After her husband's death she never remarried, but lived with her children and grandchildren the rest of her life. While visiting these relatives she often entertained them by telling of experiences she had had. Though there are no details of the stories she told, one of her great-granddaughters, Mrs. Sarah Margaret Trogdon Lambert, who listened to them, implied that they were pleasant reminiscences.[26]

There seemed to have been a very close family relationship, for young Swaim and his brothers and sisters all remained in the family circle until they were either married and had homes of their own or were established in business elsewhere.[27] The one known reference William Swaim made to his home life was that it "sheltered from a thousand storms."[28]

William, the third child and the oldest boy of Marmaduke and Sarah Swaim, was a very dutiful son. With the exception of six months of intermittent schooling he continued to aid his father in tilling the soil until he reached his twentieth year. Thereafter, until in his twenty-sixth year he was away from home only a few months at a time.[29]

While young Swaim was stretching up from childhood to boyhood, he was a handsome lad. Moreover, he was noted for "the power of his mind, the readiness of his wit, the shrewdness of his remarks, the keenness of his repartee, all set off by a continual coruscation of humor."[30] Whether or not his parents recognized his marked ability and wished to encourage the proper development and use of it is not known; but it is known that before William was twelve years old they sent him to his uncle Michael Swaim's school which was taught for two months each year in an old schoolhouse a mile and a half away. It has been said that the highly gifted, talented, or brilliant often are sensitive and temperamental, and perhaps this can explain the boy's reaction to the harness and

slow pace of formal training in the "old-field school." Anyway,
William Swaim became obsessed with a positive aversion to books,
to school, and to everything that pertained in the remotest degree
to learning and literature. Despite his avid dislike for school,
however, he learned rapidly; and at the end of the two months'
term he could read well enough to understand such books as were
then available for school use.[31]

And he had made some progress with penmanship. The first
figures he ever made with a pen were copied in 1814 when he was
twelve years of age. Penmanship seemed to have been more difficult for him than reading. He would ask his father, who wrote
a large, plain hand, to make copies for him, and by imitating these
writing examples he learned to form all the figures and all the
letters of the alphabet. On Sundays instead of joining other boys
of the neighborhood as they romped, sported, strolled about, and
learned mischief, he would settle down in some quiet undisturbed
place and apply himself, as he said, to a "laborious day's writing."[32]
For all this effort, Swaim did not develop a handwriting as bold
and clear as that of his father: his was swift and running, but
easily legible.[33]

Following this brief period of schooling, between the years
of twelve and sixteen Swaim lost all interest in getting an education.
He was going through what seemed to him a terrible personal
experience. Actually it was normal for a youth of that age, but he
thought it was strange and unusual, and his strict self-examination
produced bad results for him.

According to his own account, he was overcome with an extreme shyness, which was much unlike himself in his matured
manhood. He avoided the society of others, yet when he was
unexpectedly thrown into the company of the intelligent, he was,
as he wrote in his *Diary*, "seized with an irresistible diffidence."
In the same connection he added that he was "not infrequently
driven to the blush at his own ignorance, and shrank back with
shame and confusion from their superior intelligence." Reflecting
on this distressing situation, he almost decided to avoid the com-

panionship of the best educated boys in his community, and to abandon himself to a low and vulgar crowd among whom he could hold up his head as having equal mental strength and cultural attainments. "But happily," he wrote, "*reflection* interposed and saved me from the consequences of such a desperate determination."[34]

While young Swaim was in this state of confusion, his father, either by coincidence or by thoughtful planning, made a very wise move. There was in the county seat Town of Greensboro one occasion that offered much excitement to the people all over Guilford County, and that was the Court of Pleas and Quarter Sessions, commonly called the County Court; and once a year the elder Swaim began taking his son with him to these gatherings. There were four terms of the Guilford County Court of one week each, which were held on the third weeks of February, May, August, and November in each year. Until after the turn of the nineteenth century, court week was a special occasion in any county seat; and Greensboro was no exception. Near the Greensboro Courthouse in Swaim's day were the jail, stocks, pillories, and whipping posts. The picnic and general holiday was on Tuesday of the August term, and hundreds of people came together to enjoy the festive occasion; and, cruel as it may seem, to see the evil doers punished.[35] Since the August court was accompanied by these special attractions, and since that month was more suitable for a farmer to get away from home, it may be assumed that that was the session the Swaims attended.

All the outside goings on may have interested his father, but they were not the things that made the deepest impression upon the younger man. His main interest lay in the courtroom. It was there, as William Swaim recorded in his *Diary*, while sitting by his father in the dignified chamber and intently listening to the examination of witnesses, and hearing the arguments of the learned counsel on the varied cases that came up for trial, that his "inclination kindled into a flaming anxiety to prosecute the profession of the law."[36] It was there that his "hope leaped forward to ripe manhood, and his fancy pictured to itself the glittering honors and exalted pleasures which are to be won and enjoyed in that field of ambition."[37]

It was in the year 1819 that William Swaim had this experience which to him was a great inspiration. Judge Archibald D. Murphey was at that time a Judge of the Superior Court of Law and Equity (1818-1820), and it is possible that Swaim was influenced in his decision to become a lawyer by the wise and impressive manner of that able judge. Whatever the case, it was in the Guilford County Courthouse that his young mind received its first strong impulse to study and to grow in knowledge. It was there, too, that upon sober reflection he realized the limitations of his education, and being young, he dramatized his plight in his *Diary*. There he recorded that he had floundered in despair, and then had experienced a sort of literary conversion which "resulted in a resolution to improve the future moments that might be allotted to him."[38]

Even for that day, such an expression from a teen-age boy was melodramatic; but William was serious. He was sixteen — almost seventeen — at the time, and he entered this story in his *Diary*: "My first essay was to cuff the dust off an old Webster's Spelling Book and commence in some of its easiest lessons. 'Twas a mortifying thought, that four years ago, I was able to read the Bible and, now, scarcely qualified to spell in three letters! My resolution formed, every moment of leisure I could gain from the labor assigned me by my father, was spent in poring over my book. When the sun, which enlivened the toils of the day, would hide himself behind the western hills, I made it my business to prop my hoe in the corner of the fence, or to feed my pony in the stable, and then, to trudge to the woods and gather an armful of brush to make a light. The brush I would deposit in the chimney corner, and, with my book in hand, seat myself upon it; and by applying the brush, piece at a time, to the fire, I could keep myself a light. Thus, while other members of the family were folded in the embraces of slumber, I employed myself in learning to read. Such was the intensity of

37

my application, that I sometimes found myself severely rebuked for neglecting my business in order to learn my book."[39]

Marmaduke Swaim's library was limited to the Holy Bible and a Psalm Book. This situation presented a real problem for the eager student, for as soon as he had mastered *Webster's Spelling Book,* his mind was so whetted that he longed for something else to study. Swaim's house stood within sight of the home place of Nathan Dick, a plain, easygoing, good-natured Quaker who was fond of reading, was fairly intelligent, and was responsive in conversation. The young man sought his neighbor's company and from the elderly man first borrowed Sir Richard Blackmore's *Creation.* Swaim had had only two months of schooling, with a course of study far inferior to two months of first grade work in the 1960's, yet he read with profound interest the entire seven books of this philosophic poem based upon the intellectual philosophy of John Locke.[40] Furthermore, interested Quakers of England had established the practice of sending Bibles and other literature to the Friends of Centre Community,[41] and thus from his fellow bookworm Nathan Dick, Swaim was able to borrow other books through which he gained information and improved his reading.

Steadfastly pursuing the resolution he made in the courthouse, young Swaim broadened his knowledge from the use of Dick's library until that source was exhausted. And for a while it looked as though his future learning would be blocked by the dearth of books in his rural community. In the New World of that time, only in the cities or in the homes of the rich were resources for broad reading generally available. To be sure, the Swaims were not a very poor family, but theirs was not a home of books. And although Marmaduke Swaim thought time used for omnivorous reading was time wasted, apparently he never stood in the way of William's interest in book learning; and his major contribution to the boy's knowledge lay in the freedom to learn accorded him by his father.

A revealing commentary upon the scarcity of literature at the time is the fact that it was one hundred years from the date of

Swaim's birth in 1802 that Greensboro, the largest town within his easy reach, established a public library. In 1820 the Greensborough Male Academy established a private library which was open to the citizens of the town, but its history shows no evidence of county patronage. Though most of the men of Centre were farm owners, they did not have enough wealth to indulge in large collections of books. In fact, William Swaim was well into his twenties before there was even a newspaper published in his county for general circulation.[42]

Fortunately, some other people of Centre and adjoining neighborhoods were also interested in reading, and for their pleasure and improvement a circulating library was established. This collection was very democratically managed. Contributions were taken among the inhabitants of participating communities and a library of standard works was either purchased or rented, then the books were passed from person to person among those who wished to read or study them. All the books, which were distributed by lot, were returned periodically and alternately to New Salem, Marlborough Meeting House, and Mountain Schoolhouse. Through this exchange young Swaim was able to read and study several useful works of philosophy, history, poetry, law, and medicine; and in this way his literary craving was somewhat satisfied.[43] He had no special preference in subject matter, for he wanted to master learning in any field. He still had had only two feeble — and according to his description, he does not say why — distasteful months of schooling, yet he devoured anything and everything he could get his hands on in the way of printed materials.

By the winters of 1820-1821 and 1821-1822, either his aversion to the schoolroom had passed or he was old enough to see formal schooling as necessary. Whatever the case, William Swaim again entered school, altogether for almost four months. His attendance could not be regular, for with a family of eight children his father needed help from his eldest son; but when the weather was unsuitable for field work William went to school, oftentimes pushing his way through storms and mud to get there. Such irregularity of attendance inevitably slowed down his progress in learning, a fact he was then old enough to understand and also to regret. Then, too, he reported that his Uncle Michael, who was his teacher at both these school terms, "though an honest, well meaning man, was positively too lazy to do anything like his duty."[44] Young, alert, impatient and anxious to broaden his knowledge, however, Swaim applied every free moment he had to the business of learning.

About the same time, in the spring of 1822, he became a supporter of another avenue of learning. At that time a Sabbath School, among the first in Guilford County, was established at Bethlehem. He hastened to its opening session because he was eager to take part in any attempt at gaining knowledge. In this school there were about one hundred and fifty pupils who were governed and instructed by a superintendent, two principal teachers, and several assistant teachers. Swaim, who was then almost twenty, was appointed the teacher of a class of young boys, altogether about thirty in number. This appointment was a great encouragement to him, and he was impelled by ambition and interest to discharge his assignment well. With all his enthusiasm he directed his energy to a study of the Bible, and his chief concern throughout the week was that he might understand the lesson, and be able to answer all questions about it or explain its meaning. In later life Swaim said he learned more at this Sunday School than any other school he ever attended.[45] Of such schools he left the following observation in his *Diary*: "Allow me to say, that if parents would give due encouragement to properly organized Sabbath Schools, they would find them of infinite advantage to the rising generation. Were parents to do their duty faithfully, the education of children would not be such a burthen as many pretend."[46]

In sadness Swaim wrote that the Sabbath School through which he was so greatly benefited was discontinued when cold weather approached, or as he said, at "the fall of the leaf."[47] However, another school of the same kind was soon started at Mount Ephraim Schoolhouse; and Swaim was appointed its superintendent. Most of the people who attended this school were Quakers, and although

Swaim had always lived among Friends, he found that this intimate association with them in their religious experiences revealed even more clearly the fine principles they practiced in their daily lives. He was impressed by their attitudes and he ever afterward admired that denomination.[48]

Swaim enjoyed his position as superintendent of a Sabbath School, and enjoyed the associations afforded by it; but when winter weather set in, his school was discontinued, as were most Sabbath Schools. The short duration of these schools is accounted for by Levi Coffin in his *Reminiscences* when he wrote concerning Guilford's first ones in the 1820's that "with few exceptions Sunday Schools had no encouragement from parents and older Friends. On the contrary we had much opposition to contend with."[49]

At this same Mount Ephraim Schoolhouse, in the fall and winter of 1822-1823, another association developed that was as meaningful to young Swaim as the one with devout Friends had been. Benjamin Swaim, a cousin and about five years William's senior, was engaged to teach in a day school in the same building in which the Sunday School had been held. Benjamin was a much better educated man than William. He was a law student, and his ability and prestige as a scholar had been noised abroad, with the result that his school was so thronged with pupils that he had to have an assistant teacher. For this job, Benjamin employed William. William did not accept a salary for his work, but instead let his earnings go as tuition for three of his brothers and sisters in order that they might have the benefit and joy of additional learning.[50]

Benjamin Swaim was not only well-educated for his time, but he was also a man of very fine character and friendly disposition. Possessed of a good library for a man of small means, he shared his books with his young cousin whose appreciation of good literature had greatly impressed him. In fact, so greatly was Benjamin impressed by William's determined effort to make the most of this opportunity that he redoubled his efforts to aid the younger man with his studies. For this comradeship and assistance William remained grateful as long as he lived.[51]

**41**

It was through Benjamin's influence that William secured his next teaching position. Colonel William Dickey, who also lived in Guilford, was an acquaintance and admirer of Benjamin. In 1823, when Dickey was organizing a private school for the benefit of his own children, he invited Benjamin to be the teacher. Benjamin, however, felt it unwise to accept the invitation since he was about to begin his law practice; but he recommended his cousin William as one suitable for the position. Colonel Dickey promptly invited William to live in his home and teach six months in his family. Whereupon William, fortified by the advice of his cousin and his father, happily accepted the offer. He taught the entire six months and received fifty dollars in money, the first clear money he had ever received for himself in all his twenty-one years.[52]

Colonel Dickey was a man of considerable prestige in both his county and his state. He had served as high sheriff of Guilford for several years and had represented the county in the General Assembly of North Carolina. He was therefore acquainted with leading questions of the day. This close contact with a man of affairs offered William another type of learning — that of ever-changing current history rather than mere book learning. Already William had begun to develop an interest in political questions, and it was splendid training for him to be able to discuss topics with such a man as Colonel Dickey. This association was good preparation for a young man who was to become an editor with opinions.

His stay in the Dickey home broadened and deepened Swaim's self-reliance. The timidity from which he had earlier suffered seemed now to have been largely overcome, and he was able to talk man to man with his employer. In addition to being an intelligent man, Dickey was a genial soul who created a pleasant atmosphere in his home, and evidently put his schoolteacher completely at ease. Swaim admitted as much, for of Colonel Dickey he wrote in his *Diary*, "He was open, generous, free, and hospitable. ... He was, emphatically, a man to be loved."[53]

One characteristic of William Swaim that had become evident by this time, was his gravitation toward men who were much his senior. He wrote in his *Diary* that he enjoyed playing around with the young crowd, but that on serious questions, he usually lined up with older men. For example, he said that his first real inspiration to study and improve himself sprang from the able discussions of the lawyers in the Guilford Courthouse. He let it be known that his appreciation of the value of conversation came from talks with Nathan Dick, his near-by Quaker neighbor. And he revealed that his interest in public affairs was broadened and strengthened by his association with Benjamin Swaim, Colonel Dickey, William Adams, Dr. David Worth, Jonathan Parker, George Mendenhall of James-town, and at a later period with Benjamin Lundy in Baltimore. It is evident that he found in these older men the balance of maturity toward which he was striving.

The Mount Ephraim School experience might well be termed William Swaim's point of departure into active participation in civic affairs. While he was teaching there with Benjamin Swaim, the two young men organized a debating club, known as the "Polemic Society;" and like other young men of the whole surrounding country, William became an active member for the training it would provide in reasoning and public speaking.[54] Nor was it restricted to the younger men, for leading and well-established older men for miles around often participated in its programs. It was the same type of club as that in which Henry Clay gained a great deal of his argumentative and speaking ability, but the similiarity appears to have been entirely coincidental.[55] As the name Polemic implies, the topics selected for debate were usually ones that lent themselves to forceful arguments on both sides; and the protagonists of both sides of the questions often became highly animated in their efforts to prove their contentions. Even though the speakers were untrained, their enthusiasm for their assignments often outweighed their lack of polish. And even though they chose or were assigned to defend a position which they actually opposed, they came forward, as do any good debaters, with support for whichever side they were scheduled to uphold.

Swaim enjoyed and profited from his associations in the Polemic Society. He was interested in the variety of opinions among the members, and he liked testing his own debating skill. He left in his *Diary* a record of his personal feeling about the organization, as follows: "I took a deep interest in it, and never missed a meeting when it was in my power to attend. The debaters were principally young boys; and none of them, of course, were very eloquent, though all, who devoted their attention to it, improved amazingly. If I could impress upon all young men the propriety and profit of spending their time in this way, rather than in vicious pursuits, I would be glad to do so. Thousands of such are entirely ruined for want of some kind friend to give them a proper direction at a certain vulnerable period in boyhood and youth."[56]

The most popular as well as the most important subject that came before the Polemic Society while he was a member was the one which proposed a reform of the state constitution. Since the ratification of the federal constitution in 1789, the revision of the state constitution of 1776 had been the most long-standing issue in North Carolina. Although the original document had served very well as a unifying force during the formative years of the republic, many felt that it had become outmoded.

The more recently settled and more democratically progressive element in the western section of the state had for years felt the need for a change. As early as 1787 the question of a revision of the 1776 edition had been proposed, but there was so much disagreement on the matter that no definite steps were taken. In 1788, 1808, 1811, 1816, 1819, 1821, 1822, and 1823 definite efforts had been made in favor of reform, but they had been voted down by the ruling majority of the legislature.[57]

North Carolina was not alone in its desire for a revision, for several other states had already revised their original constitutions, a fact which now served in a way as an incentive for North Carolina to keep in line. From 1819 to 1821 the agitation became very intense. William K. Boyd in his *History of North Carolina* wrote that "the whole state was convulsed from mountains to sea. Finding their efforts [of no avail in the legislature], the leaders of the movement decided to appeal directly to the people." This decision resulted in the call of a popular convention which convened in Raleigh in the fall of 1823, immediately before the meeting of the General Assembly. According to Boyd, "after a week's session the convention adjourned. Its cause was undoubtedly a just one, but the cleavage between the extreme western and central counties was fatal; also the resort to a second convention smacked too much of a revolution. Consequently there were no effective results." When the General Assembly met two days after the convention had adjourned, it ignored the meeting in so far as positive action was concerned.[58]

The state constitution question, then, was rocking the state in the summer of 1823 when the Polemic Society was in full swing. A feature that added to the enthusiasm of the members of the society was the fact that several men of the area who were well-known to them had been recent representatives in the state legislature, and had brought back to the home scene inside news of the goings on in that body. Among such men of their acquaintance were Jonathan Parker (1800-1804, 1807-1809, 1811-1815, 1821-1828, 1832, 1834), Colonel William Dickey (1819), Dr. David Worth, (1820, 1822, 1823), William Adams, Esquire (1821), and Colonel James Neely (1824) who served in that capacity the following year and was already well versed in state politics.[59] Not only were those official representatives at fever heat over the question of the constitution, but the people in general upon every convenient occasion, either avidly defended or violently opposed constitutional reform or revision. Thus was the stage set for the young orators of the Polemic Society.

Swaim clearly understood the need for constitutional reform and was determined to express his views on the subject. It mattered not to him that he had never read as much as ten pages of grammar or seen a work on logic or rhetoric.[60] What he lacked in formal training he made up for in zeal and courage.

In his *Diary*, he wrote that "Peter Adams, son of William Adams, opposed a convention to amend the Constitution, and I advocated

45

it. Each of us warmly and earnestly maintained his side of the question, so much so that it became the chief subject of conversation between us whenever we met thereafter. At length it was proposed by one of us, I forget which now, to have the debate over again at my schoolhouse by Col. Dickey's. Accordingly, the day was appointed and notice given. Before this I had been invited by William Adams, several times, to walk up to his house [for a casual visit]. Well, I did so previous to this mighty debate, expected soon to come off between the old man's son, Peter, and myself. The old gentleman took occasion to speak of it, and endeavored to dissuade us from it. But I was 'devil-bent' and could not have been diverted from my purpose by all the magistrates of the county. At length the day came; but no Peter! The people of the neighborhood had pretty generally collected, so as to form a very respectable audience both for numbers and intelligence."[61]

With an interested audience assembled, Swaim had no thought of giving up, Peter or no Peter! The question to be considered was, in effect, "Resolved: that the constitution of North Carolina as framed in 1776 should be revised." Dr. David Worth was asked to preside over the meeting, and Colonel William Dickey was made secretary of the occasion.[62] It is not known whether the men who spoke against a revision of the constitution were expressing their personal opinions on the matter or were just supporting that side in order to promote a good program. It is known, however, that Swaim was a serious advocate of a general renovation of the original document. Dr. Worth presented as the first speaker Colonel James Neely, a prominent and highly esteemed citizen of the county; and in a clear and forceful manner he defended the old constitution as adequate to the then present needs. Swaim replied to him in a sort of warming-up speech which appears to have been extemporaneous. Jonathan Worth, who was at that time a law student under Judge Archibald D. Murphey, then further defended the negative side of the question. Whatever Worth said, and unfortunately it has not been preserved, was sufficient to impel Swaim to speak with deep conviction and convincing force, for he rose and presented his carefully prepared defense of the subject with all his might and power. And he won unanimously[63]

There is no record of those who served as judges in the debate. Perhaps the decision was by vote of the audience. Be that as it may, it was no small accomplishment for Swaim in his first public effort to win alone over his two skilled opponents — Neely, who was much his superior in age and experience in matters of state; and Worth, his same age, but who had had the best educational advantages offered in the state at that time, and was already pretty well versed in the subject of the law.

And Swaim did not do a bad job for one who had had only six irregular months of formal instruction.[*64] For that time his speech was well-written, his facts were impressively chosen and assembled, his argument was convincing, and his presentation in some places rose to the dignified eloquence of his day. On that occasion, which was very important to Swaim since it was his initial trial at writing, his speech contained ideas of great importance to the state:

"MR. CHAIRMAN AND FELLOW-CITIZENS:

"The subject of calling a Convention to amend the Constitution of your State has produced much excitement. Much irritable feeling has been manifested, both by the advocates and the opponents of the measure. Party spirit, that bane of society, has participated largely in this discussion; while reason and good sense have been almost entirely discarded. This should not be so; because the question is one which involves the dearest interests of the State, and upon its thorough and rational discussion rest our future hopes. Let us, for a moment, strip ourselves of all party spirit, discard all sectional prejudice and jealousy, and step forward in the honest candor of our hearts, for the purpose of arriving at correct conclusions respecting the real merits of this great question.

"The circumstances, under which the framers of our Constitution were convened, were at once sufficient to obliterate the hope, if there were any, of their ever being able to arrive at anything like a

---

*These six months of schooling comprise the extent of his education from the classroom; from there on he was a self-educated man.

47

perfect system of government. The delightful scenes of peace and tranquility were buried in the tremendous clangor of the cannon; the whistle of the farmer was silenced in the shrieks of the widow and the orphan; the calm, deliberate investigation of the statesmen had yielded to the bustle and tumult of the soldier; the serenity of the heavens was obscured by the smoke ascending from the half-consumed habitations of the citizens; and anarchy was threatening to destroy all civil government and engul[f] our State in the vortex of desolation! Under all these appalling scenes, in the year 1776, a Convention of Delegates assembled at Halifax, for the purpose of framing a Constitution for the government of our people. Where is the rational man that would, for a moment, expect perfection to emanate from a body of men convened under such unfavorable circumstances? Everything but faith in modern miracles would discard such an idea. But a candid examination of the current facts of that soul-trying time, together with an impartial perusal of the journals of the Convention, will satisfy us, that they intended that Constitution, by which we are now governed, only as a temporary work to protect us through the bloody scenes of the Revolution, a work for the people to examine, alter and amend, when the troubles of war should pass away and the sunshine of peace be restored.

"But if it be contended, that the Congress of Halifax designed this as a permanent Constitution, sufficient reasons can be produced to show the impossibility of framing such an instrument, at that time, as to suit the future condition of the people. The same feelings, that now are called Eastern and Western, then and long before, existed in the Province of North Carolina; and if they existed among the people, it is reasonable to presume they were not absent from that body. In the Congress, that adopted the Constitution, thirty-six counties were represented. Of these, only ten were Western. All that wide-extended range of country, lying west of Raleigh, was then divided into only ten counties. That body being thus composed, suppose an attempt had been made to fix the principles of representation on any other basis than the present, what would have been the result? Why, the same feelings, that now influence the members of the Legislature, would have at once put it down. The vote, in all probability, would have been twenty-six against ten!

"Of all the objectionable parts of the Constitution, the system of representation is the most unequal, unjust, oppressive, and anti-republican. The theory of the Constitution seems to be the representation of the people in one branch of the General Assembly, and of the property in the other: but, in practice, the people are not represented at all. Because if the people were represented, numbers would form the basis of the system. So that it is not the people, as a relative branch of the whole, but the counties, as a kind of separate governments, that are represented. Under the operation of this absurd system of representation, our government has ceased to be a republic, and become a complete and perfect aristocracy. What is an aristocracy but where the few govern the many? Is it not essential in a republic, that all the citizens of the same grade of qualification should have an equal participation in the rights and privileges of the government? — and that a majority should rule? No government where these principles are wanting in its organic laws, can merit the title of a republican government. And to show that these principles have no place in the practical operation of our State Constitution, I ask your attention to a few calculations bottomed on the census of 1820 and on the Revenue laws of the State.

"The Counties of Ashe, Buncombe, Chowan, Columbus, Gates, Green, Hyde, Jones, Lenoir, Martin, Tyrrell and Washington, in number twelve, contain a free white population of 36,525. Contrast this with the free white population of twelve large counties, viz: Burke, Guilford, Iredell, Lincoln, Mecklenburg, Orange, Randolph, Rowan, Rutherford, Stokes, Surry and Wake, in all 154,345. Thus 36,525 citizens in certain small counties send as many members to the State Legislature as 154,345 citizens living in a like number of large counties. If these twelve large counties be entitled to no more than thirty-six representatives, the twelve small ones should be entitled to only eight: Or, if the twelve small counties be entitled to thirty-six, the twelve large ones should be entitled to one hundred and fifty-seven. But instead of that, each of the twelve has an equal participation in the councils of the State.

"Let us take one more view of the subject, which will be sufficient for our purpose at present: The thirty-three emallest counties in the state contain a free white population of 138,911, lacking only 833 souls of being one-third of the free white population of the State; yet they send ninety-nine members to the Legislature, which gives them a complete majority in that body! Does it not plainly appear, that one-third of the free white population of the State governs the other two-thirds? What is this but aristocracy? — the few governing the many — one-third controlling two-thirds — making all the laws — appointing all the officers, Executive, Judicial and Military? Yet, forsooth, we must groan under this intolerable oppression, until a radical change can be effected in our present constitutional law.

"Again, the eleven largest counties in the State contain a free white population of 141,653, making 1,520 more than one-third part of the whole population of the State; and yet these counties are entitled to only thirty-three members, or sixty-seven less than the same amount of population in another part of the State is entitled to send! Is this what is called a republican government, founded upon equal rights and privileges? Yes, this is the monument of wisdom, that, we are told, is too sacred to be touched!

"It is, however, insisted, that the principle of *taxation* will give the Eastern section of the State that preponderence which it now holds. But a few stubborn facts will be found sufficient to set this notion aside and expose its authors to merited ridicule. The counties of Columbus, Carteret, Currituck, Ashe, Tyrrell, Hyde, Haywood, Moore, Brunswick and Washington, in number ten, paid a poor pitiful sum of $4,195.85 into the Treasury, at the same time, that Rowan and Orange contributed within a fraction of $5,000.00; yet these ten poverty-smitten counties send thirty members, and Rowan and Orange only six.

"Again, the counties of Hyde, Tyrrell, Haywood, Carteret, Currituck, Ashe and Columbus contribute so little to the funds of the State, that they are a clear annual expense of $4,536.66 above what their poverty-smitten condition will permit them to contribute. Thus, we have actually to compensate them for legislating against our interest!

"If each county be entitled to an equal participation in the privileges of government, it ought to contribute an equal proportion toward its expenses; and, consequently, the seven counties, last named, lack $11,748.68 of paying their part of the contingent expenses of the State government. This large sum must be paid out of the coffers of other counties to the monopolizing minority for doing their own business.

- "The above facts will be found sufficient to demonstrate that neither taxation, property, nor population, has any preponderance in the political scale; but it is the counties, and they alone, that are represented in the grand Congress called the General Assembly! Because if a county be large enough to contain a garden, a potato patch and a cowpen, and has three inhabitants, constitutionally qualified, it has an equal participation in the rights and privileges of government with the most wealthy and populous county in the State! Thus the small counties in the East have the power placed in their hands of disposing of the funds of the State as they may think proper. In short, we in the West are bound by our present form of government to give part of our money to the citizens of the East, for sending members enough to the General Assembly to take the remainder of it from us.

"Is it not time for the citizens of the Western section of the State to remember, that when the public coffers are to be filled, they pay tax according to their numbers — that when the militia are to be embodied for the public safety, they stand their draft according to their numbers — that when the horrors of war are shocking the country, they spill their blood according to numbers — and that their numbers ought to be regarded in the enactment of laws to which they are bound to be subject?

"According to our Constitution, the General Assembly convenes every year. This frequency of meeting is the cause of much unsteadiness in legislation and renders an acquaintance with the laws of the

State very difficult. Because at one session an act is passed, and the next session it is repealed, and the repealing act repealed, and re-established and repealed again, until none but those, who make the law their study, can determine what acts are in force.

"The constitutional representation of the State throws one hundred and ninety six members into the Legislature which is too many by far to transact business with any degree of facility.—According as the number of members is diminished, the responsibility will be enhanced, and the opportunity of concealing sinister motives proportionally removed. Besides these inconveniences attending a full session annually, the expense is not to be disregarded in times that labor under such pecuniary embarrassment as the present. Two sessions of the Legislature cost the State about $64,000. Now, if it were to convene once in two years, and consist of ninety six members instead of one hundred and ninety six, and continue in session forty days — the usual length of the present sessions — the expense would be only $11,520, every two years, instead of $64,000. Could this happy change be made, we would save $26,240 annually, and the State government would be conducted with more regularity and steadiness than it is, at present, with its enormous train of expenses attached to it.

"We will pass in silence over other defects existing in the Constitution, though volumes might be written or spoken upon the subject. That our Constitution is defective, all admit; and that now is the most proper time to amend it, none will deny. We are at peace with all nations; the blood of slaughtered hundreds, which once crimsoned our fields, has been washed away by the gentle showers of prosperity; the cannon's roar has long since been succeeded by the gentle notes of peace and tranquility; and our ships which were once employed in conveying hostile armies, with their leaden messengers of death, to the dreadful fight, are now occupied in transporting the rich fruits of our happy country to the remotest boundaries of the world. In short, if ever [there were a favorable opportunity] for agitating the internal concerns of our government, it is the present. Let us approach the subject, then, at once and with firmness; let us give our Constitution that honest investigation which its importance demands; and let us select a convention of delegates from among ourselves, to make such alterations as time, experience and change of circumstances have shown to be essential to the future happiness and prosperity of the entire State!"[65]

Several of the people who were connected with this debate later rose to places of influence in the state. Dr. Worth, Colonel Dickey, and Colonel Neely were already prominent public figures; Peter Adams who did not appear for the debate, can be said later to have redeemed himself by serving in both the House of Commons and the Senate of the General Assembly, and by acting for many years as Presiding Justice of the Guilford County Court of Pleas and Quarter Sessions; and Jonathan Worth, who moved to Randolph County, became a successful lawyer and financier, served as State Treasurer, represented his adopted county in both branches of the legislature, and was elected Governor of North Carolina in 1865.

As these debaters, William Swaim and Jonathan Worth, continued their lives, the North Carolina constitutional question, which they debated in the Polemic Society of 1823, became headline material for the state before it was finally adjusted in 1835.

# III

## A BONA FIDE MEMBER OF THE FOURTH ESTATE

*"These are perilous times; and a responsibility, awful as the tomb and extensive as eternity, hangs over every man who shall take upon himself the management of a newspaper; because* public opinion *is measurably formed from the* tone of the press — *the* action *of the people depends upon* opinions previously formed — *and upon* [*the* action *of the people*] *is suspended the* destinies of the Republic!"[1]

As Swaim began to take an active part in discussions on slavery, education, constitutional reform, and other social questions which then confronted the state and the nation, he put aside his former resolution to become a lawyer and decided to make printing his profession. Aware of the power of the printed word and wishing to communicate with his fellow countrymen through this medium, he had arrived at his conclusion slowly and thoughtfully, as evidenced by the fact that he was already twenty-five — well into his twenty-sixth year — when he set about to learn the printer's trade.

There was a printing establishment in Swaim's county seat, the Town of Greensboro, where he could have served his apprenticeship, but he decided to go beyond the bounds of his state to Baltimore, Maryland. He probably never before had gone as far as twenty-five miles from his home. His journey, therefore, by land to Norfolk, Virginia, thence by sea to Baltimore, seemed to him a long and lonely one. In early March, 1828, as his boat sailed up Chesapeake Bay into the harbor, he could see the tin roofs and church spires of the city made bright by the rising sun. He must have thought of another lonely young man, who in this same location had written the words to "The Star-Spangled Banner." Despite the thrill afforded by the historic spot and the grandeur of the city which lay before him, a momentary wave of his former timidity enveloped him and he felt anxious and depressed. These sensations, however, did not thwart his determination to become a public printer; and he steadfastly turned his face and steps toward the heart of the city.[2]

Whether or not Swaim had arranged in advance for employment upon his arrival in Baltimore is not known. From his recent association with the Manumission Society he probably knew that on August 29, 1817, Charles Osborne, a native of North Carolina, had started an antislavery paper, *The Philanthropist,* at Mt. Pleasant, Ohio, and that Benjamin Lundy had been one of its contributors; that in January, 1821, in the same town, Lundy had published his own antislavery paper, *The Genius of Universal Emancipation;* and that Lundy in January, 1822, had moved his publication to Tennessee, and two years later to Baltimore. He must have known that in 1824 Lundy had visited in North Carolina and had delivered his first public address against slavery at Deep Creek; had held some fifteen or twenty antislavery meetings; and, before he left the state, had counted twelve or fourteen abolition societies. If Swaim did not know Lundy personally, he certainly knew about him from their common antislavery interests. In any case, before he had been many days in Baltimore, he was at work in the office of *The Genius of Universal Emancipation,* under the direction of Lundy.[3]

He had taken this job in order to learn the printers' craft, but he showed some talent as well as ambition to try his hand at writing too, for it was not long before Lundy appointed his young employee to the responsible position of assistant editor.[4]

Previous personal contact between Swaim and Lundy had been, no doubt, very slight. In the summer of 1824, when Lundy was moving his publication headquarters from Tennessee to Baltimore, he had gone by way of North Carolina where he had family connections; and it was during this visit that he had worked on antislavery measures.[5] Swaim probably met him at this time, for Lundy later seemed to take satisfying pleasure in announcing that "He [Swaim] was one of my North Carolina converts."[6] Swaim, however, could have become acquainted with Lundy through his paper. *The Genius* at that time had a fairly wide circulation in the United States, in fact, wider than Lundy had ever hoped for, and there were "more subscribers in North Carolina than any other state in the Union."[7]

Born in 1789, a native of New Jersey, Benjamin Lundy as a young man had lived for a while in Wheeling, West Virginia. There he had seen "coffles" of slaves driven along the "thoroughfare for traffickers in human flesh," and he had never been able to forget the "wail of the captive" or his feeling for the slaves' "pang of distress." Although he had later developed a very promising business in the saddler's trade in St. Clairsville, Ohio, had married and become a father, and had built a comfortable home, he decided to give up this pleasant situation and to devote the rest of his life to the cause of the abolition of slavery. Therefore, with his family's consent and cooperation, with small contributions from friends of similar convictions, with the intermittent practice of his trade, and perhaps with some income from his publication, he began to travel over the United States, Canada, and Mexico in the hope of spreading his antislavery gospel.[8]

In this new undertaking, Lundy remained proprietor and editor in chief of *The Genius of Universal Emancipation,* but he came to lean heavily upon an assistant. As soon as the paper was well-established, he left the main responsibility of it in the hands of a junior editor, while he as senior editor contributed somewhat irregularly. Between 1828 and 1838 there were at least four such assistant editors, and William Swaim appears to have been the first one.[9]

Swaim had been associated with Lundy less than two months when he was made assistant editor. He had arrived in Baltimore around the first of March, 1828, and on May 1 of that year, Lundy began a tour of the eastern states, leaving Swaim in charge of the home office. During those intervening two months Lundy had observed that Swaim "was a very capable, intelligent and philanthropic young man."[10] In the months that followed, the editor in chief appeared satisfied with his assistant editor's work, for Lundy remained away from Baltimore for six successive months.[11]

It seems that the most significant advantage Swaim enjoyed through his acquaintance with Lundy was an opportunity to develop on his own. Also, he must have found it inspiring to know and to work for this self-made man who was kind, patient, sensitive, deeply religious, and undiscouraged by disappointments and sacrifices for his reform work.[12] It should be noted, however, that whereas the older man concentrated his efforts for reform toward the emancipation of the Negro, the younger man was to concern himself with the need for other reforms as well. Situated as they were, however, their arrangement worked to the advantage of both of them, for it gave Lundy freedom to pursue his cause, and it provided an opportunity for Swaim to broaden his practical education and to develop his talents.

In his new assignment Swaim, well-aware of his inexperience, applied himself with phenomenal zeal. His first thought was directed to his writing; but as soon as he had that obligation fulfilled, he turned to the printing and typesetting department and studied the mysteries of practical printing. So strong was his physical constitution and so inquisitive was his mind that he scheduled for himself long working hours; but he was young and could stand the greatest labor. His interest in learning, already great, received added impetus through Lundy's faith and confidence in him as assistant editor, and the hours of the day and night seemed too short to satisfy his longing for knowledge. He was elated with this first chance of acquiring a liberal and polished education. Looking over the exchanges, working in the printing department, practicing in writing, visiting the libraries, walking on the streets, or sitting in his boarding house, he was busily engaged in studying and improving his mind.[13] He seemed to prefer this method of learning to the fixed pattern of courses which at that time were required by his state's university, then the only institution of higher learning in North Carolina. He liked to find teachers everywhere and lessons in everything.

For the first time in his life Swaim now was financially on his own. Previously, his outside interests had been unremunerative; and except for short periods of earning as a school teacher, he had remained at home and looked to his work on his father's farm for support. This was also his first opportunity to prove his mettle professionally; and within an incredibly short time he learned the intricacies of practical printing and developed for himself an original and enviable style of editorial writing.

About six months after he assumed his duties on *The Genius,* Swaim was asked to return to his home in North Carolina. His father had died; and his mother wanted him, the oldest son, to settle his father's estate.[14] This was a double blow: it struck the son who loved his father and the young man who had only begun to exercise his own talents. Not once did he think of failing his responsibility as a son, but this required that he leave Baltimore and his work. He arranged, however, to remain at his desk until his employer was able to assume the duties of *The Genius.* Lundy, who was still on his tour of the eastern states, did not reach Baltimore until October 25, 1828. He wrote, "After my return, my assistant editor, William Swaim, returned home to North Carolina."[15] And so, as Swaim himself wrote, he arrived in North Carolina when "the sear and yellow leaf" was beginning to high light the forest.

As Swaim made the long and tedious journey homeward he had time for reflection, not only upon the loss of his father, but upon his recent experiences. He realized that he had enjoyed much of pleasure and profit "while he was in that beautiful and stirring city. He was greatly improved as a writer; he was a very fair compositor and knew how to manage a printing press and establishment; he had advanced considerably . . . in the world of letters, and was wiser and stronger."[16] Although completely unaware of it at the moment, this estimation was soon to be challenged to prove itself.

While acting as administrator of his father's estate, he had another opportunity quite as unexpected as that which made him assistant editor in Baltimore. Early in January, 1829, he had stepped into the office of *The Patriot and Greensborough Palladium* to pick up his county newspaper and was turning away to go about his business when T. Early Strange, editor of the publication, stopped him to propose that he buy the paper and printing establishment. Though very flattered and immediately tempted, Swaim thought such a move too serious and too expensive to allow a hasty answer. He therefore asked Strange to allow him time to think the matter over, and assured him that he would let him have an answer very soon.[17]

It would be a long step from plowboy to newspaper proprietor with only about six months of writing experience in between. Although the thought of editing his home paper greatly pleased the young man, it also overwhelmed him. He was aware of both the responsibility and the opportunity that such a position offered, but he was not yet sufficiently self-confident. And so he weighed the proposition for and against, again and again.

While in this state of indecision, he determined to visit an old friend and talk the matter over with him. In his *Diary,* under the date of January 18, 1829, he described this interview: "After laboring moderately during the week, I went to Jamestown, on yesterday, to visit my old and worthy friend, Richard Mendenhall. I found the old gentleman in a very good humor and a talkative mood. The topics of conversation were numerous and interesting. I must here be permitted to say, that his extensive information, the affability of his manner, and his communicative disposition, render him the most interesting man with whom I ever conversed. His superior intelligence, however, prevented me from figuring to much advantage! When I am in the company of those, who surpass me in useful acquirements, a kind of natural reserve, timidity, or diffidence snatches hold of the ideas in my *head* and chains them down in the bottom of my *belly*, and I am almost invariably forced to remain silent, or expose the emptiness of my cranium! This is by no means a desirable predicament to be placed in, especially when young ladies are present!

"My object, more particularly, in calling upon friend Richard, was to consult him upon the subject of purchasing Mr. Strange's printing establishment. After many unsuccessful efforts to bring the subject fairly before him, I ventured to say, that Strange designed to sell his establishment and remove to Lynchburg, Virginia. 'That,' says he, 'is your chance, if you design to set up the business in this community!' So we entered into conversation upon this subject, the result of which was, his advice to me to purchase immediately and commence business vigorously."[18]

On March 1, 1829, Swaim completed the contract with Strange for taking over the Greensboro newspaper and printing establishment.[19]

The history of Swaim's newly acquired public journal was scant and indefinite, but nonetheless unique. No one seemed to know exactly when Greensboro's first newspaper had been issued. By the process of association, using the county court records, it has been traced at least as far back as 1821. Joseph Reese, who was the first editor of *The Daily Record* (*The Greensboro Record* after 1930), wrote that he once encountered a very old farmer who peddled eggs in the village. "See here," this old man accosted Reece to say, "the [founding] date on that [*Carolina*] *Patriot* is wrong. It's 1821 and not 1825, and I'll tell you how I come to know. In the year 1821 there was a big murder case on trial at the courthouse here and I had come up to hear it. I was standing on the corner where the *Patriot* office is when along come one of the journeyman printers. He was drunk—they all were—and when he got to the corner he fell sprawling into a page of *Patriot* type put out in the sun to dry. And that's why I know the *Patriot* was published that year." Reece looked up the date of the mentioned murder case and found it was in the year 1821.[20]

Will L. Scott told a different story. He wrote in the *Greensboro Patriot*, May, 1866, that the first number appeared in 1826. "The first paper published here, we confess, was, to use a vulgar yet expressive comparison, rather a 'sardine,' ephemeral in its existence and not strikingly able in its editorial conduct. It was called 'The Carolina Patriot' and its first number appeared in January, 1826, . . . Its editors were Dr. Loton G. Watson, who will be remembered by many of our citizens as an eminent physician, though he never distinguished himself in journalism, and Mr. W. Potter, a son of Judge Potter, of Fayetteville, whose name sounds strangely to nearly all now residing here. The first number is of the size of an eight-by-ten pane of glass and was published on coarse, unclear paper, made at the paper mill of Col. Emanuel Shober in Salem. Their type, too, was indifferent, nor could they have hoped that the mechanical execution would be very handsome. But the public expected, from the promises promulgated in the prospectus, that it would be correctly edited and published. In each the[re] was disappointment. In striking off the sheets, instead of publishing them, so that the reader, in perusing them, turns them over like the leaves of a book, they printed the second and fourth pages so that he had to read them 'up' instead of 'down.' From this circumstance, it was thought, that the editors had invited the attendance, at their office on that day, of the gay son of Jupiter and Semele and sprightly John Barleycorn, who, notwithstanding their oft genial humor and glorious frolicksomeness, prove not infrequently troublesome to their friends and associates. A copy of this issue, we are informed, is lodged in a museum in the city of Philadelphia, as a 'live curiosity' in the history of American Journalism."[21]

Whatever was the initial publication date of the *Carolina Patriot*, like so many newspapers of that day it lived through only a few numbers and then ceased to be.

The idea of a newspaper for Greensboro survived, however, as evidenced by the fact that T. Early Strange purchased the unsuccessful *Carolina Patriot* from Watson and Potter and published his first issue on April 24, 1826, as *The Patriot*. He later changed that name to *The Patriot and Greensborough Palladium*. "Strange was a practical printer, a man of good sense and sound judgment, a talented writer, and an enterprising citizen; and he put out a respectable paper for those days. It was, however, made up largely of selections from other publications with very little editorial matter."[22] Strange also enlarged the paper from "demy" size to "royal" size and gave it a much better appearance.

The publication bore little resemblance to a modern newspaper. The front page of some early issues carried reprints from a Sir Walter Scott novel. The "Late Foreign News" column lived up to its title, for ordinarily it really was about a month late, and had already undergone several revisions. First, it had been brought from abroad by slow ship, and then entered in northern journals; then these journals traveled by stagecoach to southern states; and finally the news was digested and briefed by the local editor who passed to his patrons the "latest intelligence."

Advertisements were brief treatises on the subject presented. Although radio's singing and television's singing and acting commercials of the mid-twentieth century may have more vividly and liltingly pictured man's innermost parts, they promised no more than did *The Patriot's* advertisement of this conscientious physician:

### DR. J. A. FOULKES

Having returned from Philadelphia, where he has been attending a course of Medical Lectures in the University of Pennsylvania, respectfully informs his friends and the public in generally, that he intends commencing immediately, the practice of Medicine in its various branches, in the Town of Greensborough, the vicinity, and in the adjoining Counties when his services are required.

He has purchased the House and Lot owned by Dr. Watson, as well as the whole of his Medicines; These with the addition of those he purchased in the City of Philadelphia, will make, it is presumed, a Shop not inferior to any in the State. Persons from the country, can be supplied with Medicines on reasonable terms; Physicians whose assortment may be broken, will on application, be supplied at a moderate advance on the prime cost.

Those who require his professional services, may rely on his promptness and punctuality, as well as his best exertions to serve them faithfully—he can promise no more; the tests of his medical skill can only be applied by a candid and generous public, when they become sufficiently acquainted with him.[23]

Strange had hoped to make a living from his newspaper and at the same time to advance the cause of education by disseminating general information and news. So intent was he upon this last hope that at the fifty-first celebration of American Independence, when others were thinking mostly of politicians and politics, he offered this toast: "Education—the most essential of all internal improvements; the true preservative of virtue and liberty, which alone can perpetuate its blessings."[24]

However noble Strange's intentions were, his paper evidently did not bring him the hoped-for living, for he departed from the Greensboro paper with a plea to the people that they pay him what they owed on back subscriptions.[25]

That was the situation of newspaper publishing in Greensboro when William Swaim became a working member of the fourth estate in North Carolina.

When anyone planned to publish a new newspaper in the early nineteenth century, it was customary several weeks in advance of actual publication to announce through a "Prospectus" a brief summary of what might be expected when it would appear. On April 4, 1829, and in following issues, Swaim therefore published his Prospectus in *The Patriot and Greensborough Palladium*, and asked other newspapers of the state to carry it.

Any shortened version of this preliminary statement would lose to a reader the sense of urgency and personal dedication felt by the young editor. And, since well-nigh all that is known of him is his work as an editor, he deserves to be heard in his own words. This was his creed and his promise:

PROSPECTUS

of

GREENSBOROUGH PATRIOT

and

Southern Political and Literary Register

"The subscriber having contracted for the printing establishment heretofore occupied by Mr. Strange, in the town of Greensborough, proposes the continuation of a weekly newspaper in the same place, under the above title. He has it in contemplation to procure a complete supply of new materials, which will enable him to execute the mechanical part of the work in a style *equal* if not *superior* to any in the State; and his whole intellectual energies shall be exerted to render the contents of its columns both useful and interesting to every class in the community. The necessity of disseminating intelligence more generally and extensively among the ordinary ranks of society, must be obvious to every reflecting mind. An unparalleled spirit of revolution is abroad in the earth. Knowledge is running to and fro, hurling defiance in the face of DESPOTISM, and shaking his ponderous throne to the centre. Long-forsaken LIBERTY is beginning to rub the scales from her eyes and elevate immortal man to a sense of his own substantial dignity. And when we show the people of the United States their relative standing among the great family of nations, they will reform those incongruous absurdities which blot the face of our *Republican Institutions;* and thus give to the fundamental maxims of our Government, an unlimited influence abroad.

"Many of our wisest men, for the past few years, have been almost led to distrust the capacity of the people for self Government. And we admit that clouds of conflicting wrath have sometimes congregated in our political elements that might naturally give birth to fears of this kind; but to that native good sense and virtue which yet burn with fervid patriotism in the American bosom we look for a redeeming spirit that shall dispel the storm, and smile upon the approaching calm like a 'bow of promise' in Heaven's brightest sunshine. Enlighten the people—liberalize and expand the minds of the rising generation, and our almost expiring liberties will rise with renovated lustre from the crumbling verge of the tomb, and roll back that flood of intellectual darkness which has so long shielded ambitious demagogues from public scrutiny: and we may then say, without danger of being denounced for an over-heated enthusiasm, that we are 'inhabitants of time's eternal empire.'

"To inculcate a th[i]rst for moral and literary improvement among the young sons of North-Carolina — to furnish instructive amusements for the fair ones on whose intelligence and virtue rest the destinies of our country—to spread before the public a faithful account of all the events and transactions, both *foreign* and *domestic*, that may agitate the political world—to scrutinize closely the conduct of men in power, and chastise their misdoings without regard to rank—to pull the mask from the face of corruption and hold up popular vices to view in their 'native deformity'—to break the spell, which has so long palsied the energies of the Southern States, and show them the necessity of improving their advantages —and to influence our young countrymen, with warm hearts and 'lips of fire,' to 'plead their Country's cause'—shall constitute the prominent objects of the Greensborough Patriot. How far these objects will be consummated, time alone can disclose.—It yet remains with a generous public to answer the question, whether an Independent press can be sustained in this State;—and such ours Shall be, *or poverty, want and neglect* shall sink it into utter annihilation.

"In this noted age of periodicals, when so many 'scribblers for bread' are teasing the community with their 'perishable trash,' no paper can rise to respectability and command a lasting support unless it be raised above mediocrity. The limits of a prospectus, however, will not permit us to enter into a minute description of the manner in which our conduct will at all times be regulated. Suffice it to say that we shall place no restraint upon a *fair* and *free* discussion of ALL subjects that may be interesting to any considerable portion of our readers; but our columns shall not be contaminated with rancorous feelings of party spirit or personal malignity. We shall always stand as a sentinel upon the watch-tower of American Liberty, and sound the alarm of every threatened invasion. And when we fail to act as a firm and uncompromising

65

friend of the people—let us be deemed unworthy of confidence, and left to merited execration forever."

Having released his Prospectus, in April, 1829, the future editor went to Philadelphia to purchase new type in order to bring out a newspaper in every sense worthy of its name.[26] On May 23, 1829, Swaim issued the first number of the *Greensborough Patriot*. Immediately below the title he inserted the following noble sentiment: *"THE IGNORANT AND DEGRADED OF EVERY NATION OR CLIME MUST BE ENLIGHTENED, BEFORE OUR EARTH CAN HAVE HONOR IN THE UNIVERSE."* William Swaim, Editor, said that, and he meant it.

With the publication of that issue of the *Greensborough Patriot*, Swaim launched the longest-lived newspaper ever to be consecutively published in North Carolina up to 1963.[27] From the very first issues Historian Stephen B. Weeks said it became "a leader of the best thoughts of its day."[28] Moreover, its constructive influence was felt for the next one hundred and thirty-four years.

When Swaim released his first edition of the *Greensborough Patriot*, he established an editorial department:

# GREENSBOROUGH:

### SATURDAY, MAY 23, 1829

*"Truths would you teach, or save a sinking land,
All fear, none aid you, and few understand."*

ADDRESS TO OUR PATRONS. We this week present our patrons with the first number of the "GREENSBOROUGH PATRIOT." How far it will satisfy their expectations we pretend not to venture an opinion. Our prospectus will be found on the first page; and a short communication upon the subject of our paper will be found on reference to the last number issued by Mr. Strange. In this communication we promised that in our first number, we would lay before

So descriptive was Swaim's first editorial of the policies he followed in his paper, that it constitutes a fair picture of the man and his standards, both personal and professional. He had no subordinates or associates with whom to share any criticism or praise for the contents of the *Greensborough Patriot*. His paper was a reflection of himself as well as his times:

"ADDRESS TO OUR PATRONS. We this week present our patrons with the first number of the 'GREENSBOROUGH PATRIOT.' How far it will satisfy their expectations we pretend not to venture an opinion. Our prospectus will be found on the first page; and a short communication upon the subject of our paper will be found on reference to the last number issued by Mr. Strange. In this communication we promised, that in our first number, we would lay before our Patrons a more satisfactory exposition of the objects at which we aim, and the principles which shall regulate our conduct in the attainment of those objects;—We now proceed to a redemption of our pledge.

"As the broad principles of our Government are purely Republican, they can only be sustained in their beauty, and advanced *towards* perfection, by the virtue, the intelligence, and consequently, the energy and patriotism of the People. When the great mass of our citizens are enveloped in ignorance, they are liable to be hoodwinked by any aspiring demagogue, and humbugged into any measure his unprincipled ambition may suggest. Great men will play tricks for office as small ones do for smaller considerations; and, where the people are not enlightened, it is an easy matter for them to blow a whirlwind out of their own distempered throats, and ride into popular favor upon the storm. But make the people familiar with all the ordinary transactions of the Country, and those who have cried 'Liberty, independence and the rights of the People,' merely to make their designs go down the better, will retreat before the march of unassuming merit like 'midnight darkness before the beams of the sun.' Hence the necessity of a better regulated system of Education in our State than we have heretofore had. It is a source of painful regret that N. Carolina should have slumbered fifty-two years in the arms of indolence without digesting any plan for a distribution of the blessings of education among the ordinary ranks of Society. It is true, our Legislature has reared and sustained a University under its guardian protection, which readily opens its stores of science to the sons of wealth; but how will it ever be possible for the poverty-smitten thousands of ignorant and destitute children that might be congregated together in the lower ranks of life, to find access to its treasures of learning? The fact is too notorious for concealment, that hundreds of young sons of N. Carolina are growing up, even to *manhood*—in point of muscular power—without being able to read! and many of those who *can* read '*easy places*' neglect to use their '*art*' as a means of improving their minds. And the constituted authorities of our State need take to themselves no credit in concealing its truth, because many of them have used this deplorable ignorance as a hobby-horse on which to ride into posts of proffit and distinction; and this, perhaps, constitutes the best apology they could make for neglecting so long to remove it.

"It shall be our steady aim to infuse a spirit of moral and literary improvement through the State—at least as far as our influence (if we have any) can be extended. We shall not only give place in our columns to such selections and original articles as may be calculated to take hold of the tender mind, and draw it into a love of learning and virtue—but we shall endeavor to impress the people generally with a sense of the necessity of pouring the rich treasures of education into the humblest cottages of our country, until the tenants thereof shall be able to see, to learn, to know and defend their rights. No plan, however, for the consummation of an object so truly desirable will be chalked out until all that may present themselves shall have been closely examined and thoroughly investigated. Every information on the subject will be diligently sought after, and when obtained, shall be faithfully laid before our countrymen for their consideration.

"The Agricultural interests of the State will claim our particular attention. Though the science of farming is in a state of continual progressive improvement, it is yet far, very far below perfection. When our State was first settled, the inhabitants seem not to have been aware of the pernicious tendency of that system, or rather that want of system which they introduced, by prostrating the timber in every direction, and exhausting the soil by every possible means, without any regard for its preservation or improvement. They prosecuted this course until they left no inconsiderable portion of our lands in a state of dilapidation; and shrubbery growing up in every direction, as if striving to hide the general ruins: But in this age of increasing population, the people are beginning to see the necessity, not only of *improving* the lands they have under cultivation, but, of *reclaiming* those which have long since been 'thrown out.' Many able essays have been written on the subject, and much valuable information disseminated; but we yet want *knowledge* as well as spirit and energy. We profess not to be skilled in this noble occupation ourselves, but we shall make it no small part of our business to select such discoveries and improvements in agriculture as may be interesting to farmers in this section of the country. We have all the advantages of soil and climate that any other State in the Union can boast; and nothing but information and energy are wanting to place this state in point of Agricultural prosperity upon a level with the most improved of her sisters. This *information* we intend to give, and we hope it will call into action the *energy.*

"As manufacturing establishments are not only calculated to give new springs to agricultural prosperity, but to render a community more completely independent, we shall not pass the subject over in silence. Though the tariff has been severely execrated by those who were either unable or unwilling to see its advantages— yet we believe it will operate substantially in favor of the Southern States; because it will influence them to manufacture their own raw materials, of which they have an abundance. In the present condition of things, the consumer, in the Southern States, for instance, raises his own cotton, pays its freight to a Northern factory, pays the Manufacturer for spinning, weaving and bleaching it, pays for its conveyance back to our country and village Stores, and then, after giving his merchant from 25 to 50 per cent proffit, he has it ready to 'wear out!' If manufactures were established in N. Carolina and her neighboring sisters, they could call into useful exertion thousands of idle hands that are now strolling through the country, and wallowing in idleness and dissipation for want of useful employment and good wages. These labourers would have to be fed, which would furnish a market for the Corn. Wheat, Flour, Bacon, Beef, Pork and Potatoes of the farmer. This would brighten his countenance with gladsome smiles, enable him to pay his debts, and save him the trouble of trudging 200 miles with his waggon, over hills and through mudholes, to *give his produce away*, and then drag himself home, tired, and faint, and pennyless. And let it not be forgotten that these factories would create a more extensive demand for cotton and wool. This demand would give employment to an additional number of hands in rearing sheep and growing cotton—It would also diminish the number of hands engaged in the grain-growing interest, and consequently enhance the proffits of the farmer's toil. Thus they would become mutually dependent on each other, and independent of the world. Facts will hereafter be given to establish and sustain the above theory.

"The Mechanics, this useful, industrious and enterprising class of our Countrymen, shall not fail to receive their merited portion of our attention. The mechanical arts constitute no inconsiderable portion of those improvements which bless mankind and contribute to the comfort and convenience of human Society. The farmer is apt to regard his occupation as the only one that can sustain the community, and consequently, superior to all others: but he might do well to remember that without the aid of the mechanic, he would cut but a pitiful figure upon the broad theatre of an agricultural world. A mutual good feeling should be cultivated among all the *useful* professions and avocations of life. We shall carefully glean from the numerous periodicals of the day, all the improvements and original inventions that may unfold themselves in the mechanical science, and transmit them to such mechanics as may *subscribe for our paper*.

"Internal Improvements, so intimately and vitally connected with the prosperity of our State, will not be neglected. But when we say *Internal Improvement* we wish not to be understood as placing that construction upon the term which has been given to it in those wild and Quixotic Schemes which have sunk such immense sums of money, and terminated in 'pompous nothings.' We mean what the words themselves implied before they were thus grossly perverted from their original signification. It has been said that 'Bought experience is best when we pay well for it;' and if this be true, the *experience* which N. Carolina has gained in the art of improving her internal condition, must indeed be valuable. Our citizens have been so long, and so repeatedly galled and bamboozled with spacious plans of internal improvement, without realizing any, or but very little, substantial benefit therefrom that they have become discouraged, sickened, & sunk down into a kind of lethargy from which we fear it will be difficult to arouse them. In fact their expectations were wrought up to such a pitch of phrenzied enthusiasm—their calculations were so over-rated and sanguine—and the profits which they expected to realize, so immense, that no wonder, when their Fobs were drained of cash, and their 'hopes blown to the moon,' they should loathe those hated words, *Internal Improvement,* which they had once repeated and reiterated with such joyous anticipations. They now perfectly understood the maxim—*'All is not gold that glitters;'* and we hope they will profit by it. But not to be tedious—Many substantial improvements may be made in the internal condition of our State, if the people will first inform *themselves,* and act with concert and energy;—prudence will then be their guide and success will crown their efforts. The difficulty with which our sun-scorched farmers are enabled to convey the hard-earned pittance of a scanty year, to market, strikingly demonstrates the necessity of improving our roads, or of adopting other and more expeditious means of conveyance. We can promise to ourselves no very considerable advantages from removing these obstructions to navigation with which our rivers &c. abound, unless we, at the same time, give additional facilities to land carriage, and thus enable our sisters to convey their staple commodities to a market for transportation. Both are parts of the same great system of improvement, which must be consummated before that tide of emigration, which is so rapidly flowing to the west, can be stayed, or life, spirit and energy communicated to the mass of our population. All the plans on which the State has heretofore acted, those which are now in operation, and those which may be hereafter proposed, shall be candidly and impartially examined; and everything that may seem calculated to advance the *general* interest, shall find in us an humble advocate; but such schemes as may be got up to gratify the caprice, or subserve the *interest* of the 'favoured few,' at the cost of the many, shall be stripped of their spacious pretext, and lashed naked through the world.

"The fluctuating condition of our circulating medium, & the embarrassment created in our financial concerns by the mismanagement, not to say fraud and dishonesty, of those to whom the superintendence of our banking institutions have been committed, demand the strict attention and rigid scrutiny of every individual in the community. If we dally along until the year 1835,—when the Charter will expire, without providing a more steady, efficient and substantial substitute for our present Bank Notes, which have so long inundated the Country, and caused many a well-meaning man to end his commercial career in prison, and thus render an extension of the Charters indispensible, Wo to the Liberties of N. Carolina. We give the people warning in time; let them look well to their doings in this important concern. Whether all the difficulties under which we, at this time labour, might be obviated by the establishment of a bank belonging exclusively to the State, we shall not at this time determine. But one important fact should not escape our consideration—that is, the large amount of interest to the several Banks in this State. The sum paid by the people to these institutions, in interest alone, amounts to more than THREE HUNDRED THOUSAND DOLLARS *annually!* If this vast sum were paid in to the coffers of the State, instead of the pockets of the rich and insolent individuals, what important objects might we not accomplish? It would defray the whole contingent expenses of the Government, carry on an efficient and energetic system of Internal

72

Improvement, and provide largely for the education of our poor and destitute children. This subject will be resumed hereafter.

"Those benevolent Institutions of our Country, as well as of Europe and elsewhere, which have had their origin in pure and disinterested philanthropie, and which have for their end and object the general improvement of our species, are considered as worthy of the highest encomiums, and entitled to the most liberal and extensive encouragement. Man has a large bundle of selfishness worked into his composition: he is apt to regard every thing that does not contribute to his immediate interest, or the gratification of his fondly cherished propensities, as having no claims upon his purse or his labours. But a truce with preliminaries.

"Candour compels us to say that all those institutions which have been organized for the purpose of bettering the conditions of Africa's injured children, and mitigating the growing evils of slavery in the Southern Portion of our Union, so far as we may conceive them calculated to consummate these desirable objects shall have our undivided support; but we shall advocate no measures that may have a tendency to infringe upon the 'Rights of private property.' And if any declaration has ever escaped our lips contrary to this, it has been to 'Answer a fool according to his folly,' we shall never, *unnecessarily*, or *wantonly*, wound the feelings, or inflict a contusion in the sensibilities of a single individual in the community: but we belong not to that *outrageously* cautious few, who discuss the subject, four hours at a heat, and then conclude by saying—'The question is too delicate for discussion!' Its blasting influence upon the aspect of things, wherever its unhallowed foot-steps have polluted the soil, are too glaring to escape the notice of the most superficial observer. Setting aside all moral and religious considerations connected with the subject, there is not a man to be found in the Southern States, whose opinions are entitled to respect, whether he finds himself burthened with this species of property or not, who will deny that slavery constitutes the supreme political curse of this Country. It has arrayed one portion of our free and flourishing Union against the other, and engendered feelings and

73

prejudices hostile to the repose of our otherwise happy Country. Then why not discuss it freely, fairly and extensively, in order that the people may view it in all its bearings, and dispose of it according to the suggestions of their collected wisdom? But we *again* say, the subject shall not be *unnecessarily* agitated. We shall not claim to ourselves the privilege of dictating what course shall be pursued. All temperately written communications in regard to the question, whether in accordance with our opinion or not, shall find a place in our columns, and perhaps, by bringing conflicting views into collision, the s[p]arks of truth may be elicited.

"We believe it to be uniformly admitted, by men of good sense and ordinary intelligence, that female virtue alone can uphold and perpetuate the institutions of our Country. It is true, the frippery, the lightness and vanity of some, cannot be too severely censured; but it would be unjust and unmanly to condemn the whole sex for the misdeeds of a part. We speak not of those 'gay butterflies of a short sunny hour,' that spend more time and pains decorating their *persons*, than do in replenishing their *minds* with useful knowledge: but even they, weak, fickle and inconstant as they are, exert a most tremendous influence over the destinies of man. We allude to the influence of the mother in forming the infant character. It is here the mind is furnished with its *first*, and consequently, its most *durable* impressions—It is here those dispositions are engendered which will almost invariably lead to usefulness and respectability on the one hand, or shame, disgrace and infamy on the other. How important, then, that Female Education, that great bullwark of our prosperity and happiness, should receive its merited share of public consideration. Every man who has basked in the sunshine of heaven, or inhaled the atmosphere of life, no matter how stubbornly his notions may be starched with Bachelorism, if he ever marked the motions of his conduct, has found himself acting, more or less, under the dominion of *female influence*. We say not this to make the softer part of Creation more vain than they are—Heaven knows they are vain enough! Our object is, to lead them to a sense of their immense responsibility, which grows out of that unlimited influence which nature has given them. We must leave here the subject and hasten to a conclusion, but its importance will not be forgotten.

"Finally, by becoming familiar with the rise, progress decline, downfall and ultimate crash of Empires, Kingdoms and Countries, and with the causes which lead to such astonishing revolutions, we are enabled to shun those whirlpools which have engul[f]ed the most sublime specimens of Literature, refinement and national prosperity that ever shed their luster upon the minds of men. Collecting and disseminating all the foreign news that a universal acquiescence in the above position may seem to require, will therefore, claim a portion of our labours commensurate to their importance. It is to be observed also, that the Legislative and Executive Functionaries of our State, as well as of the United States, will be watched with an eye that never winks, and their actions faithfully laid before the people for their examination. In short:—All the interesting intelligence, both Foreign and Domestic—Religious and Political, shall find a place in our columns. In conclusion, we solicit communications on all the above subjects; and if they should not accord with the doctrine which we have laid down, it will not operate as a bar to their insertion, because our object is to *'Prove all things, and hold fast that which is good.'*"

Obviously Swaim subscribed to the idea that "a man's reach must exceed his grasp;" and he did so at a time when casualties among newspapers were quite common.

Though there had been adventures in newspaper publishing in North Carolina since 1751, there were only twenty-one being issued in the state in 1830 when Swaim was building up his journal.[29] Most of these championed one political party or another. In fact, many of them were born out of the desire to support an impending movement or to applaud a favorite candidate; and if either went down in defeat, the whipped publication soon withered and died. Of the twenty-one, only seven lived long enough to leave a deep imprint on the public mind—the *Raleigh Register*, the

75

*Star* of Raleigh, the Fayetteville *Carolina Observer,* the *Western Carolinian* of Salisbury, the *Hillsborough Recorder,* the *Tarborough Free Press,* and the *Greensborough Patriot*.[30] Two other impressive papers were soon added to this list, the *Carolina Watchman* of Salisbury and the *North Carolina Standard* of Raleigh. The life span of most of these was about fifty years, but the *Raleigh Register* which was published for eighty-six years, the *Carolina Watchman* which ran around one hundred years, and the *Greensborough Patriot* which under different names served the public for one hundred twenty-one years (one hundred twenty-four years if *The Patriot* is included), had the longest continuous records to their credit.

The 1830's had brought a general awakening in social, economic, and political consciousness which boldly began to assert the rights of the common man and to stir up deep feelings along lines of basic reform. In all American history there had been no period more stormy and opinionated than that which embraced the years of Swaim's editorship. In the state and in the nation it was a time of violent passions, of political party battles, and of personal hatreds. This situation in turn had brought a new epoch in the history of the printed page.[31]

Before that time, editors had concentrated upon national and foreign news, giving little attention to local and state happenings; had practiced considerable restraint in taking issue on controversial subjects; and had conducted what had passed for an editorial column with what they considered dignity and decorum. With the new age, however, a new type of editorial appeared. By the late 1820's, the previously dignified and self-controlled editorial policy of earlier newspapers, exercised on subjects of remote areas with little direct relation to the fate of an isolationist nation, had given way to an unrestrained attitude of editorial expression which burned with conviction and faced any situation uncompromisingly.[32] This change was concurrent with the increasingly heated frankness of leading men in both state and national politics.

Since the papers were usually aligned with the politicians, conflicting opinions between editors had become more and more impassioned. Editors of some of the older North Carolina newspapers, such as the *Raleigh Register* and the *Carolina Observer and Fayetteville Gazette (Carolina Observer,* 1834-1865), in the main continued to practice tactfulness and viewed with horror the state to which they thought the printed page had degenerated. For example, on May 24, 1827, Edward J. Hale, who had served his apprenticeship under Joseph Gales of the *Raleigh Register,* wrote in his *Carolina Observer and Fayetteville Gazette* that "It must be painful to every friend to the Press and Country, and disgusting to every chaste mind, to behold the entire want of decency and self-respect which many editors of newspapers exhibit in their political and party bickerings. Every day seems to break down some of the barriers of truth and propriety, and the denunciations of political opponents become more and more reckless and rancourous. Female character is attacked; the domestic sanctuary violated; epithets too gross to be applied to a condemned criminal are bandied from one editor to another, and applied to the great and good men of the country. . . . Our partialities are not so warm as to engage us in the general squabble, and to make us lose sight of the respect due to our readers and self."

To this point of view, Harriet Martineau, the intellectual Englishwoman who came to America on a visit in 1834, added her impressions of newspapers of the times: "The profligacy of newspapers, wherever they exist, is a universal complaint. And, of all newspaper presses, I never heard any one deny that the American is the worst. Of course, this depravity being so general throughout the country, it must be occasioned by some overpowing force of circumstances. The causes are various; and it is a testimony to the strength and purity of the democratic sentiment in the country that the republic has not been overthrown by its newspapers."[33]

Perhaps it was because of the turbulence of the times that William Swaim decided to enter the field of journalism instead of becoming a lawyer. Certainly his Prospectus and editorial in his first issue of the *Greensborough Patriot* reveal that he was fully aware of what was going on in the world. And whether Edward Hale and Harriet Martineau liked the prevailing newspaper style or not, Swaim joined the editors who had deep feelings, and on occasion expressed them violently.

# IV

## A UNIQUE NEWSPAPER

*"To spread before the public a faithful account of all the events and transactions, both foreign and domestic . . . shall constitute the prominent objects of the* GREENSBOROUGH PATRIOT.*"*[1]

True to his word, Swaim developed a plan of procedure for honoring the promises made in his Prospectus. He did this by the format of his paper, by his method of collecting news and special items, and by his style of writing which lost nothing from an occasional misspelled word.

With regard to format, he presented an original design, embracive and elastic enough to meet his requirements. Most newspapers of 1829, the year in which Swaim was beginning his editorship, displayed little uniformity of layout. The front page lacked the arresting and significant headlines of later newspapers; and other pages often appeared as dreary seas of type, relieved only occasionally by a one-word topic heading in capital letters. Although some papers had a few regular departments with titles, more often than not a heading was used to attract attention to some unusual feature. Some prominent publishers filled over half of their four weekly pages with advertisements.[2] Swaim, however, with an eye for style, order, and balance, departed from traditional practices and arrested the attention of his readers by setting up departments for specific types of news and articles. Such departments had definite places in his paper and they were shifted to other pages or omitted only when their space was needed for some extraordinary

79

reporting. With somewhat the same ease with which one locates an editorial page in the 1960's, Swaim's readers could locate a section of specialized reading matter in the *Greensborough Patriot*.

Although photography was unknown and illustrative sketches rare one hundred and thirty years ago, Swaim used the latter now and then. Often he emphasized a subject by introducing it with the index mark, thus: . He managed further to relieve the monotony of his pages by the artistic use of lines and the new type he had bought in Philadelphia. And he separated various subjects with ornamental dashes made by using a combination of characters from type cases:

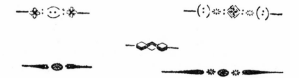

Using four pages that measured fourteen by twenty inches, with four columns to each page, he issued a newspaper that was neat and attractive as well as informative.

Across the top of the first page the title stood out in large boldface capital letters. Immediately below he presented a thesis which gave men something to ponder:

# GREENSBOROUGH PATRIOT

*"THE IGNORANT AND DEGRADED OF EVERY NATION OR CLIME MUST BE ENLIGHTENED, BEFORE OUR EARTH CAN HAVE HONOR IN THE UNIVERSE."*

VOLUME I      GREENSBOROUGH, N. C.   SATURDAY, MAY 23, 1829      NUMBER I

In this initial printing, at the top of column one, page one, Swaim established a masthead which made clear that he was sole proprietor and editor. He also stated the business arrangements under which his paper would operate:

### THE GREENSBOROUGH PATRIOT

Is printed and published every Saturday morning by
**WILLIAM SWAIM**

At Two Dollars per annum, payable within three months from the date of the first number, or Three Dollars after the expiration of that period.

Each subscriber will be at liberty to discontinue at any time within the first three months, by paying for the numbers received, according to the above terms; but no paper will be discontinued until all arrearages are paid, and a failure to order a discontinuance will be considered a new engagement.

Those who may become responsible for ten copies shall receive the 11th *gratis.* — An allowance of ten per cent will also be made to authorized agents for procuring subscribers and warranting their solvency or remitting the cash.

### ADVERTISEMENTS

Not exceeding 12 lines, will be neatly inserted three times for one dollar — and twenty-five cents for each succeeding publication — those of greater length in the same proportion.

All letters and communications to the Editor, on business relative to the paper, must be POST-PAID, or they will not be attended to.

By 1832, evidently having learned the advisability of being more specific, he added several qualifying words and phrases:

### THE
### GREENSBOROUGH PATRIOT

Is printed & published every Wednesday morning, by
**WILLIAM SWAIM**

At Two Dollars per annum, payable within three months from the date of the first number, or Three Dollars will be *invariably* exacted *immediately* after the expiration of that period. . . .

A failure to order a discontinuance *within the year,* will subject the subscriber to payment for *the whole of the succeeding year,* at rates above mentioned.

A year's subscription will be ascertained by the numbers of the paper and not by calendar months. Fifty-two numbers will make a year's subscription; and in proportion for a shorter time.[3]

With these changes, the masthead otherwise remained in the same place and with the original provisions.

In Swaim's first issue, immediately below the masthead, he reprinted his Prospectus of the *Greensborough Patriot* from which he had dropped the subtitle, "Southern Political and Literary Register." In succeeding issues that space was given to the department of "COMMUNICATIONS" — for letters and articles from his readers. The first page also carried a division entitled "SELECTED" in which were found significant lead articles, original or reprinted from other papers.

The second page carried columns entitled "FOREIGN" and "DOMESTIC" for news items, and "MISCELLANEOUS" for other articles.

Editorial material, when it was of unusual length, sometimes began on the first or second pages, but ordinarily it occupied page three. "MARKET REPORTS," "MARRIAGES," and "DEATHS" were also individually classified and followed the editorials.

The fourth page was devoted to "POETRY," "VARIETY," and advertisements. This page was lively and at first carried the paper's only illustration. The elaborate drawing was spread above the poetry section and helped to divert the eye from a column of weak writing.

When Congress and the North Carolina Legislature were in session, or when the President of the United States or the Governor of North Carolina made a significant speech, such events were reported under special headings of "CONGRESS," "LEGISLATURE," "UNITED STATES," and "NORTH CAROLINA." With this wide range of classifications, the *Greensborough Patriot* was able to cover general as well as specific developments in county, state, nation and world events.

Another unusual feature of Swaim's format was the way he used his type for presenting these various departments. The different subjects were introduced by inserting one appropriate word in bold capital letters, and that word was then fortified by its own box and descriptive poetic lines, set in very small *Italics* directly below the featured title. These quotations — and one may sometimes suspect spontaneous doggerel of the editor — served a twofold purpose: their light type enlivened the pages, and the ideas were worthy of reflection. A few excerpts will illustrate this effort to make the newspaper inviting.

While in session, the legislature had a department:

## THE LEGISLATURE

*"_ _ _ _ _ _ _ _ _ _ Illustrious all appeared,*
*Who ruled supreme in righteousness,*
*Or held inferior place in steadfast rectitude."*

### SENATE

*Monday, Nov. 19th* 1832. This being the day appointed by law for the meeting of the General Assembly, and fifty eight of the members of the Senate appearing, that body proceeded to the qualification of its members.

Swaim set up a department of COMMUNICATIONS for the people to use when wishing to express their opinions:

# COMMUNICATIONS.

*"But still remember, if you mean to please,*
*To press your point with modesty and ease."*

*For the Greensborough Patriot.*

MR. EDITOR:—I have not left my seat since I perused the first number of your paper. I like its mechanical appearance very well; and should you keep up, and improve that appearance, I have no doubt but the liberality and pride of the citizens of Guilford

The United States had its special space for featuring national news:

## UNITED STATES

*When Liberty, swift as the fiers of heaven,*
*In fury rode with all her hosts, and threw*
*The tyrant down or drove invasion back.*

### CONGRESS

In a debate which occurred in the House of Representatives on the 14th, ult. on a motion to refer to a select committee that part of the President's Message relating to the exercise of a doubtful power, the Proclamation was repeatedly spoken of. Mr. Stewart of Penn. considered it "as one of the most

The department of VARIETY which featured less serious reading matter had its own box:

---

# VARIETY.

*"Fancy has sported all her powers away
In tales, in trifles, and in children's play."*

---

*The honey-moon. Charles* had been only married a week and his wife adored him.—Oh those young wives, when they yield up their pure, deep affections, and break through the restraints of bashful fear, how they do love! And those young husbands too, when

Advertisements and fillers were the only insertions in the *Greensborough Patriot* not placed under special headings. Uncataloged advertisements, however, neatly boxed, were found on the third and fourth pages.* And the editor used *bona fide* fillers anywhere, of course, for instance:

> Some men, for fame, will write a volume:
> We write two lines to fill this column.[4]

Careful examination of extant newspaper files of the late 1820's would seem to indicate that the *Greensborough Patriot* was noticeable for its diversified and well-organized format.[5]

Swaim began his paper with a systematic plan for collecting materials. His design for various departments through which the public might speak had an immediate response. His first printing contained an article on debased practices of electioneering, a hint at long-sought constitutional reform, and a look at the disturbing state of finances, all of which were fevered topics of the day. And in the department of MISCELLANEOUS, State Senator Jonathan Parker directed a message "To the Freemen of Guilford County," in which he surveyed the last session of the legislature, especially pointing out some of the weaknesses of the Internal Improvement

---

*One or two extant editions of the *Greensborough Patriot* have advertisements on the first page, where many publications carried them, but this policy was not favored by Swaim.

program and stating that the General Assembly "had been duped by white-washed reports on the banks." He frankly concluded, "Upon the whole, although we have not done much good, I hope you will be disposed to accept the will for the deed." Of course, every important issue of the times could not be mentioned in the opening edition, but as the weeks passed the response grew and the paper developed a reader participation that was phenomenal.

If a contributor did not wish his identity known, he would sign his articles with a *nom de plume,* such as "MONITOR," "ENQUIRER," or "POLYDORE." Frequently such a contributor would write a series of articles on important issues, and thus create a point of departure which Editor Swaim would take up in his editorials. Constituting an example of this, beginning on August 29, 1829, and continuing at intervals for about seven months, were a dozen such articles in the department of COMMUNICATIONS. Signed POLYDORE, these features summarized the most disturbing conditions then existing in North Carolina.

Many North Carolinians were woefully ignorant about life in their state, and contributors such as POLYDORE served the worthy purpose of furnishing background information which was necessary for the understanding of what Swaim would later write. Entitled "NORTH CAROLINA," excerpts from the first two introductory installments will give a hint of what was to come from both POLYDORE and Swaim:

## NORTH CAROLINA, No. I

"Mr. Editor:— If you will admit the coarse speculations and humble reflections of an unpretending ploughman into your columns, I design to furnish you, at intervals, with a number on the condition of N. C.," POLYDORE began. "To view objects on their dark side is an unpleasant task; but to turn over an object, and contemplate it on all its sides, and in every light, is the necessary task of him who would arrive at truth. In the investigation I am about to make of the condition and prospects of our State, I intend avoiding no point of view, because it is overspread with gloom; happy,

85

if I can find here and there a cheerful spot, on which to relieve the eye.

"But how can an unpolished ploughman be qualified to speculate on the affairs of a State? how can he be able to express his thoughts intelligibly to his fellow-citizens? and moreover, how can he find leisure for thinking and writing? My friend, in reply to these inquiries, I will say, I am none of your ploughmen 'who whistle as they go for want of thought.' ... The life of a labourer truly has but little leisure, but as I do my thinking in the field, so during my hours of rest, I turn my thoughts into words. ...

"Love of country, and a desire for the welfare of posterity, are principles innate in the heart of man," POLYDORE continued. "On the prosperity and good government of a country, the happiness of its inhabitants depends. On the virtue, the knowledge, the industry, and economy of its inhabitants, the prosperity of a country depends. Therefore, every patriot, and more especially if he be a father, feels deeply interested, not only that the government of his country should be of the best form, and judiciously administered; but also, that public morals should remain uncorrupted; that knowledge should be disseminated among every class of youth; that industry should be fostered, and economy persevered in. ... But should he behold the signs of ruin beginning to germinate in his beloved country, he is filled with dreadful apprehensions, and will make a bold and energetic effort, (I mean in proportion to his strength,) to eradicate the evil, and produce reformation. In this situation, precisely and wholly, is the writer who is now introducing himself to the public. ...

"Evils must be pointed out and shown to be such, before reformation can be demanded. The near approach of danger must be shown, before we can alarm; and we must alarm, before we can produce a change of policy. To do effectual good, not to produce *needless* alarm, or find *needless* fault, is the sincere desire of the writer. That his progress, (should he have health and leisure to make progress,) may be crowned with beneficial results, is the ardent desire of

POLYDORE."[6]

## NORTH CAROLINA No. II

### Geographical Survey

Defining the limits of the state, "We shall find it situated between 34° and 36° and some minutes of north latitude," wrote POLYDORE. "The 35th degree runs through, or near Fayetteville. Now if we would see what countries in the Old World, or on the Eastern Continent, lie near the same parallel, we shall find the southern parts of Spain and Italy, the island of Sicily, and the northern parts of the States of Barbary, Greece, Asia Minor (now called Natolia), Syria, the northern parts of Persia, Thibet, and China. The greater part of Italy lies but a little north, and Palestine and Egypt lie but a little south of this parallel. Thus we behold our own unpretending State, placed nearly in the same latitude of those countries which were most famous in antiquity; where man attained his highest earthly perfection, and achieved the most admirable feats of invention; where a Homer invented the most sublime poem that was ever written by uninspired man; and David, the King of Israel, was inspired to compose those Holy Songs of Zion, with a fervour which enkindles devotion in the coldest climes, and in the remotest generations; and where a Virgil told the tales and achievements of his hero, in the smoothest verse, and with the most elevated pathos;— where Science flourished, and the Arts were discovered; — in short, where the mind of man developed its greatest perfection, and displayed its brightest, sublimest capacity.

"Nor are we to suppose, that the concentration of all that is grand in this particular climate, is merely a casual circumstance," POLYDORE reflected. "Doubtless the local advantages might have made a permanent occupation a desideratum; the boldness of the surrounding scenery might have inspired sublimity of thought; and the incidents of fortune might have impelled to deeds of valour; but it is to the climate itself, we are to look for the most efficient cause of human greatness approximating to a parallel of latitude. These countries are situated in the medium of temperance, between the extremes of heat and cold, . . . in a temperate climate, the bodily

87

and mental faculties, being equally vigorous and active, afford each other mutual aid. Our own State possesses, in an eminent degree, the advantages of a temperate clime.

"Beginning at our extensive sea-shore, and advancing towards the interior, the first section of country is low, level, swampy and unhealthy; yet fertile in certain places; and possesses greater commercial facilities than any other part of the State. To this succeeds the sand-hills — the land begins to undulate; and the people are less unhealthy. This section is remarkable for nothing but sterile pine barrens; however, near streams of water, the land is productive. Advancing still westward towards the sources of the rivers, you enter into a country, which, when all its natural advantages are taken into view, may, without exaggeration, be pronounced one of the finest in the world, the fictitious accounts of ignorant and partial historians and geographers to the contrary notwithstanding . . . Verdant and flowery meadows; the cool fountains of water; unbrageous forests; and the plaintive melody of the aerial songsters; all conspire to render it delightful and engaging, and to justify the above assertion; — to make it a haunt fit for the Muses, and worthy the cause of propitious Genii — In our progress westwardly we presently catch sight of the stupendous Blue Ridge, rearing its lofty columns to the skies. We know indeed that its height is nothing to compare with that of mountains in other countries; but we also know, that whether, from the country below, we view its summit, or from its summit look down on the country below, it is high enough to inspire our minds with a feeling of grandeur and awe. Beyond this range other ranges succeed; and here and there a peak lifts its head up amongst the clouds. Beautiful and cultivable valleys intervene. This is a fine and ample grazing country, and extends to the western limits of the State. These mountains are also the repository of valuable metals, especially iron.

"Thus our State has every variety of feature, from the level, uniform marsh of our maratime districts, to the lofty cliffs and profound valleys, of our mountains," POLYDORE pointed out. "The soil is no less diversified than the face of the country, and every variety of soil is adapted to its own particular production, and brings it to the highest perfection. We admit that the soil is not generally of the most fertile quality; but this is a less serious disadvantage, than if it were not so amply counterballanced by that felicity of climate, which we have already noticed; and by its capacity for improvement. No portion is so poor, rocky, or broken as not to be capable of producing something valuable, as a vine, a mulberry tree, or pasture for a herd of cattle, or a flock of sheep.

"To preponderate against all the above advantages, we can enumerate but a single inconvenience that has been imposed upon us by the hand of nature. Our whole coast is so securely blockaded by rocks, shoals, ever-changing sand-bars, and stormy capes, as to exclude us from a free access to the open ocean with large sea-vessels, and thus to cut us off from direct foreign commerce. This doubtless is a serious prejudice to the interests of the State; but [when] we consider how many natural advantages we still possess, we cannot, in reason, attribute to this solitary inconvenience, the flight of our citizens, carrying along with them our capital and enterprise; the more especially, as in time past we were flourishing maugre the barrier which nature has imposed on our commerce. That our condition is bad almost to desperation, and constantly deteriorating; and that our most enterprising citizens are emigrating with what speed they can; are facts too obvious to the most superficial observer to need the least proof. But how are we to account for these things? If the cause cannot be found in the restraints nature has imposed on our commercial enterprise, must we not look for it in the state of our social relations? That we must, is the opinion of

POLYDORE."[7]

Swaim also gathered information through exchanges with other papers. He quoted newspapers from all over the world — sometimes quoting fresh news, and sometimes quoting a point of view supporting his own previously stated opinion, or perhaps adversely criticizing it. Often he would print in the *Greensborough Patriot* an article from another journal, and then add his appropriate editorial note. His March 3, 1830 issue gave an idea of how widely he sometimes used exchanges, when he mentioned the following papers: *Edinburgh Review, Dublin Morning Herald, Boston Statesman, American Spectator, Washington City Chronicle, Milton Gazette, Doylestown Democrat, Fayetteville Observer, North Carolina Spectator & Western Advertiser,* Raleigh *Star, Yadkin and Catawba Journal, Greenville Mountaineer* (South Carolina), and *Western Times* (Indiana). On the following week there were quotations from the *South Carolina Whig, Newbern Spectator, New York Spectator, Vermont Patriot, Baltimore Patriot, Potomac Pioneer, Alexandria Gazette,* and *Raleigh Register.* He made use of *Niles' Weekly Register, National Intelligencer, New York Courier, Washington Telegraph,* New York *Evening Post, Rhode Island American,* and practically all other newspapers of the day, from the most local to the most national or international, presenting opinions both for and against on debatable questions.

In the coverage of foreign news, from the onset Swaim surveyed happenings in Europe, Africa, Asia, and all known parts of the world at that time. And under DOMESTIC in his second edition he printed twenty-five items of state and national interest. Coverage of foreign and domestic news, however, was not unusual for newspapers of that day. One reason for this practice was the fact that local news, having been passed along by word of mouth, was already known in the community before a paper could be published, whereas outside "intelligence" was news even though it might be a month or two old. Both the editor and his audience seemed to think that the meat of an edition was bred on national and foreign scenes. Swaim took this point into consideration, but nevertheless focused his attention on state, county, and town affairs if he judged them to be newspaper material. He was a cordial person and a brilliant conversationalist, and he invited people to "drop in" the *Greensborough Patriot* office to discuss measures and men; and from his discerning community he thus gathered much information and many ideas.

Moreover, he traveled over the state, attending legislative meetings, court sessions, and political rallies in order to get firsthand impressions to bring to his readers. To be sure, there were not as many avenues of information in the 1830's as there were a century and a quarter later; but such as there were, the inquisitive editor investigated, learned about, and passed along his findings to his fellow countrymen.

Swaim's mind was a veritable reservoir of ideas which he wished to get before the public, and he wisely designed his format to be a highly functional vehicle. Through his Prospectus and leading editorial he had clearly made known his hope for a change in some of the existing conditions in his state and in the nation. He made no plea for subtle reform. Nor was the plea itself subtle. From the very outset he opened his pages for free discussion on this, and all other subjects; and he invited contributions through letters, articles, and personal interviews. These might express any idea of any man, and under an appropriate heading might appear on any page of the paper, but as a rule Swaim used the editorial column for his remarks.

The "editorial" column, entitled *GREENSBOROUGH*, was the most outstanding department of the *Greensborough Patriot*. Although some newspaper editors had begun to publish startlingly frank appraisals of people and movements, others often used the editorial section for reporting happenings in the world; and in many instances as late as 1829 the editor's column was more like a brief news summary than an editorial department.[8] Swaim, however, constantly presented editorials for his readers. His editorial department sometimes covered a full page or more, and it was not at all unusual for comment on a single subject to be spread over two or three columns. On the other hand, entries might be very brief, but timely, as on April 11, 1832, when he printed thirty-six items with either outright or implied comment. To use his expression, he watched contemporary developments "with a lynx-eyed vigilence." Stripping them to their bald nakedness, he interpreted them for his readers, his comments sparkling with wit and humor or burning with bitter sarcasm.

Because of Swaim's intellectual persuasiveness, Daniel M. McFarland in *The North Carolina Historical Review* wrote: "This erratic genius at once made the *Patriot* one of the most unusual newspapers in the whole South."[9]

Swaim's primary aim was to reach as many people as possible, whether he pleased or offended them. He may not have found time to correct his Devil's typesetting errors, but he always took time to see that he brought out an edition that provoked a laugh or a frown, or excited the emotions above the normal. Under the department entitled VARIETY there were stories with surprise endings, jokes, anecdotes, and even subtle advice on how to become charming. Indeed, there was reading matter in the *Greensborough Patriot* for everybody's every mood — for the stupid and the intelligent, for the young and the old, and for the housewife and the public official. His six and a half volumes which covered the period May 23, 1829, through December 31, 1835, comprise a creditable history of those years.

# V

## FOR AN EDUCATED CITIZENRY

*"It is sufficient for our purpose, that all who are not idiots, are susceptible of acquiring a useful education. . . . Every one, therefore, how idle or stupid soever he may be, should be urged on till he imbibe the more useful parts of rudimental knowledge; . . . none but such as display signs of capacity, and inclination for learning, should be urged further."*[1]

As the year 1830 got under way, William Swaim had reason to feel proud, for he had in his keeping two precious responsibilities: a newspaper and a new wife. The *Greensborough Patriot* was progressing perhaps even better than he had expected; and within less than a year from its launching, he had met, courted, and married on April 29, 1830, the attractive Abiah Shirley, the only girl he ever seriously courted.[2] It appears to have been one of those "love at first sight" affairs which Swaim considered strictly his own private business, for although he published marriage announcements of others, he never mentioned his own. Of course the fact that Abiah Shirley (Shearley) was a remote descendant of the Royal House of Stuarts had nothing to do with the five hundred pound marriage bond that was required of Swaim, for that was a customary requirement in North Carolina at that time; but it is pleasant to know that Peter Adams, who had so utterly failed Swaim in 1823 in staging the big debate on constitutional reform, redeemed himself by backing Swaim in this venture.[3]

Abiah Shirley was a native of Princess Anne County, Virginia,

and since the death of her parents she had lived with her sister,
Mrs. Thomas Carbry, also of Princess Anne County.[4] When the
Thomas Carbrys moved to Greensboro in the late 1820's, Abiah
came with them, bringing with her a personal slave — a young Negro
woman named Mariah.[5] Also accompanying her was the story that
she was of Scottish extraction, one of her ancestors having been
named Stuart, and having been related to the beautiful and re-
nowned Mary Queen of Scots.[6] Furthermore, the name Shirley was
illustrious, for many of her Shirley ancestors of England had been
closely associated with the crown and had moved in royal circles.[7]
More important than all these facts, according to her contemporaries,
she was a beautiful young lady of "excellent sense, considerable
intelligence, and of sweet and engaging disposition."[8]

Swaim was a good match for her. Will L. Scott described him
as a "man of the rarest social qualities. Naturally he was full of spirit
and joyfulness. Conversation, in which he so excelled, was his delight. His youthful timidity and diffidence of which he was wont so
often to speak and write, had now entirely passed, and he was easy
in his manners, ready with his tongue, full of sparkling humor, and
possessed of a heart that glowed with geniality and liberality. He
was famed for his witticisms and repartee; nor were they unmixed
with poison of a bitter and deathful sarcasm. He was felt in society
— he was mighty in the field of politics and as a censor of public
manners and morals. . . . He put a mark upon vice and immorality,
which made the offender ridiculous or ignominious. He was totally
unlike those, who pass so quietly through life, that their contemporaries scarcely knew them when they were here or when they
departed. . . . His friends were always strong friends.—He loved a
pure and high-minded man and grappled him to his heart with hooks
of steel; but he abhorred the mean and dishonorable and repelled
them with scorn and disdain. The independence of his cause as a
public man is well remembered. He never knew, after he reached
manhood, the feeling of fear. As a writer, he looked only to duty,
letting the consequences take care of themselves."[9]

The young couple began housekeeping in a handsome and

spacious red brick house of colonial design, still standing in the 1960's in its original architectural design at 426 West Gaston Street in Greensboro. Here they were "able, of his own means, to live full-handed and comfortably."[10]

The ambitious young editor thus faced his future with the security of a good wife's companionship and encouragement. These were invaluable assets to one who aspired to promote reform; and certainly Swaim made no effort to hide his intention to promote reform in North Carolina.

The problems he promised to tackle were not new, but his position on them was in keeping with the advanced or liberal thought of the day. He earnestly approved and supported Henry Clay's American system, a constructive program designed to meet the growing needs of the nation. He also took his stand along with the most progressive North Carolina leaders; and began at the local level to inspire renewed interest in education, agriculture, manufacturing, mechanics and inventions, internal improvements, banking, the abolition of slavery, politics, freedom of the press, and in foreign and domestic happenings generally.

On all these subjects and more, Swaim gave his readers information, always making clear the interrelationship of the various political, social, and economic questions. He did this consistently throughout his six and a half years of editorship. In truth, his first leading editorial constituted a sort of agenda by which he was guided in writing subsequent editorials and feature articles; and similarly it has determined the order in which these subjects are presented in this book.

Fully aware of how this need for reform had developed, Swaim faced the situation squarely. He knew that the national government Embargo Acts of 1807, which were in effect until the close of the War of 1812, had forced the people of this country to make many supplies they had formerly bought from abroad; and from this necessity Americans had learned that they could live more independently.[11] When the war was over in 1814, many realized that they did not wish to return to the old way of life, but instead preferred to establish a way of their own. This realization brought about a keener interest in domestic affairs, which in turn gave birth to a new era in political, social, and economic attitudes. Thus, this country stood on the threshold of readjustment.

Personifying this new era in North Carolina was the eminent Judge Archibald D. Murphey, state senator (1812-1818) from Orange County. He observed that North Carolina had not made this adjustment as readily as some other states; and in 1815-1818 he therefore made a very serious investigation of prevailing conditions in the state. Finding humiliating and distressing situations, he reported them to the legislature and recommended practical plans for their reformation.[12]

He and his followers in this new movement believed that the state government should assume the leadership in a positive and constructive program of state development, and should take the initiative, through state aid, in the solution of state problems. Opposing this liberal viewpoint was a majority conservative group which held that all action should be left to private enterprise. Nevertheless, Murphey's reports roused the state, and revolutionized social, economic, and political thinking. Though he did not live to see his plans in practice, they formed a basis upon which the commonwealth of North Carolina has been built.[13]

By the time Swaim became a North Carolina editor, Murphey had grown old and inactive. Meanwhile, from 1815 to 1829, conditions in North Carolina had become increasingly worse, and the state was in an alarming and disreputable condition. Murphey's major emphasis had been placed on the need for a system of public education, for improved transportation facilities, and for a revision of the state constitution. Adopting these basic ideas, Swaim projected a greatly enlarged program of reform which embraced potentialities not foreseen at the time of Murphey's reports.

Swaim saw, as Murphey had seen, that one of the greatest needs of North Carolina was educational opportunity for everyone.

Through his *Greensborough Patriot,* using skillful repetition, the first thing he said in every issue was "THE IGNORANT AND DEGRADED OF EVERY NATION OR CLIME MUST BE EN- LIGHTENED, BEFORE OUR EARTH CAN HAVE HONOR IN THE UNIVERSE."[14]

Since colonial times, many North Carolinians had been deeply concerned about the widespread illiteracy among their state's popu- lation. There was the University of North Carolina (1789) with less than one hundred students; there were private academies — for both young men and young women — which offered scholastic training near the level of mid-twentieth century high schools; and there were "old field subscription schools" of the type Swaim had attended, where each student paid a small tuition; but all these were patronized by such a small number of students that educationally North Carolina stood near the bottom of the list among the United States.[15]

In the hope of alleviating this condition, Judge Murphey in his reports to the legislature had not only pointed out existing circum- stances, but also had made explicit and specific recommendations for meeting the educational needs of the white children of the state, through a state-supported system of common schools. His plan was not as broad as the later concept and practice of free education at public expense for all children, but it was the first step in that direction. The legislature, however, dominated by a majority which held that education was a private matter and was therefore the responsibility of individuals and should not be aided or promoted by the state, quickly killed efforts to put the plan into action. Under constant pressure of a few farsighted leaders, in 1825 the legislature established a Literary Fund[16] as a foundation for a public school system; but provided no system then nor fourteen years thereafter. Consequently, educational facilities in North Carolina in the 1830's had not changed much as far back as Swaim could remember.

The situation was indeed deplorable. The majority of children were still growing up in complete ignorance. Historians Hugh T. Lefler and Albert R. Newsome in their *North Carolina, the History of a Southern State,* stated that "If the Negroes and whites under twenty years of age are included, more than half of the population was illiterate."[17] Thoughtful observers believed that this appalling number of ignorant children would have to rely upon the state for educational advantages, for many parents or guardians, equally ignorant, were either too poor or too indifferent to assume the responsibility. Furthermore, they realized that the prosperity of the state depended upon educational advantages for all.

Swaim's first proposal to his readers, therefore, was "the necessity of a better regulated system of Education in our State than we have heretofore had. It is a source of painful regret," he wrote, "that N. Carolina should have slumbered fifty-two years in the arms of indolence without digesting any plan for a distribution of the blessings of education among the ordinary ranks of Society.... The fact is too notorious for concealment, that hundreds of young sons of N. Carolina are growing up, even to *manhood* — in point of muscular power — without being able to read!"[18]

Nor did he hesitate to place the blame for this distressing situation where he felt blame ought to be placed. "The constituted authorities of our State need take to themselves no credit in concealing its truth," Swaim continued, "because many of them have used this deplorable ignorance as a hobby-horse on which to ride into posts of proffit and distinction; and this, perhaps, constitutes the best apology they could make for neglecting so long to remove it."[19]

Swaim had taken his stand. Though aiming specifically at a system of public education, he fortified his position by stimulating among his readers a general interest in learning. One of his objectives in making his paper diversified was to encourage all sorts of people to want to read it, for wanting to read meant progress toward literary attainment. He must have reasoned, too, that if more people became interested in learning there would be a greater demand for educational promotion. He therefore printed a great variety of entertaining and informative articles, affording such a choice in reading matter as might appeal to different minds.

Included in this category were such items as "Ten Rules to Observe in Practical Life," which were given by Thomas Jefferson in 1825 to his namesake, Thomas Jefferson Smith; "The Origin of Yankee Doodle;" "Specific Gravity," in which were listed about fifty familiar substances, giving the number of avoirdupois ounces contained in a cubit foot; "George Washington," a letter from him to Mrs. Washington when he was made Commander in Chief of the American army; a list of the "Presidents of the United States" from George Washington to Andrew Jackson; a list of the "Governors of North Carolina," from 1729 to 1834; the "Constitution of the United States;" and "Wars between France and England." This last article was especially arresting, for it revealed the tendency toward wars. England and France, between 1110 and 1803 — a period of about seven hundred years — had spent two hundred and sixty of them in battling one another in twenty-four wars. If to this account were added the years these nations spent at war with other nations, or in civil wars, they would appear to have spent more than half their time at war during the seven hundred years.

A matter of special concern to Swaim was the importance of an intelligent home atmosphere. He felt particular concern for the part of the mother in the home. He printed articles in his paper especially designed for the ladies, and although they were in themselves entertaining and appealing to those who wished for advice, flattery, or fun, somewhere in the discussion there would often be a sentence or paragraph on the value of the educated woman. Such, for example, is this extravagant statement: "Woman is the most important sex — and if but one half of our race can be educated, let it be woman instead of man. She is with us through life. She nurses us in infancy, she watches by us in sickness, soothes in distress, and cheers us in the melancholy of old age. Her rank determines that of the race."[20] Before there was a single college for women in the United States, Swaim stressed the significance of education among women. From the *Massachusetts Journal* he quoted, "There is no subject so much connected with individual happiness and national prosperity, as the education of daughters."[21]

Advancing his stand he appealed to the pride of both fathers and mothers concerning their children, saying "This is an age in which parents seem to attend more to the external accomplishments of their children than to the formation of the minds, and endeavoring to instil into them those principles of honor and humanity which are so truly necessary for their real happiness in this world as well as hereafter. . . .

"Youth receives impressions that [it] is scarcely in the power of reason and reflection thereafter to erase; which shows the absolute necessity there is for attending minutely to the formation of an infant's mind."[22]

To emphasize this point further, as well as to show he was not alone in the thought, he quoted a paragraph from the *Journal of Education,* under the caption *"Educate Your Children Early."* This publication maintained that " 'During this period every human being is making his observations and acquiring his first experience. [He] passes his early judgments, forms opinions, acquires habits . . . [which] may be ingrained into the character for life.' "[23]

Although Swaim believed that the only way education could be made available to the general public was through an over-all state program, his advice was to get instruction in any way, every way it could be obtained. Until more satisfactory provision should be made, he urged provision of subscription schools. And he especially recommended the patronage of Sunday Schools which he knew from personal experience could be organized at little or no expense in any community. Furthermore, he believed that they could open minds to enlarged literary visions which in turn would affect moral practices; and he used his pages to recommend them wholeheartedly to his readers. Said he, "It is our firm and unwavering conviction, that if well organized Sabbath Schools were instituted in every neighborhood, and efficiently sustained by the reflecting part of society, many of those popular vices which torture the feelings of the serious, and diminish the dignity of human nature, would soon become disreputable & render a resort to more coercive means to restrain them, altogether unnecessary.... We cannot longer endure that slothfulness which has too long characterized the mass of our citizens."[24]

Nor did he let go of this subject. He talked about it as if he had been an experienced old man with a house full of children, yet he was only twenty-seven and had not a child to his name. "Let a Sunday School be instituted in every neighborhood," he urged. "Let *all* children, in every palace and cottage of our country, be taught to smile when a Sabbath appears — to grasp their books with eagerness and joy, and trip the morning dew from the the verdure of Spring in hastening to these nurseries of juvenile morality, virtue and piety.... Teach a child its duty — render that duty pleasing by a judicious course of treatment — and enable it to comprehend the reasonableness of those restrictions you must necessarily place upon its will, by teaching it *sense* and *science,* instead of *nonsense* and *pedantry* — we say do all this, and a foundation is laid on which, without difficulty, may be reared the character of a good citizen, a patriot and a Christian."[25]

So dedicated was he to the cause of education that he looked for ways to bring up the subject. Early in his editorship, on September 5, 1829, he even advised people how to eat so as to have the best control of mental faculties, emphasizing "the [stupefying] effects produced upon the functions of the mind by overgorging the stomach," and advising to partake of simple foods. Particularly addressing young men, he asked, "Would you be intelligent? Carry a book about you *always.* Not a novel — but a work of utility — a work in which you may read of realities, not fiction. Would you be wise? Open and read that book whenever you have a moment of leisure."[26] Addressing farmers, he advised, "Educate your son in the best manner possible because you expect him to be a man and not a *horse* or an *ox....* For ought you know, he may, if you do your duty by him, become the President of the United States.... [or] may enjoy an occasional intellectual feast of the purest and most exhuberating kind."[27]

Thoughtful older people were distressed about the spirit of lawlessness that characterized the restless horde of young males who

101

had nowhere to go and nothing to do in spare time. A plan was considered for organizing manual labor schools in which boys and young men would work part time to pay their expenses. The idea, however, was frowned down by the offenders themselves. School and work would not mix, the objectors argued. Swaim, who felt that any kind of honest work was in accord with learning, maintained that this attitude was entirely ridiculous, "for the whole college course is a routine of *requisition*." But no, he lamented, "such high spirited youths will never submit to the *indignity* of manual labor. ... Their lofty aspirations find vent in ... storming henroosts at midnight; barricading doors; cutting bell ropes; smashing windows; throwing fences across streets; cropping horses ears and tails; defacing monuments; strowing filth in sacred places; ... disguising their persons, and parading the streets with music of kettles, tin horns, shovels, grubbing hoes, frying pans, and whistles; maiming and assaulting peaceable citizens."[28]

He continued to print items especially intended to arouse interest in learning and to lead toward an informed public. In 1833, his cousin and good friend, Benjamin Swaim of New Salem, North Carolina, undertook the publishing of *The Man of Business*, a thirty-six page monthly law magazine which later was compiled into book form and is now a collector's item. The *Greensborough Patriot* carried a recommendation of it as a possible source of education for those in business for themselves; and advised people to avail themselves of this opportunity. " 'THE MAN OF BUSINESS' will show how to draw and execute properly all deeds and writings obligatory, such for instance, as conveyances, mortgages, trusts, conditional sales, wills, leases, covenants, contracts and agreements, touching real or personal property; also how to conduct all matters of book account and other commercial dealings. It will also contain useful sketches on the duty & responsibility of justices of the peace, constables, military officers, surveyors and processioners; together with practical illustrations of the road laws & laws relating to trespasses of stock, estrays, &c. This work will likewise be interspersed with many new and useful rules for arithmatical calculations applicable to many of the mechanic arts, statistics, tables for reference &c. In short it will be calculated to render every man his own counsellor in matters of ordinary Business."[29]

While this magazine was being published, Benjamin and William used to present in their columns examples of legal cases or other cases that were apt to come up, and to answer questions concerning them. They explained that "such an arrangement was very convenient and economical to their patrons."[30]

All these general applications of learning, these little appetizers of knowledge, were of great significance, in Swaim's estimation, for arousing public interest.

His dominant thought, however, was to stimulate interest in state aid for a system of public education — a subject on which he was always deadly serious. One of his specific efforts in this direction was to give examples of what was being done along this line in other parts of the world, in the hope of encouraging similar efforts in North Carolina. He therefore called attention to a quoted article entitled "EDUCATION IN AUSTRIA," and prefaced it with his satiric comment. "The following paragraph, copied from a French paper, we recommend to the favourable notice of our next Legislature. We have no expectation that a body of men, assembled for *good* purposes, will feel disposed to reduce such a liberty-crippling policy to practice in this land of Liberty and Independence; but we think it would not stagger the unwavering political maxims of some of them to give it an attentive perusal:

"'The system employed throughout Austria for spreading instruction among the lower orders, is attended with great success. In each village are schools, of which the masters are paid by the Government. No one is allowed to marry who cannot read, write, and have some acquaintance with arithmetic; and, under a penalty, no master can employ a workman who is unable to read and write. Small works on moral subjects, written with great care, are circulated among the lower classes. Hence crimes are extremely rare; and in the course of a twelvemonth scarcely two executions take place at Vienna.' "[31]

103

Coming closer home he reported that in 1825 Maine had 137,931 persons between the ages of four and twenty-one, and 101,325 of them attended schools. A tax of forty cents for every citizen, young and old, was required to help defray expenses for eight to ten weeks, which amounted to $137,878.57. By 1833, with 140,000 of school age, it had been suggested that the tax be raised to $1.06, and that the schools be kept open throughout the entire year. Furthermore, he announced that there were about sixty public primary schools in Boston; that New Hampshire had provided $90,000 for the support of primary schools; that New York had upwards of 500,000 children, between the ages of five and sixteen, enrolled in common schools; and that Ohio had between 300,000 and 400,000 pupils receiving instruction through state provision. "But in North Carolina, *not one!*" he lamented. "The people of this state *must* turn their attention to a more general instruction of the rising generation, or her prostration will be h[e]rmetically sealed forever!"[32]

And he let North Carolinians know that joy could come from seeing schools in operation by telling them what *The Annapolis Republican* had said: " 'We may well be proud of the success which has been achieved on the experiment made in this City of the Primary School system, enacted by the Legislature two years since. There is nothing like demonstration — there is no arguing against figures. Cost of each scholar per year, for tuition, books, stationery, and fuel, Two DOLLARS.' "[33] He also quoted from the Raleigh *Star* that " 'Upwards of *thirty-one thousand poor children* between the ages of five and fourteen years, have been instructed at the Public Schools in Pennsylvania, since their establishment in 1818;' " and then followed with the reflection that "The auspicious day that shall witness the organization of Public Schools throughout our own State, will be hailed with unspeakable delight by all her benevolent and enlightened citizens."[34]

Although Swaim knew that the subject of a public school system for North Carolina was not new, he tried to kindle new enthusiasm for it, hoping to draw to the support of public education enough power to bring it to pass.

He was very fortunate to be located in a community that backed his attitudes and opinions. His home town of Greensboro, with its three academies, was near the site of the Reverend David Caldwell's famous Log College which in its time had been one of the most outstanding schools in the South. Although the institution had been closed for several years, its influence was still felt, for there were then many of its graduates still around to encourage learning. Among these was the Reverend William Paisley who had served as principal of the Greensborough Male Academy and had established the Greensborough Female Academy, the first of its kind in the town. And there was the worthy Judge Murphey of Hillsboro who, having invested his fortune and his credit in the Internal Improvement program for building up the state, had become insolvent and about the time Swaim began his paper was imprisoned for debt in the Greensboro jail. When he was released he established residence in the town and still held to his belief in education for all. The Honorable John Motley Morehead, also a product of the Log College and a future governor of North Carolina, was a Greensboro citizen who used his influence in favor of public schools. In addition to these Log College men, prominent among other friends of education was the Reverend Peter Doub. It was he who, before there was a single college for women in the United States, founded the Greensborough Female School (around 1832) as the initial move toward Greensborough Female College (1838). This college was the first separate college for women incorporated by the North Carolina legislature and in 1963 was the second state chartered separate college for women in existence in the United States. (Around 1950 it had become Greensboro College, Incorporated, a coeducational institution.) Although some of Greensboro's citizens did not prefer public schools for themselves, intimating that they were tinged with charity, the populace of Guilford County was overwhelmingly in favor of them.[35]

It must have been a great source of satisfaction to Swaim when Governor John Owen, in his address to the General Assembly on November 17, 1829, directed his influence toward public education.[36] The *Greensborough Patriot* carried the entire speech which contained some very urgent educational recommendations:

"The influence of early education upon the well being of society, and upon the present and future happiness of the human race, is admitted by every enlightened nation of the earth;" the Governor said, "and the responsible duty of disseminating it, devolves with peculiar force upon the statesman and legislator. So completely is the formation of character under its control, that every effort should be made, . . . to direct the virtuous energies of the mind, both by moral and intellectual education, into paths of usefulness. And that the standard, both by learning and virtue, may be more elevated, a system of public education should be adopted, by which the thousands of the rising generation in our own State, . . . shall be enabled to acquire knowledge of the most useful kind. . . .

"In the present enlightened age of the world, when the favorite scheme of the philanthropist throughout the habitable globe seems to be the bountiful distribution of knowledge, wherever there is human intellect to receive it; . . . let us no longer permit the youth of our State to launch upon the ocean of life, there to shape their course without at least, the rudiments of science.

"In proportion to the ease with which an education may be acquired in other countries, and the facilities afforded by their governments for this purpose, so should . . . North Carolina attest her belief in these principles by a liberal provision for the education of her children."

Governor Owen did not leave the legislature in a quandary as to how to go about making this recommended move. He supplied a plan by a thoroughly capable gentleman, C. R. Kinney, for the establishment of primary schools in the state. Moreover, he submitted accounts of the common schools in New Jersey, and the school systems of New York, Connecticut, Rhode Island, Vermont, Massachusetts, New Hampshire, and Maine. "These several documents," he said, "are believed to contain the fullness of information upon this most interesting subject, calculated to shed all the necessary light on the path of the Legislature, in regulating this important branch of our public economy."

Swaim published in full Kinney's plan for common schools;[37] but the legislature, closing less than two months later in January, 1830, ignored it. Under the caption of "EDUCATION," the Greensboro editor then made his first downright attack upon the General Assembly.[38] In the verbose style of the day, he wrote, "The Legislature of this State has dragged itself through another 'log-rolling session,' of fifty-four days; and the question naturally suggests itself to every reflecting mind: — Who, except its own dear members and dependents, has been benefitted by its deliberations? What new discoveries have been made in political science? What measures have been adopted that can be considered as characteristic of liberal statesmen? — In short, what single act have they crammed into the already lumbered law-books of the State, that can be extended to posterity without incurring their most inveterate execration? We anticipate the answer, and the only one that can be given to these interrogatories; — 'Yes — the session of our Legislature which [has] just mingled with departing days, has immortalized itself by the passage of "An act, entitled an act to vest the right of electing the sheriffs, in the free *white* men of the state" of North Carolina!!' This is represented as a most glorious achievement, the excellence of which stands far above all earthly praise! But when we place it in comparison with the great interest of the State, we view it as but a sorry thing to brag about. If the Legislature had, by a powerful effort, bursted themselves from under the dominions of narrow-mindedness, and even made one hobbling step towards the adoption of a system of Public Education, by which the people might get their eyes open, then the argument in favour of placing all the power, might, majesty and dominion, into their most holy keeping, would wear a better face.

"Let us not be misunderstood on this point — we would scorn the idea of subtracting one iota from the assumption 'that all political power is vested in, and derived from the people only,' but we contend that a universal acquiescence in this assumption, offers an argument equally universal, in favor of enlightening a people to whom is committed the superintendence of their destinies. We believe, also, that 'political power' is as safe in the hands of the 'people' as anywhere else; because, if they are intelligent and virtuous, convenience alone can render it material, whether they exercise their power *directly*, by themselves, or *indirectly*, by their agents, the result would be the same. And if they are ignorant and corrupt, they may as well play the fool with their own business, as to elect fools and knaves to play the fool for them.

"These opinions *thus* expressed may give rise to irritable feelings; but on reviewing, we have no disposition to unsay what we have said. We intend our remarks to apply to no individual in this 'wooden world' of ours, except those to whom facts will seal the application — And they have abundant cause to be thankful that rods have not been pickled for their backs before this time.

"Governor Owen's chaste sentiments, and cogent reasonings upon the subject of public schools, seem to have produced no effect upon a truckling Legislature. The example of other States has been passed by unheeded, and North Carolina seems to be left as a 'city of refuge' for ignorance, after it shall be driven from every other portion of the world! We have been led to these disconnected observations by a perusal of the message of the Governor of New-York to the Legislature of that State. . . . The Governor says:

"'A sense of the importance of common education, has been strongly manifested by the Legislature, in setting apart a large fund for the purpose. An enlightened people will not live under a government where their rights are unnecessarily abridged, and a free government cannot be maintained by an ignorant population. . . . In our government, where every measure depends upon the public voice, our reliance must be placed upon the general intelligence of the people.'"

Disgusted with the legislature, but not defeated, Swaim came right back with this information: "A meeting of the citizens of Washington City, has recently been holden, for the purpose of adopting measures to apply to Congress for an appropriation of reserved public lands in the city, to raise a fund for the support of common Free Schools. The importance of dispensing the blessings of education among the lowest circles of society, is becoming *more* and MORE obvious. When will a modern miracle arouse North Carolina to a due sense of it? Answer: When modest, unassuming merit shall have sway in our councils!"[39]

POLYDORE, a *Greensborough Patriot* contributor who was wise to practically every part of North Carolina and who from internal evidence seems to have been Swaim himself,* appeared again at this time in the *Greensborough Patriot,* drew vivid and opportune pictures for the people of the distressing educational situation they were in, and pointed a way out of it.

On February 24, 1830, introducing the subject under the heading,

NORTH-CAROLINA No. IX

Learning:

POLYDORE wrote, "I come to consider the condition of North-Carolina in regard to Learning. I propose being a little more diffusive on this topic than I have been on former ones, because, if possible, this is more important than are any of them.†

"Though the state of education in North-Carolina is wretched

---

*In the early days of newspapers, even as he may do today, an editor sometimes wrote contributions under a *nom de plume,* if he desired the presentation of specific subjects for one reason or another. There is evidence that Swaim resorted to this method under the signature of POLYDORE. Though there is no way to know for certain that Swaim and POLYDORE were one and the same person, there are so many characteristics of Swaim's writing in the essays that they definitely lead one to believe that Swaim wrote them. In the first place there is a typical poetic quotation at the beginning of each feature (not quoted in this writing). Then there is the habit of putting many words in Italics which other contributors rarely did. The choice of words and phrases which flow and sound like Swaim is also convincing. Another clue is the fact that the last chapter which POLYDORE promised seems never to have appeared. That chapter was to have been on the situation of slavery in North Carolina, and it should have been published about the same time Swaim's *An Address to the People of North Carolina, on the Evils of Slavery* began in the *Greensborough Patriot.* The files of this paper are not complete, but there was ample time for POLYDORE's piece to have appeared, as scheduled, in the files that are available. Instead, Swaim's "Address" was included.

†This phrase will be repeated in connection with other reform issues, for reform in all the subjects Swaim mentioned in his leading editorial was so badly needed that whichever subject held the floor seemed to be, at that moment, the most important.

109

enough, and partakes in a measure, of the common gloom that clouds our prospects, yet I am happy that it presents here and there a sunny spot, which has a more enlivening effect on the spirits, from the strong contrast it bears with surrounding darkness: and still happier should I be, could I see a rational prospect that these luminous circles would gradually widen, till they come to overspread the whole State, and to enlighten every intellect with their cheering effulgence. But when I consider how much the advancement of learning depends on the policy of the government, and the general prosperity of the community; and recollect the retrograde motion which our State has taken, I can scarcely exclude from my mind the painful and melancholy reflection, that learning itself will decline; and that we shall retrograde in respect to intellectual improvement, till the *knowledge*, as well as the wealth and power of the State shall be engrossed by a privileged order. Things are unfortunately tending to this issue.

"Learning joined with religion," POLYDORE emphasized, "is the last hope of North-Carolina. If there is a redeeming spirit in the State, these only can call it into action. Whilst learning enlarges the mind, and developes its Faculties, religion curbs the licentiousness of the passions. Learning gives boldness and adventure to the mind, and produces extensive and liberal views; religion, by purifying the morals, insures soundness of principle. These form a basis for true greatness: the superstructure erected on these must possess grandeur. Religion and learning are intimately connected. . . . Knowledge and liberty of mind, are, however, necessary to regulate [religion], and prevent it from degenerating into superstition."

Looking at education from the standpoint of everyday living, POLYDORE continued. "In our observations on the subject of education, we shall not wait to discuss and decide the question, whether the intellectual faculties of all are equally capable of improvement. It is sufficient for our purpose, that all who are not idiots, are susceptible of acquiring a useful education. It matters nothing whether all are *equally* capable or not, provided all are *capable*, and it is *necessary* all should be educated.

"All men, and all women, in every sphere of life, have certain duties to perform. The more they become acquainted with their duties, and the importance of performing them aright, the better qualified, and the more disposed, they will be to perform them. In no other way can any one become acquainted with what he owes to himself, to his fellow men, and to his Creator, so well as by reading the Holy Scriptures, and other judicious writings. But in order to do this, he must first be able to read. Again, there is no one, to whom it is not important to be able to maintain an epistolary correspondence with a distant friend, or man of business; nor is there any one, who is not interested in casting up and keeping accounts accurately; but these things cannot be done without an acquaintance with writing and figures. Therefore, it is not only important, but even indispensable, that every member of the community should be able at least to *read, write,* and *cypher....*

"But besides these considerations, which render education indispensable, there are several others, which render it very important, especially to the citizens of a free and popular government. Of this kind are the following:

"1st. Education enlarges the mind, fits it for comparing, reasoning, reflecting, and contemplating, and divests it of erroneous prepossessions.

"2ndly. It furnishes an innocent, a rational, and a pleasing entertainment for our hours of vacation from business.

"3rdly. It qualifies a man for exercising, with discretion, the privilege he possesses as the member of a popular government.

"4thly. It increases and directs enterprize.

"1st. Education enlarges the mind, &c. The preceptions of an illiterate man are indistinct, contracted, and obscure; and his ideas are few and barren. His views of men and things are very partial, and his sentiments are often very illiberal. His prejudices are absurd and deeply rooted. But learning replenishes the mind with perceptions, and brightens and fertilizes the ideas. It developes the mental faculties; and opens a vast field for the mental powers to exert themselves in. The faculties of the mind, like the muscles of the

111

body, acquire size and vigour proportioned to the use that is made of them. By reading and studying the mind becomes capable of extending its views, of widening its range of thought, of combining and comparing its ideas; and thus it improves, if it does not acquire, its capacity of reflection. The studies which have the happiest effects in liberalizing the sentiments, and expanding the views, are Geography and History. A knowledge of these is so easily acquired, that any one who can read, is qualified to enter upon the study of them.

"2ndly. Learning furnishes us with an innocent, a rational, and a pleasing entertainment for our hours of vacation from business. There is no man whose life is so filled up with cares and business, that he has [no] time to devote to relaxation. Now these hours of relaxation, if spent in entire vacancy, are more irksome than even those of business; and if some innocent entertainment is not at hand, the mind is empty, and therefore open to the allurements of vice; and the man is subject to be drawn into vicious company and loose practices; where habits ruinous to health, reputation, and prosperity are acquired. How important, therefore, that every one should have some resource for filling up his hours of exemption from business, which may unite innocence and utility with pleasure. Learning is calculated to effect this in an eminent degree. What can be more *harmless* than reading *good books?* What more *rational* than the studying of *useful arts?* or more *delightful* than the *acquisition of knowledge?* Food is not more grateful to the hungry, nor repose to the weary, than this to the longing mind of man. O, knowledge! how has my soul panted after thee! How has the pursuit of thee refrained my feet from the path of vice!

"3rdly. It qualifies a man for exercising, with discretion, the power vested in him as a member of a popular government. In monarchial and despotical governments, in which common men have nothing to do with State affairs, nor any duty to perform concerning them, except acquiescence and obedience, much more limited portion of knowledge will suffice, than in a popular government, in which every man is a sovereign, and holds, in some degree, the destiny of the commonwealth in his own hands. Where such is the

112

case, every free man ought to possess an enlighted mind. He should be capable of judging for himself, what measures are necessary for promoting the security and prosperity of the State; what are the plans best adapted to carry those measures into operation; and who are the men best qualified for filling the important trusts of legislation. Without this capacity of judging for himself, a man, possessing political impunities, is obnoxious to become the dupe of any designing knave, who may approach him under the specious guise of friendship, or with the insidious sweets of flattery upon his lips; and to be rendered the instrument of his own damage. A very considerable portion of knowledge is requisite to qualify a man for citizenship, in a free and popular government.

"4thly. It increases and directs enterprize. The mind, by being habituated to study, acquires the capacity of combining and comparing its ideas, of reasoning in connexion, and of conceiving more accurately any intricate subject or proposition. Now, within the limits of possibility, whatever the mind conceives with clearness, the hands can perform with facility. Accordingly, we find nations and indivduals enterprising and inventive, in proportion as they are enlightened.

"We might multiply reasons, exhibiting the importance of education to the citizens of North-Carolina; but it would be a reflection on the ingenious reader not to suppose that when his attention is directed to this subject he can easily supply these reasons. — We arrive at this conclusion that on some accounts a portion of learning is *indispensable* to every individual of either sex and in every condition in life; that, on other accounts, it is *highly important,* especially to the citizens of a popular government.

POLYDORE."

In his second installment on education, on March 3, 1830, Swaim alias POLYDORE presented,

### NORTH-CAROLINA No. X

State of Common Schools, &c.

"I have said that North Carolina, in regard to learning, does not

exhibit all that gloom and desperation which it presents, when contemplated from other points. 'Tis cheerful enough when passing
through our country, to see the smiling 'schoolboy, with his satchel,
and his shining morning face,' not indeed, 'creeping like snail
unwillingly to school;' but bounding along in native, republican
glee, the beauty of the present, and the hope of the future. It is
pleasant, too, to enter one of our primary schools, under the superintendence of a judicious, well educated instructor . . . (and some
such the country offers) . . . Here we can find a moment's respite
from the anxiety of life,—the melancholy forebodings from the distracted affairs of the commonwealth. Again, it is a source of cheerful
hope, upon entering almost every dwelling in certain sections of the
State, to find, that at least one newspaper pays its weekly visit, and
pours out its tribute of intelligence from all quarters of the globe,
enlightening every member of the family, and assisting to prepare
him for acting his part on the stage of public life; — to see on the
shelf or the bureau, the small library of useful, and much used books;
among which the Holy Bible justly stands pre-eminent. But even in
regard to this subject, there is much, very much to deplore.

"The exertions of individuals, (I mean of such as are able and
willing to make any exertions,) are altogether incommensurate with
the great task of disseminating learning and intelligence all over the
State; and the State itself has never lent its aid to the diffusion of
general intelligence. The consequences are,

"1. That certain portions of the State are measurably destitute
of primary schools.

"2. That in parts partially supplied, the schools are in a miserable
condition.

"3. That in the most highly favored sections, there are certain
classes of children to which the benefits of these schools do scarcely
extend.

"That certain portions of the State are measurably destitute of
primary schools, is a fact that cannot be doubted by any one of much
observation. To know the extent of this destitution, is a desideratum
not perhaps in the possession of any individual in the State. It is

probably greater than many are aware of. It is not hazarding too much to say that large portions of North-Carolina are sunk in ignorance and immorality; that the people, besides being ignorant and vicious, are slothful, unenterprising, and wretched, with a state of society close bordering on barbarity.

"But in other portions of the State, partially supplied with schools, these schools are in a miserable condition. The teachers employed are an ignorant set of pretenders, who have never 'drunk deep of the Pierian spring,' nor wasted the midnight oil in penetrating the recesses of knowledge; but such as having got a smattering of education, and being too indolent to labor, have been employed as teachers; sometimes for the want of better, but often over the heads of their superiors, merely bcause their time being of less value, they have offered their services upon lower terms; and indiscriminating parents have given them a preference for no better reason. Then again, the hovels prepared for the reception of the scholars, are miserable substitutes for houses; — either open to the admittance of Boreas, or closed against the entrance of the rays of light; without any adequate accommodation of seats and tables. The children too are poorly furnished with books, paper, and necessaries for promoting their studies. They are sent so irregularly, that one portion of the time the teacher is without scholars, and the other he is overrun; especially, as from the variety of books, it is next to impossible to form a class.

"Moreover, the children are vicious and insubordinate. They cost the teacher immense pains to discipline them, if he ever undertakes it at all. In these attempts he is thwarted by the prejudices and imprudent interference of parents; some being in favor of lax, others, of strict discipline. Some being influenced by false philosophy, reject the *rod* altogether; but would introduce some wretched, incompetent substitute. Not that I would advocate a system of cruel discipline; but there is a mean in all things, and it is absurd, in avoiding one extreme, to rush headlong into the other.

"There is a set of loungers — haters of learning — who sometimes go to school for mere mischief. These, at all times troublesome to

115

the teacher, are peculiarly annoying towards Christmas, when the infection of mischief spreads from them to most of the school; learning is suspended, and disorder usurps its place. The practice of *turning out* teachers is but too notorious. The unwarranted lengths to which the practice is carried, is a strong reflection on the morality and civilization of the country. It exhibits a bad taste, and a deadly hate to learning. The scene of turning out is more than an embryo *riot,* and fosters a spirit of disobedience to salutary restraint and discipline. It is a conspiracy to mob the obnoxious individual, and that, too, for the purpose of compelling him, perhaps against principle, to do a deed for doing which voluntarily, any man ought to be severely punished; that is, to treat a collection of children with ardent spirits. Quere: Is the person of a schoolmaster, as that of another citizen, sacred from violence? Is he under the protection of the law? or does he, by engaging in that humble vocation, render himself an outlaw, liable to be mobbed, or even drowned, with impunity, by any impudent fellow who may have the outrageous bravery to want sport and a dram? Does the circumstance of their being pupils, protect them from punishment, in the perpetration of such enormities? If such be the condition of a teacher, what is it better than that of a slave? If he may be compelled to do a deed which his principle, perhaps his conscience, and most certainly his better judgment, condemns, where is the wonder, that few men of noble independence can be prevailed on to teach? If there is any law in force in North-Carolina to punish pupils for conspiring together, and mobbing their teacher, then the practice of turning out ought to be set forever at rest, by a judicial decision. If no such law exists, then one ought to be spoken into existence by an act of the legislature. Too often have I seen young men of genius, principle, and sensibility, forced by a lawless mob, to do a deed from which their noble natures shrunk; and to desert the useful occupations of teaching for which they were eminently qualified, rather than be again subjected to the like humiliation. There are many parents who encourage their children to turn out their teacher; applaud them for doing it adroitly; and are violently incensed against a teacher for making successful resistance. Generally, through the country, under the most favorable circumstances, the condition of a teacher who feels the importance and responsibility of his calling, is one of great solicitude. The children give him much uneasiness; and their parents yet more. Besides encountering all these difficulties, his nominal wages are less than can be earned by any mechanic, and are paid the most reluctantly of all debts; — whence it happens, that few men who can do any thing else, or are qualified to earn a livelihood in any other way, can be employed as teachers. Certain neighborhoods furnish exceptions, but the picture here drawn is a fair presentation of the general condition of what are termed *old field schools.*

"But in places most highly favored, there is a portion of the rising generation still destitute, that is, the children of indigent parents. Whether the poverty of the parents originates in misfortune, slothfulness, improvidence, or intemperance, the consequence to the children is, that they are brought up in ignorance. The unhappy orphan, and the still more wretched illegitimate, are found in this class. These poor children of every description, possess as much talent and genius as an equal number of any other class. Therefore, what the community suffers from a defect in their education is incalculable. POLYDORE."

On March 17, 1830, the *Greensborough Patriot* carried POLYDORE's or Swaim's third essay on education, entitled:

### NORTH-CAROLINA No. XI.
*The comparative utility of common schools, academies,*
*and universities*

"Common schools are by far the most useful to the community of any, not merely because the general mass of children can be educated in no other way, but also because every child, even though destined for the highest education, may receive his rudiments in these. Common schools, therefore, demand the first and most serious attention of the public.

"The next in utility are Academies. In these, higher branches, and branches preparatory to admittance into College, are taught.

Here, many who are intended even for professional callings, receive their final school education. Men in more moderate circumstances can support their sons in these, for a time. They also possess this peculiar advantage over Colleges, that in them there is less formality, which gives the student, or his parent, an opportunity of selecting those parts of learning, which may be more appropriate to his peculiar destination in life. Academies therefore, demand a great share of public consideration.

"I would not from this have it inferred that I consider Universities as useless. I think far otherwise. In these, young men of great genius have the opportunity of furnishing their minds with the rich stores of general knowledge. Youths, whose situation in life gives them the entire disposal of their time, may here cultivate literature, and delve in the mines of science. Therefore, these two have their claim. — Having laid down these premises, I make the following remarks, which will be found to have a more immediate connexion with the general subject under consideration, than with one another.

"Though I am of the belief, that all minds, considering only their innate structure, are more nearly of equal capacity, than some well meaning people may imagine; yet owing to external causes, and a difference of inclination, there is found a great diversity in the *qualities* of intellectual capacities, if not in their *grades*. Whence it is, that some appear to border on stupidity, who, perhaps, have naturally good minds; some have common genius, others great genius: some have a special genius, that is, a genius for a particular art or science; others a universal genius, or a genius for every art and science.

"Now where genius, capacity, or inclination, is so diverse the avocations of life should be no less various. If a child has a strong predilection for learning, and exhibits as generally happens in these cases, marks of a powerful genius, he should be encouraged, and qualified for a literary employment; for such a one will certainly succeed in literature; whereas, were the same individual destined to some other sphere of life, he might prove utterly deficient and unsuccessful.

118

"If a child should show signs of a moderate capacity, he might be encouraged, especially if his parents have the ability to support him at school. The learning of such a one, though he may never shine in the literary world, may be of more use to society, than the learning of one possessing brighter parts.

"But, if a boy exhibits no signs of capacity, or inclination for learning, nothing can be more absurd than to push him forward with the expectation of making him great by means of education. His teachers, to flatter his parents, and reap the reward, may carry him through the forms of a scholastic education; but they can never imbue his mind with knowledge, or make him a great scholar. He will be a disgrace to literature, whilst it will do him but little honor. Money and pains enough are ineffectually lavished on dronish stupidity, to elicit much talent, and make many geniuses shine, whilst these [potential geniuses] are languishing in obscurity, unnoticed and unaided.

"We have already endeavored to show, that a common education is indispensable to all. Every one, therefore, how idle or stupid soever he may be, should be urged on till he imbibe the more useful parts of rudimental knowledge; and from what we here offer, we conclude, that none but such as display signs of capacity, and inclination for learning, should be urged further.

"If the State contributes any thing to the aid of the University, except so far as it shall tend to render a collegiate education equally attainable by the rich and the poor, it is contributing to the sole benefit of the former. But the State should not contribute to the aid of one class or portion of the community, without bestowing an equivalent to the benefit of other classes or portions. If the State has already contributed much to aid the University, it is now due, that it should contribute proportionately to common Schools and Academies. Otherwise what it has done for the College, is but furthering the growth of aristocracy, to which I have observed all our institutions tend. It is a thing of rare occurrence that a man who has graduated at a University thinks of any thing but self-aggrandizement. He cannot stoop to the drudgery of those occupations which

119

are of more common use to mankind. Nothing short of a learned profession, or a dignified office can satisfy his aspirings. Not but that hundreds of them who have not the enterprise to study professions, nor the popularity to attain office, sink into oblivion, and leave no vestige of their having existed, except in the annals of debauchery.

"It is a remark that I do not remember to have seen made, but yet I believe it will appear obvious to any one upon reflection, that a University, conducted on the plan of ours, which is perhaps the common plan, is but little calculated to promote the acquisition of knowledge and literature, in proportion to the speciousness of its pretenses. There is too much formality. The same route is to be pursued by all the students, without regard to the diversity of their talents, the quickness of their conceptions, the assiduity of their application, or to their future destination in life. The only aim seems to be the acquisition of general knowledge, either profound or superficial. The student who has a genius or taste for only part of the studies, is hurried indiscriminately through all. The most diligent and the most negligent must perform their task in the same time. The student who is preparing for a particular vocation in life is permitted to dwell no longer on these branches of study which are more intimately connected with his ultimate design, than he whose designation is most opposite. This course reverses the order of nature, and prevents the students who enter the University from most of the advantages they might otherwise enjoy. It supposes every student to possess a universal genius. It injures the *constitutions* of some, and the *minds* of others. Some, by too constant and arduous an application, break their constitutions, and are rendered valetudinarians for life. Others destroy the elastity or buoyancy of their minds, & leave them broken, and in a situation difficult to define, but easy to be conceived by any one who has ever overstirred himself. Those who possess great genius and fervour are the most liable thus to fall victims. Others acquire a habit of gliding superficially over their tasks, grow more and more negligent, leave school but little improved, and are seldom heard of afterwards, except as noticed above."

Swaim, alias POLYDORE, would have approved heartily of the elective system and the variety of curricula in colleges today. So convinced was he of the inadequacy of a single curriculum for all students that he advocated reform of curriculum, whatever the cost. Wrote he: "I am not unapprised of the difficulty that would attend the attempt to adapt the classes of Colleges to the various circumstances above mentioned; but certainly the utility of such an arrangement would justify a great effort. At any rate, every student should not be compelled to go through all the classes before he is permitted to graduate.

POLYDORE."

On March 24, 1830, the subject of learning was further discussed by POLYDORE (Swaim) under the title of "NORTH-CAROLINA No. XII, *A plan for extending the blessings of education to every child in the state.*" He began by reiterating and reemphasizing "the necessity and utility of learning, and the great deficiency in the Schools and Education of North-Carolina." He concluded that the state, itself contributing some aid, should adopt a system of common schools for primary instruction. Furthermore, he advised, "at suitable distances through the state," the establishment of partly state-supported academies which would prepare students for college, and for professions, particularly teaching. In order that "indigent genius might not languish for lack of assistance and encouragement," the state should establish a fund for lending students money, without interest, and such students should, as soon as they were earning, pay back the sum to be thus used by other students.

POLYDORE said he approved of Kinney's plan as recommended by Governor Owen for the lower grades; but he suggested modifications for further consideration. Kinney's plan proposed that each county in the state should be divided into appropriate districts. These districts should raise money for building schoolhouses by a small property tax. In order to pay teachers' salaries, each district should raise by annual taxation the required sum. These were the main points of the plan, but Kinney had more to say about how it

121

should be accomplished and how teachers should be chosen. POLYDORE agreed with Kinney on a small property tax for building schoolhouses, since it would be negligible when weighed against the fact that a good schoolhouse might last for several generations. It is interesting that POLYDORE estimated the cost of such a building at $178.60, for a district four miles square. On the question of teachers' salaries, however, he agreed only in part with Kinney. POLYDORE, who estimated $75 for a man to teach four months in winter and $40 for a "tutoress" to instruct four months in summer, thought there would be much complaint of unequal taxation in different districts, for some would have in them more people unable to pay taxes than others. He therefore suggested a combination of subscriptions and taxation. Under this plan the districts should collect $2.50 per year from each pupil financially able to pay; the state should pay an equal amount for each pupil who was not able to pay plus a small fee for books, — altogether about $720 per county each year — and the balance should be made up by taxes collected by the county.

POLYDORE anticipated the question of where the state would get that much money without raising taxes, and he had the answer ready. He suggested that certain fines, and the tax on specified articles be set aside for public education. He expected the Literary Fund would increase so that the interest of it would be a constant resource. And, he wrote, "we have good reasons to expect, that the United States will . . . have a dividend of surplus revenue to distribute to us," as it did.

POLYDORE's essays on education were published early in 1830. In that same year Dr. Joseph Caldwell, President of the University of North Carolina, started publishing in the *Raleigh Register* his *Letters on Popular Education, Addressed to the People of North Carolina,* but soon discontinued them on account of ill health and other hindrances. In 1832 he released them in book form. In these essays he asserted, "I am ready to admit, nay conclusively to affirm, that [taxation] must and will be fatal to every scheme of popular education to which it is made necessary."[40] He said that the people would patronize inexpensive schools, and that the great need was for teachers. He therefore suggested an advanced state-supported teacher-training institution, not too different from POLYDORE's plan for academies, for training those who could recruit students for subscription schools.

Still, year after year passed and nothing was done about common schools. Meanwhile there were some who began to hope in terms of federal aid for education, but Swaim explained why this was a vain hope: "Mr. Richardson, of Massachusetts, on the 15, inst., introduced a resolution for the addition to the standing committee of a committee on education. This resolution elicited considerable discussion, during which the constitutional power of Congress was avowed by some and denied by others. The proposition was finally lost — 126 to 52. Of the members from North Carolina, William B. Shepperd voted *for* the resolution, and *all* others (except Lewis Williams and Abraham Rencher, who were *absent*) voted *against* it."[41]

Meantime William Swaim never stopped reminding his readers about educational progress in other parts of the Union. Here was something that had been tried and had proved to be good. Illustrating this fact was the inspiring observation that "There is no country in the wor[l]d possessing the advantages of early Education to such an extent as the Northern States of the Union. — With the exception of Scotland, no nation approaches them in any reasonable degree. Our higher Institutions may not, perhaps, possess the wealth, the riches and the long line of learned ancestry that some of the European Universities do, but the Education of the great body of the people is a point far more desirable for the advancement of general happiness, than a few splendid scholars with an ignorant people to receive the light of their great learning. Let our Colleges be supported, but let our Academies and Common Schools be guarded with a care and veneration equal to that with which we preserve our liberty."[42]

Although it was disappointing and discouraging to Swaim to see educational efforts constantly defeated by the legislature of North

Carolina, he understood the inside workings of that body. He had known for a long time that the power of the state lay in the hands of a conservative eastern majority which dominated the General Assembly. As authorized by the state constitution, this official delegation was chosen by counties, each county providing two representatives for the House of Commons and one for the Senate House. In addition there was one borough representative from each of the towns of New Bern, Edenton, Wilmington, Halifax, Fayetteville, Hillsboro, and Salisbury. Since the earlier settled eastern part of the state had many more counties than the relatively new western section, and since most of the borough representatives were from the east, the General Assembly was made up of a large eastern majority which "passed such laws and elected such officials as it wished, blocked laws demanded by the West, and dominated the state government."[43]

By 1830 the West had surpassed the East in population, but the East had the greater wealth. The West favored state improvements through state aid, but the East which was not as greatly in need of improvements, flatly put its foot down against state aid which would draw taxes from its greater wealth. Here then was a contributing factor to the conservative-East, progressive-West cleavage which throttled the state for many years. The northeastern Sound region played an in and out game with the two factions, supporting whichever had policies that most appealed to it. The southeastern border counties did likewise.

Swaim was aware of this situation when he made his first public appearance in 1823, and spoke in favor of a constitutional adjustment which would give the progressive western section more representation in the legislature. Now that he was more mature, he must have realized more keenly that a constitutional change, if it was fair, could be the means by which many needed improvements might take place in the state. Already he was seriously concentrating and publishing his views on such a constitutional revision. He meant never to relax until it came to pass, and under it, educational facilities provided for everybody in North Carolina.

# VI

## FOR SCIENTIFIC AGRICULTURE

*"A farmer cuts rather a bad figure to be seen — with his fences prostrate, or nearly so — bushes and briars over-running his plantation, and every thing around him, exhibiting marks of indolence — and he laying flat on his back, crying, 'Nothing can be done till we get a central railroad!'"*[1]

"Friend Swaim," as contributors soon began to address the serious editor of the *Greensborough Patriot,* had acute reasons for concern about agricultural conditions in his home state. Although North Carolina was almost entirely rural and predominantly agricultural, with more and more land being brought under cultivation every year, the assessed value of all the state's lands had dropped from $53,500,000 in 1815 to $43,000,000 by 1833.[2] As Swaim had pointed out in the first issue of his paper, "When our State was first settled, the inhabitants seem not to have been aware of the pernicious tendency of that system, or rather that want of system, which they introduced by prostrating the timber in every direction, and exhausting the soil by every possible means, without any regard for its preservation or improvement. They prosecuted this course until they left no inconsiderable portion of our lands in a state of delapidation; and shrubbery growing up in every direction, as if striving to hide the general ruins."

125

To complicate this situation, there was a grave lack of facilities for transporting produce to the markets; means for communicating new ideas and improved farming methods were most inadequate; and widespread ignorance greatly handicapped the people in applying constructive agricultural thoughts and opinions which did reach them.

For these reasons the efforts of the few farsighted individuals and agricultural groups who hoped to check the downward trend were ineffectual. In the 1820's, sensing the seriousness of prevailing conditions, the legislature established an Agricultural Fund to be used by the different counties that would organize and maintain agricultural societies. And Professors Denison Olmstead and Elisha Mitchell of the University of North Carolina made and published a geological survey of the state, the first of its kind in the nation.[3] Apathy unfortunately prevented these measures from stimulating interest and initiating improvements in the farm situation.

One of the chief factors contributing to this apathy was the state's loss, through emigration, of thousands of its citizens, particularly those who were young, energetic, and ambitious. Various considerations prompted their departure from North Carolina. In the first place, representation based upon an outmoded state constitution allowed the older and more conservative eastern section of the state to dominate the General Assembly to the great disadvantage of the more recently developed and more progressive western region. Almost half a century of repeated efforts to revise the constitution had failed. This disheartening political situation, plus the poor educational facilities, the impoverished soil and inadequate means of transportation, and other equally discouraging circumstances, moved thousands of North Carolinians to seek homes farther west where there seemed to be more promise. During the 1830's the migration took its greatest toll. In that decade nearly half the counties showed an actual decline in population, and the state's increase was only two per cent whereas the normal increase for that period should have been fifteen per cent.[4] Although North Carolina ranked third in population when it entered the Union in 1789, by 1820 it stood fourth, and by 1830 had dropped to fifth.[5]

The *Greensborough Patriot* gave some specific reasons for this migration: "Why is the agriculture of our state in such a languishing and unprosperous condition? is a question frequently and anxiously asked by our citizens — one answers it is for want of a rail-road furnishing the farmer with facilities for transportation not yet enjoyed in the State. Another says, our laws are radically defective, they afford not that protection to the tenant in the permanent possession of the soil, which is indispensable in an *Agricultural Community*: they give such undue & rigorous facilities to the *trader* for the collection of his debts, as are only compatible with the prosperity of a community who are altogether *commercial* in their character. And a third, after casting a despairing glance over his exhausted fields, says: 'We have here no accessible resource of lime, gypsum, or any other efficient mineral agent as a manure, the [r]enovation of our soil is therefore utterly hopeless, and I shall migrate to the West.' "[6]

Although Swaim was vexed and impatient with this state of affairs, he had faith that the damage could be mended. With courage he assessed the situation, pledged his own help, and challenged others. "We have all the advantages of soil and climate that any other State in the Union can boast; and nothing but information and energy are wanting to place this state in point of Agricultural prosperity upon a level with the most improved of her sisters. This *information* we intend to give, and we hope it will call into action the *energy*."[7]

His method of attack on the lackadaisical popular attitude was both direct and indirect. The latter, however, aimed more pointedly at the seat of the trouble. Fully aware that agriculture would receive its greatest impetus through a revised state constitution, an enlightened public interest, improved means of transportation, more satisfactory banking facilities, and progress in allied fields, he placed his major emphasis on the need for reforms in these areas. At the same time he set up in his paper the following department:

---

## AGRICULTURE

---

- - - - - *and your rich soil*
*Exuberant nature's better blessings pour*
*O'er every land.*

---

Through this section he passed along to his readers a varied mass of information for use in the home and on the farm. This department was not as regularly included as some others, for example, COMMUNICATIONS; but there was rarely an issue of the *Greensborough Patriot* that did not carry some encouraging item for farmers. Such a message might be embodied in a contributor's piece, in an anecdote, in an article that was suitable to be placed under the heading of SELECTED or VARIETY, perhaps in a little story, or conspicuously placed in the editorial column.

The agricultural division often contained good advice that might have been applicable a century and a quarter later. A typical example of its contents in a single issue would embrace such items as "The Relative Pleasures and Profits of Agriculture," "Weaning Calves," "Seeds," "Cures for the Botts or Grubs in Horses," "To Keep off or Drive away Bedbugs," "Cattle Food," on making "Composts," "Cheap Antidote," "To Preserve Vines from Bugs," and "Hints to Housewives."[8] For the most part, these discussions were short, to the point, and entirely adequate.

Another issue made suggestions for the proper care of "Trees," the art of "Soap Making" by the cold process, and a way "To restore Tainted Beef."[9] And still another carried articles on "Farmers' Work —Select Seed Corn," "Seeds for Sowing," "Weeds made Useful," "Agriculture and its Advantages," and "Skinless and Huskless Oats."[10]

Agricultural articles selected at random embraced timely discussions on such subjects as "Cultivation of the Peach Tree;" "Importance of Deep Ploughing;" "Proper Time for Cutting Grain;" "Hints to Farmers on Care of Tools;" the importance of "Manure;"

the place of the lowly "Onion;" "Apple Trees," with emphasis on good bearers, good keepers, and good flavor; the value of "Clover" as a farm product; "To Make a Good Farmer," which stressed the importance of carefully attending to the business aspect and of learning from the experience of others; and "Good Bacon," a title which was the lead for giving the proper method of raising, curing, and cooking the hickory-smoked variety. So vividly was this subject presented that as one reads about it, the odor of its frying in the country about sunup seems to well up from the age-yellowed pages of the *Greensborough Patriot*.

Nor were farm animals and their products overlooked. There were instructions on how to take care of milk, how to make good cheese, and advice on sheep culture both for food and clothing. Oxen were recognized as of immense value for work on the farm and for transporting products to market. It must have been a welcome suggestion that promised to improve the speed of these slow-motioned beasts. With amusing exaggeration it was said that at midday to feed them "with ears of corn, and for a change, give them potatoes, will make them as powerful as a steam engine on a railroad." And if to ground corn and potatoes, good hay be added for the morning and evening feedings, "oxen fed this way, with good hay to fill up, will move like a shuttle, and, make matters crack again!"[11]

These are only a few of the many subjects Swaim projected for his readers. And it is not too much to say that some of the ideas he gave to farmers one hundred and thirty years ago would make good practical programs for radio and television broadcasters of modern times.

Some excerpts from the *Greensborough Patriot* will show how persistently the editor tried to impart to the farmers the best available agricultural knowledge. He was ever alert for useful material. This is evidenced by the fact that sometimes it was reprinted from other newspapers, sometimes it was from a contributor, sometimes it came through an unsigned article, and sometimes from his own pen. In his first edition he gave twenty-five "*Hints to Young Farmers*" which might well be passed along to the Future Farmers of America. Among these were: "Consider your calling the most elevated and the most important; but never be above it, nor be afraid of the frock and the apron. . . .

"As soon as the spring opens, and the frost is out of the ground, put your fences in order. . . .

"Keep no more stock than you can keep in good order and that of the best kind. . . .

"Keep a place for your tools — and your tools in their place. . . .

"On the first of every January reckon with yourself, and reckon honestly — bring into view all the debts and credits, notes and accounts — ascertain to what amount your expenses were the last year, and enter the whole in a book kept for the purpose. Having arrived at this important knowledge, you will imitate the prudent traveller, who always keeps in view where he is next to move; you will next look forwards and calculate how and in what way, you shall best meet and prosecute the season." If this last bit of advice had not been given on May 23, 1829, a farmer of the mid-twentieth century might think it was aimed directly at him in connection with preparing his state and federal income tax returns.

Under the heading of "Select Seed Corn," the reader learned that "It is highly important that your seed corn should be selected from the best samples which can be obtained, as the offspring whether vegetable or animal will in a great degree partake of the good or bad qualities of the parent." A scientific and practical agriculturalist advised that it should be taken "from stocks that are large at the bottom, of a regular taper, not over tall, the ears set low, and containing the greatest number of good sizeable ears of the best quality; let it dry speedily; and from the corn gathered as last described, plant your main crop."[12] This method, used for many years, he said increased quantity, and improved quality of crops beyond what any person would imagine if he had not tried the experiment.

Leading staple products were "WHEAT AND CORN" and in an article under that title, men of the field were told, by argument and anecdote, that "Many of our most respectable farmers . . . seem not to be sufficiently aware that if they sow poor wheat and plant poor corn, poor wheat and poor corn they must expect to harvest. . . .

"Some years ago," said the writer, "I took pains to select from my wheat in the sheaf, enough to sow about half an acre, of the longest, fullest and most perfect heads, I could find.

"I sowed it in the same field with my other wheat, which was very good, cultivated in precisely the same manner, upon the same kind of soil, and when harvest time came I was surprised to see the difference.

"It could be plainly distinguished from the surrounding wheat at the distance of thirty to forty rods, by its height; it was heavier, and the heads were longer and better filled.

"I once let a piece of ground to a neighbour, to be planted with corn. Soon after he got it planted, I found that he had taken the corn from the crib, *'just as it come,'* without selecting or choosing.

"In answer to my telling him that each of [us] would have been dollars better off if he had planted good seed corn, he said, 'Poh? do you spose 't makes any difference what kind of corn you plant?' But harvest day told the story; and when he saw sixty bushels per acre, upon my field adjoining of good sound corn, and found upon harvesting his, that he had but forty bushels per acre, and most of that 'pig corn' and 'nubbins,' he was forced to acknowledge with sorrow the truth of my remark."[13]

"ROTATION OF CROPS" was another reform in farming that Swaim considered imperative. In the *Greensborough Patriot,* May 6, 1835, there appeared the following: "To this branch of our subject we invite particular attention; because, in our opinion, it forms the basis of all successful agriculture. Whatever pains we take, whatever expenses we incur, in collecting instruments of husbandry, in accumulating and applying manures, and in tilling the earth, all is to little purpose, unless to these we superadd a *succession of crops adapted to the nature of the soil, to the laws of the climate, and to the commercial value* of the article raised."

Giving a detailed analysis of plant life which best thrives in wet, dry, clay, loamy, and other soils, and citing the practice of crop rotation in other states of the Union, the writer concluded with tables to be used in the rotation of crops:

"Medium course in sandy soil: 1st year, potatoes dunged; 2nd, rye, with turnips after harvest consumed on the field; 3rd, oats and clover or barley and clover; 4th, clover; 5th, wheat with turnips after harvest consumed on the field; and 6th, peas, or lupins or lentils. We have by this course eight crops in six years, and five of these ameliorating crops.

"Medium course in loamy soils: 1st year, potatoes dunged; 2nd year, wheat with turnips, as in the preceding course; 3rd year, Indian corn and pumpkins; 4th year, barley and clover; 5th year, clover; 6th year, wheat and turnips as before. In this course we have nine crops in six years, five of which are ameliorating crops. And,

"Medium course in clay soils: 1st year, oats with clover; 2nd, clover; 3rd, wheat; 4th, beans, dunged; 5th, wheat; 6th, the yellow vetching."

The above advice may not be of interest to a city dweller, but to a farmer in any day and age, it makes very good sense. Thus, during Swaim's editorship, the *Greensborough Patriot* carried direct instructions as to how to handle soil, seed, and crops to best advantage. "It is to be regretted," he wrote in 1835, "that North Carolina cannot afford one paper devoted entirely to subjects connected with husbandry. Such a paper, ably conducted, would, we have no doubt, develop resources for the farmer at present entirely unknown, and stay, in a degree, the tide which is daily sweeping our husbandmen from this genial land, to the cold, uncomfortable, yet fertile forests and prairies of the west."[14] In this, Swaim was in a sense prophetic, for within four years John Sherwood began his *Farmer's Advocate* at Jamestown, North Carolina. This was followed by at least five other ante-bellum North Carolina agricultural journals which did as Swaim had predicted: they greatly aided in bringing new life into the state.[15] Indeed, the value of farm products had increased over a hundred per cent before progress was halted by the Civil War.

Not only was the editor of the *Greensborough Patriot* concerned about the practical side of agriculture, but he was also concerned for the dignity of the agricultural profession in the eyes of farmers as well as others. Running through the paper were such admonitions to farmers as "Cherish in yourselves a proper respect for the husbandman; teach your children the importance of agriculture to the well being of your country."[16] And again, warned the paper on May 13, 1835, "Let us inquire if there is not another evil agent ... dangerous to our agriculture, and which if not arrested will extend its withering influence to our political institutions, and up-loosen the foundations of our government. Is not our system of education grossly defective, and calculated to give to the mind of our youth a bias altogether adverse to the simple manners and manly virtues which are at once the offspring of agricultural pursuits, and the upholding pillars of popular government? By a system of education I do not mean a course of scholastic study: for to the eternal disgrace of the state we have not anything that deserves the name of a school system, but I mean that domestic education, those habits and modes of thinking which are inculcated by the parent and imbibed by the child in the family domicil." In a rather lengthy discussion the writer of this piece showed that he resented the way lawyers and physicians were beginning to "look down" on farmers, and stated firmly that he felt they were not to be sneered at as " 'honest Hodge the ploughman,' " but rather should be cherished with the profoundest respect.

One may well assume that the farmers found satisfaction in the fact that Swaim was one of them — that he had his own garden which he worked with his own hands. Once he inserted this information: "We have turnips — not a few — in our own garden twenty inches in circumference! Remember this is but the 17th of October, and we expect, before they quit growing, to measure some not less than thirty. We planted them in drills, and when they commenced growing we thinned them out and cultivated them with a hoe."[17]

This personal interest in turnips seems to have been brought about by a sort of game he was playing with the farmers among his

133

readers. He began early in his editorship to feature — with proper credit for growers — fine specimens of various farm products, which could come only through suitable soil conditions and proper cultivation. With Swaim this was a subtle way to induce farmers to try out their own ideas for better production; and it soon became a challenge among the farmers of the area to see who could grow the biggest of various farm items. Among the first to respond was Jeremiah Dodson, who on November 14, 1829, brought Swaim a turnip which measured thirty inches in circumference.

Farmers were carried away with the idea of growing huge vegetables, and one day some gentlemen of the Greensboro Bar stopped the court to display their horticultural success in a collection of cabbage heads of immense size. Swaim was really amused. He allowed that "Cabbage-heads in a court house, placed on shoulders, [have] become too common to excite surprise, but for a downright eatable cab[b]age, to be brought before the court for 'examination,' may well be marked down as a new era in the annals of civil jurisprudence."[18]

This contest even produced some tall stories and much fun as well as serious effort. For example, once, in 1829, Swaim reported that "Somebody has told — and we tell it again for our readers to make what they can of it — that the produce of a single pumpkin seed, vine and all, weighed between eleven and twelve hundred weight."[19] Thereafter summer after summer industrious farmers either presented the Greensboro editor with the biggest farm product they had grown, or else they told him about it.

When Swaim printed on October 31, 1832, that Zodak Tucker had given him a beet which was twenty-five inches long and twenty-two inches around, and also had brought him the largest potato he ever saw — weighing seven and a half pounds— Peter Stout gave him a bigger tale for November. "This is indeed an age of big things, as well as of big men," wrote Swaim. "Peter Stout . . . has, the past season, raised a pumpkin weighing *one hundred and twelve pounds,* and measuring *five feet three inches* in circumference. We have heard many stories of pumpkin vines being used for bridges across

Connecticut river, but to speak in sober reality, as we now do, Mr. Stout can compete in the pumpkin way with any man in this state. At any rate, we never heard of one so large before."[20]

About this time the *Rutherford Spectator* joined the fun. It reported a watermelon rind which would hold four gallons of water, and ended with a challenge, *"Beat this who can?"* Swaim, never to be outdone, replied with a tall story which would hold its own among those of any age: "Now we have a neighbor, known by the nome of Timothy Sizeable, who raised a *squash* some ten or fifteen years ago, and has stabled a large head of cattle in the rind, ever since, the door of entrance being made by means of cutting off the handle with a cross cut saw; and this is only considered a matter of common occurrence, hereabouts."[21]

And then to give double measure he told another one with the title "UNPARALLELED & UNPARALLELLABLE!" This was inspired by a correspondent of the *Dublin Morning Herald* who had said that a yawl, containing five men, has lately been crushed to flinders between the upper and the nether jaws of a whale. "This we believe to be strictly true," said Swaim, "but it is a mere trifle to the story of the man who caught a catfish in his spring branch with his dogs, so large that he used its scull for a carriage house and its ribs for Gate-posts!"[22]

The story that caused the greatest sensation of any of such yarns, however, was one entitled "TUCKER'S BEET AND POTATOES BEATEN!" Causing an excitement similar on a small scale to an Orson Wells production, some people thought the seat of state government was actually going to be moved to Greensboro, whereas Swaim was only trying to prod the legislature into doing something to help the farmers into improving their soil. "The stage drivers on the route from here to Raleigh, as well as all the other drivers that we know of, keep good teams," said this story, "and [they] drive so moderately that their horses are seldom fatigued, unless when overloaded with passengers, which, in this traveling season of the year, is sometimes the case. On Thursday last, when Jehu drove in sight, his prancers, which are accustomed to exult in the service of the general government, appeared to be almost jaded down. As usual, we set conjecture to work to ascertain the cause of such an uncommon sweating and panting. Could is be possible, thought we that the legislature had adjourned, and that the stage was crammed full of members, returning to their homes? Or had they, in fact, passed a law to remove the seat of government to the metropolis of this county, and had sent it on by the stage, with a view of deliberating on the concerns of the state, this winter, under our inspection? With this latter thought we were too much elated to maintain that equanimity of demeanor for which we have become so celebrated. This is indeed, a lucky moment, thought we. The state printing can be executed by us in masterly style; and the legislature, under our eye, will be certain to advance the substantial interests of the state. Big with these gratifying anticipations, we immediately commenced memorising a speech to be delivered by us on the annunciation of the fact, that we had been elected 'printer of the state!' But imagine our surprise, if you please, when the stage drove up to the door, and instead of unloading the state house, rolled out a huge *potatoe* which had been forwarded to us by one of the best men that ever trod shoe leather in Hillsborough! It was this massive vegetable that had wearied Cunningham's team almost to death, and created so many strange conjectures in our fruitful mind!

"Now there is no mistake or exaggeration in what we are about to say in regard to this astonishing mass of vegetable matter. We knew, if we told the truth, without a witness, we should render ourself obnoxious to the suspicion of having 'stretched the blanket!' and to guard against this we called a witness, who is, at any time ready to depose to what we say: The potatoe actually measured 22½ inches in circumference, one way and 21¼ the other. We then split it open in the middle for the purpose of ascertaining the diameter, which was exactly 9 inches! ...

"This weighty production was raised by Mr. John Christmas, Esq. in the vicinity of Hillsborough, and was forwarded to us by that gentleman as a token of his regard and esteem, which we shall reciprocate by sending him this paper, in company with our best wishes for the success of his potatoe patch next year. We cannot sufficiently admire that good feeling which pervades the community towards us; and which prompts the agricultural portion of our citizens to send us specimens of the richest productions of their orchards, gardens, and farms. May the richest showers of heaven forever descend upon the gardens of Mr. Christmas, and of his children, and his children's children, until time shall be swallowed up in the ocean of eternity.

"One incident of the affair must not be passed over in silence. Although the potatoe was designed especially for our own palate, the greedy contractor seized upon one half of it, as a compensation for hauling it up for us! Against such arbitrary exactions as this, we now, once for all, and forever, enter our solemn protestations. It was with the utmost difficulty we could keep our rage from boiling over as he and his negro man, one at each end, shouldered the biggest half, and marched off with it! A hearty dinner, however, on the remaining half has inspired us to the writing of this article!

"N.B. If this potatoe story is not more than *half* true it may be accounted for from the above fact — namely: we got but *half* the potatoe!"[23]

Although Swaim would play along in this humorous vein, he seized upon every opportunity to promote progress along serious lines. He had been greatly heartened by the response to his challenge to grow big things, and while his readers were in this co-operative mood, he reminded them "that if all the farmers in the country would strike off their habits of indolence and diss[i]pation, and turn their attention to the cultivation of the soil, and to improvements in agriculture, a more prosperous and happy people could not be found under heaven. That tide of emigration now flowing to the west would soon stay its rapid and desolating course, and cease to convey our industry, wealth, talent and enterprise to the wild woods of the west, and leave the 'raw materials' of a mighty state to crumble into ruins!"[24]

He was therefore delighted when he had news that an Agricultural Society had been formed in Pasquotank County, to act as an auxiliary to one in Raleigh. Holding it up as an example, he urged other counties to form such organizations, saying, "Man in his individual capacity, though feeble, is capable of achieving much; but when the talents of a community are thrown together, obstructions to the march of improvement that, before seemed insurmountable shrink into a mere nothingness: Hence the necessity of forming societies."[25]

If he had no specific happening on which to comment, he would attack some general subject. For instance, people in the state were talking more and more about the need for better transportation facilities, and Swaim wrote, "While every body is talking loud and much on this subject, and nothing seems to be doing, we happen to think of one species of improvement within the reach of every man who has a farm under his management: It is to improve his farm, and orchard, and vineyard, and garden. A farmer cuts rather a bad figure to be seen — with his fences prostrate, or nearly so — bushes and briars over-running his plantation, and every thing around him, exhibiting marks of indolence — and he laying flat on his back, crying, 'Nothing can be done till we get a central railroad!' "[26]

One feature of the *Greensborough Patriot* which must have been of great interest and help to the farmers was its weekly reports of markets all over the country. The places listed were not the same every week, but the range of coverage was about the same. Although the quotations would be incredible to people of the 1960's, it is interesting to observe a sample of these prices as quoted on December 5, 1829:

## THE MARKETS

*Greensborough Prices Current, Nov. 21*—Bacon 7 a 8, beef 2 a 2½, brandy 30 a 40, butter 8 a 10, corn 30 a 35, coffee 16 a 20, flour 350 a 400, molasses 50, sugar 10 a 12½, salt 125 a 150, tallow 8 a 10, wheat 60 a 70, whiskey 25 a 30.

*Nashville Ten. November 21*—Cotton 7 to 8, flour 5 to 6, lard 6 to 7, whiskey 25 to 37, tallow 8. N. Carolina bank bills 10 per cent. discount.

*Salisbury, October 3* — Cotton 1½ to 1¾ cents, corn 25 to 30, beef 3 to 4, butter 8 to 10, flour 3.75 to 4 per barrel, wheat 50 to 60, Irish potatoes 30 to 40, sweet [potatoes] do. 25 to 35, brown sugar 12 to 15, coffee 15 to 22, salt 12 to 125, homespun cloth 15 to 25, whiskey 20 to 23, bacon 3 to 10.

*Petersburg, Va., November 21*—Cotton 7½ a 9, tobacco, middling 6.00, prime, 14.00, wheat 95 a 1.05, corn 45 a 50 cts per bushel, fluor 9, bacon 9¾ a 10.

*Fayetteville, November 5*—Cotton 8 to 8½, bacon 7 a 7¾, peach brandy 55, apple [brandy] do 28 to 30, butter 10 to 15, corn 36 to 40, flaxseed 30, flour 4 to 5¼, lard 7½, molasses 32 a 34, sugar 8½ to 10, salt 75 to 80, tallow 8, wheat 85 a 90, whiskey 24 to 28, — U. S. bank notes 1¼ to 1½ per cent. premium, Cape Fear ditto ½ a 2.

*Charleston, September 21*—Cotton 7 to 9½ cents, flour 7 a 7¼, whiskey 26 a 27, bacon 6 to 7, hams 8 a 9, best kind of bagging 20 to 22, salt 34 to 50, corn 42 a 46, coffee 11 to 15 — N. Carolina bank bills 2 to 2½ per cent. discount; Georgia, 1¼ ditto.

*Richmond, September 25*—Cotton 8 a 9½, wheat 1.25, corn 45, bacon 7 to 7½, brandy apple 42 a 45; whiskey 26 to 27.

*Camden, September 26*—Cotton 7 to 8½, flour 4¼ to 5 out of wagons that from Camden Mills 6 to 7, wheat $1, corn 50 o 52½, oats 32, salt 65, whiskey 28 to 35, bacon 7 to 8.

*Baltimore, September 11*—Flour $6½ a 7, cotton 10 to 11, whiskey 24 to 25, bacon 9 to 11.

*Boston, September 7* — Cotton 9 to 10¾, flax 9 a 11, flour 7 to 7, 12¾, corn 50 a 51, cheese 3 to 5, tallow 8 a 8½.

*Cincinnati, Ohio, September 5* — Cotton 12¾, feathers 23 cents, flaxseed 37 to 40, flour 5.75 to 5.85, Kenhawa salt 50 cents, peach brandy 62, apple [brandy] do 37, whiskey 20, tallow 6 to 7, tobacco 3 to 7 cents per lb.

*Newbern, September 12* — Cotton 7.25 to 7.50, flour 6.50 to $7, wheat $1, bacon 5 to 6, salt 80 to 100, peach brandly 75, apple [brandy] do 40 to 45, whiskey 35.

*New York, September 8* — Cotton 8¼ to 10½, flour 6.87 to 7, cotton bagging made of hemp, 19 to 21, wheat 1.37 to 1.50, oak tanned shoe leather 20 to 26, hemlock do. 17 to 23, hams 9 to 10, salt 42 to 50, apple brandy 35 to 40, whiskey 21¼ to 22, leaf tobacco 3 to 5, yellow beeswax 23 to 24, — North Carolina bank bills 3 to 3½ per cent. discount, South Carolina 1 to 1½, Georgia 2 to 2½, Virginia 1 per cent. do.

*Wilmington, September 23* — Cotton 7½ to 8, flax 10 to 13, flour 6.50 to 7.00, corn 60, cheese 7 to 8, apple brandy 33 to 35, tallow 8 to 9.

*Lynchburg, Va. September 10* — Tobacco 4 to 9, Flour 4.37 to 4.50, Wheat 75, Whiskey 23 to 24, bacon 7½ to 8. — Tobacco, dull sale. Wheat has risen a little, and sells readily at 75.

Two other North Carolina products which were given much attention in the 1830's were silk and gold. Silk culture offered much promise for those who were interested in producing it, for it thrived in several states. The Morus Multicaulis, a species of mulberry, was introduced with the hope of raising silkworms. The idea was so well received that it became known as the "Morus Multicaulis craze."[27]

North Carolina also had its own mulberry trees. David Beard, a landowner of Guilford County, wrote to the *Greensborough Patriot*, "Friend Swaim:—I have made a small experiment upon the culture of silk. I had 3000 worms, which I fed altogether upon the native mulberry leaf. They have spun their cocoons in full perfection; and we have made part of the silk into sewing thread, which is the best I have ever used. I have no doubt that our *native mulberry* is as good, if not better than the *white;* and if so, every farmer may soon have an orchard of mulberry trees, if he will take the pains — as they are of a quick growth."[28]

Swaim did not overlook this opportunity for giving people encouragement to try a new experiment. He quoted the *North Carolina Journal's* approval of the venture by saying, " 'We are rejoiced to see intelligent Citizens turning their attention to this most pleasant and profitable occupation, and we hope the day is not very distant, when every family in the state will make silk.' "[29] From time to time the Greensboro editor furnished information on its cultivation and ponted out its possibilities as a rewarding enterprise.

Gold was even more important than silk; and it created great excitement, especially when gold nuggets weighing from one to twenty-eight pounds were found in the Reed Gold Mine of Cabarrus County.[30] Although all gold veins were not as promising, in the 1830's there were at least fifty-six mines in active operation in North Carolina, among them Dr. David Worth's which yielded about $20 to each bushel of soil. Swaim was pleased to report that "Tracts of land which have long went begging at *Three Hundred dollars,* have recently been sold for *Six Thousand.* We like to *hear* these things, and we like to tell them."[31] He was infuriated, however, when he learned that a gold mining company, intending to mine gold in North Carolina, had been formed in Baltimore with a capital of $100,000, and with agents "on the alert." To this he said, "Is there not industry enough in the Citizens of N. Carolina to pick up their own gold (at least enough of it to pay their debts) when it lies glittering in the sunbeams upon their barren hills where 'peas won't sprout?' Wake up ye slumbering children of indolence, and provide yourselves a better circulating medium than the Bank Bills of which you so justly and bitterly complain! 'Now's the day and now's the hour;' and let it not pass unimproved, or you'll smart for it hereafter."[32]

Gold was indeed a valuable product, ranking next in importance to agriculture in North Carolina during the ante-bellum period. Found in thirteen counties, this precious metal seems to have been extraordinarily precious, for Historian William K. Boyd in his *History of North Carolina* recorded that "It is well known that but a small portion of the gold found at these mines goes to the mint. The silversmiths of every portion of the country, north and south, purchase it up to be wrought into jewelry and plate of all descriptions. It is preferred by them on many accounts."[33] Despite this usage, before 1829 all the gold that was mined in the United States and coined at the mint in Philadelphia was from North Carolina. In that year $128,000 was coined, and double that amount was expected in 1830.[34] Swaim stated that North Carolina had gold in sufficient quantity to justify a branch of the mint five years before Congress authorized one at Charlotte in 1835.

When it was learned that Greensboro was sitting on a gold deposit, it caused considerable speculation; but Swaim's reaction to the "gold rush" around him was decidedly practical. Said he, "We cannot conveniently suppress the thought that if the Southern People would turn their attention to digging gold and *'manufacturing'* the superabundance of their raw material, they would make more 'clear money' than they can by cursing the tariff, and *'fighting'* the General Government for not replacing it!"[35] Nor could Swaim suppress the desire to utter this sarcastic prophecy, "Gold digging will soon be as profitable, in this state, as *successful* office-hunting."[36]

He also wrote a short satirical essay, entitled "Recipe for Making a Speculation," which probably was based on observation. "Go to some of the mines, or places where gold has actually been found," he advised, "and take considerable quantities of the richest ore you can come at: scatter this over the flint ridges of any worthless tract of barrens that you would dispose of to advantage, . . . and then

141

employ some kind of friend to communicate the great discovery of a new gold mine, to the Greensborough Patriot for publication. Get him to say that, for richness and extent, it is equalled by few and surpassed by none. Then . . . show . . . pieces of the ore . . . to every body who will hinder the time to look at them; . . . you had better intimate that, if you were acquainted with digging for gold, you would not touch a cent less than fifteen thousand dollars for it; but as it is, you would take (reluctantly though) twelve thousand. This will induce people to think that in truth and indeed the *golden goose* has been buried there, and that a whole litter of little *golden goslins*, were, phoenix like, growing out of her ashes. You will thus collect around you, about half a dozen men who have been smitten with the *gold fever*. You can then inform them that you have no *anxiety* to sell, but in asmuch as you are not prepared to carry on the gold digging business by yourself, you would not object to taking a fair price for it. Pretend to be very careless about it, until you ascertain the very highest cent you can get from them, and then take it, at once, before they have time to find out the deception. . . .

"P. S. Never consult your conscience on these occasions, or you might get advice that would operate against your INTEREST! and this would be doing yourself a serious injury, which would be more reprehensible than doing a like injury to another man."[37]

There is no way accurately to evaluate or even to describe Swaim's influence on agricultural development in North Carolina, and perhaps in the South; but his publication shows that he advocated the advanced methods of farming which greatly accelerated the later rejuvenation of husbandry in the state. Farm journals which began to appear in the late 1830's were in a sense enlarged versions of the *Greensborough Patriot's* farm news and advice. Certainly this editor's candid comments and vigorous attacks on agricultural conditions evoked public reactions. So clear were Swaim's arguments that it is hard to conceive of a *Greensborough Patriot* reader's not being prodded at least into thinking about the subject of improved methods in agricultural pursuits.

# VII

## FOR INDUSTRIAL DEVELOPMENT

*"Industry alone must make the South a prosperous country."*[1]

Glancing up from his desk, William Swaim saw a group of travelers he could not forget. For any editor the sight might have made a small news item, but for the Greensboro editor it meant more than news. Describing this miniature caravan, he wrote: "Eight persons passed through this place a few days ago, moving to the west — on foot. Two robust looking youths, nearly grown, led the van, with large packs on their backs. A boy much smaller followed, with a gun on his shoulder; and a woman of prepossessing appearance with an infant in her arms. Still farther in the rear marched a large elderly woman — a small girl unable to carry a burden — and a young girl about fifteen years of age, possessing all that elegance and delicacy of figure which characterize our eastern ladies, staggering along, barefooted, under a huge package which she carried on her head.

"This is moving with vengeance! — But what could they do? Must these robust, spirited youths, be compelled to labor out their existence for a landlord, reduced, personally, if not intellectually, almost to a level with his negroes? *No!* Degraded as they appear, and poverty stricken as they are; they possess remains of that pride and independence which recoils at the idea of remaining *plebians* forever. They induce a mother to leave a home, where perhaps she has seen 'better days,' and with a mixture of sullen pride and pleasant anticipation, plod their tiresome way to the west, where they can

143

find full scope for their humble enterprize, and feel themselves 'beholdin to no man.' — There is much in North Carolina especially towards the eastern part, besides the poverty of the soil, which hurries away thousands of her inhabitants each spring and fall. But it seems the remedy for this evil is 'not yet!' "[2]

As one means of stopping this draining off of her people, Swaim strongly advocated a broad expansion of industrial development in the state. He based his ideas of what North Carolinians could do upon what they had done in the past. He was thoroughly aware of the fact that though no large factories had been established, as early as the 1790's there had developed a sufficient output of home manufactures to attract national attention. For example, in 1794, Tench Coxe, former Assistant Secretary of the Treasury of the United States, and then Commissioner of the Revenue, had written that the back-country areas of the South Atlantic states had been producing more textiles than they imported from abroad.[3] The variety of fabrics reported by Coxe was surprisingly large, including "corduroys, velvets, velverets, jeans, fustians, hosiery thread, fringe cords and tassels, counterpanes and coverlets, candlewick, and callico prints."[4]

And Swaim also knew that, in keeping with Alexander Hamilton's doctrine, Coxe had urged the South to expand its home industries in the belief that manufacturing would not interfere with agriculture, but rather would furnish increased demands for farm products. That this proposal could work had been shown by the United States Census of 1810 which reported North Carolina as having produced domestic textiles valued at $2,989,140, whereas those of Massachusetts had totaled only $2,208,989.[5]

Swaim believed that industry could thrive in any section of North Carolina, but he knew that early manufacturing in the state had been largely restricted to the middle and western sections, whereas the eastern section had depended more and more on an extensive agriculture, based on slave labor. Nevertheless, domestic industry which presaged North Carolina's highly diversified manufactures of the mid-twentieth century, had made a fair showing by the early 1800's. Because of the lack of commerce in the state, which in turn was caused by poor transportation facilities and scarce capital for purchasing imported wares, many North Carolinians had turned to making their own supplies. Hats, made of genuine fur, generally esteemed in proportion to their height, and expected to last a year for each dollar of cost, were among the first successes. In 1810, North Carolina ranked fourth in the number of tanneries in the nation.[6] In addition to these enterprises, by 1815 there had been a number of small mills (many corn and flour, twenty-three iron, three paper, and one cotton), turpentine distilleries, and establishments for making guns, gunpowder, and other products.[7] Wagons, carriages, and farm implements, for which the iron was refined locally, had been satisfactorily made. Indeed, during Swaim's lifetime Ruth Worth's husband, Sidney Porter (O. Henry's grandfather), established in Greensboro a shop where he manufactured both furniture and vehicles; and Swaim's brother-in-law, Thomas Carbry, operated a similar business in the same town. Surplus grain was distilled into liquors which gained a fine reputation in the South; and Swaim's personal friend, John Motley Morehead, impressively advertised in the *Greensborough Patriot* the fine copper stills he made in his tin shop.[8]

Though manufacturing had been more prosperous in the western section of the state, from recent history Swaim knew that the eastern section could adopt an industrial program, along with its agricultural pursuits. This had been shown when the embargo acts of the national government, in connection with the Napoleonic wars, had forced the eastern planters of North Carolina to become interested in manufacturing, since their source of English goods was cut off. As soon as these wars were over in 1814, however, and the "era of good feeling" followed with advanced prices for farm products, agriculture had gained the ascendancy over all other economic activities in North Carolina. Thereafter the planter aristocracy of the East gave little or no encouragement to the establishment of industry before the Civil War.

During the legislative session of 1823-1824, however, under the pressure of declining farm prices and subsequent unrest in western

145

North Carolina, the General Assembly had considered advising diversification in both agriculture and industry; and in 1828-1829 had established a select committee to investigate the possibilities for more cotton and woolen mills as a possible relief for the state, which had reached almost the lowest point of depression.[9] Charles Fisher as chairman made an impressive report for this committee which highly recommended industrial pursuits.[10] Although largely restricted to textile manufacturing, the report created conversational interest and some newspaper publicity; but manufacturing was so odious to the landed aristocracy who dominated the state and who preferred the respectable gaining of wealth from the land, that the few who wished to establish industrial enterprises found it difficult to secure sufficient co-operation to initiate them.

In the midst of this decline in both agriculture and industry, Swaim projected his program for reform. Of course, there is no denying that at this time the stage was set for reform in industry and all of its allied fields, for in addition to the concern of the people there had been a number of influential men from time to time who had stirred up public opinion on one or more state problems. The recommendations of Judge Murphey had not been forgotten; and more recently Dr. Joseph Caldwell, President of the University of North Carolina, had published (1827, 1828) *The Numbers of Carlton, Addressed to the People of North Carolina, on a Central Railroad thru the State.* From available records, however, it appears that Swaim was the only North Carolinian at this particular time, or at any time, who independently outlined as broad a program of reform and kept the various phases of that program consistently before his readers.

Although Swaim favored a variety of industrial pursuits other than textile manufacturing, his ideas along that line did not differ materially from those in Fisher's report; and his week after week attacks on the lack of practical application of this potential, plus similar lacks in supplementary fields that would aid in promoting it, helped to breathe life into the infant idea. In his *Greensborough*

*Patriot* he kept hammering away at North Carolina's degrading problems, and his soundness of purpose could not be denied: small factories began to operate. During the 1830's, twenty-four new cotton mills were planned, to be located in eighteen different counties, and twenty of these were actually built, fifteen of which were completed by 1840.[11] Greensboro, already with one cotton mill and six other small manufacturing establishments, had stepped its diversified manufacturing up to eighteen different enterprises by 1843[12]. Other North Carolina newspapers, which up to this time had largely abstained from featuring the subject of industry because it was unpopular with the ruling planters, soon followed Swaim's example and began to speak out in the 1830's.

In support of the above statement, Diffee W. Standard and Richard W. Griffin, in a recent comprehensive study, entitled "The Cotton Textile Industry in Ante-Bellum North Carolina," cited around two hundred thirty-four references. Of these about one hundred forty-four were taken from North Carolina newspapers, but only seven of them bore dates before 1829, the year Swaim started the *Greensborough Patriot*. The seven reports were not urgent appeals for North Carolina to adopt industry, but were merely reviews of industry elsewhere. Most of the remaining one hundred thirty-seven citations were taken from newspapers of the 1830's and 1840's. It seems then that Swaim led the way in a newspaper campaign which favored industrial pursuits in North Carolina. This point gains emphasis in the conclusion of Standard and Griffin that "The years 1828-1830 mark the turning point for North Carolina's industrial future."[13]

A feature of Swaim's strategy was the stimulation of action in his own state by holding up examples of accomplishment in other states. Having learned through the *New-York Enquirer* that a cotton factory had been established at Athens, Georgia, he passed the information to his readers with the comment, "We would say to the Georgians, and to all the inhabitants of the Southern States — Improve those advantages which the bounties of Nature have placed in your possession."[14] These words were to be reiterated over half a

147

century later by a Georgian himself, the silver-tongued Henry W. Grady, who said, "I see a South, a home of fifty millions of people, who rise up every day to call her blessed; her cities vast hives of industry and of thrift; her countrysides the treasures from which their resources are drawn; . . . But agriculture alone — no matter how rich or varied its resources — cannot establish or mantain a people's prosperity. . . . No commonwealth ever came to greatness by producing raw material. Less can this be possible in the future than in the past."[15] And he painstakingly explained that agriculture could only be profitable by bringing in industry to convert raw materials into finished products and by enlarging the population through the introduction of mechanics who would consume additional products.

Swaim observed that the effects of industrial developments in the North were good. "Nothing tends so much to increase the population and prosperity of the Country as the extension of Manufactories," he wrote. "Several of our towns have from this cause doubled their population within the last ten years. In the state of New York alone there are upwards of two hundred Manufactories of Woolen goods, ninety of Cotton, and two hundred of Iron Ware. Not to mention others of less importance. What a steady ready-money market is offered to the Farmers in the vicinity of these establishments for their surplus produce!"[16]

Swaim begged, cajoled, and exhorted North Carolinians to avail themselves of the vast possibilities the state held for manufacturing. Backing his stand by bringing to their attention the highly respected opinions of *Niles' Weekly Register,* which was known for its wise and balanced judgment and fair dealings, Swaim pointed his finger to this publication which had circulated in perhaps every state in the Union since 1811 as an advocate of American industry.[17] Over and over the editor in his *Greensborough Patriot* made observations of everyday surroundings—and urged men to utilize them for their own and their country's good. "Our object is, to call the attention of our readers *again* to the subject of domestic manufactures, . . . " he wrote. "North Carolina at this time exhibits a woful picture of partial and contracted Legislation. While our Merchants are running to the north with our funds to purchase the articles which have been manufactured from our own raw materials, many of our citizens are rotting at home in vice and rags for want of employment—While our never failing, and never freezing streams are winding their profitless journey to the deep, Northern enterprise is forcing these advantages of nature to aid it in augmenting its advantages on us,— and while our citizens are sickening at the melancholy prospect, and wending their way to the west, the collected wisdom of our State are marshalling their consequence at the seat of our State Government, & — making speeches? Or — what? We leave the Acts of the next Legislature, . . . to ANSWER!

"Southern forces are congregating, and a most powerful effort will be made at the ensuing Session of Congress, to break down that system of encouragement to domestic industry which it behooves every country to promote.

"While these things are taking their course in our land, North-Carolina may DO MUCH by turning her attention to the encouragement of domestic manufactures within her own limits."[18]

Any recommendations for more intensified manufacturing, however, had to be shouted above the noisy clamor of dissatisfaction with recent tariff regulations. Although Southern Republicans had agreed to the protective tariff when it was first imposed in 1816, they soon began to change their minds and to oppose the very idea of it.[19] They contended that special duties on imported manufactures were against the interests of all agricultural states, North and South, since they increased the prices of goods which farmers must buy; and that planters and farmers would be better off to sell their produce abroad and buy their manufactures from the Old World where they were made with cheaper labor at less expense and hence at lower prices. After the tariff rates had been raised in 1824 and again in 1828, exasperated southern planters hotly objected to the measures which they said were placed upon them by northern bankers and manufacturers. Dr. Thomas Cooper, President of the College of South Carolina, expressed the prevailing southern sentiment when he said it appeared to him that "'the farmer and the planter are to be considered inferior beings to the spinner, the bleacher, and the dyer; that we of the South are to hold our plantations as the serfs of the North, subject to the orders of the master minds of Massachusetts, the lords of the spinning jenny, the peers of the loom, who have a right to tax our earnings in order to swell their riches!' "[20]

Swaim ran headlong into a nest of southern hardheads when he advocated southern industry under protection. From the beginning of his newspaper life in North Carolina, however, he made clear that he was in sympathy with Congressman Henry Clay's American system which was designed to promote general national development. The plan, he contended, was simple in construction, but large in significance. Its two leading features were a protective tariff and internal improvements. He explained that a tariff would encourage the establishment of American industry which in turn would create an expanding home market for the produce of American farms; that internal improvements, made possible through federal appropriations, would furnish transportation routes for the necessary exchange between producer and consumer. He believed that the system would bring such great development of internal trade between the states that it would justify the federal expense. Painstakingly he described the economics of the program. The system's collateral constituents were the establishment of a United States Bank and a land bill. A strong national bank would provide a stable currency for facilitating intersectional trade; and a land act would provide for distributing among the states the proceeds from the national sale of public lands for financing internal improvement projects. The American system was so designed, he said, that as soon as manufactures had become firmly established, the protective tariff could be reduced.[21]

Having stated his position on manufacturing in his first editorial of the *Greensborough Patriot*, Swaim pursued his point in the second, May 30, 1829, with factual answers to some of the more prevalent arguments advanced by southerners against the tariff. "We promised in our last," he wrote, "that we would from time to time, produce facts in support of the opinion that this measure of the General Government which has created so much factious discontent in the Southern States, would not operate against our interest — but on the contrary, would show itself to be fraught with the most beneficial consequences. The objections against the tariff of 1824 have all turned out to be without foundation. The result has proven that the predictions respecting it emanated from a source not hereafter to be relied on. The tariff of 1828 [known as the "Tariff of Abominations"], in the fashionable slang of the day, is called a 'Yankee trick,' but the vote in the House of Representatives, shows a large majority of Yankees opposed to it! The vote of six New-England States stood as follows — 15 *for,* and 23 *against* the tariff of 1824 and [16 for and 23 against in 1828]."[22]

Continuing this discussion in a lengthy, convincing editorial, Swaim quoted figures to show that neither imports nor exports had been entirely cut off, as had been predicted, but instead had run into vast millions. And to the argument that "our commerce will be ruined and our ships rot in their harbours," he cited figures that proved commerce was increasing. "How will our upright, pure and holy patriots & Statesmen, get around these facts," he challenged, "when they wish to make the people believe that the tariff is riding in 'fretted ruin's fiery car' over the shipping of the United States?"[23]

In connection with the tariff, a rumor had circulated abroad that direct taxes might be imposed for defraying the contingent expenses of the national government. Swaim realized, as he said, "that the people will not endure the idea of having our country infested with a hungry clan of tax-gatherers — Uncle Sam might as well demand their *souls* as the scanty contents of their *pockets.*" In answer to this rumor, he presented statistics which showed a decided increase in customs despite the restrictive system. "Here is 'destruction of the revenue' for you!" he sarcastically proclaimed. "Save, O, Save! or we sink!' "[24]

No one took the preservation of the Union more seriously than William Swaim. If all the states co-operated toward general national development, he said, he could foresee a glorious future for the country. Reminding southerners of how they "wrote and swaggered and threatened resistance to the strong arm of the United States, for palming upon them the obnoxious TARIFF," and how they passed resolutions to buy nothing manufactured north of the Potomac, he informed them that they were, in truth unwittingly, breaking their resolutions. Some southern merchants, he said, were sending home trunks and bales of cloth made in the North, and were selling these as English goods in order to command a ready market and a full price. These northern materials were of sufficient fineness and beauty to satisfy the most fastidious taste, he assured, but were being palmed off as English because fashion had so long given preference to imported cloth. " 'So it is with American carpeting,' " Swaim quoted from *Niles' Register*. " 'Not a yard of it can be found in any store in New York; *it is all* English!'

"Baltimore is also preparing to manufacture *English* calicos, for our southern Anti-tariffites, upon a large scale," Swaim continued. "An entire new establishment, to contain one hundred power looms, impelled by steam, is now partially in operation in that city and will soon be complete — for weaving stuffs for calicoes. These looms will make about 15,000 yards a week."[25]

While southerners were being led by their agrarian politicians to oppose the tariff, northerners were making and selling cloth to an extent which caused the English to lament that their cotton manufacturing had decreased one third on account of the American tariff. These facts, Swaim pointed out, should convince southerners that protected industries would mean better employment for labourers in home industry and would give a home market for cotton. Some might have doubts with regard to the immediate effect that tariff would have on the South, "but common sense must teach them that the ultimate effect will be good," he maintained by quoting from the *Pawtucket Chronicle*. "What matter it to them whether they sell their cotton to the English or the Yankees? — The market is as sure and the pay is as good. They can even do better than to sell it to either; — let them spin and weave by the help of steam and their slave population. It would be opening a new field of labor for those troublesome servants, who are so rapidly outnumbering their masters; and instead of exporting raw cotton they could export it manufactured into cloth.—Such a course would raise the value of their real estate. Their corn and their rice planters would find a home market for their crops; in fact, the whole South, instead of going behind every year as it does now, would thrive. And what is more, their habits would be improved—from a profligate they would become an industrious people; and consequently a virtuous one. These facts are known to the southern politicians. Every individual of them is aware that industry alone must make the South a prosperous country — they know that ease and indolence has enervated her, and nothing but labour of mind and limb, will restore her to a healthy state."[26]

The author evidently felt a little pang of conscience at having so cheerfully welcomed the news of a decline in British manufacturing, for when he had finished his discourse, he laid this apologetic wreath: although Americans "feel for the distresses of the English brethren, yet charity must begin at home."[27]

The Greensboro editor did a very intelligent piece of reporting on the tariff question. As sources, to mention only a few, he gathered arguments for and against from all over the United States and from abroad, quoting from such newspapers as the New York *Morning Herald*, the *New-York Enquirer*, the *Providence American*, *Niles' Weekly Register* of Baltimore, the *National Intelligencer* of Washington, Leed's *Mercury* of England, and various southern publications. He left no doubt as to the stand different leading public figures took on the issue — such gentlemen as President Jackson, John C. Calhoun, Henry Clay, and Daniel Webster. And he brought the subject directly home to his fellow North Carolinians by showing the damage they might do by supporting some misinformed politician for office. Such misinformation was aptly illustrated by a circular issued by Abraham Rencher, twice elected to Congress from a North Carolina district. In this circular, Rencher stated that under the pretense of raising revenue for the government, northern manufacturers had "filched" from southerners.

153

Having read Rencher's piece, Swaim paid his respects to the Congressman: "He jumps in and nails the tariff by the throttle, and belabours and worrys it most unmercifully. This is the course pursued by every demagogue south of the Potomac. Every man feels the pressure of the times; and every man who wishes to *feel* his way into congress, finds it the easiest way to *inform* the people that the tariff and that alone, has 'brought death and all our woes!' The worthless scoundrel who has wasted his substance and reduced his family to beggary by intemperance, and who has become too besotted to labor, jumps at the chance of saddling the cause of his beggarly condition upon the damned tariff; and becomes vociferous in support of the candidate who has been so kind as to frame for him this beautiful *excuse*. . . . Now we should be pleased to learn, by some means, how much longer this ridiculous position will be assumed by men who pretend to know any thing about the history of the tariff.[28]

"Previously to the tariff of 1816, northern capital was vested, to an immense extent, in *commerce*," Swaim explained, "a duty on foreign commodities was laid, at that date, which amounted to a partial prohibition, and cut off a large portion of that commerce in which our brethren of the north had embarked. This measure was taken for the openly avowed purpose of protecting manufactures in the United States, so that we *might* be what we *pretended* to be 'INDEPENDENT' of every other nation. It was insisted, and justly so, by Mr. Calhoun, the great apostle of nullification, and of whom Mr. Rencher seems to be an humble disciple, that infant factories could not compete with the capitalists of Europe without protection — it was given. The south might then have turned this protection to their own account by immediately erecting factories to work up her own raw materials; but she had done the wind work; and rested 'therewith content;' while the north enterprisingly and resolutely adopted that policy which we had urged her to pursue, contrary to her own consent. She soon became rich. We envied her: and swore that the . . . *system of plunder* should be repealed. . . .

"Before Mr. Rencher nibs his pen to write another circular, or clears up his throat for another speech in congress; we want him to as[c]ertain from some school boy, the difference between a duty levied on, and collected *from* foreign goods, and a tax levied on the people of the United States. He seems to be ignorant of this difference himself, and it is so great, and so material, that he ought to adopt some such means of making himself familiar with it, before he gets so far in advancement to renown that he cannot turn back to learn these *small matters!*[29]

Meanwhile dissension over the tariff continued to rise, particularly in South Carolina; and nullification was as freely spoken of as ordinary household matters. The *Greensborough Patriot* took on a national tone. Swaim gave his readers the benefit of diverse opinions on the subject, although he warned that "The passion once let loose in South Carolina — will cause a desolation that men shall turn pale at."[30] The different attitudes are well defined in this 1832 excerpt: "At a public dinner given at Savannah [Georgia] on the fourth of July, the following professional toasts were given.

"By Dr. J. C. Habersham — *Nullification* — The only drastic and efficient purgative for that abominable intestine disease, the Tariff.

"By Dr. R. D. Arnold — *Nullification,* like other 'drastic purgatives' when improperly applied, producing death instead of a cure.

"By Dr. Giradon — *Nullification* — When *Doctors* differ who then can agree?"[31]

Of greater interest to Swaim than the Georgia toasts, however, was the fact that the noted Englishwoman, Mrs. Frances Trollope, had lined up with the nullifiers. In 1832, she had "achieved notoriety and roused violent resentment by her caustic book, *Domestic Manners of the Americans,*" and she was at the time very much in the public eye.[32] Evidently Swaim did not approve of the critical Englishwoman, for when she passed through Greensboro, he gave her a sort of satirical brush off. "It is said," he opined, "that Mrs. Trollope passed through this place day before yesterday, in the semi-daily stage from Martinsville, on her way to New England to raise troops, to assist South Carolina in nullifying the government. She was *at-*

155

*tended* by Doctor Cooper, principle of the South Carolina College! Their carriage was drawn by a *barefooted negro.*"[33]

Within about a month after this event, South Carolina under the leadership of John C. Calhoun passed an ordinance nullifying the tariff laws of 1828 and 1832. Since Calhoun had begun his political career as an advocate of the Union, a supporter of tariff, and a believer in internal improvements, Swaim considered him an opportunist and explained his reversal of opinion on tariff this way: "But his hopes of ultimately reaching the presidency, have all melted into fog, and his prospects of promotion, now depend upon the success of his attempt to effect a severance of the union, and to establish a great southern republic. He would rather 'reign in hell than serve in heaven.' "[34]

Although North Carolinians in the main did not approve of South Carolina's attitude, in the course of the controversy Charles Fisher supported it in the *Western Carolinian* of Salisbury; and Swaim wrote that Fisher tried to get that section of the state to align with South Carolina. Among other things, Fisher contended that the United States government should not resort to force to bring South Carolina into line, for the constitution gives it no such power. On December 12, 1832, Swaim replied, "Now we should suppose, if the constitution of the United States, indeed be a monument of wisdom, it must allow that government which springs legitimately from it, to possess power sufficient to *enforce* the execution of its own laws. Without this *right,* the constitution, together with all the institutions growing out of it, had better be blown out at once, and let each state set up business for itself! It is the most ridiculous thing that can be imagined, for congress to spend from three to six months each year solemnly enacting laws for the good government of the people, if she has no right to provide that these laws shall be executed! It is admitted by this expounder of laws and 'ordenances,' that the general government has power to put down 'combinations of turbulent individuals, in any part of the country, who resist the laws;' but when a whole state becomes 'turbulent' and refractory, and offers resistance to the laws, there is no help for it! The laws of the Union must cease to act; while daring treason, in the face of day, must be suffered to unfurl its hell-sta[i]ned banner with impunity!

"Another s[o]phism, worthy of its *author*," continued Swaim, "must not be passed over: He says 'the STATES are *parties* to the federal compact; they created the federal government, are then *principals*, while the *government* is only the *agent!*' And then to 'nail the basket,' he asks with an air of triumph, is the *agent* greater than the *principal?* Now so far from the *states*, being either *party* or *principal* to the federal government, they are wholly out of the question — and entirely unknown to that government. The constitution of the United States was not formed by STATES, but by the *people*. The states had no hand in it. After the constitution was formed it was not even *ratified* by the *states*, in their capacity as such; but by the *people* of the states in convention assembled for that purpose. The people of the United States, called the general government into existence; and no power short of that which gave it being, can alter or extinguish it. A convention of the people of the United States, can either new [model] or demolish the government; but a sickly convention of nullies, representing less than one fiftieth part of the whole people, can no more change or resist the legitimate action of the government, than they can create a world! nor is it right they should do so unless *one man,* in a particular section of the country, where *mush room and politician* are synonymous, ought to have more political influence than fifty men who are known to enjoy the use of reason!

"We will here take occasion to remark that this same people, who formed the constitution of the United States, ordained that a supreme court should be instituted, to whom should be submitted the final decision of all questions arising under the constitution — Hence the decisions of that tribunal, are, in all cases, the supreme constitutional law of the land; and can only be annulled by that semi-omnipotent power of the whole people, whose voice called them into being!

"If the general government has no power to coerce a state, then

**157**

is the bonds of our happy and prosperous Union, nothing but a wisp of fog that may be broken by the breath of any political scoundrel that may think proper to blow upon it!"[35]

Swaim was deeply concerned about the significance of South Carolina's action. For that reason, he had only praise for the firm decision of President Andrew Jackson, whose attitude on many previous national questions he had considered irritatingly noncommital. When the President issued his Proclamation which carried the sentiment, "THE FEDERAL UNION MUST BE PRESERVED," Swaim reported the speech most favorably. "HUZZA FOR GENERAL JACKSON!!!" he wrote. "The time has been, when we never expected to feel justified in uttering the exclamation which we have placed at the head of this article! but we now do it in the solemn sincerity of our heart. It gives us pleasure, almost too big for utterance to say, that one act of General Jackson's whole life, has met our cordial & undivided approbation!"[36]

In addition to his editorial comment, Swaim put out a special edition of the *Greensborough Patriot* and printed the Proclamation in full, making clear that he did so because of the principle involved. "Though it may not form a plaster as broad as [Jackson's] former transgressions," he said, "yet it will '*cover a multitude of sins!*' . . . and we but echo the voice of the community in which we reside, when we say that thousands of patriots who honestly opposed his re-election, will stand by him in carrying out the principles of his proclamation 'while there's a pea in the dish!' We are opposed to taking the tariff from a single button, until this affair is put forever at rest!"[37]

Almost from the beginning of his editorship in Greensboro, low-tariff people had accused Swaim of disloyalty to the South. A typical example appeared in the South Carolina *Camden Journal* which said that he had been "in the constant utterance of language towards the whole South, and more especially towards South-Carolina, which one would think the brazen face of insurrectionary hardihood itself would blush at."[38] To this attack Swaim replied, "we deny the imputation of any unfriendly feeling 'toward the whole South,' or any part of it; but in speaking on the subject, we have uniformly declared that all our partialities are listed in favor of Southern interest, and that our days, be they many or few, should be spent in *advocating* that interest, and in opposing every thing that might come in conflict with it. And this constitutes the reason why we oppose the high-pres[s]ure movements got up by Southern Demagogues, for the purpose of building their ruined political fortunes upon the ultimate annihilation of Southern prosperity and happiness."[39]

After that dogmatic answer to a dogmatic accusation, Swaim asked the editor of the *Camden Journal* to mind his own business, hereafter, and to let him alone. Otherwise, he promised his readers, in his own brand of invective, and with his own favorite weapon, "we intend [to use a] 'gun-powder sling, stirred with a lightning rod,' and drench him [the Camden editor] with that!... We shall leave him to crown his empty noodle with all the laurels he can reap from his foulsome punning and obstreperous ranting!"[40]

Early in 1833, all eyes were upon Henry Clay's compromise tariff bill in Congress, a measure to ease tensions. The President had advised that something of the kind should be worked out, and Clay and Calhoun had put their heads together; but Swaim, not willing to lower the tariff, took a dim view of their conclusions. Calhoun had been among the first to say that industry in America must have protection if it would succeed, and Clay had been the embodiment of a program for national prosperity. Now these men advocated compromise, a word omitted from Swaim's vocabulary.

Following a leading editorial of around 1,320 words on Clay's and Calhoun's new attitude on a protective tariff, Swaim concluded: "The more we think of the bill introduced by Mr. Clay to reduce the tariff, the less we like the project; and the more we examine the speech he delivered on its introduction, the less confidence we have in the man. The pitiful and ridiculous sophisms resorted to by him, to sustain his positions, and excuse himself for turning his back upon a policy of which the American people have always proudly hailed him as the champion, are, indeed, unworthy the heart that conceived them, or the tongue that gave them utterance. He says, that unless the tariff be gradually reduced this session, it will be annihilated in the next, and with it all the hopes and prospects of the manufacturers. This argument clearly places him with one foot upon the North and the other upon the South, and his eyes imploringly fixed on the next presidency!"[41]

Pointing out what he considered the weaknesses of Clay's speech, Swaim observed that Clay occasionally resorted to that "transcendent eloquence, for which he has been so long and so justly celebrated. These things we say, in honest sincerity; and we regret the necessity which compels us thus to speak of a man whose talents and integrity have always claimed our highest admiration."[42]

One of William Swaim's chief characteristics was his frank appraisal of men and things as he saw them. No matter how high a person might stand in his estimation, or in that of others, he never hesitated to put his principles above personal feeling. His rules for human behavior were exceedingly rigid, and he felt it his duty to consider in his newspaper the character of any aspirant to public office in order that the people might see the one in whom they were being asked to place their trust. He thus applied his pen to the great and the small, sometimes in praise, sometimes in condemnation. In his opinion, to disagree with his point of view was to err. Thus he explained the actions of his former colleagues in reform: "It is said that Clay and Calhoun have 'kissed!' This is not difficult to account for. They both find their political prospects cut off; and have concluded to join their fortunes together, and make one more *dead set* for power. When the rebellious angels were expelled from heaven, for coveting too much power, they formed a league in hell, to make war upon the realms from which they had been driven, and to use the language of Milton, 'Devil with Devil damned, firm concord hold!' Clay and Calhoun have both abandoned their principles, and we care not now, how soon the people abandon them."[43]

After Clay's compromise tariff bill had become the law of the land, Swaim took particular pains to let the people know how the House and Senate had wangled their way out of the "scrape," as he called it; for although he admitted that he had never witnessed the passage of a measure that gave him more surprise and regret, he still believed that progress would come through an enlightened people. Swaim was indeed a dedicated partisan reformer, with the reformer's characteristics — dogmatism and optimism.

Amid the preoccupation with the tariff question, a very significant enterprise was taking root two or three hundred feet from Swaim's back yard. Henry Humphreys, a fellow Greensboro citizen, who also believed in industrial development, was in the process of building the Mount Hecla Steam Cotton Mill, the first to be operated by steam in North Carolina. Somewhat earlier (1818-1825) Humphreys had operated a cotton mill outside Greensboro where he employed the water power of a dam he had formerly used for a grist mill. This simple beginning apparently excited little attention, or perhaps Humphreys withheld news about it, for it was merely listed in a newspaper article as "one of the four mills in the state" in the 1820's; "but from this humble start, the second largest mill in ante-bellum North Carolina soon developed."[44] Swaim had but to look up from the back door of his own home to see the imposing structure, built of brick and containing four stories and a basement. It was one hundred and fifty feet long and fifty feet broad, and housed twenty-five hundred (later three thousand) spindles and seventy-five looms. Sheetings, shirtings, and osnaburgs were woven, and cotton yarn, put up in five-pound packages, was sold throughout the country to be woven on old-fashioned looms. When the mill was first established this yarn was so popular that country people came into town and camped all night around the factory, waiting for it to come off the machinery. Other products of the mill were hauled in large wagons to Virginia, Tennessee, Kentucky, and western North Carolina.[45]

The building was started in 1828, and the mill was opened in 1833. Meanwhile, Humphreys appealed to the legislature for an exemption of taxation until he could bring his experiment to a paying basis, and Swaim strongly urged a favorable hearing. "The establishment of similar factories throughout the southern country, will turn the fruits of the protecting system into our coffers," he argued. "Our soil with proper culture will produce the raw material, and our streams and forests will afford advantages of water and steam power, for the propelling of machinery, unknown to the north; and we want but enterprise, such as Mr. Humphreys has shown himself to possess, and an adequate *protection* for that enterprise, to turn the tariff to our own account, and enable us to live within ourselves."[46]

Humphreys was not granted a tax exemption, however, and Swaim fearlessly attacked the legislators for what he said was lack of vision. Disclaiming any connection between his opinions here and his friendship for Humphreys, he contended that the state would ultimately benefit by withholding taxation until industrial firms could report a measure of progress. "North Carolina will never come out of the kinks, until legislative encouragement be given to men of enterprise," he said. "Such encouragement would invite capital from abroad, and soon make us rich, respectable and powerful. But we fear a short-sighted, niggardly and parsimonious legislature will forever keep the nose of the state on the grindstone, unless men shall be found with fortitude enough to burst through that incubus which has always palsied our energies, and become public benefactors in spite of such *spare-rib* and *scape-tail* legislation!"[47]

This big cotton mill in the South made national news under the heading of "STEAM ENGINS!" Swaim could restrain no longer his swelling pride when the *Pennsylvania Advocate* of Pittsburgh and *Niles' Weekly Register* of Baltimore took notice of the enterprise of his home town. It appears that Humphreys had asked the Greensboro editor to wait until opening time for publicity, but once the news was out, Swaim wrote, "We have been chaining our pen for some time on the subject of this factory. Our quill has been restless ever since the splendid building was reared . . . so anxious did it seem, to speak in high terms of the enterprising spirit which first prompted Mr. Humphreys to embark in it. We have been admonished, however, not to fire at random. But one thing we will say, if we should get indicted for it, namely: the building for the reception of the machinery is nearly completed, and men who have seen factories as 'plenty as blackberry,' declare that this surpasses anything of the kind they had ever seen. Greensborough is evidently coming out of the *kinks*."[48]

Accompanying a large scale industrial development in the South, Swaim foresaw the infiltration of mechanics and inventors for advancing the work, and he did not overlook this important group of people. Industry was no newfangled, untried idea to him. He had grown to manhood in a community that was partly agricultural and partly industrial. Cut off from profitable transportation, his family and neighbors, in addition to farming, had developed various crafts. There were among them weavers, tanners, cobblers, harness makers, hat makers, carpenters, brick masons, millers, and smiths. The latter became so expert that they could make needles, pins, and scissors; and could draw a wire fine enough to make cards for carding wool and cotton.[49] With the exception of weaving and the making of clothes, which arts were practiced in nearly every home, usually one or two experts in the various crafts would serve an entire community.[50] From actual experience and observation of craftsmen, then, Swaim could envision the significant place that mechanics would come to hold as the country developed, and he therefore made a place for them in his paper.

Nor did he withhold information about problems that might accompany mechanics. His first news item for this group was entitled "Hard Times." It dealt with a condition in New York City where many excellent mechanics "have been compelled to abandon the city," and "many who have visited the city in search of employment have been totally disappointed," because the "present high price of provisions of all kinds operates very grievously" on the laboring classes.[51] Within a few months, however, he had the pleasure of reporting a brighter side of this picture. The mechanics of New York City had been organized, a house of worship had been appropriated, the group had been recognized as constituting an

163

important part of the population, and it had been acknowledged that "much of the happiness, character and prosperity of the city depends upon the influence they exert."[52]

Since the main circulation of the *Greensborough Patriot* was in an agricultural area, Swaim did not give as much space to the discussion of mechanics as he did to other subjects which directly touched more people of the South. Mechanics were both newer and fewer in the South and consequently there was not as much to be said about them. However, when he sensed any sign of prejudice against them, which was so typical of southern agriculturists of that day, he would let fly with a stinging rebuke to such snobs. "A portion of the world profess to regard mechanics as one degree below those individuals who have a living offered them without manual labor; but that position is a small and weak one, . . . " he affirmed. "In point of science, moral virtue, and even practical politeness, the operative mechanics of the United States are second to no class of people. The work shop has produced as many great men as the college hall; it has done as much for natural philosophy, and more for religion, than the counting room; and has done as much to develope intellect as [to] hoard wealth.—The individual, therefore, who stands up in the face of the world, and judges his fellow citizens by their ability to subsist without labor, must be destitute of one or two very necessary qualifications — experience and common sense. With these on his side he would be able to see that INTELLECT makes the man, and the operation of moral causes upon that intellect, the gentleman."[53] Thus Swaim let the mechanics know that he was their friend.

Although during his editorship most of the mechanical inventions were of minor significance, Swaim took pride in reporting them for the promise they held in the field of experiment. And it takes very little imagination to associate mid-twentieth century luxuries with the stories he published about inventive efforts. Take, for example, the mechanical English gig that could run a mile in three minutes with three passengers aboard. It was drawn by a wooden horse, mechanically operated, so that the pull came through the hind legs, and was guided by a single rein attached to the horse's mouth.[54] These principles were not unlike those that control a modern automobile.

And there was the foot warmer. The Reverend Jeremiah Dodson of Guilford County had a very warm heart, but it did not heat his very cold feet as he rode on horseback to church in the winter time. He, therefore, invented a foot-warmer that would fit into the stirrups of his saddle. It was a sheet iron box, fitted with a cast iron heater which could be "taken out from time to time, and het in the fire to suit the temperature of the weather," and it cost fifty cents.[55] To be sure it was less expensive than an automobile heater, but it served the same purpose and got people in the habit of keeping their feet warm.

Then there were the attempts to fly. In 1829, a report came through Vienna that a Frenchman had really brought to perfection the long desired art of flying in the air. He was said to have reached a height of more than nine hundred feet, and to have then proceeded with perfect ease for a great distance horizontally.[56] Five years later Swaim covered the ascent of Mr. Mason's flying steamboat in Cincinnati. He reported that it was equipped with a two-horsepower engine which turned four vertical shafts projecting over the bow and stern, into each of which were fixed four spiral silken wings which were made to revolve with sufficient velocity to cause the vessel to rise. An adjustable silken cover aided in the control of the flying boat. It weighed sixty pounds and cost $300.[57] Sixty-nine years later Orville Wright first flew at Kitty Hawk.

Despite the fact that all these attempts were simple, they were hopeful beginnings, and to Swaim they represented potentials for future mechanical developments.

There were many other inventive entries in the *Greensborough Patriot*. For instance, there was the announcment of a machine for making wrought nails, the rights of which sold for $100,000; the story of a knitting machine that would make two pairs of long woolen stockings per day; the report of a successful solar heating system in which a steak could be cooked in its own gravy; the account of a shingle machine that would cut sixty shingles in a minute; the discussion of a plow so ingeniously designed that it sharpened itself as it worked; and the notice of a snuff box in the shape of a pistol, which, by the help of a spring, threw snuff up the nose without 'snuffing.' One can almost hear Swaim chuckle as he penned his comment on this snuff box: "This is quite an invention. We hope soon to hear of another to convey the tobacco smoke down the throats of certain frequenters of certain places, as in that case they would get the good of it, and others would be freed of its annoyance."[58]

Such playful touches as this may be found running all through the paper. Although utterly serious about encouraging inventions, Swaim was not too dignified to introduce a refreshing bit of humor on the subject. The following squib would probably bring a spontaneous smile to the face of any reader: "NEW DISCOVERY. It has recently been ascertained, by the practical experiments of several scientific gentlemen, that an application of soap and warm water, is an infallible cure for that very prevalent disease called the — dirty face!"[59]

The phosphorous match, the mowing machine, and the Colt revolver were among the inventions produced during Swaim's editorship. And, in addition to those already mentioned, there were other smaller developments which he reported from time to time, so that altogether the subject of mechanics and inventions became a live and interesting part of the Greensboro paper.

For proclaiming his views on manufacturing and mechanics, Swaim was well located in Greensboro which was becoming more and more industrially inclined. In addition to his neighboring Mount Hecla Steam Cotton Mill there were other promising industrial developments which combined hand craftsmanship and power-driven machine work — a tannery, a gig and carriage shop, a furniture shop, a handmade hat shop, a tailor shop, and a tin shop which featured stills, but also manufactured various household utensils. Furthermore, his fellow citizens were keenly interested in education, religion, politics, agriculture, and other live subjects of the day. Therefore the editor was never wanting for some understanding and sympathetic person with whom he could talk over situations, personalities, and plans.[60]

Swaim became a resident of Greensboro in 1829, when the village, generally called "The Pine Barrens," was only twenty-one years old. Its history was well-known to this young man of twenty-seven. It had been established as the county seat of Guilford County in 1807-1808-1809, with 1808 as the official founding date since the plot of land on which it stood had been purchased during that year. It was situated at the surveyed geographical center of the county to insure impartial travel distances to taxpayers and others who might have county seat business. This location was no coincidence. When Guilford County was established in 1771, its capital was temporarily lodged in the dance hall of Robert Lindsay's home while waiting for a courthouse to be erected. The building, located in the northwestern section, was completed sometime after 1774 and the county metropolis was called Guilford Courthouse (originally Court House. Later onetime Governor Alexander Martin and Thomas Henderson bought all the land surrounding and whereupon the courthouse stood and changed the name to Martinville. Because Martinville was not located near the center of the county, some citizens were upset at having to travel farther than their proportionate mileage to replenish the public treasury. Consequently, they drew a plan for a new town, vigorously electioneered in its favor, and carried the decision to move the county business to the very heart of Guilford. They named the new location Greensborough in honor of General Nathanael Greene who had been in command of the American soldiers in the significant Battle of Guilford Courthouse, about six miles away.[61]

In the municipality's brief lifetime, Swaim felt it had made unusual progress. He had lived in the village less than a year when, on March 24, 1830, he published his impressions of it in the *Greensborough Patriot;* and since a man's environment so greatly influences

167

his work, it is appropriate for the reader to see Greensboro exactly as this man saw it:

"The situation of Greensborough is beautiful beyond description. The order, the taste, the regularity, and the splendor of its buildings are surpassed by no inland town in the whole southern country; and others are continually springing up as by magic, on every street. The citizens, in point of intelligence, enterprise, and respectability, have no cause to shrink from a comparison with an equal number of citizens in any other section of the State. Heretofore we have had no buildings constructed for the separate and exclusive purposes of divine worship. The Gospel has, however, been faithfully, and in many instances, *ably* preached in the Court House and Academies, by the different denominations, ever since these buildings grew up to supply the place of a prostrate forest; and it gives me unfeigned pleasure to say, that two splendid churches are now in the state of forwardness, and will probably be completed during the ensuing summer.

"In a government, which can only be upheld by the wisdom and virtue of its population, we are not to overlook the institutions of learning, in our estimate of the advantages possessed by particular cities, towns or neighborhoods. And fortunately for us, we are blessed with a male, and a female Academy, now under the superintendence of preceptors and preceptresses inferior, in point of qualifications, to none; — these Academies are, at this time, on the 'full tide of successful operation,' and want nothing but that encouragement which they deserve, to place them among the first institutions of the kind in the country. To these may be added, a Sabbath School, at the female Academy, under the superintendence of the Misses Hoggs. We would feign hope the young men of the place have energy enough to imitate the laudable example placed before them by these young ladies; but we have our doubts!

"We must be here permitted to express our surprise and regret at the wide contrast between the moral instruction and deportment, of the boys and girls of this place! On Sunday morning we see swarms of little girls, with clean and smiling faces, pacing arm-in-arm, and book in hand, to church or to school; while the other sex (with too few exceptions) are strolling through the streets from morning till night, or learning mischief elsewhere! Sabbath schools shed a genial influence around the hearts of children; and parents stand in their own light, or they *would* encourage them! ...

"We yet have to speak of another institution, which deserves the undivided support of both town and country: we allude to the 'Greensborough Library Society.' Although the active operations of this society have been, for a short time, suspended, yet we anticipate the most beneficial results from its recent resuscitation. The Library embraces almost every work that young men should read [altogether over fifteen hundred volumes], aside from works of a professional character."

Explaining that books could be secured anywhere in the state through Library Societies and circulating libraries, such as he had used while in Centre Community, Swaim concluded that by proper use of these facilities anyone could look to literary improvement. "And then, instead of wallowing in those sinks of vice and sin which blot the reputation of our country, they may spend their idle moments, in laying the foundation of future usefulness and respectability."

The wayward boys whom Swaim mentioned in his description of Greensboro, were typical of the "restless horde" which he referred to in connection with manual labor schools. These are more specificailly described in a *Greensborough Patriot* notice of 1831. Under a large capital letter heading of "$15 REWARD," Thomas Carbry, C. Winburn, and William Adams offered the reward money to anyone who would furnish information on the "nocturnal raiders who infest this Borough; and who, in defiance of law and public order, are in the practice of committing various excesses." In this instance, they had removed a sulky from Carbry's shop, had torn down Winburn's sign, and had demolished Adams' fence. Furthermore, they had "made a practice of insulting and annoying Elisha Mendenhall," and had engaged in other "nightly disturbances which have so much annoyed the peace of our village."[62] Indeed, it might be a question for debate: Whether the teen-agers of Swaim's day were more "out of hand" than were those of the mid-twentieth century!

Some of Greensboro's beautiful buildings which impressed Swaim were still standing to be admired by citizens of the 1960's. Among them were the Reverend William Paisley's house (1819), which in Swaim's day stood on the location on which a new post office was built in 1933 (Paisley's house having been moved to 109 Hillcrest Drive); onetime Governor John M. Morehead's home (1825), which later housed The Keeley Institute at 447 West Washington Street; and Henry Humphreys' home and place of business (1830) of three majestic stories rising at the southwest intersection of North, South, East, and West Streets, later Elm and Market Streets. So out of the ordinary was this towering structure that it soon became known as "Humphrey's Folly," but having been renovated inside and out, its main original walls adequately housed a portion of twentieth century progress. The house in which Swaim lived was perhaps the most beautiful residence in the town. For four years he resided with his kinsfolk, the M. S. Sherwoods, whose home was built before 1829 at what later became 426 West Gaston Street. This building, constructed of red brick with a front portico and large white columns, was an impressive colonial structure.*

Sherwood family tradition relates that the Swaims' only child, Mary Jane Virginia, who was to become the mother of O. Henry, was born in this house on February 12, 1833. After her birth, in May of that year, the Swaims bought a house and moved to the first block of what later became North Greene Street. Thereafter they often visited at Sherwood House, then a little over one long block away; and their child played in the yard, under the tree which still stood over a century later, old but sturdy, at the edge of the sidewalk.[63]

The Swaims were soon well-established in their new home. Of

---

*Directly across the street lived the Sidney Porters who had moved to Greensboro around 1830. In the early 1820's Porter had come to Guilford County as a clock agent from Connecticut, had met Ruth Worth of Centre, and had married her in 1824. Their oldest child was Algernon Sidney, who later married the Swaims' daughter Mary Jane Virginia; and this couple became the parents of O. Henry.

this situation Will L. Scott wrote that "Severe as [Swaim] was as a public journalist, yet he was a man of infinite good humor and of the gentlest affection. His home was a sort of loveland . . . His family was his all . . . a flattering promise of long happiness with his dear ones buoyed him in his industrious and arduous walk in the business and political world. His fortune was better than that of Midas. Whatever he touched turned not to gold only but to that prosperity and felicity which gold only cannot give or purchase."[64]

Of Abiah Shirley (Mrs. William) Swaim, Scott wrote, "she was a woman of rare graces of character . . . beautifully cultivated . . . She was a member of the Methodist Episcopal Church," her Greensboro membership having been in what later became the West Market Street Methodist Church. She was a leader in her community, particularly in the "application of loving kindness;" and her influence was felt in her personal associations and in society.[65]

The home of this small family after May, 1833, was just around the corner from the *Greensborough Patriot* office. This residence became the setting for informal gatherings of Swaim's friends with whom he discussed ideas and plans for the progress of the state and the nation.

At that time Greensboro was a small southern village in its original boundaries of about a quarter of a mile in width and a little over a quarter of a mile in length. It had three streets running north and south for three blocks and three streets running east and west for three blocks. Its water supply came from two public pumps, installed on two different streets. The pump that was nearest to Swaim's home while he lived with the Sherwoods was over four town blocks away. There was a spring, however, that rose about where the Greensboro post office was built in 1933, and its overflow formed a brook which trickled through the Swaim-Sherwood back yard; and doubtless that water source was used in emergency. After Swaim moved into his own dwelling he was about two village blocks from the nearest pump. The population within the corporate limits numbered 369 inhabitants, enlarged by an additional 115 living around the town.[66]

The actions of the people were regulated by a Board of Commissioners, composed of five men elected by voters of the municipality; and the Commissioners elected one among them to serve as Constable. Although the state legislature had authorized Greensboro to organize into a self-governing town in 1824, which it appears to have done, there are no specific records of the proceedings before early in 1829. In that year William Adams, originally of Centre Community and Swaim's good friend of long standing, was made Constable of the municipality; and in April, 1829, Adams with four commissioners drew up nine regulatory ordinances for the citizens to observe.[67] By the time Swaim became the village's editor in May, these ordinances were no longer news; but in 1830 when the board added a tenth regulation for the benefit of hogs in the town, and set up a patrol system for the benefit of the people, that became real local news. A list of these rules, signed by William Adams as chairman of the board, and Peter Adams as secretary, were carried for several weeks in the *Greensborough Patriot*.[68] A glance at these gives an idea of the simple living conditions as well as the aggravating problems which existed in the community.

## ORDINANCES

*For the regulation and government of the town of Greensborough adopted by the Commissioners of said town.*

1st. Every person who shall exhibit a Stud Horse or Jack in any of the Streets of this Town, nearer to the Court House, than the first cross streets, shall be subject to a fine of Five dollars — Provided such offender shall first be required by the Officer of Police to remove said Horse or Jack. And any person, letting or trying a Mare to a Stud Horse or Jack, within the corporation, shall be fined Five Dollars.

2nd. Any person known to keep Wood, Stone or Lumber, in the two main Streets, crossing at the Court House, within the corporation, unless for purpose of building, (and then not more than thirty feet of said street,) for twenty four hours, shall be fined Two Dollars, and shall be subject to a like penalty for every twenty four hours such wood &c. remains in the streets afterwards; and on the cross streets, no person is allowed to take up more than eight feet on the side of the streets, for their wood or any other lumber, under the penalty of Two Dollars for every twenty four hours they may exceed those bounds.

3d. Every person living within the incorporation, shall be subject to a fine of Five Dollars, for every ten days his Chimney or Chimneys shall remain less than two feet and a half above the comb of his house or houses.

172

4th.   Any person known to drive or stop a Wagon, Cart or Carriage of any description, in any Street within the corporation, at any public time, for the purpose of selling any article or commodity whatever, shall be fined One Dollar, and be liable to a like penalty of One Dollar for every hour they remain within the street or streets — Provided, that they are first notified by the Officer of Police, any one of the Commissioners, or the Secretary.

5th.   Any Wagoner or any other person who may feed his team or horses, within the two main streets crossing at the Court House, shall be fined One Dollar for such offence — Provided, that, they are first notified by the Officer of Police, any one of the Commissioners, or the Secretary.

6th.   Any person known to fire a gun or pistol (the Cannon excepted) anywhere within the corporation of the Town, shall be fined One Dollar.

7th.   Any person throwing Shavings, Straw, Leather, Ashes or any other kind of litter in the Streets shall be fined One Dollar for every such offence.

8th.   Any person watering a horse on the Platform of either of the Public Pumps, shall be fined One Dollar for every such offence.

9th.   The Officer of Police shall at all times attend to the removal of any nuisance, when required by any of the Commissioners, under a penalty of one dollar for each neglect.

10th.   No person shall feed a hog or hogs in any of the streets within the corporation, under the penalty of one dollar for every offence.*

The high esteem in which Swaim was held by his town was shown in 1833, when he was elected to its Board of Commissioners "whose duty it will be to keep matters straight in Greensboro for the next twelve months."[69] Since 1828 the village had been upset because the board had made no move toward establishing a fire department, and the officers of 1833 were elected on a "fire ballot." The new board acted immediately and thus Swaim became one of the original organizers of the Greensboro Fire Department.[70] At that time it was a simple arrangement. Every owner of a house or houses was ordered to have two ladders for each building, "one of which shall reach from the ground to the eves of these houses, the other to rest on the top of the house, to reach from the comb to the eves ... [and] the Treasury have made immediately ten fire hooks for the benefit of the corporation."[71] Citizens were further ordered to clear all rubbish and nuisances from their back yards; and failure to cooperate with the department automatically brought a five dollar fine.

----

*The local newspaper also carried the plan, in thirteen sections, under which the newly organized patrol system would function.

While Swaim was a town commissioner, he served as secretary for the board, and, in the absence of the Constable, he acted as Constable *pro tem.*[72] In 1833, acting in this capacity, he gave a hand to the new Fire Department by "ordering" that John M. Logan and W. R. D. Lindsay, two of the town's most respectable citizens, "go with the Police Officer this evening and see that ladders are provided and put up agreeable to law."[73] This meant that these men were to check all homes to see that each one had ladders ready for immediate use in the case of fire. He also printed fifty copies of the town laws in order that the citizens might be properly informed concerning the conduct that was expected of them; and he employed a man to repair the west town pump and supervised the work, all for the sum of $10.55. And, at the commissioners' request, he made out a list of all the taxes that were supposed to be paid into the town treasury at that time.[74]

In the early 1830's it was not customary for newspapers to include very much local news, for accounts of such happenings were usually spread by word of mouth before they could be put into print; but the *Greensborough Patriot* often took notice of home town affairs. Possibly the fact that its editor was on the town council had something to do with his more careful coverage of the town news. An example of this was the story of Postmaster Dr. John A. Mebane who got into a misunderstanding with stagecoach mail carrier Thomas Carbry about a schedule for mail leaving Greensboro. The whole town was discussing it, and columns of the *Greensborough Patriot* were devoted to the subject. Moreover, local educational and religious meetings, court cases, political events, and candidates for public office were often announced and reported upon. And at Christmas time, 1832, the fiery reformer-editor printed the following notice in his paper: "We stop the press to announce that the Greensborough Candy pulling Association will assemble this evening at the public square, on Piety Hill, at the tap of the drum. All unmarried Folks, young people, gals, boys and children, are requested to bring each a bottle of molasses, and participate in the festivities of the occasion."[75]

174

Swaim's concern for Greensboro included not only its government, safety, and education, but also its appearance and cleanliness. On the subject of hogs in the streets, he vented his spleen in his own inimitable sarcasm under the one-word title of "HOGS." He wrote: "The citizens of Greensborough, who have located themselves in the town for the purpose of raising pork for market, are informed that such of their hogs as run at large in the suburbs, and are rather inclined to the woods, are in a starving condition — that it would be to their advantage to keep them confined to the limits of the corporation, as there are not more than five hundred hogs at present fattened in the main streets. It is presumed that five hundred more might be kept here in town to great advantage, without any inconvenience to the inhabitants.

"Should there be any gentlemen in the neighbourhood who make a business of raising pork for market, they are earnestly solicited, to locate themselves in the center of this town, it being set apart by the commisioners for the sole and exclusive purpose of raising hogs — not that kind of *swine* which is fattened in *swill* shops — but the real four-footed grunters. I know of no improvement that could be added to the place, except a rail road, with which the citizens would be so well pleased, as to have constantly in their view, a large quantity of hogs rooting round [their] doors, especially in *wet weather*."[76]

Mrs. Anne Royall, a noted jaurnalist and a correspondent for the *Morning Courier and New York Enquirer* and the Washington *Post*, supported Swaim in this essay. When touring the South, on February 21, 1830, she wrote, "As I drew near Greensboro, the land grew thin and sandy, more pine, but well watered, and vast droves of hogs."[77]

Troublesome hogs, however, did not prevent Swaim from witnessing the successful operation of the Mount Hecla Steam Cotton Mill and other smaller industries in his home town, as proof of the possibilities of the program he favored. A prophet a century and a quarter ahead of his time, he envisioned an industrial development for North Carolina and the South which unfortunately did not take a firm hold until the 1950's. As a result of his campaign for industrialization, however, manufacturing showed a decided increase in North Carolina between 1840 and 1860. This development was interrupted by the Civil War. Though there has been progress in manufacturing in the whole South since his time, agricultural interests have remained dominant. Since the Great Depression of the 1930's, Swaim's plan for a better balanced economy, which included processing raw materials to their finished products in the South, has been more widely practiced; and definite programs have been organized to carry this idea forward. Swaim used his newspaper for spreading an industrial gospel, and as his pages yellowed and the print faded, his prophecy began to be fulfilled.

# VIII

## FOR IMPROVED TRANSPORTATION

*"Let us not act as did the poor Hypochondriack, who perished, though in reach of victuals, from immagining that he had lost the use of his arms."*[1]

Since the close of the War of 1812 with England, a keener interest in domestic affairs had been felt throughout the United States. Among the chief concerns that claimed the continued attention of the people was a system of better transportation facilities for both trade and travel. Although other states had made notable progress along this line by Swaim's time, North Carolina had made small advancement over pioneer days. Natural waterways had been little improved; and roads, which were scarcely more than trails rambling through fields and forests, were almost impassable in wet weather. This condition especially handicapped the western Piedmont and Mountain areas of the state which were largely dependent upon land travel, for it rendered access to markets both difficult and expensive. Many considered a solution to this problem North Carolina's greatest need, and the demand for better transportation became increasingly urgent. Swaim supported Henry Clay's American system which included joint state and federal action in the development of transportation facilities within the states and between the states of the Union.

Swaim knew the transportation situation he faced was deplorable, but he also knew that the one great effort that previously had been made to solve this problem had ended unsatisfactorily. He knew that Judge Murphey, in his famous reports to the North Carolina legislature from 1815 to 1818, had outlined a transportation plan which would have opened travel routes to all points in North Carolina by connecting dirt roads, canals, and navigable rivers. The plan called for developing Beaufort and Wilmington as large commercial centers where North Carolina products could be assembled for export, and from which imports could be distributed throughout the state. Such a development would render North Carolina independent of the ports and markets of Virginia and South Carolina, a freedom Murphey very much desired; for he felt that North Carolinians had come to lean too heavily upon these states, particularly on Virginia, for economic and political advice. Murphey's recommendation had been calculated also to increase the productivity and value of farms; to reduce freight rates; to raise the per capita income and wealth, which in turn would raise the standard of living; to bring in more revenue for general state development; and to stimulate state pride and thus check the tide of emigration.[2]

Swaim knew, too, that Murphey and his followers had believed that the state government should take the lead in such a state-wide program of transportation improvements, for previous efforts by local county governments or by private means had failed.[3] This idea had met with a more favorable response than his recommendation for public education; but even so his support had come largely from the Piedmont and Mountain regions which so desperately needed outlets to markets, and from the eastern towns and areas near the sites for the proposed improvements. The General Assembly, however, dominated by the East with its navigable rivers for transportation, had proved very indifferent in the matter.[4]

Yet, in 1815 the General Assembly had passed an act which provided for the employment of a surveyor to study the state's situation, and to make recommendations for improving transportation facilities. Meanwhile there had been great excitement over the outlook, and the state had subscribed $112,500 for stock in navigation and canal companies, the larger portion going to the

East, although the West was in far greater need of help. During the next few years additional state appropriations had been made for public works with the result that the East, still theoretically opposed to state aid, had received $123,030 to the West's $13,300.[5]

Swaim was about sixteen years old when most of this had taken place—about the time when he had determined to make a man of himself—and he must have heard his politically minded western community discussing the matter with grave concern.

And it was well within Swaim's comprehension, that about 1819 a surveyor from England, Hamilton Fulton, had arrived at the state's request and had made investigations and suggestions for transportation projects. In that same year a Fund for Internal Improvements and a Board of Internal Improvements had been established. The fund was to be raised from the sale of one million acres of Cherokee Lands which the state had acquired from the Indians; from income of the Bank of Cape Fear and the Bank of New Bern in which the state held stock; and, as it turned out, some from the general revenue of the state. The board was to administer this fund.[6]

Although both were clothed in glowing prospects, neither the fund nor the board had met with great success. Collections from the sales of public lands had been slow and income from the banks had fallen off because of hard times. The board had had no experience by which to guide its efforts, and no engineer to direct operations. Moreover, the urgent demands of local groups for improvements in their own vicinities had caused the board to undertake local projects at so many different points that few could be completed. And thus the whole program had been rendered practically useless. Out of sixteen projects in which the state took part, only three had been rewarding, and they for only a short time—the Cape Fear Navigation Company, the Roanoke Navigation Company, and the Buncombe Turnpike which connected Greenville, South Carolina, via Asheville and Hot Springs, with Greenville, Tennessee.[7]

Thus, while a young man, Swaim had been impressed that thousands and thousands of dollars of the state's money had been spent with next to none of the desired improvements accomplished.[8] Living among the general public he had watched a great prejudice develop against the subject of internal improvements and he had seen citizens who had a real vision for the future advancement of the state become greatly depressed and disheartened. Nevertheless, they had not abandoned the idea; through personal interviews and writings they had kept the subject alive.

As time passed, rivalry between the state's political groups had become more and more pronounced. Whenever a debatable subject was under consideration, sometimes the entire East would become aligned against the West. At other times the wealthy middle East would become aligned against a combination of the West, the northeastern Sound region, and perhaps the southern middle border counties—depending upon the issue. On the subject of internal improvements, however, basically the cleavage had remained East against West. In general the wealthy middle East, favored by rivers for transportation and well-satisfied with itself, still strongly opposed state spending for internal improvements, because it would have to bear the major expense of such a program. The Sound region, although willing to accept federal aid for the major projects of opening Albemarle Sound and constructing an inland waterway in its own vicinity, always felt that it would not greatly profit by lesser internal improvements, mostly in other parts of the state, and it therefore stood firmly against state aid. The southern border counties which had an outlet through Fayetteville were not so hard pressed. The West, however, which included the more democratic Piedmont and Mountain areas, was woefully handicapped for access to markets and had sought better transportation facilities through government participation.[9] The West had contended that a big movement for the benefit of everybody, such as a transportation system, should be supplemented by state and federal aid, since it would be too much of an undertaking for private enterprise or local communities. But the East had controlled the General Assembly and by the early 1830's it had become even more averse to granting state aid.

After 1829, however, the West had a new champion and a new weapon for waging its battles. The *Greensborough Patriot* became the outspoken voice of the so-called back country. Before its publication in May of that year, there were only two newspapers of any consequence west of Raleigh—the *Western Carolinian* of Salisbury and the *Hillsborough Recorder,* both founded in 1820. In the early 1830's the *Western Carolinian* lost prestige because it favored nullification, and the *Hillsborough Recorder,* mildly liberal in its point of view, did not greatly arouse public spirit. Although at times other men and newspapers expressed their opinions on the subject of internal improvements and other needed reforms, Swaim was the only North Carolinian who in the early 1830's presented a specific program of over-all reform and made week by week reports as to its progress or otherwise.

Insofar as actual work and accomplishments were concerned, the internal improvement program was near a standstill in North Carolina when Swaim revived interest in it through the pages of the *Greensborough Patriot.* In the passing years, to Murphey's projected plan for connecting roads and waterways had been added the hope for a system of railroads as well; but as late as 1832 no lines had been laid in North Carolina, and in that year only the one-and-a-quarter mile Experimental Railroad was undertaken near Raleigh. In keeping with his policy of providing for his readers a sort of historical background to the issues he presented, Swaim presented a clear picture of the lamantable pass to which North Carolina had come for lack of internal improvements. He did this through the following summary by his faithful "contributor," POLY-DORE:[10]

### NORTH-CAROLINA, No. VII.

#### Internal Improvements

"It is not my belief, that any internal improvements which could be made, other things being the same they are, could wholly relieve

North Carolina from her present embarrasments. By Internal Improvements here, I only mean the effecting of facilities from rivers, the opening of canals, & the erecting of Rail Roads or other roads. But though these improvements might not wholly relieve us, yet, by affording a cheap conveyance for the interchange of productions in different portions of the State, and for throwing the surplus into the mart of the world, it could not fail to have a potent influence over our prosperity and enterprise.

"When flour is worth $7 per barrel at Newbern, and wheat is plentiful in the upper country, say 2 or 300 miles from the market, no man would be indemnified in wagoning his flour to market; for it would cost him nearly half its value to get it there; and the balance would not justify the undertaking. But if the farmer could get his flour to market for less than one dollar per barrel, he would realize a profit, which would impart new vigour to his enterprise. Again, salt frequently costs but 50 to 60 cents per bushel in Wilmington; whilst, in the upper country, it always more than doubles these prices. The difference is owing to the expense of carriage. These two instances sufficiently illustrate the subject, for the comparative effect is nearly the same in other instances, according to the weight and bulk of the commodity.

"As things are, the active citizen of this State has many and strong inducements to emigrate. He may remove to very distant States, and yet, if North-Carolina offers the best market, he may compete with her own inhabitants. In verity, when the improvements now in progress shall be completed, the citizens of Ohio and Indiana may rival us in our own markets. They will be, in effect, nearer to our trading towns, than we of the upper country. *The narrow policy* of our Statesmen is a by-word and a reproach among our Sister States. They have so far outstripped us, in the honourable race of improvements, that we have shrunk back to the gaol, oppressed with an incubus.

"We owe this state of things, in part to the monopolizing, self-aggrandizing projects of a few speculating aspirants, who were, a few years ago, at the helm."

POLYDORE was writing this summary on November 7, 1829, and it was the fifteen preceding years to which he referred. He stated that the politicians and their supporters, in their "avidity to see splendid works, and to reap splendid profits," rushed into improvements without knowledge. They secured charters, purchased, at high prices, land for their operations, and went to work without system, or experience, or skill. Meanwhile the state invested heavily in "these ill-concerted schemes. Extravagance marked every step;" POLYDORE continued, "and what was done, was done to no purpose. The funds were squandered; the romantic projectors were involved in difficulty, and bankruptcy. Ruin and consternation spread around; for, in their fall, they were not alone, but with them they carried others, whom they had involved as securities. Like the falling of mighty oakes, they crushed all within reach of their widespread boughs.

"Then commenced another scence. The public mind having been excited, to an unusual degree, with the anticipation of something great, was now suddenly depressed with disappointment. Artful and designing men were ready to seize on this state of public feeling, and to convert it into a stepping-stone, from which to elevate themselves to power. Abusing the ignorance and versatility of the people, inveigling mightily against internal improvements, not discriminating between the greatness of the object to be attained, and the impropriety and inadequacy of the measures adopted for its attainment, and being aided by those who were yet sore with the wounds received in the attempts already made, they have succeeded in turning the current of popular opinion altogether against internal improvements, and have raised themselves to places of honor and trust, under the promise of opposing every attempt, how judicious soever it may be, at the bettering of our internal commerce. This game is still played with success. Meantime the best interests of the State are suffering for the want of something effectual being done. An enlightened people can discern the difference between economy and parsimony; whilst ignorance is naturally short-sighted and penurious.

"The people are gravely told by these electioneering stump-orators, that they have nothing to take to market; that it is non-sense to be at the expense of making provisions for carrying off their surplus produce, when, so far from having anything to carry to market, they are in want of every thing; that they should first turn their attention to improvements in agriculture; and that, perhaps after the lapse of a century or two, some improvements of the facility of commerce may become necessary and practicable. They have even gone so far as to make some regulations, and offer some premiums, to encourage improvement in agriculture. This is a sample of the extreme fatuity *of our little Statesmen*. Who will, or who can, be at the expense and trouble of improving his land, whilst his surplus produce will do nothing towards remunerating him for his troubles, and defraying the expense? Notwithstanding our wretched modes of culture, the exuberant productions of the coun-try are often a burden on the hands of the cultivator. The amount to which our productions could be swelled, would they yield us any profit, is incalculable. It is the vilest absurdity to talk of our having nothing to carry to market. Our grievance is not that we have nothing to spare, nor altogether that there is no market, but that nothing, under existing circumstances, will bear carrying to market.

"We are in a quite critical and desperate situation; constantly growing poorer for the want of a convenient market, and already too poor, (or rather I should think, too indolent and penurious,) to engage in improvements. Whilst the subject is so unpopular, and the legislature composed of men, who have gained their eminence by giving a pledge to hold the purse-strings, to suggest any thing to be done, would be *'to cast pearls before swine.'* "

Taking note of the argument that it might be better to use harbors of other states to avoid the social problems attending the growth of cities, POLYDORE went on: "It might be added, that were we void of debt, ignorance, sloth, pride, dissipation, and in-justice, and possessed of their contraries, independence, in-telligence, industry, humility, economy, and justice, we might be very happy, with even less commerce than we now have. But, as an improvement of the facilities of internal commerce would advance our prosperity, and assist in the acquisition of some of the desirable objects above enumerated, without rendering more difficult the attainment of any, the subject certainly is worthy the notice already taken of it; and should the period ever arrive, when our greater grievances are redressed, and popular attention is aroused to the redress of this, I shall rejoice, if still alive, and able to wield a pen, to add my pittance towards the advancement of so great a good.

POLYDORE."

In sympathy with POLYDORE's contention that "facilities of internal commerce would advance our prosperity," during the first months of his editorship of the *Greensborough Patriot*, Swaim analyzed for his readers some of the main water routes of the nation to show that they were helpful in promoting progress. He called attention to those of New York, Pennsylvania, Delaware and Maryland, Virginia and North Carolina, South Carolina, Louisiana, and Ohio; and he stated that the property value in New York state alone had been increased over $100,000,000 by its routes. He also listed twenty-two canals by names, giving mileages and connections.[11] With special reference to the Pennsylvania Canal, he wrote, "It is said that since the commencement of this canal, about sixty buildings have sprung up like mushrooms along the line from Marietta to Columbia. This shows the advantage of improvement. Capital will always flow where prospects of proffit are flattering. Why do not towns spring up as by magic in N. Carolina? because her politicians legislate upon the log-rolling plan! But her citizens will not sleep always!"[12]

One project under the plan of internal improvements in North Carolina was that of draining the swamps of the eastern part of the state so that rich harvests might be reaped from the lands then left to the wilds of nature. Swaim, who had launched his paper as an open advocate of the abolition of slavery, was soon confronted with a proposition which to him seemed very unwise. Governor John Owen in his inaugural address on November 17, 1829, stated that

185

every patriot and enlightened citizen of the state would like to know why the spending of so much state money had brought so little progress to the state. As a way around this dilemma, the governor seriously proposed that, since the most prosperous eastern part of the state was being worked by slave labor, the same method might be employed to advance a program of internal improvement. "Slaves constitute the only effective force," he declared. "With them our swamps must be drained, and our rivers opened, or the former remain the abode of noxious animals, and the latter, a mere apology for navigable streams."[13] He then informed his audience that to employ white labor to drain the swamps would not be successful, for white men did not have the physical endurance for such work; that the state must either give up all effort toward internal improvements or else make an appropriation for the purchase of slaves for carrying the program forward.

On November 28, 1829, Swaim published the governor's speech in his paper and in the same issue ridiculed the top executive mercilessly. He said that he had always admired John Owen, but he could not sanction his "proposition so gravely made and so *plausibly* urged, to purchase snail-pacing slaves to carry on a *vigorous* system of internal improvement! When freemen, propelled to industry by *State pride* and a prospect of *remuneration,* have been unable to make commerce flow at their bidding, we are advised to resort to the happy expedient of supplying their place with —SLAVES! and this too, by PURCHASE!! Our statesmen have been employed for many years in taxing their brain to invent some efficacious method of rousing into action the torpid energies of the State; but it has been reserved for this *glorious* age of invention to make the discovery that slaves constitute the only part of our population that can be depended upon!! . . . Whether Governor Owen has any of these *smart* negroes to *sell* to the State we are left to *conjecture,* without making it our business to enquire. And while the guardians of our destiny are fondling over the delusive dream, that slave labour will make us rich, and wise, and great, and powerful, the citizens of the State would perhaps act prudently in ascertaining whether it has not uniformly produced a contrary effect. [Swaim wondered if others in power had slaves they wanted to sell] and consequently find it convenient to make the discovery that if the slaves were *bought* instead of *hired,* they would soon convert North-Carolina from a 'desolate wilderness' into a 'blooming Eden!' "[14]

Having warned that if this plan should be considered seriously he would be heard from again, the editor expressed satisfaction when the governor's recommendation to the legislature was turned down as an imprudent investment. Wrote he, "*So far, so good!*"[15]

Another though quite different event related to the matter of internal improvements constitued exciting news in its own right, though it bore no known connection with the current nullification disturbance. Labelled officially as a secret government experiment, of which the object has remained secret, the event created about as much of a sensation as did the launching of sputnik in 1958. In midwinter, 1833, an express stagecoach was dispatched from the City of Washington to Charleston, South Carolina. Newspapers were soon notified of the speeding coach, and the *Greensborough Patriot* quoted an account of the journey from the *National Intelligencer* of Washington: " 'The express was speeded to Charleston, and returned to this City, within the compass of five days. We are entirely out of the secrets of the executive, and therefore have no knowledge of the special object of this unusual dispatch. We have some doubt however whether it was anything more than a first experiment, with a view to future use of the same facility of conveyance, in preference to the slow and uncertain mail carriage, should any immergency arise to require it. From what we hear this express was intended to be a secret transaction. Such a thing as a *secret express,* . . . is a thing so obviously impracticable, where it is so rare, that we wonder it should have been thought of for a moment.' "[16]

The feat was indeed spectacular, for the travel time was forty-eight hours for a distance of five hundred forty-four miles; and this during the time of year when dirt roads would have been about at their worst. The purpose of the express, therefore, became secondary to the performance. There was, however, much speculation about it, and Swaim informed his readers that it was thought to have borne a message from the President of the United States to the state officials of South Carolina; though he doubted that to have been the sole purpose of the movement which still remained a secret.[17]

Whatever prompted the unusual dispatch of that stagecoach, it served the purpose of demonstrating the maximum speed that could be achieved by horses and a stagecoach on dirt roads. Moreover, it also supplied a point of comparison in favor of railroads which were still in the experimental stage, but were already beginning to supplement dirt roads.

In *The Numbers of Carlton. Addressed to the People of North Carolina, on a Central Railroad thru the State,* Dr. Joseph Caldwell proposed that a railroad be built from New Bern, North Carolina, to the Tennessee line. The plan also included a provision for access to the Atlantic Ocean by enlarging the connecting water route from New Bern, North Carolina, to Beaufort, North Carolina, which was located favorably for a seaport. All this he estimated could be financed by a tax of thirty-seven cents for seven years on every taxable poll, "with like sums to be subscribed annually by capitalists, returnable in five years after the work is finished."[18] At that time trains of cars were being successfully drawn by horses along steel-plated wooden railroad tracks in some parts of the world, but not in North Carolina. By the 1830's, however, horses began to be replaced by locomotive engines which greatly accelerated both speed and capacity in transportation. Although Swaim continued to give information on other possible internal improvements, it seemed to him that the railroad offered the most hope for the most pepole in the state; consequently it was most discussed by contributors and furnished the most novel newsaper material.

The *Greensborough Patriot* followed what has become an accepted method of reporting in that it supplied details of development as the subject progressed. Since public thought in North Carolina was directed toward railroads, Swaim, as was his policy on any subject he introduced, published a brief history of their gradual expansion.[19] He stated that rail cars had been used first near New Castle upon the Tyne in England about 1650, and that a locomotive engine propelled by steam had been employed on the Merthy Tydvil railroad in Wales in 1804. He mentioned the important railroads in the world; and through a correspondent supplied facts on the United States' railways in 1829:

## MISCELLANEOUS.

*"Tenets with books, and principles with times.*
*Manners with fortunes, humours turn with climes"*

FOR THE GREENSBOROUGH PATRIOT.

MR. EDITOR As the people are beginning to seek information on the subject of rail roads, I have thought proper to furnish you with a list for publication, of the length of the principle rail roads finished and in progress, in the United States. It is as follows:

| | |
|---|---|
| Baltimore and Ohio rail road | 270 miles |
| Kattskill to Ithica, N. Y. | 167 |
| Charleston to Savannah | 135 |
| From Philadelphia to New York | 96 |
| From Lexington to Cincinnati | 75 |
| Camden to Amboy | 60 |
| Baltimore to Susquehannah | 48 |
| Boston to Providence | 43 |
| Boston to Worcester | 40 |
| Baltimore to Washington | 38 |
| Hollydaysburg to Johnston | 37 |
| Ithica to Oswego | 29 |
| Boston to Lowel | 25 |
| Elizabeth to Limmerville | 25 |

A contributor made railroads seem a grave necessity by relating his personal observation of transportation needs. "I have seen

189

several wagoners lately from Fayetteville," he wrote, "with horses half dead; and some had been compelled to leave their loads behind. I think this a very proper time for all the members of the assembly, elect, to turn out with a heavy load of flour, and drive, themselves, with a grass fed team, [to market], and I will bet two dollars to one, that they will come home . . . [and vote] for a railroad forthwith."[20]

In connection with this observation Swaim calculated a man's time at the prevailing wage of fifty cents per day, plus other expenses, to show that freight rates by railroad when compared with those by wagon would give the farmer $25 more profit on every ten barrels of flour sold, if it had to be transported across the state. And he called upon men to use their reason. "Now seven dollars and fifty cents on each taxable poll would build a railroad from Beaufort to the Tennessee line," he explained. "And where is the patriot who would not pay that sum, even to try the *experiment,* if success was doubtful? The complete success of railroads, however, is no longer a matter of speculation!"[21]

As proof of his last statement, Swaim called attention to a train that had traveled from Liverpool to Manchester, England, carrying one hundred tons and drawn by one engine. The distance of about thirty miles had been covered in one and a half hours, averaging about twenty miles per hour. Compare this system with that of the dirt road, he challenged. "An eight horse wagon on a common road, is capable of carrying only eight tons a day. Consequently, it would take one hundred horses working for one day on a turnpike road to perform the same work as was here accomplished by a single steam engine in an hour and a half on the rail-road."[22]

Such accomplishments were not limited to England, he pursued. In our own country, on the route from Baltimore to Philadelphia, " 'eleven cars, containing 200 persons and a vast deal of baggage, were whirled along by a single locomotive engine, at the rate of fifteen miles an hour, and occasionally a mile in three minutes,' " he quoted from the *Examiner.* " 'It appears to us that it needs only the sight of these things to convince any North Carolinian that the true policy of his state is to fall in with the spirit of the age and to construct rail roads wherever the extent of the business will justify it.

"'Cannot our citizens be roused to make a beginning in the great work, by undertaking at once, and with a proper spirit the construction of [railways?] . . . It would not only be a profitable and valuable investment, but would tend to [stimulate] other more important enterprises. Depend upon it, we must better ourselves or our trade will take to itself wing.'"[23]

On the advantage of swift railroad transportation over the more commonly used slow methods of the day, Congressman David Crockett had something to say from his own observation; and Swaim gave his readers the benefit of Crockett's experience. "'I can only tell you my notion of the speed of a railroad car in this way;'" the *Greensborough Patriot* quoted the Congressman as saying inelegantly, "'I put my head out to spit, and overtook it so quick that it hit me smack in the face!'"[24]

Internal improvement organizations, at times almost languishing in hopeless despondency, began to revive at this time and to push measures for railroads and other developments by seeking state aid to help finance them. Indeed, William Swaim himself became secretary of Guilford County's Internal Improvements. After appeals of these organizations to the General Assembly had been repeatedly ignored, Swaim fearlessly attacked the official body for what he called its pusillanimous attitude. In an editorial of December 15, 1830, he wrote: "Mr. Bynum, for want of better business, or to keep himself in fashion, we don't know which, has introduced a series [of] resolutions, denying in toto the constitutional power of congress, to appropriate funds for works of internal improvement within the states. We hope the lgeislature will give him all due credit for his zeal in the matter, and for the flowery eloquence with which he has bedaubed his resolutions, and then after paying the public printer his bill for printing them, let them fall stillborn from the press. We are not disposed to do the lgeislature the in- injustice of charging them with possessing more discernment on this subject than they ought to possess; but we think Mr. Bynum will find

191

himself too late in the day to pass his resolutions by a very decent majority. If he wishes them passed by a unanimous vote, he had better present them to some dinner party in South Carolina."[25]

Such an open attack in print, added to similar previous ones, disturbed the members of the legislature. It was recalled that Swaim had written a scathing rebuke of the General Assembly after it adjourned in January, 1830, because he said it had done nothing toward solving the state's problems;[26] and now he had started assailing the legislators again. As a consequence on December 25, 1830, a resolution was introduced in the North Carolina House of Commons for arresting and bringing Swaim before the official body for contempt of the legislature. When the editor learned of the legislative action concerning himself, he told the whole story in the *Greensborough Patriot*. Reporting it in a more revealing attack upon official incompetence than he had embodied in the editorials which prompted the action against him, he said that "Rather than have their deeds dragged into the sunshine, [members of the legislature] were disposed to convert themselves into a court of judicature, and then sit as Judge and jury *in their own case!* The mighty subject was first introduced by a gentleman from Chatham, as we are told, for a *Christmas frolic!* His resolution proposed, that we should be sent for, to the bar of the house of commons, and there atone for a contempt of the Legislature. And what is this but the hall of the house of commons converted into a *theatre,* the members of a grave assembly transformed into political mountebanks, ourself the object of the *play,* and each man acting clown for himself. A man of the first respectability informs us, that certain men had drunk too much *egg-nog,* or some other kind of *stimulant,* to comprehend the object of the *farce,* and were accordingly disposed to make a *serious* business of it. They had *washed* the *rust* from their *genius,* and were determined to say a speech while they felt like it. The mover of the resolution, after returning to his senses—if he ever had any—withdrew his *plaything,* and hugged it again to its own kindred bosom. A disciple, however, still big with the subject, introduced another resolution, having in view the same object, the passage of which was advocated with much *zeal & ability*. Here drowiness came over the house like a cloak, and they all fell into the arms of Somnus, and left the resolution to take its luck on the table. — Next morning, matters having *cooled off* a little, this bantling was withdrawn and *another* introduced which was [mentioned] in our last.* Seven mortal speeches were pronounced, and here the matter *ended!* Thus the time of the members, and the funds of the people, are squandered; and woe be to the hide of the fool who shall dare to expose such scenes to the world."[27]

The reason for the abrupt ending to which Swaim referred was the fact that George C. Mendenhall, a representative from Guilford, who had treated the whole matter as a joke, suddenly realized that his fellow legislators were in earnest and really desired to punish Swaim. He advised them that "they had better abandon the thought of such a thing; for, if they arrested, or caused Swaim to be arrested, they would regret it only once and that would be always— *that he[Swaim] would lampoon them to death!*"[28]

At this point Swaim's mind was on internal improvements which he hoped would be made possible by federal and state aid; and he meant to let the people know what their representatives in Raleigh had done, or rather had not done, and why so little was known of legislative actions.

Apparently, criticism did not disturb Swaim who realized that criticism as well as praise would attract attention to the subject he was promoting. Therefore, when the General Assembly adjourned, within less than a month after the House of Commons had considered arresting him for contempt of the legislature, he dared to expose even more forcefully what he considered to be legislative dawdling. He said that North Carolina stood just as she did on the day the body met, in so far as sound laws were concerned. "But mark North Carolina's dejected look—she is fifty-five days *older* and thirty-five thousand dollars *poorer,* than when the last swarm of vultures commenced preying upon the small remains of her

---

*The issue of the *Greensborough Patriot* carrying the editorial "mentioned in our last" seems to have been lost from the files.

vitality, . . ." he declared on January 12, 1831. Becoming more and more emotional as he lambasted the press of North Carolina for not daring to expose legislative weaknesses, he continued: "The political concerns of North Carolina have been badly managed for the past ten years. Many of the people have known this, and some of them have even dared to complain; their displeasure, however, has been much restrained by a hope that a coming year would atone for the follies of the past; and that prosperity would smile upon a wide spreading delapidation, reanimate the skeleton of decay itself and recall that spirit of enterprise which once promised to spread power and respectability around us:—But, alas! each succeeding year has been but a refinement upon the miserable management of the past. Would to heaven the ghastly reality were anything else than what it is! Enterprise has taken refuge where industry and perserverence can be respected and rewarded—talents have sickened at the prospects and fled to more congenial climes— and that guardian genius, which constitutes the sinew of the land is pluming his wings for eternal flight.

"The people have *murdered* themselves, and are now haunted by their own *ghosts!* Once in every twelve months, a political reel is danced in each county—a lottery is drawn: and three men turned up—more frequently *blank* than otherwise—to whom is committed the guardianship of our institutions! And thus the *sport* goes on from year to year, while North Carolina is marching with measured step toward irretrievable ruin and not a struggle is made to check the rapidity of her course or prolong the period of her coming fate. And why are these things so? Because something is radically defective in our system of legislation. And why have not the people discovered and corrected this defect? Because the alarm has not been given by those who have placed themselves upon the watch-tower![29]

"Millions have been squandered upon local and partial legislation; but North Carolina is not five dollars better off than she was twenty years ago! Though her legislature has always been possessed of a few towering and gigantic minds, yet the morbid mass of inert matter ballanced against them, has always nuetralized their efforts for the general and public good. Why has not the PRESS sent forth a reprehending voice against these things? Because printers are cowardly as well as other men; and cowards dread to come in conflict with power. Dishonest and effeminate politicians dread nothing so much as the *'homeliness and holiness of truth:'* but while the press can be held in awe, the people can be kept in ignorance, and our disobedient servants are screened from chastisement.

"This brings us to the subject before us," Swaim continued as he now turned his forthright commentary to the North Carolina press. "We have no disposition to insinuate that the *Star* and *Register* [of Raleigh] willfully misrepresent the fact of which they dare to speak; but we do believe, that whoever reads either, or both of these papers, with the expectation of finding the *whole* truth, will be much mistaken. Our reasons are these—The conductors of the Register have been already severely schooled, and subjected to the necessity of *locomotion* for the *freedom* of their publications; and if the maxim be true that *'a burnt child dreads the fire,'* we have but little to *hope,* and the legislature has but little to *fear* from anything they may publish. . . ."[30]

"And as almost all the other papers in the state imbibe their tone in a greater or lesser degree, from the two above named, it is not surprising that the people are left almost as much in the dark respecting *realities,* as if no paper was published in the state. If the veil could be lifted at once, from the dark and deadly corruptions which are rankling in the heart of our political system, it would astonish the people as a peel of ten-fold thunder upon the stillness of meditation! Every thing that has the appearance of benefitting the state, even in a remote degree, seems to be shunned with marked and studied caution. The great interests of education, by the proper advancement of which, our citizens might assume a tone of enterprise and respectability, have been trammeled under foot, . . . Works of internal improvement, which if properly pursued, might render the commerce of the world tributary to our interests, occupies but a small portion of the public notice. The subject of a penitentiary, and of a circulating medium, have been passed off as a dream of the night.—In short, the legislature of this state has been principally employed in authorizing the building of gates, lauding the purity of Jackson's administration, electing officers, and restoring men to credit, who never had any to loose!"[31]

Since Swaim's primary concern was to stimulate such popular approval of state aid to railroads as to constitute irresistible pressure upon the legislature, he welcomed discussion from any and all sources. Even though the first railroad charters in North Carolina were granted seven years after railroads had been chartered in other states, it would seem that his efforts did help to hasten the beginnings of improved transportation in the state. According to *Laws of North Carolina,* during the legislative session of 1831-1832, a charter was granted to the Cape Fear and Yadkin Rail Road Company, to construct a railway from Wilmington to Salisbury. And a charter was granted for the North Carolina Rail Road Company to build a route, beginning near Beaufort and running by railroad and canal through New Bern, thence to Raleigh and on through the central part of the state as far west as practicable. The penurious legislature granted only aid for the railway surveys, "not exceeding $4,000 for each route," but Swaim felt that a beginning had been made in the right direction.

It was the hope that these projected roads might be built by private subscriptions, and the books were soon opened to the public for buying stock. Swaim promoted these private subscriptions and week by week reported the amount of stock purchased here and there in the state. He printed such public appeals as the following: "We congratulate the public on the brightening aspect that this animating project is assuming. To us in this vicinity, it is a matter of thrilling importance. We have a hardy and industrious population, and as fair fields as the sun ever shone upon; and yet, the products of our labor avail but little for the want of a market. . . . The proposed route is admirably convenient to the construction of this work, and the means of our citizens are ample to accomplish it. . . . There is no doubt, not the shadow of uncertainty even resting on

196

the practicability and success of this measure. Come forward then people of the West, with the resolutions of men, show that the spirit of enterprise and vigorous thrift, is not dead within you. Let not our children, when they review the prosperity of New York, New Jersey, Pennsylvania and the other states who have gone forward in this goodly work, have cause to reproach their fathers with lameness of spirit, or faintness of heart. Let us not act as did the poor Hypochondriack, who perished, though in reach of victuals, from immagining that he had lost the use of his arms. Come forward your self and get your neighbor to come with you and contribute all that you can do without for the present, to this only work that can redeem you from your present dejection and be assured that it will speedily return to you with 'increased triple fold.' "[32]

For a short while after the Cape Fear and Yadkin and the Central Railroad Compaies were chartered, encouraging reports were made in the *Greensborough Patriot*. Then Swaim quoted from the *People's Press* an excerpt which carried a description typical of enough citizens to account for the defeat of the two measures: " 'Every body seems to be sensible that some energetic measures are requisite for the salvation of the state; and whenever any public improvement is proposed, all nod assent; and they continue to nod, nod, nod, till they get fast asleep—dream of ruin—get the night mare—wake up in a fright—rub their eyes—feel in their pockets to see if they've been robbed—inquire how much the rail-road progresses, and whether the bridge is built—but never put in a cent nor stretch forth a hand, to aid in works calculated to prosper the state and enrich themselves.' "[33]

After having advanced for over a year, every known encouragement for building the two chartered railroads, Swaim sadly announced in 1833 that the plans had been abandoned. "At present there is too little capital and public spirit in North-Carolina, unaided by government, to effect any great scheme of internal improvement,"[34] he lamented. But he did not put the matter to rest.

True to his policy of keeping the *Greensborough Patriot* an independent paper, Swaim published arguments on both sides of the question of railroads; and he reported how different legislators had voted on the subject. Every few weeks he alloted several columns in the *Greensborough Patriot* to Jonathan Parker's reasons for opposing state aid for any state development, specifically railroads. It was the same old argument, that reform measures should be accomplished by private enterprise. This opinion Parker even more forcefully proclaimed because so much money had been wasted on attempts at internal improvements. And there were others to whom Swaim allowed space for airing similar views. Frequently the worth of these opinions was assessed by another contributor to the *Greensborough Patriot* rather than by Swaim himself. One convincing reply to Parker came from Dr. David Worth, Parker's lifetime neighbor.

Outlining a plan of proposed railroads over the state and showing how their income would pay for them, Worth contended that "by a judicious and liberal system of policy, these stupendous works may all be completed without taxing the people a single copper; and when finished, the profits arising from them, will be sufficient to pay the whole expenses of government, and push the system of improvements as it were, to almost every man's door.

"Improvements of this kind in the great state of New York, have been completed, have paid for themselves—and now yield a revenue to the government of that state, sufficient to pay all its expenses, and for all the purposes of extending their system of improvement and education, without taxing their citizens a single groat. And when these great works were first talked of there, De Witt Clinton, their great projector, was made the very butt of sport by some, and was mobbed on many occasions by others; but now the people witness in *reality* what he only saw by *anticipation;* and his memory will be revered by the citizens of that state, to the latest generations."[35]

To Dr. Worth's level headed evaluation of the advantages to the state, Swaim added the more personal benefits which would accrue to the people. He proclaimed: "Our state is susceptible of improvement to an extent which shall place her in proud comparison with her now vaunting sisters. All she wants is an outlet from the mountains to the ocean, for the rich productions of her soil. [O]ur citizens will then feel themselves to the soil, and remain content within her borders. As soon as our wandering population can be induced to determine that their bones shall be laid beside those of their ancestors, and that their offspring shall inherit the fruits of their labor, *in this state,* they will commence a system of agricultural and mechanical improvement that shall cause our state to bloom as the Eden of a new world."[36]

Pressure was growing stronger and stronger from those who wanted the state to participate in the movement of railroad building. Internal improvements organizations which had been established in the various counties of the state came forward to support the measure openly. When the Central Railroad and the Cape Fear and Yadkin Railroad failed to develop for lack of state aid, agitation reached a climax. In 1833, forty-eight counties sent delegates to Raleigh where they met and adopted resolutions, asking the legislature for state aid for internal imrovements to the sum of $5,-000,000.[37] Again the controlling East closed its ear to the call.

In October, 1834, just before the legislature was to convene in November, through a contributor Swaim called attention to the fact that here were 1,189 miles of railroads, finished or under construction, in the United States,[38] whereas North Carolina had only the little local Experimental Railroad.

Early in November, 1834, about the time the General Assembly convened, a meeting of Guilford County's internal improvement organization was called. Court adjourned in Greensboro to give time and place for several hundred determined citizens to take action. With Dr. David Worth as chairman and William Swaim as secretary, there was no mistaking the seriousness of the occasion. John M. Morehead, future governor of North Carolina, who had previously asserted that the people should "either determine upon some plan proper to be pursued, or else put the matter forever at rest,"[39] delivered an impressive address on the importance and possibility of internal improvements. Furthermore, he introduced

199

thirteen resolutions to the effect that "the spirit of internal improve-ments, which pervades every other state in the union, should not be permitted longer to slumber in this state;" that there should be an end to demagogical legislation which grants charters to indi-viduals for what the state should do; and that legislators should be advised to support wholeheartedly the internal improvement move-ment.[40]

Despite this agitation, there was still no state aid forthcoming. The Wilmington and Raleigh Rail Road Company was chartered in 1833-1834 to connect those two cities; but when Raleigh failed to support the railroad, it was rerouted from Wilmington to Weldon where it could connect with a railroad from Richmond and Peters-burg, Virginia. With this change, the Raleigh and Gaston Rail Road Comany was chartered in 1835 to connect those two points, and also to connect with the railroad from Petersburg, Virginia. There was, however, no railroad for the West; and it soon became known that even these two eastern routes could not be completed by private means.

It was now completely obvious that as long as North Carolina remained under the influence of the conservative East, movements for over-all state progress could not go forward. Consequently, there was an increasing demand from the more progressive landlocked West for a revision of the state constitution with special attention to representation in proportion to population. This revision was now considered by some as the most important single issue in North Car-olina. The East, however, stubbornly refused to permit the call of a convention to revise the constitution. It was unwilling to surrender its cherished dominance of the legislature to a poorer and less ex-perienced section whose economic and social policies might be in conflict with its own. The West, on the other hand, had had enough of the East's selfish and inconsiderate power; and it made known in no uncertain terms that there would be a constitutional revision (Chapter XI), and under it, internal improvements.[41]

Although Swaim still promoted principles rather than parties, the rising Whig party (1834) of the nation was supporting reforms similar to those he had wanted for North Carolina. And the rising Whig party (1835) in North Carolina, with policies in harmony with Swaim's ideas and hopes, found in Swaim a hard working friend,[42] and became the vehicle which carried forward the program he had long advocated.

While all these considerations were receiving state-wide attention, there were some proposed federal projects that were of particular interest to North Carolinians. Chief among these were a national highway from Maine to Louisiana, a new inlet to Albemarle Sound, and an inland waterway from Boston to Savannah. The highway would be especially beneficial to the isolated western part of the state, while the new inlet and waterway would be advantageous for the Sound region. But the slaveholding, planter aristocracy of the middle eastern area, with Nathaniel Macon as its mouthpiece in Congress, stood in bitter opposition to these proposals because his constituents would be taxed for improvements located elsewhere. Macon, who had been in the national House of Representatives from 1791 to 1815 and in the United States Senate from 1815 to 1828, obstinately resisted the whole national program as embodied in Clay's American system, declaring it absolutely unconstitutional. And he championed the *laissez faire* economic policy within the state, abhorring what he termed the high-flown notions of public education, internal improvements, and a revised constitution. Although the tendency in the United States was toward a concentrated effort for developing and strengthening the nation, the majoriy of North Carolina Congressmen, following Macon's lead, adhered to a more conservative policy of State rights, strict economy, and the minimum of federal action. Only Congressmen from the West and Sound region of the state supported the constructive program of internal improvements through federal expenditures. Thus, even though Macon was no longer in Congress when Swaim became a North Carolina editor, his influence obtained in the state as well as in the nation; and it became, as it were, a battle royal in North Carolina between what western North

Carolinians considered the outmoded spirit of Macon and his school and the flaming forward motion of Swaim and his followers.

By 1835, the West and the Sound region of North Carolina were adopting Whig politics, and Swaim could see hope for the ideas in which he so firmly believed. These sections had at first supported Andrew Jackson for President, for they had thought he would favor a national program of internal improvements. They lost their enthusiasm for him and the Democratic Party, however, after he vetoed the Maysville Turnpike bill and Clay's Distribution Bill, which proposed that the proceeds from the sale of public lands be distributed among the states for internal improvements and other needed reforms; and they then lined up with the Whigs. Evidently Swaim thought David Crockett had summed up the situation very well, for in his paper he quoted Congressman Crockett, who at all times supported internal improvements, as saying, "I do not consider it good sense to be sitting here [in Washington] passing laws for Andrew Jackson to laugh at; it is not even good nonsense."[43]

# IX

## FOR SOUND BANKING AND CURRENCY

*"Whilst we wish and demand no more than justice, to rest satisfied with less would be to act with unfaithfulness to the public weal."*[1]

William Swaim had assumed his newspaper responsibility in serious times, filled with controversy about finance. The Second Bank of the United States and all North Carolina banks were under fire. So interrelated were their operations that the actions of one affected the actions of the others.

The history of the Second Bank of the United States (1816-1836) is more than the story of an institution. It symbolized "the clash between merchant capitalists of the East and agrarians of the South and Southwest, between the forces of nationalism and of States' rights."[2] Since this development took place in a transition period amid several domestic controversies in which political principles often bowed before economic considerations, the question of the renewal of its charter in the early 1830's had politicians and demagogues behaving remarkably alike, particularly in their vituperative arguments. In fact, the problem itself was so complicated that it made impossible any neat division of opinion on the basis of Right and Wrong.

Swaim, being relatively unversed in the subject of economics, did not claim to have the answer to these problems, but he conscientiously presented information regarding conditions in the state due to bad banking practices, and the action or inaction of the state legislature. Moreover, he made quite clear his disapproval of President Jackson's stand against the renewal of the charter of the Second Bank of the United States. He knew that United States Treasury certificates were often at a discount below that of state bank notes; he knew, however, that the federal government could use state bank notes only in the area of their origin because they were badly depreciated; also he knew that the Second Bank of the United States by law had to transfer its funds to different parts of the country without regard for differences in the value of state bank notes; and he knew that the latter practice had forced the national bank to insist that state banks honor their notes in specie. Above all, he knew that the whole intricate business added up to a national bank whose ownership combined investments of government and private citizens, with the degree of government control very slight, the value of specie in the country at a premium, and the money and banking problem itself cursed with incompetence, dishonesty, monopoly, and disorder.

One of the causes of wide antagonism to the Second Bank in the 1830's, when its rechartering came into question, was the practice of permitting its branches to issue drafts on the parent bank in Philadelphia. These branch bank drafts were signed by their respective officials and at their discretion. These co-called national bank "notes" tended to cut down the circulation of state bank notes, thus reducing the profits of the state banks.

When President Jackson, however, reduced this problem in politics, business ethics, and economics to the simple slogan, "Democracy versus a Monster," meaning the Second United States Bank, Swaim considered him reckless and said so.[3] In his reporting of developments in the bank controversy just as in his advocacy of internal improvements, Swaim, the responsible and democratic editor, emerged as a forerunner of North Carolina's Whig politics. Always he insisted that no institution should exist for the privileged few, but that merely destroying a corrupt institution seldom automatically solved the problems it had created.

"The fluctating condition of our circulating medium, & the embarrassment created in our financial concerns, . . . demand the strict attention and the rigid scrutiny of every individual in the community," wrote Swaim in his first editorial for the *Greensborough Patriot*.[4]  He was referring to the growing dissatisfaction over the years in connection with banking policies in North Carolina and to the bank controversy which had dominated the legislature of the state during its 1828-1829 session.  At that time there were only three banks in North Carolina—the Bank of Cape Fear (1804) in Wilmington, the Bank of New Bern (1804), and the State Bank of North Carolina (1810) at Raleigh—all private banks, each with branches elsewhere,[5] and each with the state as a large stockholder.  Their methods of operation had caused a fierce conflict between creditor and debtor classes and their respective sympathizers.  As was to be expected, the former constituted the conservative political group which favored the banks, and the latter, the so-called radicals, who were against them.  Contention between the two groups had become so heated that it threatened to undermine confidence in privately owned banks in North Carolina.  The legislature even appointed a Joint Select Committee of eighteen members, with Robert Potter as chairman, to investigate the matter.

Swaim had returned to North Carolina just in time to observe the controversy at its height while this investigation was under way.  A brief summary of what took place inside the legislative halls will explain what he meant when he referred to "embarrassment created in our financial concerns."

During the session of 1828-1829, Potter's committee, reflecting the division in public opinion, submitted majority and minority reports, both of which were printed in the Greensboro paper.  The majority, with George Spruill as leader, was concerned largely with the immediate problem.  In his report, Spruill admitted that bank officials had taken unauthorized liberties, which he said seemed harmless and for the best interest of the public, and recommended that the banks be compelled to "pay specie on demand for their notes," a policy abandoned in the state in 1819.  The minority, with Potter as leader, dug deeper into the matter, charging that the charters of these several banks had been willfully disregarded and grossly violated, and recommended that the attorney general of the state institute proceedings against them.[6]

As background evidence for the accusations, the minority's report contained the following information: Whereas the capital stock of the Cape Fear and New Bern Banks was to be paid in gold or silver, these banks soon managed to get possession of nearly all the paper money which had been issued on the faith of the state, and which, being at the time a legal tender, enabled them to evade demands for specie. When in 1814 their charters were extended and they were authorized to increase their respective capital to $800,000—New Bern adding $575,000 and Cape Fear $525,000—it appeared that the whole of this additional amount was manufactured by the banks themselves. Moreover, in many instances, favored individuals were permitted to acquire stock by merely signing their names and putting their notes in the bank, without advancing a single dollar of actual capital. It followed that the whole amount of the interest drawn from the people, on the loans made on this fictitious capital, was a foul and illegal extortion; for by the use of their notes which intrinsically were of no value at all, the stockholders of the two banks had drawn from the people by way of interest thousands and thousands of dollars.[7]

On the State Bank of North Carolina at Raleigh, the minority report stated that its charter directed books to be opened to receive subscriptions, three fourths of which was to be paid in gold and silver, and one fourth in currency issued on the faith of the state. The bank began operation in 1810, however, before the authorized amount had been paid in specie. Thus, at a time when they had in circulation nearly twelve dollars in notes for every dollar of specie in their vaults, and when most obviously they were unable to redeem their notes with specie, they purchased the notes from the holders by the sale of stock which the directors created by the mere act of subscription. The minority committee conceived such practices to have been "a most flagrant and fraudulent violation of their charter."[8]

In 1819 the three banks had entered an agreement not to pay specie, and the minority committee reported that a "scene of extortion and usury ensued, which had no parallel in the annals of avarice—the strange spectacle of monied institutions exacting specie in exchange for the notes, which they themselves refused to redeem in specie."[9]

Furthermore, the minority report pointed out that through various manipulations, the interest collected by these banks had sometimes reached twenty-six per cent. In conclusion, it noted that the people of North Carolina had already paid into the banks a total profit of about $4,000,000 on their stock—of which three fourths had been manufactured by the banks themselves in a fictitious and fraudulent manner; that they had already paid this immense sum, exceeding four times the amount of actual capital stock ever paid into the banks according to law, and that they still owed these banks on notes more than $5,000,000, about four times the amount of the whole circulating medium of the state.[10]

Having made this list of accusations, the minority of the committee submitted a bill, known as "Potter's Bill," which requested that the General Assembly direct the attorney general forthwith to institute in the State Supreme Court a judiciary inquiry into the conduct of the banks; and if in this procedure the banks should be found guilty of violations, the court should take over their accounts and hold them for further order of the court or the legislature. Meanwhile redemption of the notes and debts of the institutions should be guaranteed by the state.

Whether to adopt the majority or minority report led to one of the memorable debates in the legislature of North Carolina. The ablest speakers took part in the arguments, employing both eloquence and ingenuity. Those who defended the banks admitted that spurious methods had been practiced, but they forcefully contended that the financial institutions had been driven to such actions because of popular demands for additional currency and

207

because representatives of the people in the General Assembly had forced an increase of capital stock against the directors' protests. Moreover, they said that the amended charters of the banks of New Bern and Cape Fear did not require that specie be paid for the new stock and that paper subscriptions made to the State Bank were necessary, for at that time the other banks had a monopoly on the specie in the state. Thus expediency rather than a desire to defraud, they said, caused their violation of sound banking. And they gave explanations which made appear less objectionable some of the other dealings which the minority of the committee had condemned.

Despite the able defense of the banks, sentiment in the General Assembly remained almost equally divided on the subject. Potter, in the hope of making a wider appeal, declared that the State Bank had been the greatest offender, and modified his bill so as to remove the Bank of Cape Fear and the Bank of New Bern from the contest. When votes were cast in the House of Commons, after the first and second readings of Potter's Bill they showed, respectively, 66 for, 54 against, and 62 for, 54 against its adoption. On the third reading, 59 voted for and 58 against its adoption.[11] Speaker of the House, Thomas Settle, Sr., desiring to spare the banks an open inspection, exercised his right of voting, cast his ballot against the bill, produced a tie, and declared the bill rejected for lack of majority support. Following this action, Swaim, under the name of POLYDORE, said, "The legislature in chartering the Banks, produced a hideously rapacious monster, which forthwith sprang into enormous magnitude, refusing control; and from the contemplation of which the stoutest hearts recoiled."

The recommendation of the majority of the committee to pay off obligations in specie was taken care of in the process of liquidation of the banks which followed.

After this battle was over, in writing for the *Greensborough Patriot*, staunch old farmer Jonathan Parker, who had sat in the legislative halls of his state longer than any other man of his day, allowed that the bank situation caused the greatest excitement of any in the session. "It was a hard trial . . . the General Assembly had hitherto been duped by whitewashed reports . . . [the findings] were worse than had been anticipated . . . [the bank officials] have speculated rather too long already, and if wise measures are not speedily pursued will ruin the state."[12]

With the banks saved from judicial proceedings, the minority group was soon drawn into another battle when the banks asked for an extension of their charters from 1835 to 1838. Under the caption "OUT OF THE FRYING PAN INTO THE FIRE," Swaim gave his opinion of the situation. "Our readers are already apprized of the fact that the Legislature, at its last session, in the overflowing of their 'abundant loving kindness' towards the people, the whole people, and nothing but the pepole, have condescended to extend the charters of the several banks from 1835 to 1838! It would stretch the powers of conception in twain, to imagine a more consumately ridiculous 'come off,' than we find in the face of the act providing for this extension. The preamble of the Act sets forth, in *honeyed* strains, the out-pouring sympathy felt by the Legislature for those of their constituents who might have the misfortune to be involved in debt to the Banks; but the body of the law shows that a *large* majority of the Legislature were either looking one way and trotting the other, or else that they were gulled into an unenviable state of survile favoritism, by the all-subduing influence of a moneyed aristocracy.

"The preamble very *plausibly* represents the object of the extension, to be the means of enabling the Banks to wind up their concerns without oppressing the people. If this be the *real* object, why did they not strike the Banks (together with their long catalogue of claims against the people) from existence at once, and thus save the people from ruin, and punish these corporations for violating their charters? We anticipate the objection to this, however, 'that if the Banks are blown to the moon, the value of their paper currency will follow them, and we shall be left without a circulating medium.' To this it *might* be replied—'dissolve their corporate powers and continue their corporate responsibilities— make their property responsible for the redemption of the notes

209

with which they have fraudulently inundated the country.' This
will be feeding them with the fruit of their own doing; and what
objection can they have, to be dealt with as they have dealt with
others? We anticipate a castigation for this sentiment, from somebody,—we don't know who—nor we don't care."[13]

While Swaim was thus reporting the current bank news and
expressing his editorial opinion, his "contributor," POLYDORE,
was carefully preparing an explanation of how all this financial
trouble had developed in the state. Entitled "NORTH-CAROLINA,
No. VIII," with the subtitle "The Banks," it was one of a series of
chapters on North Carolina history which was published in the
*Greensborough Patriot* in order to give its readers information
on subjects that were discussed in the paper.[14] Swaim saw to it
that his patrons were told what had been, what was, and what he
thought might be. And upon many occasions, POLYDORE was
an able assistant in giving this information, as he did now in connection with the banks.

With regard to the bank question at this time, prevailing
conditions having been summarized in legislative reports, POLY-
DORE concentrated on historical background. He explained that
soon after banks were chartered a great number of influential men
became stockholders and a still greater number became bank
debtors. "The stockholders were tempted to surpass the limits
of their charters for the sake of deriving large dividends from their
investments. The Bank debtors were induced to favor the Banks,
for the fancied benefit of indulgence, which rendered the future
downfall and disgrace more inevitable and complete from having
fluttered awhile in borrowed feathers." This situation was particularly true after the War of 1812 which was followed by an
"era of good feeling." "The overflowing abundance of money, and
the ease of acquiring it, introduced general extravagance," POLY-
DORE noted. "The unexampled emoluments of trade, produced
a universal spirit of speculation. The cheapness of every article
of clothing, introduced a taste for show in the ornaments of dress."[15]

Meantime men of smaller fortunes became indebted to the bank debtors. "The moment a man becomes *deeply indebted*, he becomes a *cowering slave*. If the Banks are in any way pressed upon, necessity, as they say, will compel them to press upon those who are their debtors;" POLYDORE continued, "and if those indebted to the Banks are compelled to pay, the like necessity will compel them to press their debtors. Thus is produced a vast dependence, by which the Banks have been enabled to maintain their ascendency over the Legislature."[16]

"The inquiry naturally offers itself," he questioned, "which deserves the most unqualified censure, the Banking Incorporations for surpassing the provisions of their charters, or the State Legislature for suffering them to do it? or may not these bodies be so interlinked, and, in some way, identified, as that, to censure the one, will be to condemn the other? This appears to be the easier and more probable way of accounting for the management of these concerns. Otherwise, I should unhesitatingly give it as my opinion, that the Legislature merits the greater share of the blame. The Banks are but a creature of the Legislature. They were spoken into existence by that body, and the moment they transcended the condition of their birth, they were virtually dead; nothing but a legal investigation being necessary to sink them into utter annihilation. This investigation the Legislature should have procured to be made. But the Legislature either suffered itself to be deceived by the artifices of *these unnatural creatures*, or it winked at their fraudulent proceedings. To suppose the Legislature deceived, is to suppose it a composition of imbecility; for it was from time to time warned. To suppose its connivance, is to suppose it a mass of corruption; for no other conclusion is rational. Now if I knew which was the less disparagement from the character of a Legislature, imbecility, or corruption, I would, in so extreme a case, incline in my judgments, to the side of charity."[17]

Granting, then, that both the banks and the legislature were to blame for the shocking financial predicament, POLYDORE further held that one of the worst features of the bank situation was its influence over elections. He claimed that a man deeply indebted forthwith became "a cowering slave;" and thereafter it was an easy matter to direct his vote toward the side of his creditor. "I will leave my reader the easy task of drawing his own inference, concerning the facility of converting this servile dependence into an instrument of intrigue," POLYDORE warned.

"I have not the desire, had I the ability, to conjure up a tempest;" he continued, "but I can say to my fellow-citizens, behold! a portentous cloud is lowering, in our horizon, which has already given signs of being fraught with deleterious vapours, and threatens to inundate us with universal ruin. If we have one particle of energy remaining, let us be on the alert. . . . . Whilst we wish and demand no more than justice, to rest satisfied with less would be to act with unfaithfulness to the public weal. The subject deserves to be well understood, and vigorously acted on. . . .

"Let us for once arouse, and stand to our post.

POLYDORE."[18]

As may be seen from PLYDORE's piece, legislative debates on the subject did not allay the disturbed popular feeling concerning money. There was an increasing demand that new banks be organized to take over as soon as the charters of the old ones expired, and since the 1823-1824 session, bills for a state-owned bank had been introduced and defeated. In 1830, because the North Carolina Senate sent the bill for a state-owned bank to the House of Commons with some spaces blank, the two houses began "cavilling," as Swaim said he supposed for he purpose of killing the bill by delaying it. "When will they Legislate according to the maxims of common sense," he exclaimed, "and not according to the suggestions of Logical *non sense?*"[19]

Many people were impatient; and they voiced such sentiments as did a contributor to the *Greensborough Patriot* who, signing himself "A VOTER," wrote: "The time, I think, has nearly arrived for the *free men* of North-Carolina to say, whether they will continue to submit to such an unjustifiable imposition, as our present

*Above,* first general hospital in North Carolina, showing Dr. David Worth's home, office (right), and cabins (left), all used for patients. *Below,* birthplace of William Sydney Porter (O. Henry) near Polecat Creek.

*Upper left,* Abiah Shirley (Mrs. William) Swaim, grandmother of O. Henry. *Upper right,* William Sydney Porter (O. Henry). *Lower left,* Dr. Algernon Sidney Porter, father of O. Henry. *Lower right,* Mary Jane Virginia Swaim (Mrs. Algernon Sidney) Porter, mother of O. Henry. There is no known photograph of William Swaim.

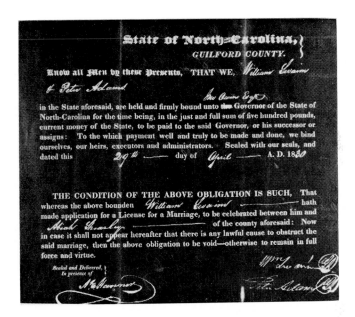

*Above,* marriage contract of William Swaim and Abiah Shirley (Shearley). *Below,* Sherwood House, 426 West Gaston Street, the first home of the William Swaims.

Friends of Swaim. *Upper, left to right,* Judge Archibald D. Murphey, Lyndon Swaim, and Henry Humphreys. *Center,* Governor John M. Morehead. *Lower, left to right,* the Reverend Peter Doub, Governor Jonathan Worth, and Peter Adams.

*Above,* Mount Hecla Steam Cotton Mill, as it appeared on Henry Humphreys' scrip. *Below,* Blandwood, 447 West Washington Street, the home of Governor John M. Morehead, Swaim's lawyer and political co-worker.

William Swaim's desk. With only candles for a light and a goose quill for a pen, from this desk he edited the *Greensborough Patriot*.

Ordered, that the treasurer pay Carroll & Worth $15.00 for
repairs done to the market-house.
Ordered that the treasurer pay David Woodburn 75 cents for
making two well buckets.
Ordered, that the treasurer pay Larry Brown $6.00 for re-
pairing and cleaning out the wells, at sundry times,
up to this date.
Ordered, That the present Secretary, William Swaim, make
out a list of taxes due for this year, and give it
to the officer of police, who is hereby directed to collect
the same, forthwith, and pay it over to the treasurer.
Adjourned.
William Swaim, Sec.

Greensborough Dec. 17th 1838.
The list of Taxable property, and Taxables was made out, according
to the above order; and this morning handed to the Town
Constable, together with the order for immediate collection.
William Swaim Sec.

*Above*, sample of Swaim's handwriting, taken from minutes he wrote while Secretary and acting Constable of the Town of Greensboro. *Below*, sketch of a gig similar to the one owned by William Swaim.

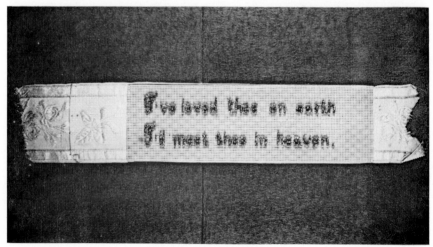

*Above,* sideboard from a suite given by William Swaim to his bride, Abiah Shirley, in 1830. *Below,* Mrs. William Swaim's bookmark.

banking institutions have been rendered; or whether they will have a Bank created and settled on the more broad and solid basis of the commonwealth?"[20]

When nothing came of the state-owned bank bill in 1830, Swaim turned the mirror of publicity so that legislators might see themselves as others saw them. "Stupidity itself will assent to the position that something ought to have been done during the past session of the Legislature, besides making speeches," he declared. "Our Legislature is postively ten years in the rear of public opinion. Some towering spirits may be found in that body; but they are like angel's visits—'few and far between.' Every succeeding session becomes less determinate. The people have looked in vain for a reformation of their moneyed concerns. The [legislators] have become completely subjected to the relentless dominion of Bank influence. This influence exerts itself, more or less, through every department of society. Whether all the printers in the State are bank debtors, whether they have been furnished with a little of the 'wherewith' to hold their peace, or whether the materials of their composition are so yielding as to be moddled according to the wishes of money made nabobs, it seems difficult to determine; but certain we are, that 'something is rotten in Denmark.' Some editors are silent as the mansions of the dead upon the subject, some go all the way round every thing to get to nothing, and leave the subject where they found it—in the dark, while others come out in the open face of day, and manfully defend that system of consummate fraud and knavery so long practiced with impunity by the banking institutions of our country. . . .

"The Legislature may spend 8 days in settling a mere quibble; and the Banks themselves endeavor to fortify their precarious foundations by a lavish distribution of bribes; but the day of their doom draweth nigh, and the wickedness of their ways will yet be visited upon them. Let them take heed!"[21]

Desultory talk about the state of finances dragged on. Swaim announced almost every week some step, some move, some plan in connection with the winding up of business in the three banks whose charters were about to expire. Through him the people of western North Carolina had a voice that was being heard. Even though they did not know much about the general subject of banking, they knew when money jingled in their pockets, and they were greatly encouraged that they had a newspaper behind them that demanded fair play in money matters. The legislature also realized the influence of this newspaper. It knew it had a critic who would probe to the core of its every action.[22]

Meanwhile, Swaim remembered to publish his customary history of the subject under considration, and his brief summary on banks makes interesting reading. "Banks were first established by the Lombard Jews in Italy, [in] 808," he wrote, "the name taken from *Banca*, a bench—benches having been erected in the market-place for the exchange of money &c." He then mentioned famous banks that had been established over the world, among which he listed the Bank of the United States (1791) and the Second Bank of the United States (1816).[23]

Time was drawing near for the legislative session of 1832-1833. Year after year the movement for a state-owned bank had been defeated. The old State Bank was winding up its business and soon would be ready to close, a fact which made more urgent than ever provision for a bank to take its place. When they convened in November, 1832, Swaim let the legislators know what was expected of them. "The establishment of a bank by which the state may be furnished with a sound currency for all the purposes of commerce, we think will not—cannot be neglected by the present session. . . . Let not conflicting views and interests prevent the establishment of a bank *of some kind*. Let all the members unite upon the best plan they can digest, and give us a bank, *at all events*."[24] Two weeks later he again reminded them that "In this subject, of all others, the state is, at this time, the most deeply interested. All classes in the community are looking to this session for relief from the thickly gathering gloom that over-hangs our country."[25]

Six bank bills were introduced at that session, and the one finally adopted provided for a Bank of North Carolina whose officers, after the first year, would be elected by the legislature. From the outset, Swaim, who understood the people of the state, doubted that this bank plan would meet with success. Moreover, he said as much, first by suggestion and finally by positive statement. Almost immediately he intimated that some future legislature would have to take the matter in hand. In February, 1833, he wrote: "We cannot help believing, that except the new Bank (Books of Subscription for which are at present open in the several towns of the state) go into operation; or some other be established by a future Legislature, before the whole of the demands of the present closing Banks upon our citizens be satisfied, money will become a distressingly scarce article in the state."[26]

By May of that year, Swaim was emphatic in his insistence that a new bank would have to come from some future legislature. The requisite sum for establishing the Bank of North Carolina had not been subscribed. Governor David L. Swain issued a proclamation, directing that books be reopened for subscriptions. To this Swaim commented that "The Governor is doing his duty according to act of assembly; otherwise he might have spared the trouble of issuing this second proclamation—for everybody knows, by this time, that the stock will never be taken. Though it was *proclaimed* in the Raleigh papers that stock had been *liberally* taken in that place: and though 'the man what prints' in Milton, said the same for that place;—*yet the first dollar has never yet been subscribed,* and we fear never will be!"[27]

Swaim was right. The capitalists of North Carolina reacted as capitalists of any other state would have acted: they would not be parties to a banking institution whose officers were elected by the legislature. Reporting the legislative session of 1833-1834, he could supply proof of his contention, for other and different efforts were made by the legislature to relieve the financial crisis. This was accomplished through the chartering of a "Bank of the State of North Carolina," the renewal of the charter of the Bank of Cape Fear, and the chartering of the "Merchants Bank of the Town of Newbern" and the "Albemarle Bank in the Town of Edenton."[28]

The charter of a Bank of the State of North Carolina proved to be more accetable than that of its immediate predecessor, for it provided that of its ten officers four only should be appointed by the state with the state treasurer as *ex officio* member. Gleefully Swaim quoted the *Raleigh Register*: " 'The opinion seems to be generally entertained that the Charter is an excellent one, and that it is so, is evidenced by the fact, that Capitalists of other states, are availing themselves of its provisions.' "[29] He then urged local people to take stock so that it would be what it purported to be, a "Bank of the State of North-Carolina."

Even with these provisions for a number of new state banking institutions, it still remained for supporters of both conservative and radical banking policies to watch, as Swaim would say, "with a lynx-eyed vigilance," the conduct and administration of banks in North Carolina. It appeared that with such tireless scrutiny the people at last might have a satisfactory circulating medium.

While all these local bank affairs were rocking the state, Swaim also called attention to financial problems on the national level. When Andrew Jackson became President of the United States in 1829, he declared war upon the Second Bank of the United States which had been chartered in 1816 and was scheduled to expire in 1836. He said that this institution was contrary to the national constitution; for it gave special privileges to the rich, but was against the interests of the plain people.[30] The Greensboro editor reported in 1830 that "The stock of this Bank fell, at New York, from 125¼ to 120, immediately on the receipt of the President's Message. It has not recovered from the shock. . . . There is a report that extensive speculations were made in anticipation of the message!"[31]

In spite of Jackson's known opposition, however, Congress in 1832 passed a bill for renewing the charter on its expiration. This was definitely a political move, coming as it did about the time for another presidential election; for the main supporters of the bill thought the President would not dare oppose it, lest such action might lose votes for him, or his party. Meanwhile Jackson had made his position clear to a friend and Swaim so informed his readers. He quoted Jackson as saying: " 'Sir, I have entered for the presidential heat upon the principle of opposition to that Bank; and I mean that the people shall decide whether they will have Jackson and no Bank, or the Bank and no Jackson.' "[32] In July, 1832, Jackson vetoed the bill to renew the charter of the Second Bank of the United States.

The veto came as a great shock. The President's position was esspecially difficult to understand since the United States Government before it established a bank had lost by its deposits in local banks nearly half a million dollars. Through a reprint from the *Raleigh Register* Swaim released information to the effect that since the establishment of the national bank, out of the $440,000,-000 deposited by the government at various times, not one cent had been lost. " 'And yet, those in authority seem bent on its destruction. The property of the bank, as is shewn by a report recently made to congress, exceeds the whole amount of demands against it by $43,058,143—and yet the President would withdraw the public funds from its vaults, on the ground of it being an unsafe depository! It has frequently been remarked, that "prejudice is strong as death, and narrow as the grave"—and never did there exist a stronger illustration of its truth than the hostility manifested towards this institution by General Jackson.' "[33]

To this opinion Swaim added that "Nothing the present executive has ever done has so effectually roused the people as the late nullification of the bill for renewing, in a modified form, the charter of the bank of the United States. He has, as we predicted, emphatically nullified *himself*. He has long been attempting to stand astride of two stools; but this *jostle* has prostrated him between them."[34]

A few days before Congress met in 1832, the Bank's stock fell from 115 to 110. At the time, this drop was not understood, but it became very clear when Swaim later explained that "it is now confidently stated, that it was owing to some person or persons being favored beforehand with a knowledge of what the message would contain on the subject. On the receipt of the message, nearly two millions of the stock were sold at 104½ to 105."[35]

The *Greensborough Patriot* carried President Jackson's Veto Message in full, covering the front pages and half of the second of two issues. Introducing it with a contempt seldom shown the least petty county officer, Swaim briefly remarked, "We commence, this week, the publication of the message of President Jackson on returning the United States Bank Charter Bill. The document is not worth one fourth part of the space it occupies; but we have thought proper to publish it entire—that its several parts may condemn the whole."[36]

At the conclusion of the veto message, Swaim observed that much of the President's "reasoning is flimsy and fallacious, and many of his deductions are drawn from false premises. But even if his premises had been correct, his inferences as clear as the sun at noon-day, and his objections, whether constitutional or otherwise, as permanent as the mountain which sustained Noah's Ark after the flood—they would not save the several states composing the Union, and particularly North Carolina, from bankruptcy, and ruin, if the whole concerns of this mighty institution should be wound up in the short period of three years. . . .

"The most unpleasant aspect in which the subject can be contemplated, is, that the United States' bank and the [North Carolina] banks, will be compelled *simultaneously*, to wind up their business. The charter of the former extends to the 3rd of March 1836, and from that time it is allowed two years to close its business. The charters of the latter extend to January 1st, 1835, with three years further to wind up. So that the whole must be closed, almost at the same moment. Without the application of some remedy, this would produce unheard of embarrassments in the monied operations of the people of the state;—not the merchants only, but every individual, of whatever class or occupation, will feel its ruinous influence."[37]

The veto had supporters and opponents, and Swaim printed

the opinions of both. In his own inimitable fashion, he showed the seriousness of the situation by giving the conflicting opinions of two unidentified citizens of the United States, as follows: "LOGIC! We here cite two parallel passages, as samples of the new logic employed in the veto message; they show how to take a luminous view of both sides of the subject, by reasoning two ways at once. [Said one], 'We have in the result of our legislation, arrayed section against section, interest against interest, and man against man, in a FEARFUL *commotion,* which threatens to *shake the foundations* of our Union.' [Said the other], 'In the difficulties which surround, and the dangers which threaten our institutions, there is cause for *neither* DISMAY nor ALARM!' "[38]

Under the headline "CROCKETT OUT DONE," Swaim quoted still another version as coming from a stump speech oration of a candidate for public office. Speaking of the President's bank veto he said: " 'If the President should Veto the New Testament and destroy the ordinance of Baptism and the Lord's Supper, there [are] persons who would still shout that they saw through him the dawning of a glorious mill[en]nium.' "[39]

While Jackson was going ahead with definite plans for closing the Second Bank of the United States, there were some who held on to the hope that he would reconsider and approve its recharter. In support of this opinion, Swaim wrote that "The impression seems to be gaining ground that the Bank of the United States will again be re-chartered, though no one can certainly foresee the manner in which it is to be effected. Perhaps the belief springs from a conviction that its continuance is indispensable to the prosperity of the nation, and that therefore public opinion will sustain it. If the Institution should be destroyed, we cannot see how the National Revenue is to be colleced, or public funds transferred from one extremity of the Union to the other, without the certainty of great loss, to say nothing of the absolute benefits which it confers on the community at large, or of its efficiency in maintaining a sound and uniform currency."[40]

Within a short time Swaim reported Jackson's way out of this dilemma. At a cabinet meeting, the President, having listened to several proposals for action, tersely stated that he had already decided what to do. With that announcement, he requested William J. Duane, Secretary of the Treasury, to sign the circular to the officers of the customs, directing the removal of the deposits. Secretary Duane replied that he had duly considered the subject in all its bearings, and he could not consent to the issuing of any such orders; "whereupon the President, who, as his fl[a]tterers tell him, 'was born to command,' turned from his minister of finance with a cloudy brow, and directing his eyes to the attorney general, said— Mr. Taney, *I appoint you as Secretary of the Treasury.* There was no mistake in this delicate insinuation—Mr. Duane was no longer Secretary of the Treasury—Oliver Cromwell could not have done it in better style."[41]

Swaim's prediction of financial turmoil was soon to come true, By the middle of December, 1832, the *National Gazette* numbered the broken state banks in the Union at ninety-seven, and that did not include all the states. By 1834 Swaim wrote that "petitions, and memorials, loud and long are continually pouring into both houses of congress, setting forth the pecuniary distress of the country, too plain to be misunderstood. Not unfrequently ten or fifteen of these memorials, signed by thousands, are presented in a single day; and yet the executive turns a deaf ear to all these complaints; and congress, insead of acting efficiently to relieve the wants of the people, as they might do, are yet harping away upon the subject, without any prospects of coming to a termination, before fall, if ever, 'God save the republic!!' "[42]

Swaim did not profess to have solutions for all the banking problems of the state and the nation. He did try, however, through his printed pages to keep his readers aware of develpoments during this period of financial turmoil. He kept them informed on the actual termination of the Second Bank of the United States, the rise and fall of bank stock, the failures of banks in other states, the per capita amount of specie in circulation in the United States, the reports of the different North Carolina banks, and various other items of financial news. He hoped, by his honest reporting and dissemination of information on the subject of general finance, to help the people of the country to come to intelligent decisions in the matter.

# X

## FOR SOCIAL JUSTICE

*" 'What a stupendous, what an incomprehensible machine is man! who can endure toil, famine, stripes, imprisonment, and death itself, in vindication of his own liberty, and the next moment be deaf to all those motives whose power supported him through his trial & inflict on his fellow man a bondage, one hour of which is fraught with more misery than ages of that which he rose in rebellion to oppose.' "*[1]

The antislavery influence which surrounded William Swaim as he grew to manhood in Centre Community was immediately reflected in his newspaper, for in his first *Greensborough Patriot* editorial he took an unequivocal stand against the institution of slavery. At the same time he made very clear that he would not support irresponsible abolitionism. "Candour compels us," he affirmed, "to say that all those institutions which have been organized for the purpose of bettering the conditions of Africa's injured children, and mitigating the growing evils of slavery in the Southern Portion of our Union, so far as we may conceive them calculated to consummate these desirable objects shall have our undivided support; but we shall advocate no measures that may have a tendancy to infringe upon the *'Rights of private property.'* "[2]

This bold and unprecedented antislavery attitude of a North Carolina newspaper editor was indeed daring. Although no newspapers in the state earnestly supported slavery, few championed the antislavery cause. With its main purpose of promoting gradual emancipation, the General Association of the Manumission Society of North Carolina had been organized in 1816. Members of the organization hoped to establish better social, economic, and political conditions for Negroes and thus to prepare them for the proper use of their freedom when it came. One aim of the society was to widen its influence by getting its views before the public through newspapers; but it had been unsuccessful in this at first, as is evidenced by the following reply to a member from Joseph Gales, Editor of the *Raleigh Register* which was the strongest newspaper in the state at that time:

> Dr Sir—I recd by a young man who passed thro' this place some days ago an Oration delivered before your Manumission Society, with a Request, that it might be inserted in the Register, Star, and Menerva. I am not willing to insert it in the Register, it is on a subject which the people of this State will not bear discussed with temper at present, it might also produce consequences of a direful kind by getting into the hands of Slaves, for many of them can read—I wish with you, that an end could be put to Slavery, but it will be of no use to attack the people's prejudices directly in the face, it must be brought about by slow, but gradual means—if you wish the copy returned say so.
>
> Yours respectf—
>
> J. O. GALES[3]

Raleigh, Septr 6th 1816

Gales' attitude was largely typical of the North Carolina press. Though he relented a little in the 1820's, he became proslavery in the 1830's.[4]

On the other hand, when Swaim set up his *Greensborough Patriot* it was distinguished from the outset for his stand against slavery.[5] Before he became owner of the Greensboro paper in 1829, it had had no editorial policy in favor of emancipation, but occasionally it had carried reports of the Manumission Society meetings. Moreover, in the 1820's some other North Carolina papers had become more tolerant of antislavery sentiment. When a Virginia town on July 4, 1829, had offered a toast to *"Emancipation and Colonization—dictated alike by humanity and expediency,"* Swaim wrote that "the people are turning their attention more and *more,* towards this all important subject. Twenty years ago such

a toast could not, or *would* not have been published in this state;
but it is *now* drank with applause, and published in more prints
than one! and, so far as we have learned, the publishers have not
had their heads struck off yet!!"[6]

The *Greensborough Patriot,* however, was the most avowed
advocate of the antislavery cause in North Carolina, and Historian
R. D. W. Connor wrote that its editor, William Swaim, "was
distinguished by his bold and aggressive stand against slavery; his
paper was popularly regarded as the unofficial organ of the North
Carolina Manumission Society."[7]  Although the eastern section of
North Carolina had by far the larger slave population, there were
slaves in the western section.  And although the western section
was far more antislavery, there were some people of the East who
favored emancipation, for example, Judge William Gaston of Craven
County.[8]  Generally speaking, however, views concerning slavery
finally drifted into the state's familiar pattern of East versus West.
Nevertheless, Swaim offered the pages of his paper to everyone,
East and West, for arguing the subject.  "Then why not discuss it
freely, fairly and extensively," he questioned, "in order that the
people may view it in all its bearings, and dispose of it according
to the suggestions of their collected wisdom?"

Scott observed that Swaim was a man of no ordinary ability and
he had "returned to his native state, fully determined to exert his
influence at whatever business he engaged, on the side of universal
freedom.  He was honest in his opinion as to slavery and had
strong faith in its ultimate extermination.  About this time he
penned, in his private correspondence, this prophetic paragraph:
'America will yet shake off that fatal incubus, which has so long
palsied her energies,—she will yet say to the friendless negro:
Let thy body stand redeemed and disenthralled from the shackles
of slavery, and let thy soul walk abroad in its Majesty!  Great
events are yet slumbering in the womb of futurity!  We know not
what a day may bring forth!' "[9]

This "fiery crusader for freedom and humanity," when his paper
was about one month old, under the heading of "DECLARATION

OF INDEPENDENCE," wrote the following antislavery appeal: "Fifty-three years ago this day [July 4, 1829] the most illustrious body of statemen that ever assembled under Heaven, declared to a listening world, that the thirteen colonies . . . were 'Free Sovereign and Independent States.' At the sound of this declaration, every American heart responded, Amen! and the proud Monarch of three Kingdoms trembled upon his tottering throne! This declaration, which jeopardised the lives, liberties and fortunes of those who signed it, and of those whom they represented, was based upon the broad principle 'That all men are *created equal*, and endowed by their Creator with the *right* of pursuing *life, liberty* and *happiness.*' Who, after reading these everlasting truths, and seeing them hung in gilted frames throughout the United States— after witnessing the joyous enthusiasm that burns in the American heart . . . after reading a register of orphan's cries and widow's tears produced in their defence—after viewing, with an eye of fancy, the thousands of our kindred, slaughtered like dogs for supporting them—after beholding . . . old soldiers . . . who exposed their almost naked bodies to the whizzing balls of a merciless British soldiery, that their descendents might be FREE—we say who, after all this mass of concurrent testimony, staring him full in the face, would believe for a moment that a SLAVE would be permitted to breathe in this 'LAND OF THE FREE, AND HOME OF THE BRAVE'? . . .

"Our object is not to reproach nor to irritate—but to pursuade our fellow citizens not to permit less important things to divert their attention from a question which, it has justly been said, is 'Big with the fate of this Union!'" A little later the *Greensborough Patriot* again called attention to this subject: "Slavery! what a solecism in a free government! Absolute slavery! How deplorable the condition of him who is under the absolute control of another! Hereditary slavery! It is not enough that the unhappy slave must drag the galling chain through life, he is destined to see it riveted to his posterity."[10]

Such a courageous avowal shocked some of Swaim's more

reserved readers. He had established at the beginning of his editorship a policy of presenting opinions of various readers on all sides of each public issue, and communications to the paper were usually signed with such pseudonyms as "Monitor," "Scrutinizer," or "Enquirer." Monitor responded immediately to Swaim's invitation to write for the paper and indicated that he had read every word of the first edition of the *Greensborough Patriot* and liked it very much, but that he hastened to warn the editor against assailing the "highly sensitive" subject of slavery. "I am an enemy to the *principle* of slavery myself, . . . " he stated, but "Upon the whole, I think it would be better for your individual interest, and perhaps nearly as well for the community, if you would close your columns absolutely, against all interference with it, or any of its concomitants. . . . The people are so sensitive upon even the most distant allusion to the subject, that it might, and probably would, check the circulation of your paper, and thus operate against its usefulness, to meddle with it at all."[11]

In the second edition of his paper, Swaim published Monitor's communication with an appropriate expression of appreciation for the friendly advice. Then he added: "Thus far, and no farther, can we walk hand in hand with our correspondent; but when he touches, though not with a 'rude and unskillful hand; that *string* which vibrates terrible discord,' we cannot join the *chorus*. He says he regards the existence of a coloured population in vassalage among us, 'as the greatest calamity that ever Divine Providence permitted to visit the earth,' and yet would prevail upon us to close our columns against its discussion! . . . We conclude by giving our friends to understand that we *will not* be *admonished* from a straight-forward course—at least as *straight* as our obscured and flickering vision can *direct us*."[12]

Typical of the policy of presenting opposite views expressed by various patrons of the paper was the following answer of Scrutinizer to the advice of Monitor: "Without much preamble I can at once inform 'Monitor' that on the question [slavery], I am as far from his opinion, if that be, in truth, his genuine sentiments, as the east is from the west; and while he professes to have his eyes so widely open, as to view *slavery* 'as the sorest evil that ever Divine Providence permitted to visit our world,' I do deeply regret that the *beam* is not still further removed, so that he could see the great need there is for people to enquire more into . . . the consequences of this corroding evil. . . . Indeed, I cannot see how he . . . considers slavery as the greatest scourge of the nation, and yet desires all tongues to be mute, and all hands to be motionless in endeavoring to avert impending destruction. These things do not coalesce."[13]

Scrutinizer had something more to say. He told Monitor that if he expected tacitly to wait around for a mighty storm of vengeance from heaven to pour down upon the heads of slaveholders and through plagues of flies, mosquitoes, scorpions or some other fatal catastrophe to relieve those in bondage, disappointment would be the likely result. He predicted, however, that if the rigors of oppression were not softened, or if the sin of slavery were not abolished, a mighty distress in some form or other would come upon the people "before even half a century should be rolled away."[14]

About two weeks later Enquirer contributed a constructive thought toward the solution of the problem, when he declared that "if we are alive to our best interests, and the happiness and prosperity of our offspring, we must see it is high time to be aroused to the labour of doing away [with] the wrong; and not to promote any to public honor or proffit, or to the House of Legislation, who are not friendly to its abolition; but only such who, evince they are true patriots, by being willing to aid what they can in saving their country from impending ruin."[15]

Words of plain, outspoken wrath, and happy approval of the readers were thus prominently inserted, and these free expressions of opinions made the paper a powerful voice of the people. Citizens took pride in seeing their beliefs in black and white in a newspaper; and they were aroused by seeing those of others, whether they liked them or not. It would have been an odd person, indeed, who would not have experienced a surge of enthusiasm for one or the other of the two following countrymen who openly blasted away their grudges and appeared in public, perhaps for the first time in their lives. Said a North Carolinian, "You may stop my paper at the end of the present year. I like every part of it exactly well, except the slave question, with which you seem to tinker rather too freely. I admire your independence, but damn your principles, in regard to that matter."

Immediately following, came this message from Fredericksburg, Virginia: "I . . . wish to become a reader of the *Greensborough Patriot*. The avowal of your intention of devoting a portion of your paper to the improvement of that long-neglected, and much injured portion of the inhabitants of our country,—the *colored people,* increases my desire to see your paper. I am particularly well pleased with that sentence in your prospectus, which says:—That your paper shall be in the broad and most unqualified sense of the term—*a friend of the people,* and an unwavering defender of their rights."

And no less thought provoking was Swaim's amused comment on the two opinions, when he said, "If any person doubts the similarity of a printer's condition with that of a 'hen on a hot griddle,' let him read the above and believe."[16] He was pleased, however, to have this frank response, for, believing that ultimately the majority would favor the abolition of slavery, he welcomed open discussions which he hoped would lead to intelligent decisions.

Levi Coffin in his *Reminiscences* wrote that "William Swaim, a young man of rare talent, . . . advocated the manumission of slaves, and though he met with a storm of opposition and was assailed by other papers, he continued his course boldly and independently. He received letters from various parts of the State full of threats and warnings. These he published in his paper, and replied to them in editorials. Many public speakers and writers engaged in discussion with him, but they could not cope with him, and generally retired from the combat much worsted."[17]

One such attack which came from a South Carolina reader will serve to illustrate this point. By way of introduction to the threat, Swaim cleverly wrote that a copy of the *Greensborough Patriot* had been returned to his office, and on it had been written "all about round the margin of our paper like chasing the devil round the stump . . . the following very polite insinuation: 'If the Editor of this sheet had traveled as far south as this paper, he would have learned that such slang and principles as it contains were "no go." Reform your manner, friend [Swaim], or faith keep your paper and your principles to yourself.—Tar and feathers are plenty here, and any man who aims at abolition, under however specious disguise, is entitled to a coat of it, free, gratis, and for nothing.—Look out. Asmoden.' "[18] In good humor Swaim replied, in effect, that if the South Carolinian had hoped to frighten the North Carolinian from his antislavery attitude, the threat had completely missed its target.

In addition to contributions for his paper, Swaim used various methods of keeping the question of slavery always before the public. In articles on the history of slavery, he traced the custom from the middle ages to the practices of his own day. Negro slavery, he said, had been first introduced into America in 1501, by Spanish slaveholders, who emigrated with their Negroes; and a royal edict of Spain had authorized Negro slavery in America in 1503. In a rather lengthy article, he presented different aspects of Negro slavery which had been introduced into Colonial Virginia in 1619, concluding with the fact that in 1820 there were in the United States 233,400 free Negroes and 1,764,833 slaves, many more African slaves than he listed in all other Negro slaveholding countries together.[19]

News about Negroes who had gained their freedom also had a place in the *Greensborough Patriot*. Illustrative of this position, a case which greatly disturbed Swaim came up in the legislature within a few months after he became editor. It concerned an adjustment of the law for electing sheriffs of the state, and the legislature precluded free Negroes from casting their votes in such elections. Under the heading of "SHERIFF BILL," Swaim hurled this dart at the official body: "The bill to vest the right of electing sheriffs in the free *white* men of the State has become a law. A motion was made to strike out the word 'white' in the title, but it was lost 93 to 36. We cannot well see what business that pretty *leetle* word, *white,* has in any part of the bill: We think the Legislature would be detained at least a fortnight in drawing a line of distinction between *white* & colored."[20]   He emphasized his feeling on this matter by saying that if free Negroes were not allowed to vote, then they should not be taxed; for no man, black or white, ought to be taxed without being represented.

Special happenings in connection with enslaved peoples furnished other angles for consideration. The Greensboro paper often carried short notices concerning the slave trade that was being carried on surreptitiously. Despite the fact that protests were being made against it, the date of 1808 having been the deadline for importing slaves into the United States, and despite the fact that some vessels cruising the Atlantic were making an effort to supress the practice, Africans were still being entered.[21]

Nor did Swaim withhold the horrors of the slave trade. Describing the experience of an eye witness at the unloading of a Spanish ship which the English had captured, the *Greensborough Patriot* carried the following insertion: "Such a heart rending sight I never before beheld, nor could I believe that human beings could survive the hardships and cruelties those poor creatures did. [Altogether two hundred and seven, including boys, girls, and adult men and women] were stored away in a place in the hold in the vessel scarcely large enough for one quarter of their number, and that not more than 2½ feet high; . . . they were all entirely naked, and great numbers of them completely crippled by being confined below; . . . when we consider the distressing situation of the poor creatures; . . . it is enough to make any one shudder at the idea. . . . They used to feed them just as they would cattle—about a dozen of them would sit around a dirty tub of boiled rice, which they had twice a day, and about a pint of water each."[22]

In direct contrast to this terrible story, the Greensboro editor held up fine examples of the emancipation of slaves by individual masters. People who had given the question serious thought were aware that the topmost men of the nation had been in favor of freeing the Negro and had done so with their own slaves in their last wills. He cited the *Washington City Chronicle* which affirmed that "Mr. Clay's efforts for oppressed Africa[ns] will be remembered when all the monuments of selfish ambition shall have perished from the earth."[23]  And Swaim announced upon the death of John Randolph of Virginia that this colorful and conspicuous statesman had provided in his will for the emancipation of all his slaves. The aged and infirm were to be cared for during their lifetime and the children were to be supported until they were able to take care of themselves. "This is an act reflecting the highest credit on Mr. Randolph's benevolent feeling and it is with the greatest pleasure we announce it to our readers."[24]

Swaim's most effective reporting on the question of slavery, however, was in connection with the General Association of the Manumission Society of North Carolina, with his paper as its chief spokesman.  John Spencer Basset in his *Anti-Slavery Leaders of North Carolina* wrote that "some of the state newspapers took the side of emancipation. This was noticeably true of the *Greensborough Patriot*, then edited by William Swaim. Here was a man of strong talents and much ability in writing."[25]  Moreover, his positive antislavery convictions at once impressed the Centre branch of the Society, and it sent him, within less than a year after he joined, as a delegate to the semiannual meeting of the General Association, held at Hopewell Meeting House in Randolph County. Within less than two years he was made secretary of the General Association of the Manumission Society of North Carolina, a position which he held from 1826 to 1832. Thus when he became editor of the *Greensborough Patriot* he was already in a key position thoroughly to know and to understand both the institution of slavery and the Society's attitude toward it.[26]

In the *Greensborough Patriot* the General Association of the Manumission Society of North Carolina for the first time was given a medium through which it could publish its proceedings and dispense its doctrines to the public without restraint. The paper carried accounts of various developments in different parts of the world, such as the welfare of freed slaves who had returned to Africa, or had gone elsewhere; the feeling of slaves themselves on slavery; laws concerning slaves in the southern states; and antislavery articles, announcements, and addresses to the General Association of the Manumission Society of North Carolina.

These addresses, one of which sometimes covered several columns on the front page of the *Greensborough Patriot,* were impressively marked with a depth of feeling and a gentle handling of the subject, yet they were very positive and determined in their intentions. A typical one was that of Benjamin Swaim, president of the General Association in 1829. In speaking to representatives from the various branches of the Society, after outlining specific plans for petitions to Congress and the North Carolina legislature on behalf of slaves and urging a more concentrated effort in broadening the work of the Society, he emphasized that the Association must be careful to regulate its course of procedure with a proper mixture of firmness, prudence, and forethought. "Gentlemen, this is no trivial occasion. Let us awaken to a due sense of its momentous importance, . . ." he earnestly entreated. "The fate of many millions of human beings is at stake. The revolutions of time are not more certain than this—that the hour of Negro-Emancipation is fast approaching. It must and will assuredly come. And all that we can do, is, to prepare for its approach, by a timely and gradual improvement of their debased condition . . . Aided by Divine assistance, we may fearlessly encounter all the opposition of our enemies, and confidently stand forth, the advocates of truth and justice, with such unyielding firmness and determined purpose, as no earthly interest, power or prejudice, can successfully resist."[27]

For many years Manumission Societies in North Carolina counties and elsewhere had discussed various plans for gradual emanci-

232

pation; but none of the members had spoken of or seemed to think of immediate and unconditional abolition. Nor had they seriously considered colonization. It is true that under the pressure of the American Colonization Society, for a short while (1817-1824) the North Carolina antislavery organization had changed its name to Manumission and Colonization Society; but when genuinely conscientious members had perceived that some slaveholding members favored making colonization a condition of freedom simply to eliminate what they considered the disturbing influence of freed Negroes upon slaves, North Carolina members dropped "Colonization" from the title. Thereafter, apparently in the belief that all antislavery causes should work together, some members brought colonization up again, but it found no support in the meetings.[28]

While William Swaim was secretary, and his cousin, Benjamin Swaim, was president, the position of North Carolinians on this point was thus clarified: "Although we do not, in a social capacity, recognize either Emigration or Colonization as fundamentally within the sphere of our deliberations, yet they are incidental subjects, which occasionally claim our attention as circumstances justify."[29]

At first Benjamin Lundy, a national antislavery leader, had thought the Colonization Society might serve a good purpose in helping those free Negroes who wished to go to Africa, Canada, or some other place outside the United States; but he never considered colonization as a condition of freedom. When he became more familiar with the ulterior motives which had developed within the Colonization Society as it grew in strength, he became openly hostile to the organization and declared "that its existence had been only productive of evil."[30] And Evan Lewis, Lundy's assistant editor, and forty-five years an opponent of slavery, said he had, "from the commencement, considered the influence of the Colonization Society more injurious to the cause of emancipation than all other causes combined."[31]

Antislavery leaders in North Carolina had no objection to free Negroes going of their own will to any part of the world that was open to them, but to compel them to go as a condition of their freedom was strongly opposed. On colonization, the *Greensborough Patriot* carried this simple statement, "We sincerely hope that the liberality of the American People will become sufficiently extended to enable all the coloured inhabitants of this Country, who may wish to do so, to return to the land of their fathers." Swaim made clear his understanding of this situation by later adding that "All that the Colonization Society *can* remove will be no more than a drop from the bucket."[32]

Furthermore, Swaim's paper carried the reactions of freed Negroes to colonization when they pronounced it as an ill-fated and sinister operation which was radically at war with their vital and dearest interests.[33] In short, Swaim wanted Negroes to be free; and at liberty to leave the country if they wished. He did not wish their freedom to depend upon their leaving.

At a semiannual meeting in March, 1829, the General Association of the Manumission Society of North Carolina took an inventory of itself, concluding that it had not accomplished all it had wished, but that it had done enough to justify its continuance. It recognized that the work it hoped to accomplish might take years. And it lamented the deep-rooted prejudices of some, the ignorance of others, and still more the sordid avarice of many, all of which had to be overcome. To combat these and other attitudes, the organization decided, now that it had an outlet through Swaim's printing establishment, to publish a special address to all branches of the Society and to citizens of North Carolina, urging a concentrated effort to spread information about the organization and to enlist active members. Robert W. Hodson, Amos Weaver, and Benjamin Swaim were appointed to draft the address to be approved by the General Association.[34]

For carrying on the work of the General Association between its semiannual meetings, its chief agency was a Board of Managers, first appointed in 1825, with a membership which varied from three to nine. Its responsibilities were to look after the business of the organization, to draw up petitions, to prepare essays, to act as an advisory group on many important discussions which came before the meetings, and to submit all their actions for approval by the General Association when it convened semiannually. William Swaim, as secretary, was an *ex officio* member of this Board of Managers in 1829-1830; and Amos Weaver and William Reynolds were the other members selected. It was the duty of this three-member board to review the above mentioned address and present it to the General Association for final approval.[35]

The committee appointed to write this particular address was an entire year in preparing it. As mentioned before, the General Association required that the Board of Managers submit to it "the whole of their proceedings . . . to be approved, amended or disposed of as that Body may adjudge expedient."[36] Under that ruling, the committee's address would have been heard at the General Association's semiannual meeting, beginning on March 12, 1830, its first meeting after the work had been completed. It is not known whether or not the address prepared by the committee was ever published, for on March 10, 1830, Swaim apparently on his own, had started publishing an address on slavery in the *Greensborough Patriot;* and when Weaver as chairman of the Board of Managers later released an address as authorized by the General Association of the Manumission Society of North Carolina, it was the same as the one published in the *Greensborough Patriot.* In a small book entitled *An Address to the People of North Carolina, on the Evils of Slavery,* it was published over the signature of "The Friends of Liberty and Equality." It soon became common knowledge, however, that Swaim was the author of the work, which was regarded by some as his best piece of writing.[37]

The *Address* was so highly regarded by the opponents of slavery that about thirty years after its first publication it was reissued. And in 1882 Lyndon Swaim, who followed William Swaim as editor of the *Greensborough Patriot,* received a letter from Daniel R. Goodloe, a newspaper editor of Washington, D. C., with this interesting inquiry: "William Swaim in 1830 published a pamphlet entitled 'An Address to the People of North Carolina on the Evils of Slavery' with mottoes in Latin and English. The imprint is

'William Swaim, Printer, Greensboro, N. C. 1830.' Some twenty-seven or thirty years ago the abolitionists of New York republished, I suppose, a *facsimile* of the original [as similar to the original as could be done], and Mr. Spofford, the librarian of Congress, has procured a copy. He asked me who was the author, as it is a rule with him to give, as far as possible, the name of every author. I should have quoted in the title that it purports to be written and published 'By the Friends of Liberty and Equality.' William Swaim introduces the address with a few words over his signature, stating that it emanates from the 'Board of Managers of the Manumission Society of North Carolina.' I will thank you to write me all you know of this Manumission Society and of the authorship of this pamphlet. The pamphlet does great honor to all concerned with it, and their names should be known in this day of universal liberty."[38]

Although the address contained sixty-eight printed pages, about five by seven inches in fine print, a brief resume will give some idea of the main thoughts Swaim presented in the hope of moving the public to support gradual emancipation.[39] A reproduction of the title page is shown on page 237.

On the second page there was this neat statement:

*To the people of North-Carolina.*

The Board of Managers of the Manumission Society of North-Carolina in General Association, feel it their indispensable duty, respectfully to address, not only their immediate constituents, but with them, the people of the State in general.

WILLIAM SWAIM, *Sec.*

Guilford, March 1830.

Introductory remarks followed, stating that the author had gone into the subject with every caution and reserve, never ventur-

AN

## *ADDRESS*

## TO THE PEOPLE OF

# NORTH CAROLINA,

### ON THE EVILS OF

# SLAVERY.

---

BY
*The friends of*
*LIBERTY AND EQUALITY.*

---

"Anne, liceat invitos in servitutem dare."—DR. PICKARD.

"Not only the Christian religion, but nature herself cries out against a state of slavery:"—POPE LEO. X.

⁎§⊛§⁎

WILLIAM SWAIM PRINTER,
*Greensborough, N. C.*
**1830**

237

ing to discuss rashly any aspect of it and professing to have considered the matter on all sides and to have made every due allowance for the peculiar situation of all parties concerned.

The body of the address was presented in five propositions:

## PROPOSITION I

*"Our slave system is radically evil.* The truth of this proposition is generally admitted, and it would be still more generally avowed were its pernicious effects less." He added that one of the ill effects of the system was that it tended to render man more destitute of a true knowledge of its enormity, and thus to efface "from his understanding those ideas of social order and reciprocal justice engraven on the mind by the God of nature."

## PROPOSITION II

*"Our system of slavery is founded in injustice and cruelty."* This discussion, covering forty pages and embodying the main issue, is divided into two sections. Section I, *"Of the injustice of absolute slavery,"* deals with the inhumane methods of procuring slaves, with the wrong practiced in committing a fellow creature into absolute slavery, and with slavery as the violation of the laws of nature, and thus of God, as expressed in the Declaration of Independence, in the Bill of Rights, and "in some way or other set forth in some part of the Constitution or Laws of perhaps every State in the Union." Section II, *"On the cruelty of slavery,"* points up the ruthlessness of foreign and domestic slave trade; shows the lack of state legislation in connection with the marriages, the property, and the personal treatment of slaves; and calls attention to the lack of proper interpretation and execution of such laws as did exist.

## PROPOSITION III

*"Absolute slavery is a fruitful source of pride, idleness and tyranny."* Here Swaim described briefly the bad effects that slavery had on the white race. By having slaves at his command, he

explained, the white man imagines himself, from childhood, as being a part of a superior race of beings; and feeling superior, he expects his slaves to support him while he basks in a sort of idleness, and meanwhile drifts toward a type of tyranny not only over his slaves but also over his indigent white neighbor, "or any one else over whom he may have gained an advantage."

## PROPOSITION IV

*"Absolute slavery increases depravity in the human heart, and nourishes a train of dark and brutal passions and lusts, disgraceful to human nature and destructive of the general welfare."*

This section portrays the gross ignorance into which nearly all slaves were sunk and describes the deplorable corruption of morals everywhere seen among them, as well as among the whites in their relation with them. Swaim ended this particular discussion with this summons: "Let the *people*—the virtuous, the intelligent *people*, call 'loud and long' for redress on this subject, until virtue triumphs over vice, and humanity over cruelty."

## PROPOSITION V

*"Slavery, absolute and unconditional, is no less contrary to the Christian religion than to the dictates of justice and humanity."*

In this last proposition, Swaim answered the attempts to reconcile slavery with the teachings of the Bible and with Christianity. His concluding words on this were, "May the spirit which inspired these holy men of old, who wrote the sacred text as they were moved by the Holy Ghost, save us from 'wresting it thus to our own destruction.'"

In conclusion the address contained a definite and specific plan whereby the General Association of the Manumission Society of North Carolina proposed to bring about the gradual emancipation of slavery:

"The following principles, most of which are deducible from the foregoing remarks, we give as the primary principles held by

239

us as a Society—together with a brief outline of the plan which we would adopt for the abolition of the evil complained of: and

"*First.* We hold, with the venerable [founders] of our republican institutions, that liberty is the *unalienable birth-right* of every human being; and that God has made no difference in this respect between the *white* and *black.*

"*Secondly.* We believe that, in a national and individual point of view, the negro is entitled to the same measure of justice with the white man, and that neither his skin, nor any other material consequence attending him, can afford a reasonable pretext for his oppression.

"*Thirdly.* We believe that the evil is one which affects every part of the community, in a greater or less degree; and may therefore be termed a national evil; and that both emancipation and colonization are necessary to its removal.

"With regard to emancipation, we hold 1st, that it should be gradual; so conducted as not to interfere with the rights of property; —But 2ndly, that it should be universal. This however, is not enough.—The debt which we owe the negroes is not sufficiently paid by merely suffering the oppressed to go free. We believe it to be the duty of our countrymen, to use all possible means to enlighten and elevate the minds, ennoble the hearts, and improve and elevate the character of the negroes among us, that they may be prepared both to enjoy and appreciate liberty, and to discharge the important duties assigned them by their creator, as well to himself as to their fellow creatures, with honour to God and benefit to mankind.

"In order to remove this alarming evil which is threatening in its aspect, and which if continued long enough, must be so destructive in its consequences, we would recommend the following:

"*First.* Let a law be enacted, preventing the further introduction of slaves into the State for sale or hire.

"*Secondly.* Let a law be enacted, facilitating individual emancipation, by allowing such masters as wish to liberate their slaves, to do so; provided the liberated slave be capable of earning a comfortable livelihood.

"*Thirdly.* We would recommend a law to facilitate individual emancipation still further, by authorizing negroes to make contracts with their masters by which they may purchase their own freedom.

"*Fourthly.* We would recommend the passage of laws imposing still further restraints upon the abuse of slaves, and affording the unlawfully abused slave, at the same time, easy means of redress.

"*Fifthly.* We would recommend a law providing for the instruction of slaves in the elementary principles of language, at least so far as to enable them to read the Holy Scriptures.

"*Sixthly.* We would provide by law that all children in this State after a certain period, should be free at a certain age; and from and after the passing of said act, no negroes should be removed from the State in such a way as to lose the benefit of said act upon their posterity."

Such an outline could hardly do justice to the address, for the lengthy treatise was couched in logical, vivid, forceful, and convincing language, filled with deep conviction and emotion. To any thoughtful person, the case appears well defined; and the proposals for gradual emancipation reasonable and workable.

It should be remembered by those who read the address in its entirety that a great deal of light has been thrown on the subject of slavery since this treatise was written. Swaim and his contemporaries, who evidently approved of this approach, which accented the injustices of slavery, were certainly aware of the system's economic disadvantages. Why the author did not dwell on this side of the question may be anybody's conjecture. One explanation might be that although the economic arguments versus slavery had been touched upon, they had not been clearly defined when this plea for redress was published. Nor would it have been easy to write a saleable argument against the labor system of the South. It would seem, however, that the main reason for not touching upon the econmics involved, was the fact that another address was published about the same time on on this aspect of the subject.[40] It is also noteworthy that Swaim did not elaborate on the word "colonization" as he did on "emancipation," which seems a silent indication that he believed a freed slave should be allowed to make his own decision on that point.

It is indeed regrettable that consecutive numbers of the *Greensborough Patriot* for the last half of the year 1830, almost the entire year of 1831, and most of 1832 have not been preserved, therefore it is not possible to determine accurately the reactions to the address as carried by the paper. The extant numbers, however, do contain some very significant information. When the legislature met in the fall of 1830 after the release of the address in March of that year, out of its forty-six Public Acts, at least ten applied to slaves, making the laws concerning them more strict; and at least three Private Acts contained regulations of the same kind.[41] No one could say positively how much influence the address had on the lawmakers, for about the same time there appeared a pamphlet entitled *Appeal in Four Articles,* by David Walker, a Negro native of North Carolina then living in Boston. Walker's intention was to arouse the slaves to efforts at progress and even insurrection,[42] and on his pamphlet has been placed the major responsibility for the more rigid laws. There was, however, much aversion to Swaim's plan for gradual emancipation; and since the slaveholding East had control of the legislature, it appears that quick action was taken to make slavocracy more secure.

One of the main objects of the Manumission Society was to encourage slaves to look toward supporting themselves once they had gained their liberty. A school had been established for them at New Garden,[43] a community much interested in education, and other schools for Negroes had been recommended. George C. Mendenhall of Jamestown had purchased slaves for the sole purpose of teaching them self-supporting trades and then setting them free.[44] Sallie W. Stockard in *The History of Guilford County, North Carolina,* recorded that from 1820 to 1845 Mendenhall "had a large system of industrial labor on his farm. His slaves were all special workmen. Being taught a trade they worked at it, not running around from one thing to another. . . . In his store a negro clerk sold and bought goods. His harness shop was kept by a slave, a set of whose harness before the War took first premium at the State Fair. His carpenter helped to build the capitol at Raleigh, N. C. His caterer was sent to wait on President Buchanan when he visited the University of North Carolina. George Mendenhall had a shoe shop; a work shop in which were made plows, rakes, hoes, etc.; a large flouring mill, cotton gin, tan yard and farm, all worked by specially skilled negro slaves."

How much influence these small adventures in education had on the legislature can not be known, but it is known that the intention of one of the Acts of 1830-1831 was to prevent all persons from teaching slaves to read or write, the use of figures excepted. Any persons who should be found guilty of breaking this law would be subject to a penalty; if white a fine of not less than $100 nor more than $200 or imprisonment; if a free person of color, a fine, imprisonment, or whipping, not exceeding thirty-nine lashes; and if a slave, thirty-nine lashes on his or her bare back.[45]

When this legislation was made known, Swaim published it in the *Greensborough Patriot* and wrote that "*Certain* men in *this* state, and others of the same *complexion,* have become so squeamish on the subject of '*Slaves, free negroes and mulattoes,*' that we are not certain whether we would be *safe* in *publishing* the acts of the last legislature on the subject, but we intend to risk it. We this week copy the act prohibiting the *education* of slaves; and we shall, from time to time, publish such acts as may be best calculated to shed *light* on the subject."[46]

The following week he published an "Act to Prevent the Circulation of Seditious Publications and for Other Purposes." This act provided that any person who should circulate written or printed materials which might excite insurrection, conspiracy, or resistance in slaves or free Negroes would be subject to a penalty: for the first offense, imprisonment for one year and "put in a pillory and whipped;" second offence, death without benefit of clergy. Or, if anyone should speak so as to cause such excitement, the penalty would be, for the first offense, thirty-nine lashes on his or her bare back and imprisonment for one year; for the second offense, death without benefit of clergy.[47]

As soon as this Act was published, the editor of the *Western Carolinian* wrote, "It has been very confidently predicted that 'Friend Swaim' Editor of the Greensboro' Patriot will fall the first victim to the new law on the subject of seditious publications. [Exactly one month earlier, the legislature had spent an entire day in discussing whether or not Swaim should be punished for publishing seditious literature, but had postponed the matter indefinitely.] It will certainly mortify us very much to see one of the 'Editorial Corps' dangling in the air, or in plain English—hanged. For the credit of the corps we hope he will take timely warning and correct his 'ca-co-lo-gy' . . . if he does not, and they ever catch him about the 'flats of Wilmington,' we will [underwrite] for him, that he will never issue any more 'Seditious publications.' "[48]

Other Acts had to do with intermarriages of whites, free Negroes, and slaves; with harboring runaway slaves; with free Negroes selling their products; with gaming among slaves or free men of color; and with regulating emancipation laws. Under this last Act, slaves might be emancipated only by giving bond of $1,000 that they would leave the state within ninety days; and if they ever returned, they would be sold into slavery again. One exception to this law provided that free Negroes over fifty years of age might remain in the state on the grounds of "meritorious services."[49]

The law that forced free Negroes to leave the state placed Swaim in a particularly trying position, for when he married Abiah Shirley in 1830 she owned two slaves, a Negro woman, Mariah, and her daughter, Hannah; and Rachel, Jane, and Henry were born to Mariah by 1835. Slaves could not be freed to live in North Carolina; and the master and mistress could not bring themselves to send these dependents, who were unprepared to provide a livelihood for themselves, into a world completely unknown to them. Consequently, while Swaim was proclaiming his rabid abolition doctrine, he was at the same time a slaveholder. To those who did not know the circumstances, he might have appeared as failing to meet his own standards. Swaim's concern, however, was for freedom of all slaves, and his personal situation was a part of the total problem.

People of the South were becoming more and more conscious of proslavery and antislavery divisions. Swaim could see proslavery sentiment gaining ground with frightening rapidity. Before 1830, many southerners had been favorably inclined toward gradual emancipation on the ground that slavery was morally wrong and that its abolition would be best for both master and slave. And there had been some tendency to soften the rigidity of slave codes. By 1830, however, the proslavery forces were gaining greater control. Cotton had become king and slavery seemed fastened upon the South. Rising market prices added to the value of slaves as property, a fact which strengthened proslavery thought. Restlessness of the Negro population, as evidenced by the Nat Turner insurrection (1831) which was said to have had ramifications in North Carolina,[50] caused the southern states to take on a harshness never before practiced. All these things lent impetus for more restrictive legislation, and thus led away from any plan for gradual emancipation. Another factor which stimulated reactionary attitude was the northern dissemination of abolition literature in the South —literature, such as the *Liberator,* which called for immediate and unconditional abolition of slavery.

The *Greensborough Patriot* carried an account from the *Boston Courier* which referred to the indictment of the publisher (William Lloyd Garrison) of the *Liberator* " 'at our late Superior Court.' " The *Boston Courier* noted that " 'The contents of the *Liberator* may be of an inflammatory character, and its circulation in the South may be extremely dangerous, but we are not aware of the existence of any law which can stop its publication, so long as it dos not disturb the peace in this State.' "[51] The matter of disrtibuting seditious literature in slaveholding states was brought up in a Boston municipal court, however, and Judge Thatcher, stating that this was a new offense, never before presented for the consideration of a New England jury, charged his jury to consider it. No decision was recorded in the Greensboro paper, but the *Liberator* continued to be printed. Postmaster General Amos Kendall took care of the matter by agreeing to a censorship by southern postmasters of all abolitionist literature in the mails.[52]

Restrictive legislative measures of 1830-1831 had practically blocked all efforts at intelligently preparing slaves for freedom in North Carolina. At the following session an act was passed which prohibited free Negroes from preaching to colored congregations. And Swaim declared that the legislature "has attempted to usurp the dominion and prerogatives of Omnipotence, when a man, labouring under the suspicion of a colour, [who] is commanded by heaven to preach the everlasting gospel . . . . must prostrate himself before the assembly of this state, and implore permission to obey that command! . . . We do not insist upon the propriety of giving countenance to the obstreperous rant of every ignorant and begoted religious pretender; but we deny the right or the propriety of any legislative interference. Public opinion is the proper corrective of this evil. For any other to be exacted is tyranny."[53]

The Quaker Law of 1830-1831 which required men of that sect either to report for military duty or pay a fine, also had a devastating effect upon antislavery efforts. As a result of that law, emigration to the West became so pronounced that it took most of the young men who had been active in the Manumission Society and that organization had its last meeting in 1834.[54] The outlook was grim. Swaim wrote bitterly that "So far as we have been able to understand the laws of the state, it has become an indictable offense to *dream* on the subject of slavery; and much more so to *write* or *speak* on a subject so exceedingly 'delicate.' We believe, however, that the day is not far distant when people will *feel* on the subject. We have no disposition to fly in the face of *authority*, but the evils of slavery must [and] shall be discussed. We have been almost silent on the subject for some time, not because the argument has been exhausted; nor because our opinion in relation to this *national sin* has changed; but because we never thought it best to be forever harping on one string!"[55]

Swaim had fearlessly and steadfastly opposed slavery, but always with dignity and without agitation for violent change. He did not approve of the northern abolitionists, who looked on from a distance and aggravated a situation which they did not understand. He could foresee utter turmoil which was bound to follow if the Negroes, without any preparation whatsoever, were set free upon a society which was no better prepared to admit them than they were to be admitted. Of northern abolitionists he wrote that "However we [may] admit the justness and pertinency of many of their positions and observations, we cannot approve the recklessness and precipitancy of their fulminations against a generation, who have, in a manner, had the evils of slavery forced upon them. Truth, however admissible, is rendered of little or no effect whatever, when urged with too much of vituperative and uncharitable zeal. The abolitionists seem not to appreciate the independent and chivalrous feeling of the southern people, when they propose their uncompromising doctrines of immediate emancipation, amalgamation &c. And they do not act wisely nor candidly in seizing upon every circumstance of individual barbarity which they can get hold of . . . and holding them up to the public as true specimens of the general conduct of the southern slaveholders. There is no man with correct ideas of natural justice, and whose observations have been candid and unprejudiced, with regard to its withering influence on the general prosperity of the south, who will for a moment recognize the right [of] the policy of slavery. Yet he knows not what is to be done. The laws forbid him to emancipate his slaves here, if he were so disposed."[56]

These discouraging reflections did not mean that Swaim and other southerners who opposed slavery had any idea of quitting. It became necessary, however, to adopt some new approach in the place of the defunct Manumission Society if southern antislavery hopes were ever to be realized. This was a long range plan; but antislavery thought turned toward getting control of the legislature.

Although the General Association of the Manumission Society had had no written law concerning the use of the ballot, several times in the minutes of the organization the idea had been mentioned as though such a method had been practiced through consensus of opinion.[57] And Joshua E. Murrow, a Quaker whose forebears were among the original settlers of Piedmont North Carolina, in April, 1959, said that he had learned from his grandfather, William B. Hockett, and other older men of Centre Community, that members of the Manumission Society understood among themselves when voting for representatives to the legislature they would cast their ballot for antislavery men. In this muted yet powerful force, there still remained some promise. Through the revision of the North Carolina Constitution in 1835 (see Chapter XI) which provided for the redistribution of seats in the General Assembly, the western part of the state, which was largely antislavery, would have a more nearly fair representation in the General Assembly. The new constitution provided that the governor and members of the House of Commons were to be elected by all adult white male taxpayers; but to vote for a senator, one had to own fifty acres of land. This property qualification needed to be removed before all adult white male taxpayers could fully express themselves. That handicap was overcome in 1857, thus opening the way for the antislavery West fully to assert itself. Historian John Spencer Bassett in his *Anti-Slavery Leaders of North Carolina,* wrote that with all these advantages in voting privileges, combined with the righteousness of the antislavery cause in the abstract and the superior strength of the vigorous western counties, "it cannot be doubted that the West would finally have removed the stain of slavery from the State"[58] through a policy of peaceful abolition. But the Civil War intervened.

At the distance of a century and a quarter, it seems that Swaim could hardly have handled the subject of emancipation with greater tact at that time, or have prophesied with greater accuracy its future effect upon the South.

William Swaim's concern for underprivileged peoples did not stop with the Negroes, for he made clear in the beginning of his editorial career that "Those benevolent Institutions of our Country, as well as of Europe and elsewhere, which have had their origin in pure and disinterested philanthropie, and which have for their end and object the general improvement of our species, are considered as worthy of the highest encomiums, and entitled to the most liberal and extensive encouragement."[59]  Here, there, and everywhere running through his paper were notices of suffering among the Indians, the mentally ill, the deaf and dumb, the blind, and the imprisoned.

He was deeply perturbed about the Indians, and followed them step by step in their struggles against the domination of the white man. He told of different tribes, their situations, their successes or failures in battle, and at times their attitudes toward their enforced western retreat.  "It seems the 'talk' of President Jackson has not been sufficient to quiet these injured people," he once wrote bitterly.  "They have been denounced as a barberous and unfeeling race of beings, undeserving the sympathy of their *white* brethren; and although they have not had their hearts mellowed into tenderness by the *corrupting* influence of *civilization*, yet their disposition to resist the encroachments of injustice cannot be extinguished, but with the spark of vitality which burns upon the altar of their hearts."[60]

Swaim further described the Indians' refusal to yield to white claimants the peaceable possession of their lands. After giving his readers a Congressional report as a summary of the situation, he continued: "In recent reports on the Indians, the reasoning contained in the [reports of Congress]—if they can be said to contain any reason—is neither connected, lucid or conclusive, and is principally employed to sustain these three prominent positions: *First*— that we have the  power to compel the  Indians  to leave their im-

249

provements and their habitations,—to drop the last tear upon the graves of their ancestors;—and to take up their residence in the wild and uncultivated woods beyond the Mississippi:—*Secondly*: That it would contribute to our *convenience*, and to the futherance of our *wishes* and *inclinations* to call that power into prompt and vigorous exercise:—And *thirdly*: that whatever we have the *power* to do, provided it be *expedient*, we have the *right* to do!"[61]

Another group of unfortunates whom Swaim tried to help through the influence of his paper was the mentally ill. The desperate need for a "lunatic asylum," as it was called at that time, had already been forcibly brought home to the people of Swaim's immediate community. Three of the brightest children of Dr. David Caldwell, teacher, preacher, physician, and statesman, were suffering from mental illnesses; and there was no place in which to hospitalize them. When, in 1830, a bill was introduced in the state legislature to establish a lunatic asylum by using money in the amount of $30,000 which the United States owed North Carolina for advances made during the War of 1812,[62] Swaim hopefully reported the bill in the *Greensborough Patriot;* but he was later forced to acknowledge that this much needed measure became lost in the entanglement of legislative speeches.

A similarly vague proposition, brought before the United States Congress, was reported by Swaim. In 1830, Congressman Augustine H. Shepperd of North Carolina presented a bill to aid in the education of indigent deaf and dumb persons.[63] He proposed to finance such a move by granting to the states specified tracts of land to be sold, the proceeds from the sales to be used for building such institutions. The entire procedure was to be accomplished within the forthcoming ten years; and Shepperd very cautiously included in the bill a provision that these land grants would be for the sole and only purpose specified. This proposition, too, only served the purpose of keeping the idea in the public mind.

And Swaim kept hammering away for repeal of the law that threw people into prison for debt. About the time that he came to Greensboro to live in 1829, Judge Archibald D. Murphey was committed to the Guilford County Jail. Murphey had invested his entire fortune in projects for internal improvements which he believed to be good investments for himself and for the state; but in that haphazard program he had lost everything he owned, and had been overcome with debts. As a result, Judge Murphey became the central figure in what Historian R. D. W. Connor called the "most noted case of imprisonment for debt in the history of North Carolina."[64] Swaim cited other states which had abolished such laws, and he called loud and long: "Is North Carolina asleep? or does she expect that her citizens can earn money to pay their debts while locked up in prison? It's time she'd look to this!"[65]

The Greensboro editor also pleaded for a state penitentiary, since North Carolina had none. He used as argument the case of Thomas Norman, a man convicted of bigamy at the spring term of the Guilford Superior Court, 1829, and sentenced to be executed the following November 21.[66] This case pointed up several evils which Swaim thought North Carolina should remedy. He insisted that if the state had a proper penitentiary, criminals could be given prison sentences rather than the death penalty, which was the punishment for at least twenty-eight crimes in 1817, and at least thirty-three crimes in the early 1830's.[67] For his readers, the dramatic story of Norman not only held interest as an installment thriller, but it also brought to their attention the problems of too drastic punishments, of the great need for revision of the criminal code, and for the provision of physical facilities for handling criminals.

Swaim reported the Norman case dramatically and in detail. For six months Norman waited in the Greensboro jail house for his day of doom. Came November. His friends petitioned Governor Owen to stay the day of death until the legislature would meet and reconsider. There were more days of waiting, during which Swaim asked: "When will North Carolina establish a Penitentiary, and make punishment proportional to the degree of crime?—*Answer* —when little mean, and contemptible county bickerings shall cease to influence elections; and when talents of a high order shall be made the test of fitness, instead of that *swinish* prostitution of

251

principle which has so long influenced our approach to the ballot box. A reformation must be effected in our mode of electioneering, or the day is not distant when our General Assembly, instead of embracing the tallent and wisdom of the state, will be composed of the very *scales of ignorance, frailty and corruption.*"[68]

More time passed. The bill for Norman's pardon was introduced in the state legislature, but the day of execution arrived and no pardon had been granted. Swaim reported every move. Norman was taken from the death prison, was placed in a vehicle upon a coffin that had been prepared to hold his mortal remains, and was driven under the gallows. "A large concourse of people had assembled to see the *'fun!'*" Swaim continued, "The Rev. Messrs. McDonald and Caruthers, lifted their petitions to Heaven in his behalf. [Norman] then briefly the addressed bystanders, in a voice so low, that we were unable to understand what he said. He bid farewell to his intimate friends, and to those who stood near him; and just as the sheriff had placed the rope around his neck, for the purpose of extinguishing the spark of vitality which was burning upon the altar of his heart—*a pardon arrived!*"[69]

With penetrating sincerity, Swaim made all these problems of the state, the South, the nation, and the world look ugly, hateful, and mean. And he held them before the people so consistently that even those who wanted to do so could not forget them. Since this man lived only a total of thirty-three years, and published his paper for only six and a half of them, he lived to see few of his hopes fully materialize. North Carolina did not immediately build a penitentiary after the Norman case, but it did build one in 1875. Democracy often requires a succession of William Swaims to prepare an electorate for proper action.

# XI

## FOR CLEAN POLITICS

*"We have no connexion with party spirit. — We deny the existence of such feelings in our bosom.—We have no other motives than our 'country's good' and our own interest where it can be promoted without a prostitution of principle. Our guide shall be naked undisguised truth, where it can be obtained, and when its opposite finds its way into our columns, unintentionally, a generous people will pardon it"*[1]

William Swaim and the *Greensborough Patriot* were independent of any man or any political party. To the extent permitted by his membership in the human race, he was an objective critic of his times and of the men and issues that shaped them. It is true, however, that in 1835, the year of Swaim's death, the Whig party in North Carolina adopted a platform which included well-nigh all the major political, social, and economic beliefs and proposals consistently endorsed by him during his editorship of the Greensboro paper.[2] In 1839, William's apprentice Lyndon Swaim, as new editor of the *Greensborough Patriot,** declared its

---

*Within the three years succeeding Swaim's death, the *Greensborough Patriot* underwent a half-death, several changes taking place in the editorship and the ownership of the paper. Until April, 1836, it was edited by Alfred E. Hanner for Swaim's estate. At that time Hanner and Mrs. William Swaim's first cousin, C. N. B. Evans from Milton, North Carolina, bought the business. When Hanner died in the summer of 1837, E. S. Zevely became associated with Evans. Zevely had his own paper, the *Southern Telescope,* which was consolidated with the *Greensborough Patriot,* the name becoming *The Telescope.* After a few months Zevely's interest was purchased by John D. Clancy of Hillsboro and the paper again became the *Greensborough*

253

political affiliation to be with the Whigs, and stated that his late cousin William had "no small influence . . . in developing and strengthening views and doctrines of the Whig organzation."[3]  In North Carolina this meant more than in many states where Whigs were opponents of President Andrew Jackson, but seldom in agreement as to what they favored; for in this state the Whig party initiated a quarter of a century of remarkable progress—the first genuine advancement in the history of the state.[4]

This awakening of North Carolina from a state of depression and degradation into a state of hope and prosperity was brought about by a concentrated effort in which the press played a significant role.  From a careful review of North Carolina newspapers in 1828 and early 1829, it appears that William Swaim's *Greensborough Patriot* was in the vanguard of the liberal press which promoted this great change.  Other North Carolina newspaper editors had reported and lamented conditions in the state, but up to that time none had equalled Swaim in boldness and fearlessness of effort to inspire the people into action for their own good.

Although Swaim maintained his political independence, his influence helped to bring about the incorporation of his practical proposals for reform into the policies recommended by the rising Whig organization of North Carolina.  It is especially noteworthy that Whigs generally represented the monied and cultured classes throughout the nation, and in North Carolina they had some following in the wealthy Sound region, but in this state their real strength lay in the poor, undeveloped, progressive western section where Swaim's work complemented that of his fellow townsman and friend, John Motley Morehead. In fact, Morehead, who served two terms as Whig governor (1841-1845) of North Carolina, was among the few men whom Swaim never criticised adversly.  Swaim died the last of December, 1835, the year before the Whig party came

---

*Patriot.*  Greensboro citizens, however, missed the superior editorship of William Swaim, and in 1839 they asked Lyndon Swaim to return to Greensboro and edit the paper, which he did for fifteen years.  He purchased it with M. S. Sherwood who became its business manager.  And in 1842 he married Mrs. William Swaim and became a devoted and exemplary stepfather to her daughter, Mary Jane Virginia.

into power in North Carolina, but he had so firmly established his program in the organization that the reforms he advocated were carried forward by that political party; and during the next fifteen years its administration marked an unprecedented era of progress.[5]

In the first place, the rising Whig party in North Carolina supported a constitutional revision which, among other advantages, gained for the western counties a more nearly proportionate number of representatives in the legislature. This enabled the West to influence progressive legislation, to be put into effect by the help of state aid—something the East had heretofore refused to permit. Because the North Carolina Whigs sponsored measures for development of the entire state, they attracted a following in every county, and public questions tended to arouse party interest rather than sectional interest. This response did not entirely obliterate East-West sectionalism, but it helped to reduce it by inspiring citizens to work together for unified progress throughout the state.

Soon after North Carolina Whigs formally organized in December, 1835, and came to power in 1836, the state treasury was greatly replenished (1836) by the federal government's distribution of its surplus funds among the states. North Carolina received $1,433,757.39. This additional reserve greatly aided the Whigs in their plan for the state to grant aid or to participate in private, county, or state undertakings for reform. Consequently, once in power, this party moved forward with its progressive program. Knowing how Swaim had spent his mature years in efforts to incite North Carolina out of its lethargy, one can but feel the dominance of his spirit as there were established the long-sought state system of public education (1839), a school for the mute deaf (1845), an institution for the mentally ill (1849), and a school for the blind (1851). Although there were some variations, the underlying principles of the provision for a public school system were more nearly patterned after those presented by POLYDORE (Swaim) than those of any other previously suggested plan. Nor was Swaim's influence felt any less in plans for various internal improvements, particularly the building of railroads, for it will be remembered how he persistently urged the people to avail themselves of this mode of transportation. By 1840, supplemented by state aid, the Wilmington and Raleigh Railroad (later Wilmington and Weldon), stretching one hundred and sixty-one miles, the longest railroad in the world at that time, and the eighty-six mile Raleigh and Gaston Railroad—both in the East—were completed. By 1856, the North Carolina Railroad from Goldsboro by way of Greensboro to Charlotte was completed, providing western counties an outlet to the markets of the world. In addition to these major projects, progressive legislation was enacted for building a new state capitol, and for reforms in the fiscal system, the criminal code, and the legal status for women. Along with all these improvements came a noticeable advance in agricultural achievements, a more satisfactory currency, and promising beginnings in industry.[6]

By 1850, however, the Whigs' strength was waning in North Carolina, and the Democratic party was gaining control of the state. Long opposed to reform through state aid, this party now experienced a rejuvenation and a change of heart through its young, forceful, and enterprising members who were sensitive to public sentiment and who were determined that the party should promote a constructive, progressive program. Consequently it adopted the popular reform program which had been launched by the Whigs, and enlarged upon progressive measures until the Civil War.

Such a change of political leadership had been greatly aided by the *North Carolina Standard* of Raleigh, a paper, ironically, first published in November, 1834, for the purpose of fighting, not supporting the forces of reform. But during the 1840's William W. Holden had become its forceful editor. Originally a Whig, Holden had joined the Democrats because of his impatience with the growing aristocratic tendencies of Whig leaders in the state, and because the Democrats were changing their policies to favor reform. Holden promptly adopted the sarcastic and satirical technique that Swaim had so successfully employed in the *Greensborough Patriot* in the early 1830's when he was getting a constructive program of reform initiated. And thus as Swaim had used his *Greensborough Patriot* to launch this great program of reform in the 1830's, Holden used his *North Carolina Standard* to back the Democrats in carrying the program forward in the 1850's.[7] Swaim had hated the *Standard* when it was organized to fight the things he believed in and worked for, but independent that he was, he most certainly would now have approved of Holden's effort to continue reform in the state.*

The role Swaim played as a precursor of this reformation began with the *Greensborough Patriot* on May 23, 1829. His technique for instigating change in the *status quo* was to avoid devious and delicate approaches. Instead, he aimed immediately, directly, unhesitatingly, and fiercely at the heart of the trouble. His out-sized sense of responsibility moved him to attack the legislature of the state with a boldness and daring that startled men out of their lethargy and incited them to positive action. The evils he assailed were not new, but his technique was such as to congeal public opinion, and thus to help bring about within a relatively short time that which other leaders had been working on in some instances for half a century. To do this, he dwelt not only on the actions of the legislature, but also on the type of men chosen for that body, on the responsibility of the voters who placed men in the General Assembly, on the methods of electioneering, and on the part the people should play by letting their representatives know what was expected of them.

In the tradition of Archibald D. Murphey, whose progressive record is well-known to North Carolinians, Swaim took his stand; but in his newspaper he had one great asset which Murphey lacked: although Murphey's recommendations for reform were print-ed, they did not have the week by week, month by month, and year by year press publicity that Swaim could give his program. The *Greensborough Patriot* was the only newspaper in the state which

---

*When the Whig party was no longer active, the *Greensborough Patriot* thereafter supported the Democratic party.

proposed such a broad program of change in 1829 and followed it up in the early 1830's. Other publications favored various changes, from time to time, but on the whole they did so less violently and less consistently.

To speed improvement, Swaim applied his verbal whip without restraint. Among his strongest attacks was that upon the North Carolina legislature. This assemblage was controlled by a majority of conservative representatives from eastern North Carolina who were satisfied with conditions as they were, and who stubbornly and consistently voted down any proposed progressive measures. The more progressive members, who were from western North Carolina, felt indignant and imposed upon, as they repeatedly witnessed defeat of their efforts. Sometimes they were discouraged almost to the point of giving up the fight. Swaim began at once to break up this impasse by publishing the stark truth about the legislature. No other newspaper editor had dared as outspokenly to call the official body undignified names, and to point up its failure to solve state problems. The people of the western counties gloried in Swaim's outspoken wrath. Those of the eastern counties, however, were disturbed by and afraid of this fiery spirit filled with such conviction and sincerity, and they tried to thwart his efforts.

As has been previously shown, the first legislative assembly to meet after Swaim became a North Carolina editor was severely castigated by him for failure to establish a system of public education. Other opportune attacks on the legislature followed from time to time on various subjects. He did not wait, however, for a session to be under way or a special question to be under consideration. He was apt to burst forth at any time in a tirade, as he would say, "to pull the folly of the legislature about their ears."[8]

One constant target of these attacks was the amount of time and money wasted by governing bodies. He was greatly concerned for the many North Carolina children growing up in ignorance and carelessness, with little to arouse their curiosity or ability. The legislature met in session year after year without providing these children stimulants for their wholesome growth or schools for their development. Swaim lamented all the time and money wasted with so little accomplished. Suppose, he wrote, that all this useless spending on legislative meetings for the last twenty years "had been employed in teaching the alphabet to the *infants* and lessons of morality and industry to the *youth* of our country, how different would have been the aspect of things at this time! We do not mean that no legislation is necessary, but if all the time which has been *wasted* during the above named period, in discussing questions which they were incapable of comprehending and which had no connexion with the subject of legislation . . . had been employed in works of *usefulness*, the people of the state might have clapped their hands with joy, instead of folding them in despair as they now do.

"To make this remark, if possible, more plain,—suppose the people should *instruct* their public servants—or rather *command* them . . . to *work more* and *talk less*—to aid the education of youth by precept and example—to encourage *industry* by being *industrious*—to discourage *intemperance* by being *temperate*—to *strengthen perseverance* by *bursting through difficulties*—to *advance* the cause of internal improvement, by *laboring* for the means—to improve the internal condition of the *state* by improving their *own* condition and that of their *neighbors*—to build houses *on the earth* and not castles *in the air*— to drive *intreague* and *corruption* from the state, and cease to fight *windmills* and *chimeras*. We say *let all this be done*, and factories of every description will spring up in the twinkling of an eye—the tariff will strip off her horrid deformity and clothe herself in the smiles of a beautiful face, desolation, in the agonies of despair will leave us forever—prosperity will light up her torch of sun beams, and the cry of '*sedition*' will not be heard in all our borders!"[9]

As an indication of the lack of real understanding of state needs, one Mr. Wilson, a member of the General Assembly, early in one session introduced a resolution for the body to adjourn on December 20, whether or not anything had been done. Presuming

259

that he made this move in order to remain popular with his constituents, Swaim soon let him know that his plan would not work. "He
thought that if the session should happen to be a long and fruitless
one, as it probably will be," Swaim wrote, "he would have this
*sweet* morsel with which to *sugar* his countrymen into favor with
himself! He can tell them that, although much time and money
has been spent to no purpose, the fault is not his—that he *done
his best* at an early part of the session, to fix the period of its
existence; but all in vain! This is not the way to render a session
*short* and *fruitful.* Instead of *protracting* it by *resolutions* for
*adjournment,* each mother's son of them, should roll up his sleeves,
take hold of the *business necessary to be done,* and hang on . . .
until it [is] accomplished, and then adjourn. If they are employed
as the represntatives of the people *should be,* we shall not grumble
to pay them as long as it may be necessary for them to remain in
session; but if they expect to follow in the track of their predeces-
sors, and do no good for themselves, nor their constituents, they
ought to adjourn tomorrow!"[10]

By 1832 the legislators had become well aware of Swaim's
attention in their direction, for he wrote that the *Greensborough
Patriot* was much in demand among them. This gave him faint
hope that they might mend their ways. He waited impatiently to
see if any important legislation would be accomplished, but toward
the end of the session he could withhold no longer. "This body
seems, indeed to be doing a *cash business,* about now—that is, for
themselves! It is, indeed, impossible to record the proceedings of
that body, without sometimes permitting a generous indignation
to arise in the bosome. They have been in session nearly fifty
days, at an expense of 700 dollars per day, and but seven or eight
public laws yet passed! It has become proverbial throughout the
Union to speak of North Carolina as a degraded state; and when
we take into consideration the character of her legislative functionaries, God knows, this proverb is not to be *grinned* at! It is neither
*seditious* nor *libellous* to say, that the last legislature was one
hundred per cent. worse than nothing; and the present session is

fifty per cent. worse than the past! If the present legislature contains the 'assembled wisdom,' the people, may well exclaim— *'Save Cassius or we sink!'* "[11]

Before the 1833-1834 General Assembly met, Swaim predicted that it would "do nothing for the relief of the state."[12] He said he based his assumption on the way its members had been elected. He kept in close touch with the candidates through their speeches and printed circulars, and he said he knew that three fourths of the members of this particular body had been elected by promising " 'all things to all men. . . .' We need never calculate upon *any thing* from the legislative body, in any country," he declared, "whose members ride there on *hobbies* instead of *liberality*, intelligence, and merit! Would to heaven it were otherwise. It pains us to thus speak of our country men—but the *naked truth* had as well be told, *at once!*"[13]

Nevertheless, he gave them every opportunity to prove his prediction to be wrong before he reported their doings. But they dawdled along with granting permits for gates, building fishponds, and attending to other small matters until they wore out his patience. "This gate-making and fish-trap concern seems to have improved in point of the facility with which their work is *executed*," he reported sarcastically. "It took them at the commencement of the session, three separate sittings to authorize the building of a gate; but such is the state of improvement among them, that the wind-work of a gate can now be built in one day. They only have to say 'go to it Jerry,' and the work is done! Samuel Latham, as soon as he can get the timber seasoned will have a 'lawful' gate in Pitt County. It is not specified, we believe, in the act authorizing the construction of the same, whether it is to be fastened with a *lock* or a *latch;* neither is it defined, what kind of timber shall be used, or whether it shall be *cut* or *sawed.* Some difficulty may yet arise before the *enterprize* is completed!"[14]

While all the petty arts of the legislature were thus being practiced, progressive leaders were bringing up bill after bill for the development of the state, only to see them postponed indefinitely

or voted out of existence by the dominant conservative members of
the East. Evidently somebody said to Swaim that legislative
doings were not worth printing. Swaim, however, felt differently.
He wanted the legislative record broadcast, and he wanted people
to talk about it. "If any person should be so inquisitive as to
enquire the reason why we have published the whole of the
'gate,' 'Fishtrap' and 'Frog-pon' bills passed by the last session of
the legislature," he explained, "our answer will be, we have all
along said the session was a *trashy* one, principally engaged in
doing a *trashy* business; and we have thought proper to publish
the whole of the *trash* of that *trashy* assemblage, for the purpose
of showing that we have not been mistaken!"[15]

Swaim paused in his censure of the legislature long enough to
point out that the main reason why this body was so inefficient
was the type of men often chosen for its members. He warned
against electing representatives not fitted for public positions; and
he drove his quill after such candidates and exposed their lack of
qualifications without fear and without mercy. Remembering
when legislative members from the more western counties were
once passing through Greensboro on their way to Raleigh, he
shook his head in deep concern. "Some of them," he described,
"as if to make up the want of intellect by a surplus of extra em-
bellishment, had washed themselves with strong soap suds and
scoured their ancles with cornshucks. Some, as if their wisdom
lay in their beards, had not shaved for three weeks, . . . In fact,
so far was this indifference carried by many, that they seemed not
to have *washed their faces* or *shifted* their *shirts* since the last
August election! Some appeared to be men of intelligence and
weight of character; & other simpletons, seeming to have barely
decernment enough to know that they ought to be wise, rendered
their ignorance the more rediculous by their silly attempts to
*conseal it. 'God save the State!'* "[16]

People should consider more seriously the type of men they
send to the legislature, Swaim reiterated. To illustrate this point,
he had previously written one of his famous "No!" editorials, many

of which ran effectively all through his pages, and had shown the political weaknesses of one G. T. Moore, a candidate for the State Senate from the West. Swaim had read Moore's campaign literature which was filled with high-flown rhetorical flourishes about the blessings of liberty. The Greensboro editor became highly dramatic as he exposed this man for his lack of practical vision. "Does he mark out the course of policy by which these blessings [of liberty] can be secured to us and extended to posterity? No!" Swaim questioned and answered in the same breath. "Has he introduced the subject of a circulating medium, by the proper regulation of which alone, the people can be saved from ruin? No: Is any part of his mental labours devoted to the subject of a common school system, by which our country can be saved from the wilting tread of knaves and demagogues? No: Does he call upon his countrymen to examine their constitution, and be prepared to say at a proper time, whether they may wish it altered or amended? No: Does he bring before them the subject of Internal improvement, and tell them that by a proper application of their resources they may soon become independent and powerful? No: Does he tell them that industry and application to business, will form the best antidote for the hard times, so much complained of? No: [Does] he, indeed, take any stand, on which an honest politician would not blush to be found? No, He circulated his *bottle* until the people became sufficiently *innebriated* to swallow any other filth that might be presented," and then wandered off into generalities about the national government, with not a constructive thought about what might be accomplished in the North Carolina legislature.[17]

Nor did representatives from the eastern counties escape Swaim's scrutiny. From among many specific examples which he pointed out as poor material in the legislature from the East, was Senator Josiah Houlder of Johnson County. The Greensboro editor introduced him by saying "the soul of such a man . . . might be put in a nut-shell and then have 'room to let!'" There had come to Swaim a copy of Houlder's political pamphlet in which the senator had proudly announced that several projects had been before the last legislature to provide for amending the state constitution and that his vote had been recorded against all of them. One of the projects was to ascertain the wishes of the people on whether or not the majority wished the constitution amended, and he had voted against that. In his wondrously illogical explanation, Houlder said that he "was affraid for the wishes of the people to be known, for fear they, the *people*, would get the power out of the *people's* hands, and give it to a few individuals! . . . When the *people* are allowed to get the power out of the hands of the *people*, into their *own hands*," he said, "they will have the power to filch *from themselves* money to build railroads and unite the church and state!"[18]

What can be expected, Swaim implied, when the legislative halls contain such men?

In order to be completely fair and to show that he held no personal grudges, over and over again Swaim warned about being careful when selecting a public representative. "Many — nay thousands of men," he declared "are to be esteemed for their private virtues and moral worth, who are no more fit to fill the station they sometimes seek, than a drunkard is to inhabit the Kingdom of heaven;—Hence, we can consistently write, speak and *act* against a man's promotion, and yet esteem him as a worthy private citizen."[19]

Along with his attacks upon specific legislators and legislation Swaim had much to say on the methods of electioneering which often placed unworthy and inadequate men in positions of responsibility; and in this the people came in for their share of criticism for not being sufficiently wide awake to avoid such pitfalls. On this angle in 1830 Swaim wrote, "We hope that the citizens of this state have had enough pueril and childish Legislation to convince them of the fact, that a reformation is badly needed in the character of men who have heretofore had the *honor* of representing us, and by whom we have had the *dishonour* of being *represented;* & that ordinary discernment which Providence has withheld from but few, will satisfy them that this reformation can only be effected through the medium of the ballot-box. The people may speak in vain to their representatives after they are once clothed with power; but let them speak through the ballot-box, while that power remains in their own hands, and their voice will be heard like the speaking of many thunders. And why not speak *now*."[20]

Two years later, on August 29, 1832, Swaim again appealed directly to the people to use the power that had been granted them. "The great cause why North Carolina has not long since called into fruitful activity her ten thousand prolific resources," he reminded, "is want of intelligence, firmness and independence among the people. When the bone and sinew of the land shall close their eyes to men, and guard with a lynx-eyed vigilance, those measures and principles, which had they been sustained would have long since, exalted our state to a proud eminence among her sisters—then may we hope to see better days; but while elections are conducted with a view to sectional or personal predilections, while the public feeling and taste are such, that a seat in the legislature cannot be obtained without wading 'belly-deep,' through falsehood, slander and vituperation, honest, intelligent and honourable men will turn aside, and give place to beings whose intrusive presumption can only find a parallel in the magnitude of their ignorance."

One electioneering method which Swaim abhorred was the practice of distributing whisky to influence votes. Under existing conditions, conscientious and upright men had little chance of being elected to the legislature. A contributor to the *Greensborough Patriot* who signed himself "AN OBSERVER," seriously questioned, "What can we expect where the 'quart bottle stands for the hour glass,' & a considerable number give their votes agreeably to the last drink of grog they have swallowed, any previous promises to the contrary notwithstanding? We must expect, under such circumstances, that those who have the least real candour, and the most duplicity, provided they are the most liberal in treating with ardent spirits, will have the preponderance over other candidates, whose lofty minds soar above these base, these low subterfuges."[21]

Swaim therefore insisted: "Let it be proclaimed to the world, from the ballot box, ... that no man can obtain the confidence of the people, who will have the meanness to resort to any other method of securing his election than that of his own merit, and a frank and fearless avowal of his own sentiments. The practice of treating, previous to the election, and of making every sotish Devil drunk on that day when of all others, he should be most sober, shall first be torn limb from carcase & thrown in mangled fragments to its native hell; ... All the evils growing out of this vile sin shall be held up to view in their native deformity. We shall freely, fully & fearlessly expose the conduct in this respect of all those who may become candidates without regard to the rank they hold in society. Let them take heed to their ways!"[22]

And he was as good as his word; for if any would-be public servant showed he was not worthy, Swaim would hold him up to public view, even if he were an intimate friend. He had so much to say about the type of men whom people should choose to represent them that within a year after he started his paper, under the heading of "GOOD NEWS THIS WEEK!" he reported: "[Guilford County candidates] have resolved that they will not treat people with spiritous liquors during the whole of the present fly time, or electioneering campaign.

"We have received several communications on the subject. . . . All . . . go to condemn the practice, and applaud the manly spirit which prompted our candidates to turn their backs upon it."[23] And three years later a *Greensborough Patriot* reader assured Swaim it was generally admitted that he had done much toward stopping the detestible practice of treating in Guilford. Moreover, other counties in the state separated drinking and voting.

In tackling the subject of electioneering, Swaim also condemned the practice of smearing the good name of a candidate by bringing up the illegal or immoral transgressions of his relatives. If in so doing, he could also condemn the transgression itself as a public or private problem, he always did so. For examples, in a series of articles which stretched over a period of several months he assailed the evil of illegitimacy itself, and also the manner in which, indirectly but falsely, it had been used by Solomon Spain-hour of Stokes County against Augustine H. Shepperd, a candidate for the Congress of the United States. And although Swaim did not approve of David Thomas for a member of the General Assembly, he avidly defended him against the falsehoods that were being circulated for his political detriment—that he was a Deist, and that he had no Bible. An agent had started these tales because he was mad at Thomas for not buying a Bible from him. Swaim explained that Thomas was a generous churchman and owned already more than one Bible.[24] Thus, in line with his reform movement, Swaim always asked for serious consideration of the problems he revealed.

After elections were over, he thought the people should instruct their representatives on specific measures they wished enacted. Consequently, Swaim and others had warned members of the 1834-1835 General Assembly that, among other legislation, provisions for internal improvements and constitutional revisions were expected. The General Assembly convened early in November, 1834; and legislative bills for these important measures were presented, but laid aside. Swaim wrote on November 26, "We have as yet heard but little from these wise men; but we have heard enough to take away—entirely efface and obliterate—the small remaining hope we had in that soop-tailed assemblage! For ten years, we have been looking to the General Assembly with a faint hope that something would be done to redeem the state from her sinking character and condition; but each year has been but a refinement upon the miserable policy of its predecessor! We have no room to multiply words here, but we intend to take the bull by the horns in *good earnest*, before the session terminates! We have never yet put our columns in mourning; but we expect before next spring to sing the funeral dirge of the state!"[25]

On December 17, 1834, Swaim obliquely let the legislature know that its actions were being watched with his "lynx-eyed vigilence," by saying, "Should the reader ask what has been done? the answer is ready—nothing! A more contemptible set of men

267

perhaps never assembled in the state. They embrace the very rag-tag and bob-tail of our population!"

With urgent bills waiting for action, the executive body turned again to playing politics and wasting time on trivial matters. It had allowed George B. Greer to use its time in getting his credit restored. Restoring credit or otherwise taking care of its members seemed to have been one of the benefits to be obtained from the legislature, for Swaim had cited case after case since 1829. Particularly noticeable were the cases of James Call[o]way and Abraham Brower who had been members of the General Assembly. According to Swaim, Brower, on his return home "got *drunk* and broke his thigh! He applied to the Legislature for renumeration and got it! Mr. Call[o]way was a member, became *liquor-sick*, and had the grace to ask the State to pay his grog-bill—his tavern-bill —and his physician's bill. Such men instead of the respect and confidence, deserve the deep and damning execration of the people. Brower ought to have had his neck broke instead of his *thigh,* and Callaway ought to have died during his *indisposition.* We presume the State would have defrayed their *funeral expenses* without *regret.*"[26] And then with highly important state questions lying on the table, legislators again turned to exasperating piddling on behalf of Greer's credit. Swaim facetiously remarked that "A thought here strikes us, that much good might be effected, in a short time, by the passage of some general law on the subject, in the healing benefits of which all might participate. They seem to have an inexhaustable fund of credit on hand: Any person may steal a sheep, or swear a lie when he will. He has nothing to do but to ask the legislature to vote him a *clever fellow!* But to our project:

"We propose that a law be passed, restoring to credit the state of North Carolina, and all her gallows dodgers, *en masse;* and as they have been trying to patch up the present tottering administration, it might be well to include it, and let the whole be restored at once. Any dirty scoundrel might then come into the pool and wash."[27]

When January, 1835, was wearing on and no legislation of importance had been enacted, Swaim again spent his fury in the direction of the General Assembly. "We have never been accused of speaking more highly of this body than we ought to have done," he wrote. "It is true, we have never entertained a very high opinion of the collected wisdom of the state; and we generally make it a point to speak about as we think, not caring who may be displeased, or how our interest may be affected by such a course. We would rather restle with poverty, and be FREE, than to be the SPLENDID SLAVE of any man, or any government."[28]

Insofar as the assembled legislators were concerned, he reported they were "at least three hundred per cent. worse than we have ever represented them to be. [There are] some highminded and honorable men in both houses; but they are in so small a minority, that all their efforts to do good terminate in nothing but a futile waste of time.—so that all they can do, is to look on and mourn over the murderous course pursued by the majority!

"It is no uncommon thing, for either house to take up some private bill, to regulate the patrol in some eastern county, or prevent FISH from getting into the FRYING PAN—and gravely discuss its details for three or four whole days in succession! Those immediately interested, generally take an active part in such important discussions, while the ballance have nothing under heaven to do, but drink liquor and smoke cigars!"[29]

Swaim practiced no reserve on what he termed this maddening dillydallying. He warned that "The people must open their eyes and look into these things; and purge their legislature of pill-boxes, demagogues, quacks and miserable, third rate county court pettifoggers, or their liberties will cease to exist even in name."[30]

These attacks on the legislature had purpose. Swaim intended that the people should have their eyes opened to what was going on in their state and in their legislature, for he realized that the success of his undertaking would require the support of the General Assembly elected by the people. With the make-up of that body as it was—the conservative East controlling a weak General Assembly—he could have little hope for change. From the beginning he realized his most important move, then, was to work for an acceptable revision of the state constitution, which, among other things, would provide for greater representation for western counties in the General Assembly. With the progressive western section allowed its rightful voice in state affairs, great progress could come. At every opportunity Swaim therefore eased in a sentence, a phrase, or a forthright editorial to remind the people that their outmoded code of laws was the root of all their evils.

The old North Carolina constitution provided that each county, regardless of size, wealth, or population, should have one member in the Senate and two representatives in the House of Commons; and seven towns should each have one borough representative. Since the East had more counties and more towns than the West, it therefore had the majority of representatives and thus controlled the General Assembly. Although the East had the greater wealth, by 1830 the West had the greater population. And it was particularly galling for the more populous progressive West to have to bow to the less populous conservative East.

This situation had grown increasingly more difficult by the early 1830's. All progressive measures for state development were blocked by the controlling East which preferred to keep the state as it was, lest it lose its power and find its greater wealth taxed for public improvements. Eastern North Carolina was favored by rivers as natural outlets for its commerce, but the western part of the state had no suitable roads, railroads, or rivers for carrying on prosperous enterprises. Yet, the East would not sanction any proposals for a sizeable expenditure to benefit the West. The East was fully conscious that the West, now more powerful in population and deeply anxious for an opportunity to improve its backward condition, was continually striving for its fair representation in the legislature so that it might have some voice in determining the situation of the state. But for almost fifty years the East had cast its majoriy vote in the legislaure against every move of the West toward constitutional reform.

The original constitution contained no provision for amendment. The only way it could be changed was by a constitutional convention called by the General Assembly or by the people. The last great move on this subject had taken place in 1823, when twenty-four western counties sent forty-seven delegates to a convention at Raleigh where they drew up proposals for the legislature to consider. "Even the approval of Thomas Jefferson, published in the papers of the time, had no effect." The legislative body rejected this popular demand.[31]

Agitation on the subject had subsided since that discouraging defeat, but when Swaim began his *Greensborough Patriot,* page one of his initial issue carried a hint that the subject was going to be revived. As he kept bringing the subject up, other North Carolina newspapers began to support him. Although the *Western Carolinian* had taken constitutional revision as its theme in its Prospectus of 1820, more recently it had been quiet on the subject. Only the *Greensborough Patriot* dared to take the lead in this new approach.[32]

Swaim always worked to encourage the people to take an active part in any movement for their own betterment. His first step was to make and keep them conscious of the need for specific reforms—reforms which all thoughtful people knew could be brought about only if progressive members controlled the legislature. Constitutional reform, then, was of primary concern. Swaim let the people express their opinions about it through his pages until he felt they were ready and determined to fight it through.

He did not, however, leave the question entirely up to the people. In Chapters III, IV and V of "NORTH CAROLINA," by POLYDORE, who on this subject appears almost conclusively to have been Swaim himself, the case presented for constitutional revision was very impressive and powerful. These chapters appeared in the *Greensborough Patriot* on September 12, 19, and 26, 1829. Through them the writer clearly showed why constitutional

271

reform was imperative, enumerated the arguments that had been used against a revision, and with strength and dignity explained their weaknesses.

In three weekly discussions on why this constitutional reform must be made, POLYDORE concluded that "If it was the privilege of our ancestors, fifty years ago, to convene for the purpose of framing a Constitution on which to base their rights, it is no less ours, now, after the experience of half a century has shown that this instrument does not secure equal rights to all our citizens, to meet in Convention, for the purpose of amending it. We have in support of this opinion, all reason, together with the practice of all, or nearly all the original States. Most of the States, that formed their Constitutions during the confusion and trials of the Revolutionary struggle, have since found it necessary to hold Conventions for the purpose of amending them. Then where is the wonder, if the like necessity be found to exist in North Carolina? . . .

"Meantime *imperious necessity* demands . . ." he continued, "[that] a Convention [be] called as sooner or later it certainly must be, if North Carolina is destined eve[r] to emerge from its present groveling obscurity. . . . [When it is called] Let no polluted hand touch this instrument. Let no sot, no gambler, no prodigal, no horse jocky, or other kind of knave; no trader in the souls of men, no fraudulent stockholders, or indulged bank debtor, no intriguing politician, nor any religious bigot, come near. Let only such as have clean hands, clear minds, liberal principles, and unbiased judgments, dare approach. — If a Convention of pure-minded patriots could be assembled, we might safely submit the whole Constitution to their disposal, either to amend, or to substitute a better in its stead. This should be returned to the people for their ratification or rejection. . . .

"It may as truly be said, that we of N. C. live under a despotism, as if we live under an absolute monarchy, and even though we may not be oppressed, (which by the way is not admitted,) it does not follow that we have no just cause of complaint or apprehension.

272

We live under a despot, who may at pleasure become a tyrant and oppress us. We are deprived of sovereignty, which is justly ours.

"Some seven or eight years ago [1823], as must be recollected by every one who was then arrived at years of observation, there was great excitement on this subject; the whole argument was familiar in the mouths of every one; it seemed to be fast acquiring popular favour, and rapidly maturing for a crisis; when wonderful to tell! it vanished like an apparition at the matin cock-crow, and has never been heard of since, till now, I have started it afresh, scarcely knowing what I do; whether any patriot will respond a cordial amen; or, whether 1 stand isolated on enchanted ground; whether the excitement is only smothered, and wanting a gentle breeze to fan it into a refining fire; or, whether apathy and sloth have totally extinguished it.

"I have ever thought it betrayed a degree of baseness, thus to abandon a reform, which the emergencies of the times so imperiously demands; the question of which, is incontrovertible, and the attainment of which seemed just within our grasp. I have often mentally exclaimed, poor North Carolina! Thou are governed by a minority! Thy many are subservient to thy few! Thy energies have sipped a narcotic potion! Thy enterprise is driven into exile! Thy good tends to evil, and thy evil to worse! Thou art prostrate, and pinioned; and hast neither nerve to exert, nor tongue to cry!— And then I whistle back my errant thoughts.—I have not, however, abandoned the hopes, that there is yet a redeeming spirit in North-Carolina, the beloved land of my nativity.

POLYDORE."

As his dynamic fellow worker in this democratic move, Swaim had the Reverend Amos Weaver* of Greensboro, who was elected to the House of Commons for the sessions of 1830-1831 and 1831-1832. Weaver was a personal friend, as may be remembered from their co-operation on antislavery measures; and his position in the legislature enabled him to keep Swaim informed on the inside workings

---

*The Reverend Mr. Weaver was the first permanent pastor of the First Baptist Church of Greensboro, after it was founded in 1850.

of that body on the constitutional subject, as well as to discuss it with other legislators who were friendly to a revision. A bill for a convention had been introduced in 1830-1831 and again in 1831-1832, but as usual was defeated. In the summer of 1832, before legislature convened in the fall, Swaim published a long and forceful defense of revision which Weaver had made before the House of Commons during its last session. He published an equally impressive address by Weaver to the people. These addresses were reinforced by similar ones by other intelligent legislators, such as Jonathan Parker, Allen Peeples, and John D. Toomer.[33] There was also an address to the sheriffs of North Carolina on posting over the state public notices about the proposed amendment; and there were communications from the public in general, all of which were printed in the Greensboro paper.

In Weaver's addresses he reiterated with penetrating impact the same arguments that POLYDORE-Swaim and others had been presenting. Having given examples to support his statements, Weaver asked in sincerity, what to do? It appeared a futile effort to seek redress through the General Assembly. If the West asked for more counties so as to give it more legislators, the East would demand more counties to increase its legislators in proportion. Weaver compared the situation of the West with that of the United States before the Revolutionary War, and added that it was "unworthy of, and disgraceful to the sons of American Revolutionary Patriots, thus tamely to submit to such a state of things as now exists,—to have our liberies wrested from us by an unfeeling—or to say the least, an unbrotherly aristocracy."[34]

In connection with Weaver's addresses, in the summer of 1832, the *Greensborough Patriot* presented a concrete working plan for revision. First, the people through their representatives should ask the 1832-1833 session of the legislature for permission to find out at the next general election, by a referendum, whether or not the majority wished to call a convention to amend the constitution. But if the legislature would not grant this request, then those legislators who favored a revision should organize, while still in

Raleigh, and should formulate definite plans whereby the people of the state, without legislative consent, could vote on the question.[35]

Meanwhile, in the summer of 1832, the *Greensborough Patriot* suggested that the people meet at the county courthouses and take a stand on the matter. Typical of such organizational meetings was the one in Guilford County where Jonathan Parker was made chairman and William Swaim secretary.[36] At this gathering, Weaver advocated an unlimited convention, to be called by a vote of the people, the constitution to be amended by that convention, and the revision to be approved by a vote of the people. Thereafter an unlimited convention seems to have been fixed in the minds of ardent revision supporters. They preferred an unlimited convention because it would be free to make whatever changes it thought best, whereas a limited one would be required to revise certain articles that would be specified in any act which provided for the calling of a convention for constitutional reform.

By 1832 other leading newspapers of the state—*Raleigh Register, Carolina Observer and Fayetteville Gazette, Newbern Spectator, Hillsborough Recorder,* and *Western Carolinian* of Salisbury —were giving added emphasis to the subject. Since the *Western Carolinian,* established in Salisbury in 1820 primarily to promote constitutional revision, had lost much of its influence by 1832 for having favored South Carolina's nullification movement, the *Carolina Watchman* of Salisbury had been launched in July of 1832 to support a constructive program. The editor of the *Carolina Watchman* was a lawyer, Hamilton C. Jones, who, with John M. Morehead had represented Swaim in 1831 in a libel suit involving freedom of the press.[37] The Prospectus for the *Carolina Watchman* was carried by the *Greensborough Patriot* several months prior to its launching on July 28, 1832. On October 17, 1832, Swaim wrote, "We have laboured night and day that we might convert [Jones] from the error of his ways—that is, from *Jackson Van Burenism*— and initiate him into the good old cause of 'our country—the constitution—Union.'" In this mission Swaim was finally successful,

275

for in 1834 Jones withdrew from Jackson and later joined forces with the rising Whig party. Thereafter, through his *Carolina Watchman,* he gave able support to the same reforms which had been outlined in the *Greensborough Patriot* Prospectus in 1829, had been urged in Swaim's opening editorial in 1829, and had been consistently promoted in the *Greensborough Patriot* columns for five years. Thus Swaim's convert became a leading disciple for constitutional revision.

Soon after the General Assembly convened for its 1832-1833 session, Swaim wrote that "The subject of calling a convention has found its way into the house, at this early period of the session. On this question we anticipate much angry and fruitless discussion."[38]

This prediction was correct. When nothing came of the bill, some of the legislators who were in favor of a convention followed the suggestion that had been made in the summer of 1832 in the *Greensborough Patriot.* While still at Raleigh in January, 1833, they met out of session and decided to take a vote of the people at the next annual election in August, 1833, on those *for* and *against* calling a convention for amending the constitution. The results of the proposed referendum were to be passed to the governor who in turn should pass them on to the legislature. These interested legislators also decided to publish an address to the people; to set up Committees of Correspondence in the various counties to see that the address and other information reached the people; and to appoint Richmond M. Pearson, Romulus M. Saunders, William H. Haywood, Jr., and Thomas Diews (Dews) to prepare that message.[39]

The address to the people was an enlightening and convincing presentation of the subject, covering one and three fourths pages of the *Greensborough Patriot.* Other state newspapers also carried it. This address enumerated the different revisions that were considered imperative; answered arguments against revision and underwrote arguments in favor of it; cited almost all the original thirteen states which had already revised their first constitutions;

and defined the meaning of a limited and unlimited convention. In conclusion, the commitee declared, "We sincerely believe that the speedy settlement of these questions involves the destinies of the state; that it will restore harmony where there is discord; that it will be the means of developing the internal resources of the state, without any recourse to additional taxation; that it will economize the government, so as to bring its expenses below the regular ordinary revenues; that it will destroy the divisions of *East* and *West*, and disengage our representatives from the strifes of sectional party; that it will stimulate them to higher and more promising exertions, for reviving the hopes and advancing the prosperity and honor of the state."[40]

This address, psychologically timed, was published in the summer of 1833, before annual elections—and before the popular vote, promoted by the 1832-1833 legislators out of session, was to be taken on constitutional reform. When the people had voted on this urgent question, the results showed 30,000 *for* and 1,000 *against* a convention.[41] Even in the face of this overwhelming majority vote, the 1833-1834 legislature again failed to respond to the popular demand. This time, however, the West did not accept defeat as it had in 1823. Just before the 1834-1835 legislature convened, Swaim let its plans be known by saying that "the WEST will make but one more appeal to that body for a redress of their grievances. Disappointed in this, they will certainly take the matter into their own hands, and instead of asking for an inch, they may hardly be satisfied with an ell."[42] Two weeks later he made this intention more positive by declaring with the *Carolina Watchman* that " 'If the Legislature refuses to grant us our rights at the next session; then we go for a different mode of redress. Then let the people of the west rise in the majesty of their power, and teach those who are not disposed to harken to their remonstrances, that they, as free citizens will have their weight in the legislative branch of the government in which they live.

" 'Rash and violent measures should be avoided, by all means; but let us say to the East, *our political rights you must allow us.*

277

WE WILL HAVE THEM.' "[43] And every word of that warning meant business.

These definite plans Swaim published in August and September, 1834. When the legislature convened the following November, he again repeated the intention of the West by saying, "On this subject [of a convention] it behooves the present [session] to act efficiently. We want, we need, we can have, and we will have an amendment of the state constitution. We have petitioned and remonstrated long enough. We say with the Carolina Watchman, —'This is the last appeal that will ever be made to the legislature!' If they refuse to hear ou[r] voice, we of the West have determined to try our strength! Let the East beware how they hang back!"[44]

Soon after the 1834-1835 General Assembly convened, a bill providing for constitutional revision was introduced, and Swaim gave it an important place in the *Greensborough Patriot;* but for days and days no definite action was taken on it. On December 24, 1834, one anxious member stood up and reminded the legislature that it had been convened for thirty-eight days without passing any measure of importance, while the convention bill and "other measures of deep and vital importance to the people, now remain upon the table, neglected & undisposed of."[45] He then moved the adoption of a resolution, urging the legislature to consider the convention bill and other measures pertaining to the general good of the people of North Carolina. This resolution was lost 32 to 27.

About this time, Swaim went to Raleigh, where Senator Jonathan Parker of Centre Community, Representatives Jesse H. Lindsay and Ralph Gorrell of Greensboro, and other friends over the state were members of the General Assembly. He did not report what they did and said, but he did report that before the third reading of the convention bill in the Senate "A great number of amendments were proposed, and a very animated discussion arose on their respective merits."[46] And, on January 14, 1835, he was able to announce in the *Greensborough Patriot* the passing of "AN ACT:"

---

### NORTH-CAROLINA.

---

*"Let wisdom through her councils reign,*
*And her's shall be her people's gain."*

---

#### AN ACT

Concerning a Convention, to amend the Constitution of the
State of North Carolina:

WHEREAS, the General Assembly of North Carolina have reason to believe that a large portion, if
not a majority, of the freemen of the State, are anxious to amend the Constitution thereof, in certain
particulars, hereinafter specified; and whereas,
while the General Assembly disclaim all right and
power in themselves to alter the fundamental law,
they consider it their duty to adopt measures for
ascertaining the will of their constituents, and to
provide means for carrying that will into effect,
when ascertained: therefore,
*Be it enacted by the General Assembly of the*
*State of North Carolina, and it is hereby enacted*
*by the authority of the same,* That the Court of
Pleas and Quarter sessions of each and every
county in this State, at the first term that shall be
held after the first day of January, one thousand
eight hundred and thirty five, shall appoint two
inspectors to superintend the polls to be opened at

---

The Act (January 9, 1835) called for a limited convention,
that is, it stated specifically how certain amendments must be made,
that certain others be left to the discretion of the convention.
The Act was clearly defined, and every one by reading it, could
learn something of what results to expect. It also provided for the
people to vote on whether or not they wished a convention called for
the purpose of revising the constitution according to the Act. If
the majority favored calling a convention, the Act provided for
electing delegates to the convention; and for submitting the work
of the convention to the people for approval.

North Carolina's Historian William K. Boyd wrote that the
threat of revolution, the power of the press, and the change in
attiude of some eastern leaders were effective in influencing the
passage of the bill.[47] Although the Whig party was not to be
organized officially in North Carolina until December, 1835,[48]

279

sentiment in its favor was growing rapidly, and there were potential Whig members in every county in the state. The future Whig leaders of North Carolina favored Swaim's over-all reform program for the state and were incorporating reform projections for public schools, agricultural improvements, industrial advancement, internal improvements, sound currency, and constitutional revision into the platform they were planning. This constructive program captured the West and Sound region, and the West thus gained some eastern Whig support and won its fifty-year battle for constitutional amendments.[49] Swaim's influence had been effective in this long-fought battle, and now came his moment of victory.

It was not, however, an easy victory. The future Whigs knew that a constitutional revision was necessary, if they were to be fully represented in the General Assembly and thus were to be able to carry on the program of reform which they were anticipating. It is not surprising then that those who favored a revision wanted to be very sure of the convention bill's passage before a final vote was taken on it. It is not surprising that certain eastern legislators agreed to vote for a convention if the West would vote for an eastern railroad measure. And it is not surprising that there had been much political maneuvering with the result that the bill was so adjusted as to receive the support of some eastern legislators. The *Journal of the Senate and House of Commons, 1834-1835*, shows amendments in both houses before the first, second, and third votes were taken; and finally a joint committee from the two houses was appointed to iron out their differences.[50]

It appears that all this bargaining had come as no surprise to Swaim, for he turned immediately to his next duty. Although he had hoped for an unlimited convention, he spared his wrath on the Act that called for a limited one, gracefully accepting the compromise, and vigorously applying his efforts toward convincing his western friends that the Act was the best that could have been passed at the time.[51]

The favorable vote on the bill did not begin to be the end of work, for the Act provided that, first, the people of the entire state must vote on whether or not they wanted this particular kind of consitutional revision. There was still great uncertainty as to whether the East or West would win a popular majority in this struggle. If the majority voted for a convention, then they would have to have another election for choosing delegates to represent them in that convention, and still another to pass on the work of the convention.

"The convention bill, as it has passed into law, will be found in another part of this paper," ... wrote Swaim. "We propose to take up the subject, in a series of editorials hereafter, for the purpose of setting the matter in its proper light before the people. ... the convention question is an important one, and the people will soon be called to the polls to *vote* upon it. On its issue is suspended the future prospects of the state; and we intend to spread before our subscribers, a light on the subject, as broad as the heavens!"[52] It was not all the reformers had wished, he admitted; but it was the result of a compromise, "as advantageous to the West, no doubt, as could be effected." Then he continued, "The people will soon be called upon to ACT on the subject; and before they ACT they ought to THINK, —and to think profoundly; They ought to think—not for themselves, only, but for after ages."[53]

If there were ever any doubt of Swaim's absolute conviction that the revision of the constitution was essential to the progress of his state, and particularly to his section, the following story would dispel it. The state asked all North Carolina newspapers to print the Act until the convention should meet in June for the total fee of ten dollars, when in fact Swaim said it was worth one hundred and twenty dollars. At this proposition most of the presses balked, and carried the Act only once or twice. Swaim said that for the legislature "to spend about 50,000 dollars in passing a law; and then offer the printers of the state ten dollars apiece for publishing it five months, is really *hoggish and mean!* If it were not that the people ought to be informed on this subject, we would see the members of the legislature *hung,* as a majority of them deserve to be, before we would stick a type for any such a purpose."[54] All evidence indicates that

Swaim printed it at his own expense much longer than other leading state papers.

And he did another thing at his own expense which must have been very meaningful. Since the Act called for a limited convention, whereas the West had set its heart on an unlimited one, many ambitious westerners bitterly resented such a restriction, and were about ready to throw up the half bargain and try again for a better one. As soon as Swaim thought they had had time fully to absorb the provisions of the Act, true to his promise, he began a series of editorials in which he painstakingly explained all articles of the existing constitution and balanced them off against the provisions for the new one. Admitting that the Act was not all the West had hoped for, he explained that the West would not lose, for the finished document was to be submitted for approval.

This series of long, weekly, detailed editorials continued for two months, leading up to the time to vote on whether or not the convention Act would be accepted. Swaim's sense of mission about keeping the people informed was highly dramatic; and his persuasiveness was not easy to ignore when he presented many times in different ways this thought: "We again entreat the people not to let any consideration, divert them from attending to this most important of all questions on which they have been called to act for the last twenty years!! ... They should not suffer themselves to be diverted from this purpose, by any ordinary considerations ... We [impress upon them] the importance of turning out to a man.... Again we say — *To the polls!* TO THE POLLS!!"[55]

And Swaim also had a word of advice for the East. Although he expected the people of that section to vote *"en masse"* against a convention, he warned that if they did, the West had the power to demand an unlimited convention. He made clear that the "West is determined to have a convention at all hazards." It was his opinion that the West would put up with a compromise, "but let the east hang back until this project falls through, and the west shall FORCE an unlimited convention upon her; and she will find it too late then to talk of a compromise! ... [Thus] we shall run the hazard of having a convention brought about by STORM; and unlimited in POWER and DURATION! Hence, we say, to vote FOR the present plan is SAFE— To vote AGAINST, *is* UNsafe!"[56]

By the middle of February, 1835, Guilford County was well organized for the campaign, and Swaim had been made secretary.[57] (It is noticeable that being an intelligent and serious person as well as a good penman, he held this position in every important group in which he participated.) The object of the organization was to instruct every voter in the county about the good that could come from a convention, and to urge him to vote *for* a convention. Sub-committees were appointed to convey this information virtually to every man's door, laying it fully before him, at his own fireside. Within a week an address to the people was printed and distributed far and wide. It explained the many advantages that could come from a convention, among which were provisions for future amendments to the constitution, for the election of the governor by the people, for a more satisfying representation in the General Assembly, and for lessening sectional strife by extending more equal opportunities to the people in every part of the state. The address therefore urged every citizen to remember "that his vote on this question involves more deep and lasting considerations than all the votes he has given for the last twenty years; because it affects the fundamental law of the land." In conclusion it reminded, "For want of this opportunity we have suffered much, for the opportunity we have struggled often and hard. Justice to ourselves, — duty to posterity — the interests of our state — all conspire, and call aloud, for us to avail ourselves of this opportunity . . . and vote for a convention."[58]

The vote *for* or *against* a convention was to be taken on April 1 and 2, 1835, about two and a half months after the legislature authorized it. Anticipating this event, Swaim issued a warning to all North Carolina sheriffs who were to provide for the referendum, saying, "They can never be forgiven, 'neither in this world, nor the world to come,' if they neglect, or pass over this most important of all duties devolving upon the office they have assumed."[59] And in his own inimitable fashion he urged that "an imperious duty devolves upon the people, to attend, and let their voice be recorded. . . . We hope that, on this occasion, all *demagogues*, like their kindred owls and bats, will confine themselves to the shade, and that the whole affair will be managed with a single view to the prosperity of the state, the whole state, and nothing but the state."[60]

After the vote was cast, with the slow communication of the time, it was three weeks before the final results were known — 27,550 *for* and 21,694 *against*, a 5,856 majority in favor of the calling of a convention to revise the constitution.[61] The vote of the West was much smaller than expected, not from any abatement of zeal, but because many felt that a limited convention was a niggardly dole when compared with what they felt was their political right, and thus was unacceptable. Jonathan Parker on the other hand expressed the majority opinion when he said it would be better to have half a loaf than no bread at all.[62]

With a convention authorized, the governor placed upon the sheriffs of the counties the responsibility of opening polls for electing delegates to the convention. This matter weighed heavily upon Swaim, for he knew how important it was to elect responsible men. There were to be two representatives from each county, without regard to taxation, territory, or population. That meant the East which had more counties, would have a majority of delegates in the convention — the very same situation that the West had so bitterly complained about in the legislature. Swaim, anticipating that westerners might fear the consequences, reminded them that the act provided for representatives to take an oath. He referred to the delegates' pledge, as required in the Act, to be fair and not to evade limits fixed by the Act. And he added that if any of the delegates were to try to take advantage of the others they would not be able to, for all provisions of the Act were so clearly expressed that none but idiots could misunderstand.[63] Swaim further explained that the most important step at that point was to elect delegates of fine character and high ideals. Again and again he urged the people all over the state to send their most capable representatives to the constitutional convention.

Swaim said he believed the East would be disposed to write a constitution that would be ratified by the people; for the East knew that the West, with its population majority, could easily vote a constitution to oblivion, and take the subject into its own hands, in defiance of the East. Moreover, he said, the East knew that the West would do that very thing. But he disliked to think of prolonged sectionalism, and hoped each particular section of the state would work for the good of the whole.[64]

On electing delegates to the convention, Swaim again reminded that a man might be ever so highly esteemed as a gentleman, and yet not be a forceful politician. And "in this case we need our strongest men — our heaviest metal." Swaim fortified this position by quoting from the *Carolina Observer*: ... " 'Let the body be remarkable for its weight of talents and virtue. It is no ordinary occasion, and there should be no ordinary men [deputized] to represent the people in it.' "[65]

When the convention assembled on June 4, 1835, Swaim promised to give a full report of all the proceedings, if it took him until Christmas. Extant consecutive issues of the *Greensborough Patriot* through July 8, 1835, show that he began to publish all the major discussions so that the people might be prepared to vote intelligently when the finished constitution was submitted for popular referendum. The convention completed its work by July 11, 1835, but since consecutive copies of Swaim's paper are available only through July 8, his final words on this major subject cannot be quoted. As he predicted, however, the revised document was "acceptable." It was accepted by a majority vote of 5,165.[66]

The following significant changes were thereby made. Whereas the old constitution had made no arrangement for constitutional amendments, the revised edition was to contain such provisions. The poll tax was to be uniform — that is, the same amount for everyone subject to it. Provision was made whereby public officials might be impeached. Retaining the highly controversial article of

285

the old constitution which required religious tests for public office, the word "Christian" was substituted for "Protestant." Borough representation was to be completely abolished. The privilege of voting for public officials was to be withdrawn from free Negroes, to which Swaim uttered the one-word comment, *"Damnable!"* The governor was to be elected biennially by the adult white male tax-payers instead of annually as heretofore by ballot of the General Assembly; which thereafter was to convene biennially. Equal county representation in the General Assembly was to be abolished. Instead fifty members of the Senate were to be elected biennially from districts whose inhabitants paid equal amounts of state taxes; however, to be able to vote for a senator, one had to own fifty acres of land. And one hundred and twenty members of the House of Commons were to be elected biennially and were to be distributed among the counties in proportion to federal population, with each county guaranteed at least one representative in the legislature. All white male adult taxpayers were to be eligible to vote for members of the House of Commons. The East with its greater wealth would control the Senate (27 to 23), but the West with its larger pop-ulation would control the House of Commons (65 to 56).* This situation would undoubtedly lead to the necessity for compromise in legislation, but it would also lead to more carefully planned legislation.[67]

The 1835 revision of the constitution was a victory for democ-racy and a turning point in North Carolina history. It opened a way for the state to enjoy an era of social and economic progress. No North Carolinian had made a greater contribution to this par-ticular victory than had William Swaim.

Swaim had no better opinion of the Congress of the United States than he had of the legislature of North Carolina. In order that

---

*These figures were based upon an East-West division as set up by Wil-liam K. Boyd in his *History of North Carolina, Volume II, The Federal Period, 1783-1860*, pages 146-147; and upon a list of North Carolina counties, sena-torial districts, senators, and representatives (121) in the House of Commons for 1838, as supplied by Thad Eure, Secretary of State in 1959. (Death or resignation was probably the cause of the one added representative.)

his readers would not feel that he was neglectful, time after time he would insert such a warning as the following: "The proceedings of Congress are crowded out this week; but our readers will not be vexed at this omission when we tell them that little or nothing has been done since our last date, except spinning long yarns!"[68]

It was not surprising, however, to learn from the *Greensborough Patriot* that Congress in the 1830's was confronted with the problems of postage rates and the budget. On the latter a resolution had been introduced in the House of Representatives to cut expenses by lowering salaries of officials. This gave Swaim an opening to say what he thought. "We can't, somehow, get the notion out of our head," he wrote, "that the most effectual means of retrenching the expenses of Government, would be ... for the members *all* to leave thair hairsplitting, talkative dispositions at home for their children to play with, & enter the House, clad in a plain & decent business costume. It is ridiculous, almost beyond endurance, that men who claim the confidence of the people, should so shamefully abuse the trust reposed in them, as to retard the business of the House by rehearsing their long and fulsome speculations, like 'a thrice told tale, vexing the dull ears of drowsy men!' We will hazard our reputation upon the assertion, that the time which *has been* and *will be* consumed in *unnecessary* speaking during the present Session, will not cost the United States less than *two hundred and fifty thousand dollars!*"[69]

It was not long before he was reporting a specific case of long drawn out speeches, in connection with Samuel Houston of Texas and Representative William Stanbery of Ohio. In one of his orations, Stanbery had asked, was not the late Secretary of War, John H. Eaton, removed from his position because of his attempt fraudulently to give Houston the contract for Indian rations? Because of such an accusation, Houston, upon seeing Stanbery on a Washington street, promptly accosted him.

" 'Are you Mr. Stanbery?' he asked.

" 'Yes, sir.'

" 'Then you are a damned rascal,' Houston cried, giving [Stanbery] a lusty whack on the head with his cane."[70]

The attack caused a national sensation. Houston was arrested and brought before the House of Representtaives for trial. Although Francis Scott Key was the official attorney for Houston, the Texan conducted his own case. The trial lasted four weeks, and finally the House of Representatives voted for Houston to be reprimanded. This duty fell to Andrew Stevenson, Speaker of the House, who had been Houston's "drinking partner" the night before the final speeches. After an encomium, Stevenson said, "I do reprimand you accordingly."[71]

Swaim was utterly disgusted with such carryings on at the national capital. After laying the facts before his readers, he wrote: "to lay aside all the important measures upon which the people called them together to act; and spend three or four weeks, at an expense of not less than fifty five thousand dollars in discussing the case of Houston, whose whole hide and *tallow* are not worth the *candle* by which we write this worthless article, is too insufferably rediculous and contemptible!...Considering the distracted condition of things at Washington, and the luke-warmness of the people in regard to it patriotism has cause to be ALARMED![72]

Convinced of the great need for progressive social and economic legislation at national as well as at state level, Swaim felt that Congress should direct its energies toward this end. Usually when measures along these lines were introduced, however, they were worn out by long, wearisome discussions on whether or not they were constitutional or were infringing on State rights. For thirty-seven years North Carolina's Nathaniel Macon had used his influence against practically every progressive measure in Congress —holding rigid economy, State rights, and a strict interpretation of the United States Constitution above the national program of internal improvements, protective tariff, sound currency, and national defense -- and his influence still obtained.

Regarding the tendency to avoid reform measures, to think in terms of personal gain, and to use State rights as a shield against reform and criticism, Swaim wrote, "When such feelings and such sentiments, and such motives regulate the legislation of a free people, and obtain a mastery in the halls of Congress, it is time to recur to the great lights of the revolution, and take a new departure on the road to national greatness."[13]

No one could have been more serious than Swaim in this matter of honesty, efficiency, and vision in government officials; but following an occasional practice which combined humor with seriousness, in this manner he brought home his criticism of Congress: "UNREASONABLE PUNISHMENT. A person in some part of the world—we forget, or never knew where—was brought before a Judge for murder in the first degree. The circumstances divulged by the evidence were of so aggravating a character that everybody thought hanging was too good for him. In order to meet this difficulty, the prosecuting officer proposed to his honour, that the convicted offender, instead of undergoing the comparatively mild punishment of death, should be condemned to *read a congress speech from end to end!* The Judge, however, after some desultory conversation with the bar, urged as a conclusive reason for declining to pronounce such sentence; that the constitution would not justify the infliction of any '*cruel or unreasonable punishment.*' "[14]

Not stopping with his analyses of the state legislature and the national Congress, Swaim extended his estimates and criticisms to include the highest officials of the United States. Being politically independent, and apparently unafraid of losing subscribers, he was free to appraise all men exactly as he saw them. Believing that the great object of government was to improve the condition of the people by well-considered and positive actions, he expected those who were placed in positions of public responsibility to give the most they had to their assignments. He kept his "lynx-eyed vigilence" constantly focussed on the national capital, and consequently his paper was spotted with the names of John Quincy Adams, Henry Clay, John C. Calhoun, Daniel Webster, Martin Van Buren, and Andrew Jackson. He admired Adams who felt the national government should function as an agency for economic, intellectual, and moral improvement. He thought well of Henry Clay and his American system until Clay sacrificed some of his principles in the hope of political gain. He was painfully disappointed in Calhoun for his attitude toward nullification. He was lukewarm on the subject of Webster. He had little use for Van Buren. And he did an honest job in reporting Jackson.

Swaim wrote very little about Thomas Jefferson, and when he mentioned him he did not try to tie Jeffersonian and Jacksonian democracy together. Whenever he referred to Jefferson he used the most respectful language, such as "The immortal Jefferson, whose name will hold a conspicuous place in the annals, not only of Virginia, but of the world, till time shall be no more."[75]

It was natural that President Andrew Jackson should be more in the spotlight than any of the other leading political figures during the editorship of Swaim. Speaking of his presidential message in 1829, Swaim said, "We find in it much to admire, and much to condemn. . . . The picture of the condition of our country, as it stands connected by its commercial relations with other countries, is very beautifully and perhaps accurately drawn. If the high toned feelings here manifested, had characterized his observations upon our internal concerns, he might justly claim the character of an exalted Statesman."[76]

The Greensboro editor was greatly annoyed, however, by what he considered Jackson's vague position on such important issues as the tariff, the disposition of funds from the sale of public lands, the United States Bank, and internal improvements. In this connection Swaim wrote, "Take the whole business together, and we are unable to compare it to anything more appropriate than the *satisfactory* answers of the negro when his master asked him where the plow was. Cudjo answered: 'Long a de harrow massa.' 'And where is the harrow?' interrogated the master. 'Long a de plow massa.' 'And where are the plow and the harrow both?' continued his master. 'Why bose togedder massa! Ha'nt I tole you tree time afore?' "[77]

Although Jackson was not his favorite person, Swaim very soon made clear that his paper would deal honestly and openly with him. When "ENQUIRER'S" article, containing unduly rough criticism of Jackson, came to Swaim's desk, he refused to publish it, saying, "We think it not only unnecessary, but ungenerous, in weighing the merits of our Chief Magistrate, to throw into the ballance his conduct previous to the election. Before he came into power, it was prudent to examine his public and private character, as a test of his fitness for the appointment; but since he has been crowned with the distinguished honors of the Nation, we say: — let everything sleep in oblivion but his public acts, by which his administration alone should be judged."[78]

Some of Jackson's public acts, however, had greatly shocked Swaim before his first term was out. The president had practiced the policy of political patronage to an extent hitherto unknown. Swaim said that he had removed within eighteen months one thousand, four hundred and seventy men from public office — many honorable and useful men along with those who should have gone— in order that he might promote those who had supported him for president.[79] Among those favored were some of the newspaper men who had used their presses to elect him, and Swaim thought offices thus "purchased" were a disgrace to the country.

In 1832, a committee from Swaim's county came together to consider whether it would support Jackson or Clay for president. Members of the committee reported that in looking toward permanent duration of the government, they felt that Jackson had exercised too much freedom in rewards and punishment through patronage; that up to that time he had not asserted himself on nullification; that he had disturbed the nation by his bank attitude; and that his term had been so strongly marked by his most self-willed and partisan feeling that the whole Union was in a state of excitement. Consequently Guilford County came out for Henry Clay for president. At that time Swaim was a great admirer of Clay. The nearest the *Greensborough Patriot* ever came to having a twentieth century headline was when it printed Guilford's decision to back Clay for president.

---

# The Patriot,

"LIBERTY — THE CONSTITUTION — UNION"

---

## PEOPLE'S NOMINATION.

### FOR PRESIDENT,

# HENRY CLAY,

## OF KENTUCKY,

### FOR VICE PRESIDENT,

## JOHN SARGENT,

## OF PENNSYLVANIA[80]

---

An interesting incident occurred in June, 1832, when Jackson supporters in Guilford were trying to get organized. The county had favored "Old Hickory" in 1828, because it thought he would promote internal improvements. When he had moved slowly on that and other much needed reforms, Guilford citizens had turned to Clay. At a court session when hundreds of people from over the county were assembled, a meeting was called for the purpose of nominating an elector on the Jackson ticket. When the appointed hour arrived, after much bell ringing and court crying, about 40 people ambled into the courtroom. When the chariman of the meeting tried to procede with the business, because of heckling he found it difficult to get positive action. He then requested that all anti-Jackson men leave the courtroom, and all but eight men left.[81]

When Jackson was re-elected, Swaim announced the outcome without comment.

Swaim resolved to be tolerant of Jackson during his second term. "If it should hereafter turn out that he has determined to consult the real interests of the Union, and restore the government to its primitive purity and permanence, we have determined to do as the boy did that attempted to cypher — Rub out all the past and take a new start!"[82] By the time of the next presidential election, however, Swaim admitted that even though he approved of some acts of Jackson's administration, he loathed with a "bitter distilled vengeance" the President's choice of Van Buren for the next president.

Col. David Crockett was a member of Congress during Swaim's editorship, and he was quite as colorful as a real life figure in the 1830's as he was as a mythical figure in the mid-twentieth century. Swaim liked Crockett's ideas, and quoted him on his dislike of nullification, his approval of internal improvements, and his clever description of President Jackson's latitudinarianism. In speaking of Jackson, Crockett said he supported the Chief Magistrate until he " 'changed the principles he professed before his election. When he quit those principles, I quit him. . . . I am still a Jacksonian, but General Jackson is not, he has become a Van Buren man . . . Although . . . [he] changed his course, I will not change mine — *I would rather be politically dead than hypocritically immortalized.*' "[83]

A national condition which worked to Swaim's disadvantage all through his editorship was that of bad mail service. In his avowed desire to promote general improvmeent throughout the country, he made an early effort to get this matter adjusted when on July 18, 1829, he published in his paper the following account: "Post Office Department. We hear many and loud complaints from many parts of the country respecting the *management* of this Department. It was instituted for the accommodation of the people; and any thing tending to weaken their confidence in its safety, will cast a 'drowsy pall' upon the intercourse of the Nation. We have, as yet, no practical evidence that the whole Department will be prostituted to the base designs of a party, but we know that such *suspicion* has gone

293

abroad in the land: and we say, *destroy* the confidence of the people, and you destroy the establishment itself, with all its thousand facilities.

"Postmasters appointed under the new administration have threatened to stop the circulation of newspapers that shall dare to give their readers correct information of the powers that be — men have so far lost their confidence in offices connected with the department, that they send their letters to other offices to be mailed, or have them endorsed in a handwriting other than their own—"

This brief notice was copied in the *National Intelligencer*, which Samuel Ashe in his *History of North Carolina* said was considered the most important of all the newspapers in the country; in the *New York Courier and Enquirer;* and in the *United States Telegraph* of Washington which called the *Greensborough Patriot* a "*contemptible village sheet*" for calling attention to unsatisfactory mail services and political pressure.[84] Whereupon C. K. Gardner, Assistant Postmaster General, on August 4, 1829, wrote to Swaim, asking for proof of his statements that (1) postmasters have threatened to stop the circulation of newspapers, and (2) men have so far lost confidence in some offices that they have endorsed their letters in a handwriting other than their own or have sent their letters to other offices to be mailed. Moreover, Gardner said he was instructed by the Postmaster General, William T. Barry, to get the names of postmasters thus accused.[85]

In reply, on August 24, 1829, Swaim quoted from two recent issues of the *National Intelligencer*: first, " 'the Wiscasset Citizen says that one of the new batch of *reformed* Postmasters has had the impudence to threaten *openly* to "restrict the circulation" of a paper called the Kennebec Curier merely because it disapproves of the proscription.' " Second, postmasters have been known to cause business " 'letters to be endorsed under envelopes, in the handwriting of others; . . . whilst other persons send their letters to postoffices ten miles off, to avoid corresponding through their own which have been "reformed." Those facts have occurred to our knowledge.' "

In conclusion, Syaim wrote Gardner that "These facts from the Intelligencer I hold to be sufficient to sustain the averments made in that article from the Patriot which elicited the letter of yours now before me; but I shall shortly exhibit to your inspection, facts relative to the *management* of the Post Office *nearer home*."[86]

Here the matter rested for a few weeks while Swaim collected proof of the disorderly situation of the mail around him.

Meanwhile, one New Yorker wrote Swaim that "In looking over my Courier & Enquirer of this morning, I observed, in quite a conspicuous place, an extract from a *Greensborough* (*N. C.*) *Patriot*, about the Post Office Department. I immediately walked to the office of the 'Courier & Enquirer' and ordered them to stop my paper for degrading themselves so far as to notice a pitiful, contemptible paper edited in the back-woods of N. C.!"[87]

Swaim informed his readers that "The letter was concluded with a concatination of vulgarisms that would not sound well in your *courtly* ears," and jestingly took notice of this letter by saying if the man did not watch out the North Carolina editor would enlighten and enrich all the citizens of his backwoods and collect them into a great town big enough to overshadow and eclipse New York! "Guess the New-Yorkers will feel *pretty cheap then!*"

Within about a month, on September 23, 1829, Swaim had ready his reply concerning the mail situation in Greensboro; and he addressed it directly to Postmaster General Barry, assuring that he was prepared to sustain every accusation by judicial testimony. Entering seven complaints, he gave the names of highly respectable citizens who had witnessed or experienced such mismanagement.[88]

*First.* The Greensboro postmaster, being a practicing physician, was absent from his office about two thirds of the time, and no person was regularly left in charge. People coming many miles from the country to get their mail might wait three or four hours and then go home without it. For proof contact John Hoskins or Peter Adams, Greensboro.

*Second.* The postmaster was frequently absent when the mail arrived, and the mail bags were thrown out of the stagecoaches at the postoffice door, and there they lay for hours. For proof, ask Jacob Hubbard or John Hoskins, Greensboro.

*Third.* He has frequently assorted the mail so carelessly that many of the packages were sent in the wrong direction, and letters and papers were delayed in reaching their destination. For proof, consult Thomas Moore, New Garden.

*Fourth.* He has time after time intercepted letters to others and has allowed them to remain almost three months in the Greensboro Post Office before he advertised they were there. Thus business men have sustained much injury since such letters often needed prompt attention. For proof, inquire of A. Geren, postmaster Geren's Store, and Dr. David Worth, Centre.

*Fifth.* He has exchanged United States notes which had been turned over to him to mail for a patent on a grater, and has sent North Carolina money instead, which was at the time about seven per cent below par. When brought face to face with the accusation, he acknowledged the act, saying. "that they could make nothing more of it than a breach of trust." For proof, consult Camm Moore, Jacob Hubbard, Moses Mendenhall, and John A. Smith.

*Sixth.* When postage has been paid to him for mailing letters, he has apparently put the money in his own pockets and sent the letters with postage to be collected. For proof, ask Harmon Armfield and John A. Foulkes of Greensboro, and Samuel Browning of Guilford County.

*Seventh.* "His conduct in regard to the office has been of a kind so suspicious that many individuals are afraid to correspond through the office, but mail their letters at other offices, and direct their correspondents to send their communications to offices in the neighborhood. For proof write to T. Early Strange, Jacob Hubbard, William Adams and Peter Adams, *Greensborough.*"[89]

Again addressing Barry, Swaim offered to furnish more evidence if wanted. And he further suggested that if there were any doubt in the Postmaster General's mind about the integrity of the citizens whose names he had supplied, he might consult Congressmen Augustine H. Shepperd and John Long for verification.[90]

Sometime after sending the above facts, Swaim heard indirectly that Barry had the subject under advisement. When this was made known, Greensboro citizens, then Jackson supporters, but later for Clay, sent Barry a petition "setting forth their grievances and praying for their redress." There were only one hundred and twenty-five males over twenty-one years of age in Greensboro at that time. And this petition carried more than one hundred signatures.

Meanwhile two Greensboro citizens wrote the Postmaster General that the "Postoffice at this place, [is] managed with as much correctness and fidelity as any other Postoffice in all the Southern country."[91] Apparently that gave Barry the excuse he wanted to do nothing about the matter; for the Greensboro postmaster was left in his job.

Swaim placed the disturbance completely in the open by publishing all the letters and information on the first two pages of the *Greensborough Patriot.* He said he had not wanted to make complaints against a neighbor, but public pressure had forced him to do it. He fortified his stand and gave insight into his upright character by saying, as he always did in controversial situations, "Any person who may feel himself wronged or aggrieved by anything contained in these articles . . . shall have the use of our columns, to the full extent of space we have here occupied, to vindicate himself from false charges and false imputations. Anything communicated shall be faithfully and honestly inserted."[92] No one, however, accepted this challenge.

Thereafter he kept publishing complaints which were known to him personally or which he quoted from other papers over the country. In 1835 he announced that Barry, whose incompetence as Postmaster General had even been admitted by Jackson, had been replaced by Amos Kendall. Of this appointment Swaim observed that "many predicted that he would bring order out of confusion; but our opinion then was, and continues to be, that he will render corruption itself more corrupt. The difference between him and his predecessor we believe to be this: Barry was corrupt, without the sense to conceal it; — Kendall is ten times more corrupt, and has engenuity enough to prevent detection!"[93]

State and national affairs were not the end of the Greensboro editor's interest. Swaim's coverage of foreign events was both interesting and extensive. This subject occupied a rather large section in practically every weekly issue of his paper. He covered details from the death of royalty and the distribution of the crown jewels to threats of war that would entangle the United States. He reported on meetings of royalty and other officials from time to time; on various European revolutions in the 1830's; on political reform bills and strikes of weavers in England; on a Franco-American debt question, growing out of the French debt to the United States for services in 1806-1807; and on civil wars in Latin America. This material he reprinted from other papers, generally from out of the state, or secured firsthand from travelers to foreign countries; and he managed to keep his readers informed on foreign as well as national, state, and local affairs.

In placing all these matters before the public, Swaim was living up to his promise when he said that all important news would be collected and published and that "the Legislative and Executive Functionaries of our State, as well as of the United States, will be watched with an eye that never winks, and their actions faithfully laid before the people for their examination."[94]

# XII

## FOR FREEDOM OF THE PRESS

*"Congress shall make no law respecting an establishment of religion, or prohibiting the free exercise thereof; or abridging the* freedom of speech or of the press; *or the right of the people peaceably to assemble and to petition the Government for a redress of grievances."*—Bill of Rights, First Amendment, Constitution of the United States.

The hardest battle that William Swaim had to fight was in defense of his right to speak and write his convictions. From the beginning to the end of his editorial career, he repeatedly told his readers that his course would be that of an independent, and he clearly defined this stand. In 1831 he announced that "The Patriot shall continue to be what it has always been, free from the control of any mortal except ONE. The despot may frown — the tyrant may scorne—the nabob may threaten—and the critic may sneer—but we give them to the winds, or place them under our feet and pass on in that course which nothing but want of patronage shall ever interrupt." In 1832 he elaborated on this position: "That we have erred, in numberless instances, both in point of *fact* and *opinion*, we are as ready to *admit* as our enemies are to *charge;* but we will meet the world in the teeth, in defence of the rectitude of our intentions. We have never 'bowed to the knee of Baal' nor *licked the dirt* from the feet of the *popular idol* of the day. If we had taken this course, the probability is, we should have received *'fewer kicks* and *more coppers;'* but we should have robbed ourself of that peace of

299

mind which a *quiet conscience* alone can give; and which we would not *barter* for all the *political bubbles* that have ever bursted upon the ocean of time, since *created order* sprang from *chaos*.

"When we first commenced the publication of a paper in this place, a disposition was made by the *Nabob Gentry*, to *seduce* us from an independent course, and by their *friendly advice*, to *warp* us into their service; but finding us not composed of *materials* so *pliant* as they first expected, their next attempt was to *intimidate* by threats, not of *violence*, but of *withholding*, and persuading others to *withhold*, the *needful!* They soon learned from our tone, however, that we would sooner crawl on our hands and knees, and beg for sustenance — *and be free* — than to *compromise our principles*, and *sacrifice our freedom of opinion*, for a seat among the tawdry and tottering *thrones of corruption!*

"Still bent, however, upon the fell purpose of preventing, if possible, an *unshackled press* from growing into *public favour*, our enemies have even ransacked hell, from the centre to the circumference, for slanderous fabrications; and these have been heaped upon us without *cause*, without *measure*, and without *mercy*. But thanks to a generous public — they have thus far sustained us 'through evil as well as through good report' ... [and in gratitude for this support, Swaim declared that] before we will relinquish our right to think, speak, print, and publish our own *deliberate opinions*, in relation to *public men* and *public measures*, so far as the same shall be authorized by the mandates of *constitutional law*, or required by the *interests of our country* — we say, before these privileges shall be *relinquished*, we will *renounce existence itself!* Take away our *rights* as a *free man*, and *life has no charms for us!*"[1]

After all that, he again affirmed, "In short, our paper shall be, in the broadest and unqualified sense of the term, *a friend of the people*, and *an unwavering defender of their rights*." Earlier he had warned that "We will *praise* where we can, and *blame* where we *must*."[2] He proudly took this stand from which he never retreated, confident that his security lay in the first amendment to the Constitution of the United States.

By "independent," he said he meant that he considered himself free at all times to print news faithfully, taking no stock in half truths about men or their actions, whoever and whatever they might be. He believed then as Gerald W. Johnson believed a century and a quarter later that "the highest attainable freedom is contingent upon the fullest and most accurate information, since reality and reason hang upon information."[3]* Within the limits of human reason, it was his intention to present the truth without bias. When a measure for public welfare was under consideration, however, he reserved the right to uphold the position he felt to be wiser or more nearly right.

Swaim realized that few men have the magnanimity to tolerate in an editor or anyone else the expression of opinions different from their own, especially if those opinions are in favour of a higher tone of moral duty than they are willing to adopt. Hence, he said, the difficulty in making a press, in reality, an engine of moral reform. In order to keep his promise to present all aspects of the news and of all issues, he proposed that "Those of our readers with whom we have the misfortune to differ in our political opinions, who will be kind enough to extend liberal indulgence to our errors of judgment, shall at all times have the use of our columns to defend their favorite sentiments, as a friendly turn for their liberality."[4]

"To conduct a leading newspaper well, is not so easy a matter as many idlers imagine, . . ." wrote Swaim of his self-imposed standards. "To make a good editor requires the essence of thirty members of congress, twenty fourth-of-July orators, and about a dozen modern poets, to say nothing of the thousand flowers caught from the 'living [waters] as they rise' — from men of the world — from

---

*Swaim complained that particularly the Raleigh editors at the seat of state government dared not tell all they knew. What they did tell was generally true, but they did not always present the cause of conflict and people were left to accept a statement of fact without knowledge of contributing forces and developments, and therefore they could not, intelligently, think things through for themselves.

Wall Street — from Broadway, &c. &c. An editor must always be with the people — think with them — feel with them."[5] He maintained that above all people on the earth, the editor must be most alert and aware. He agreed with the *Boston Galaxy* that, "Like the Jackall, he must hunt diligently to satisfy the appetite of that lion, the world. He must be an indefatigable caterer for that huge and fastidious epicure, the public. He must sleep to dream about the mails, and wake to examine them. Up early and down late, it is his task to present an epitome of the various intelligence from the four quarters of the globe, the sad and the merry, the gloomy and the gay, the revolution of empires, and the growth of squashes, the adventures of kings and great men of the little drama and large world."[6] Whatever it took, however, Swaim was determined to publish a creditable sheet.

In the third issue of the *Greensborough Patriot*, dated June 6, 1829, he warned that there was reason to watch closely recent developments in connection with the press, for there were some editors who, in the hope of appointment to office or prestige, were tying themselves to political parties which might dictate what they should or should not say. "The freedom of opinion, of the pen and of the press, have been regarded as the great pillars of our national freedom and happiness," he wrote. "While these remain uncorrupted the people are secure; but when power or self is used to render them subservient to the caprices of party, let the people be alarmed for their safety; and let them prepare for shielding their neck from the trample of tyrants. Never, since the organization of our Government, have we seen such a reckless disposition to corrupt the sources of intelligence, and render it impossible for the people to be impartially instructed in the things that pertain to their interest or the perpetuation of their National existence, as has been manifested by the President of the United States and his understrapping coadjutors in their mad career of political regeneration."[7]

Here Swaim was referring to Jackson and the spoils system. Some of the most flagrant examples of this system were Duff Green,

Editor of the *United States Telegraph,* who was made Printer to the Senate and House of Representatives; Amos Kendall, Editor of the *Argus of Western America,* who was appointed Fourth Auditor of the Treasury; Maj. Mordecai M. Noah, Editor of the *New York Enquirer,* who was made Surveyor of New York; and Dabney S. Carr, Editor of the *Baltimore Republican,* who was given a "comfortable" place in the Custom House in Baltimore. They had plucked these large plums from the political pudding because their papers had supported Andrew Jackson.[8] In such a liaison between politics and the press Swaim could see the danger of prostitution of the press. "When the Executive of the United States promotes to office the little-souled editor of a *party,* merely as a reward for services rendered to such a *party,* he ceases to be a President of the U. S. and becomes the President of a *party.* . . . If this principle which ought to be trampled in scorn beneath our feet, becomes adopted, where shall we look to for independence of the PRESS? . . . If every party scribbler must have a crum for each *lie* he may palm upon the community, the people may abandon all efforts to obtain correct information, and bid farewell to the liberties of their country!"[9] Whatever the outcome, Swaim steadfastly pursued his determination to court neither friend nor foe, but rather to take for his guide truth as he saw it.

At the end of his ninth month of publication, he began his serious defense of a free press. This challenge presented itself when Francis Todd in 1830 brought a libel suit for $5,000 damages against the editors of *The Genius of Universal Emancipation.* In the absence of Editor Benjamin Lundy, Assistant Editor William Lloyd Garrison charged that Todd, a Yankee of Newburyport, Massachusetts, and owner of the ship *Francis,* had carried from Baltimore, Maryland, a cargo of slaves for the New Orleans market. Although Todd was within the law, Garrison declared that he was at war with the common sense of mankind and that God and good men regarded his action with abhorrence, and "resolved to cover with thick infamy all who were concerned with this nefarious

303

business." Whereupon in the Baltimore City Courts, Garrison was indicted for libel, convicted, and sentenced to pay a fine of $50 and costs of prosecution.

Early in 1830, Swaim printed the leading paragraph from Garrison's article, with this comment: "This is the paragraph for the publication of which the prosecution has been commenced; and we can now inform Mr. Todd that, if he wishes to get his 'belly full of law,' he can institute a suit against us for copying the article from the Genius."[10]

The matter was also taken up by the General Association of the Manumission Society of North Carolina, of which Benjamin Swaim was president, and William Swaim, secretary. The president, evidently backed by the sceretary, stated that it was of the highest importance that the liberty of the press be understood and appreciated, and appointed a committee to consider whether Garrison had gone beyond the privilege guaranteed by the liberty of the press. Members of the committee reported that they did not consider Garrison's statement libelous, they did not think he abused the liberty guaranteed to the press by the Constitution of the United States, they did consider public protest against the illegal and unconstitutional decision in the case to be quite in order, and they definitely favored the publication of this position of the Manumission Society in the Greensborough Patriot.[11] Swaim's rejoinder in this case would be remembered later, in connection with his daring in other matters.

There was a quick reaction from Scotland Neck in the eastern part of the state to Swaim's stand, when by return mail a reader wrote that "Not until very recently have we in this part of the state, known that there existed a press conducted on such liberal and honorable principles as we are happy to find govern the Greensborough Patriot. Your boldness in courting a collision with the slandered Mr. Todd cheers us.... Your paper has been shown to several in this section, all speak of it in the highest terms of commendation, & many will subscribe no doubt by the next mail or so."[12] The writer further stated that people in his vicinity thought a man of Swaim's talents and ability should move to Washington City. "They think you will be able to hold Duff and others of his kidney in check. . . . Your talents and indubitable courage are very much needed there." And he even said within eight years Swaim "will certainly stand a good chance for the presidency."

Such flattery, however, could not outweigh the fact that the admirer failed to pay postage on his compliment. Swaim printed the compliment; and under it the oblique half-joking reminder: "We can only say that, inasmuch as the postage was not paid, our fears have given birth to doubts whether money could be started to pay the *subscription*. When we receive another letter from him, postpaid, and on opening it, smell *two dollars*, he may look out for— anything he wants! even a calf-rope!"[13]

Some of Swaim's intimate and interested friends told him that his insistence upon absolute Puritanical standards, and his open criticism of personal character might hurt him as well as the one he assailed. Swaim, however, was willing if necessary, to sacrifice himself for his undertaking. He maintained that "to attack *principles* successfully, it must be done through the *persons* who embrace those principles."[14]

This attitude which he considered free and frank was soon to land him in a libel suit instituted by one Zimri J. Emery, an apprentice bound to him. Emery for his own reasons ran away; and in advertising for his return, Swaim described the boy too unreservedly to suit the young fellow. In the 1830's, however, apprentices were governed by very strict laws which were carefully explained in the *Greensborough Patriot*.[15] Apprenticed young men were under the absolute control of those who contracted to keep them a specified number of years while teaching them the trade. It was considered a serious offense for an apprentice to leave his employer before the expiration of the term of the contract; and anyone who hired a "runaway" apprentice laid himself liable to a heavy fine. It was not unusual, however, for an apprentice to run away. Nor was it unusual for the employer to advertise his actions. Newspapers of the day carried notices of warning against the employment of specified "strays." Naturally such notices contained descriptions which were hardly pleasant appraisals. And Swaim, as was his custom, said just what he thought about Emery's abrupt departure in language that was definite beyond question.

With fingers pointing conspicuously to the title, he placed the following vitriolic notice in the *Greensborough Patriot*:

## A RUNAWAY!!

"On Tuesday, the 30, ult. An Apprentice boy, named Zimri Jorden Emery, took himself away from my employment, without any provocation or cause of complaint, except what grew out of the circumstance that he got above his business, or too big for his clothes, and became self willed and disobedient, for which, as in duty bound, I gave him a moderate and reasonable flogging. This he conceived to be *indigestible* without some *exercise* and accordingly hung his feet to his ancles and walked off.

"He is about 18 or 19 years of age; about the ordinary stature; complexion yellow, especially about the mouth; long and lantern jawed; down cast, sneeking looking; slovenly gaited; slow motioned; much addicted to telling tales, particularly such as are not true; with more conceit than good sense; and not more honesty than he should have. I give this description, not through prejudice, but because I conscientiously believe it to be a correct one.

"Said apprentice was bound to me by a voluntary agreement, entered into and even *urged upon me* by himself and his mother, on the 20, of November last.

"He was to be entitled to all the privileges, and subject to the liabilities and restrictions of an endented apprentice, during the term of three years, except his clothing, which was to be furnished by his mother, and for which I was to pay an equivalent of $75.00.

"I have been told since his elopement, that he has it in contemplation to offer himself as a *journeyman printer*, at some office in this state. This is the reason why I am thus particular in describing his person, together with the circumstances of his connexion with me. I want no printer, to be imposed upon by a wirthless

Devil, as I have been — they are already cursed with an undue portion of the ills of life, without this intollerable torment super-added.

"I hereby caution all persons against harbouring, trading with, trusting, or employing him, under the 'pains and penalties in such cases made & provided,' as I am determined to prosecute, to the utmost rigor of the law, any or all, who may thus offend.

"I will give *two and a half cents*, IN CASH, to any person who shall deliver said runaway at my office in Greensborough; or twenty-five cents for confining him in any jail, and sending me word.

"All the printers in this State, together with the Yorkville Whig and the People's Advocate, in S. C. are requested to copy this notice a few times, and the favor shall be promptly reciprocated.

WILLIAM SWAIM"[16]

This notice bore the date of July 7, 1830. Soon thereafter Emery entered suit for libel against Swaim. Early in November, 1831, the two met in the Guilford County Superior Court where a case, the *State vs Swaim* for publishing a libel against Zimri J. Emery, was tried. Solicitor General John Scott and William A. Graham, Esq., were counsel for the state; and Hamilton C. Jones and John M. Morehead, Esqrs., defended Swaim on the basis of freedom of the press. With Judge William Norwood presiding, the case lasted an entire day. The jury, having been charged by Judge Norwood, retired, and in a few minutes returned with the verdict of "guilty." Swaim's counsel then entered a motion for a new trial. The *Raleigh Register* reported that the request, "being refused, an appeal we understand, *was taken* to the State Supreme Court."[17] It appears, however, that there was a misunderstanding on that point, for the *Supreme Court Reports* contain no record of the case.

In March, 1834, Swaim published in his paper what seems to have been the outcome of the case, and one of his venomous out-bursts against the Solicitor of the Court, John Scott. In the intemperate and lengthy finale, he demonstrated both his strength and his weakness; the courage to publish what he thought; but also the tendency to allow anger and contempt to possess him. One may wonder at times whether Swaim would have been as scurrilous in this attack, had Scott been only a reprehensible public servant and not a reprehensible public servant who prosecuted William Swaim.

In his own inimitable high-voltage language, Swaim paid his respects to Solicitor Scott: "We have already mentioned the fact, that this *high minded* and *honourable* prosecuting officer, commenced a suit against us, for an alleged libel, in the superior court for this county, some three or four years ago — that, after shaking this prosecution over our head, in order to *intimidate,* and running the county to three or four hundred dollars cost, he entered a [*nolle*] *prosequi,* without solicitation on our part, and contrary to our wishes; that before the prosecution was commenced, he *disgraced* himself, by *meanly* exerting what little influence his *official station* placed at his disposal, to turn the current of public prejudice against us; and that he even talked of 'tar and feathers,' and hinted to the good people of this place the propriety of making such an application!!

"During the pendency of this suit, we could hear of his *'libellous'* and slanderous tongue, running like a *mill* [*clapper*] wherever he went. At Stokes superior court, he was heard to hint something very much like taking a *walking stick* to us when he got to our court. A lawyer brought us the information; and our reply was that if Mr. Scott would withdraw all his *prosecutions* against us, and make up an *issue* to be settled with *walking sticks* we would be content to adjust the matter in that way. Court came; and with it came the solicitor general! We passed and re-passed him several times during the week, but did not even receive a *flogging for our pains!*

"On Friday of our court, however, this hero of the 'green satchel' and 'walking stick,' remarked in his own room, in the presence of several lawyers, that he understood we had been locked up at home *crying* all the week, for fear of being *chastised* by him! We was in the courthouse when a member of the bar brought us this information, directly from Mr. Scott's room; to which we replied,

308

that even if we had been *crying* all the week; we had never risen between midnight and day; and went into the rooms of members of the legislature and *'cried' for office,* as he had done, for the appointment which he was so wholly unfit to fill.

"Finding it impossible to make us cower at his lordly feet, either with his *snake-pole indictments* or his *walking stick,* he *dismissed* the *scare-crow,* and we envy him not the laurels he has reaped from the contest. Such *victories* are not very flattering to his reputation, as a prosecuting officer, if he did *cry for the appointment.* If ever the 'liberty of speech and the press' is to be successfully assailed in this *free country,* John Scott is not the man to do it! He is as wholly unfit for a prosecuting officer, as he is for a seat at the *left* hand of God!"[18]

That outburst seems to have been Swaim's masterpiece of invective. It prompted one of his friends to warn him against such intemperate language. No one, however, denied that Scott was a sorry specimen of public servant.

The *nolle prosequi,* which Solicitor Scott entered, produced one of those rare records in court history, the interpretation of which required the authority of the Honorable Dillard S. Gardner, Marshal-Librarian of the State of North Carolina Supreme Court Library. Wrote Gardner, "Since a nol. pros. is not appropriately entered after a verdict which has not been set aside, a nol. pros. after a verdict would be irregular but would stand until challenged for irregularity. When a case has reached a verdict, it has been tried — and the judgment of the court upon the verdict would finally dispose of the case."[19] In this case no available record shows reference to the case again, indicating that evidently it was indefinitely postponed.

The conflict between Swaim and Emery which provided the occasion for the editor's appraisal of the Solicitor General had dragged on for almost four years. While this case was pending, several others which also tested the freedom of the press were instituted against the outspoken editor. Conspicuous among these

309

was an attempt of the state legislature to silence their harshest critic.

In the session of 1830-1831, that body was turning out a sizeable block of restrictions in connection with slavery. While these various bills were under consideration, Swaim published an editorial and a communication which brought legislative wrath down upon his head. Since these articles were read in full or in part before the House of Commons, it will give clearer insight into the disturbance to reprint them here. In the editorial column, Swaim wrote that "Mr. Mears,... [a member] from the joint select committee relative to slaves, ... who, from present appearances, may safely be dubbed, 'the negroe's Devil, ...' has reported something like half a gross of bills against these miserable outcasts from human commisseration."[20] Referring specifically to some of the bills, Swaim added, "But we must walk lightly over this ground, and not blunder upon the truth, lest we might render ourself obnoxious to another bill which was conceived and brought forth by the same committee— namely, 'a bill to prevent the circulation of seditious publications.'

"The same *select* committee gave birth to a bill to prevent masters or owners of slaves from learning them to read or write.

"While this bill was under consideration, our Senator, Mr. Dick moved to strike out that part of the bill which prohibits slaves from being taught to read; but his motion was lost by a large majority. He then moved to exclude Guilford county from the operation of the bill, but this motion was also lost, and the bill passed its sceond reading without a division.... If this bill becomes a law we intend to commence the study of low Dutch; for it has been said ... that a person can swear harder in that language than any other!"[21]

As secretary of the Manumission Society, Swaim used his newspaper to fight slavery. And antislavery sentiments hardly endeared the editor to those who preferred the *status quo*. In the same issue that contained the low Dutch wisecrack, Swaim published the following communication signed "Father Abraham:"

"Mr. Editor: There appears to be a dissension among the journals of the day concerning the besetting sins of our country. Some are exclaiming against the mal-administration of President Jackson, and others against Clay and his bargains, eating parties, the tariff, etc.

"That there are great moral and political evils extant, there can be no doubt; but that Jackson and Clay are the cause of all these evils, is entirely a mistake. There is one evil in existence of greater moral and political turpitude than any other, and yet the Journals say but little about it; although I am inclined to think that it is the real cause of dissension among many of them — that is the evil of slavery.

"That slavery is the greatest moral and political evil that has ever yet disgraced the features of a free and enlightened republican government, is apparent to every one who suffers himself to reflect soberly upon the injustice and cruelty of the slave system, as practiced in the United States, and the consequences arising from it.

"1st. Slavery is a moral evil, because it is inconsistent with the principles of human nature.

"2nd. Because it gives one man absolute power to domineer over another, and frequently to men of the most despotic dispositions; men who are addicted to intemperance, and every other species of vice that can possibly be named.

"3rd. If the Bible is to be taken as a standard by which to regulate our moral conduct, we shall find slavery inconsistent with the tenor of it also; and to say 'a slaveholding christian' is as great a solecism as to say, a drunken christian, and yet every religious society will exclaim against the vice of drunkenness, and many of them tolerate the slave system, of which even Pope Leo the tenth said, 'not only the christian religion but nature herself, cries out against a state of slavery.'

"4th. It is a political evil, because whatever is morally wrong never can be politically right.

"5th. It is inconsistent with the very essence of our republican institutions, and is the cause of most of the prejudices which exist among the states: and I fear that the spirit of nullification has sprung from slavery, if the true cause were known.

311

"6th. It keeps many of the states continually on their guard in order to prevent insurrection.

"7th. But one of the greatest evils attending it is, the deadening influence it has upon the agricultural interests of our country.

"8th. Slave labour is not so profitable as free labour which can be easily proven by mathematical demonstration.

"Mr. Editor, these are a few of the evils that attend the slave system of our country; yet many more might be adduced. Seeing that the features are so apparent, what shall we say of that man who tells us that he is sent by his maker to declare the 'whole council of God,' and declaims against vice of every kind, with the logic of a Paul and the eloquence of a Cicero, until he comes to the sin of slavery where he is entirely mute, or says but little about it for fear of hurting the feelings of the people? Though he should have the tongue of an ang[el] and declare not against the sin of slavery, what is he? Nothing, I fear, but a time-serving, truckling counsellor who cares not for the flock but the fleece.

"Or what shall we say of the politician who declares to his constituents that he is in favor of everything that will tend to the good of his country without dreading consequences, and yet when the subject of slavery is presented to him in the legislature, he will say that 'it is inexpedient to legislate on the subject at present.' What is he? He is a poor, cringing, dodging devil, who cares for nothing, I doubt, but his popularity.

"And the man who admits that slavery is an evil and yet says, what can we do? We have them here and what can we do with them? shows that he is insincere, or dreadfully ignorant.

"I expect, sir, that this production will prove unsavory to some of your readers, yet these sentiments have not been written for the purpose of creating any excitement, but that the attention of your readers may be drawn to a subject in which they are so much interested is the wish of

FATHER ABRAHAM"[22]

On July 7, 1829, and occasionally in subsequent issues of his paper, Swaim had inserted notices about the *Genius of Universal*

*Emancipation,* a publication bitterly hated by slaveholders. He had even ventured to say that Benjamin Lundy, its editor, had contributed more to the cause of emancipation than any other man in the United States. And he had prophesied that "though the pointed shafts of malignity may, for a time, be hurled against [Lundy], his most [s]anguine hopes *will* be consummated."²³

This accumulation of concrete evidence of Swaim's efforts to promote antislavery sentiment, together with *An Address to the People of North Carolina, on the Evils of Slavery* which Swaim had written and published for the Manumission Society, proved too much for the legislature. As a result, Spencer O'Brien of Granville County submitted a resolution in the House of Commons "that the Attorney General of this State be and he is hereby directed to commence a prosecution against William Swaim, Editor of the *Greensborough Patriot,* for the seditious and libellous publications contained in his paper of the 15th December, 1830, and in papers issued from that office on previous dates."²⁴

The *Raleigh Register,* on December 30, 1830, contained an interesting account of the proceedings: "On Saturday [December 25] the House of Commons were engaged almost the whole day in discussing the Resolution submitted by MR. O'BRIEN, directing the Attorney General to institute a prosecution against the Editor of the Greensborough Patriot, for the publication of certain seditious articles in his paper. For the purpose of presenting the case on its true merits, we would copy the objectionable passages which were read to the House, but that we deem them highly indecorous and improper. It is sufficient perhaps to say, that they consisted of free comments upon the bills before the Legislature in relation to persons of colour. A communication in the same paper, under the signature of 'Father Abraham,' was animadverted on, as containing sentiments of seditious import.... The principal arguments advanced against it were, that the contest was an unequal one, that if a prosecution was commenced, there was no certainty of a verdict for the State; and that the acquittal of the Defendant would operate only to increase the evil complained of, inasmuch as it might

313

encourage other editors to pursue a similar course; that it would only serve to lash an obscure individual into notice, the very thing perhaps he desired; that the course proposed was without precedent, and that the Legislature could expect to gain nothing from the contest. Much was said of the general and proper bias of jurors in favor of the liberty of the Press which would operate much in favor of the Defendant, — on the other hand, it was contended, that the time had arrived when a signal example should be made of those persons who, residing among us, disseminate doctrines calculated to lead to the most deplorable consequences; that unless some check was interposed, the evil would soon become too great for remedy; that Editors occupied an elevated station in Society, and if the opinion was entertained that they were beneath the attention of the Legislature, that opinion was unsound; ... [Finally] on the question of postponing the resolution indefinitely, the vote stood 88 to 33."

Swaim probably did not fear any great loss of readers, since this type of publicity tends to increase them. Such a person would hardly be very concerned about the injury he and his paper might suffer from sedition and libel suits, since he was convinced that there was something bigger at stake than personal pride and business prosperity. "The liberty of the press, so watchfully guarded by the framers of our Constitution, is placed in jeopardy," he wrote, following his brush with the legislature. "Tyranny & despotism always seek to break down the press, or awe it into contemptible silence, and then their work of ruin becomes easy. — This work has already been commenced in North Carolina; and it remains with the people to say whether it shall be 'nipped in the bud,' or whether it shall be suffered to overshadow the land and extinguish our liberties. An evil spirit is abroad in the land, and we admonish the people to guard themselves well against its influence. We shall not cease to 'cry aloud and spare not,' while the freedom and prosperity of our country are threatened with annihilation; nor shall we *court* the *smiles*, or *dread* the *frowns* of any man on earth. We shall speak of men and things *as they are* — and on our devoted head be the consequences! If the people are willing to sustain us in this course, our thanks are always ready in return for their patronage. But if, through their cold and chilling neglect, we are delivered up to our persecutors, be it even so! Our press shall remain forever unawed by power while under our control. *It shall be independent* — and may this declaration be printed with the blood of the first tyrant who may be arrayed against any branch of this great bulwark of American Freedom!"[25]

Sometimes the flamboyant style and messianic tone of Swaim's writing would indicate that he tempted Fate or counted very heavily upon what the *Raleigh Register* called the "proper bias of jurors in favor of the liberty of the Press." In any case, within less than a month after this experience with the legislature he came across a distressing report about slave traffic as practiced in and around Washington City. He reprinted the report with the following introduction: "If we were not affraid of an indictment for sedition we would publish the following article from the American Spectator and Washington City Chronicle."[26] No one accepted that dare. And in 1832 Benjamin Lundy expressed high gratification that Swaim "still ventured to write against slavery, although the Legislature of that state had passed a law to muzzle the press."[27]

William Swaim was a public printer as well as a newspaper man, and among other things he printed all sorts of pamphlets, broadsides, court blanks, and electioneering material for candidates seeking public office. Through his printing establishment he was drawn into a spectacular libel case with Robert Potter, who, while a member of both the General Assembly and Congress, was widely known for his leadership among antibank forces.

In 1831, Potter became involved in a fight with two of his wife's relatives whom he severely injured. The victims were said to have been preachers of Granville County which was also Potter's county. For these offenses Potter was indicted and convicted in the Superior Court of Granville, and was sentenced in one case to two years imprisonment; and in the other case to $1,000 fine. Potter was a powerful and magnetic public speaker, and he had gained such a large following among the country people both for his antibank position and his charming personality that it was thought not safe to confine him in jail at Oxford in Granville County. He was therefore sentenced to serve his prison term in Hillsboro in the adjoining county of Orange.[28] Incidentally he was re-elected to the legislature in the midst of this upheaval.

Potter complained bitterly of what he considered the injustice of his treatment by the Granville Court and the more influential citizens thereabouts. While residing in the Hillsboro jail, he therefore wrote *An Address to the People of Granville* in which he claimed he was provoked into the conflict with the two men he had thrashed. Moreover, he alleged that both the committing magistrates and the Superior Court Judge, Robert Strange, had denied him his constitutional and legal rights and had obtained his conviction by the most infamous abuse of their power. He cleverly referred to the judge as "Mr. Justice Strange who is certainly a Strange Mr. Justice."[29] The *Address* was published in pamphlet form, five by seven inches in size, eighty-six pages in length, and in very fine print. And Potter employed Swaim to print it. There is no intimation in available records that it was anything more than a business transaction.

No reference was made in the Greensboro paper to the printing or libel for it until September 25, 1833, when Swaim released the story in the *Greensborough Patriot* under the heading of "LIBEL SUIT." This is his version of the affair, couched in his own style, serious, courageous, and at times repetitious and well-nigh hysterical: "I have heretofore omitted to mention that Robert Potter and myself have had the honor of being associated together in an indictment, charging us with having 'written, composed, printed and published, or caused to be written, composed, printed and published,' certain false, scandalous, malicious and defamatory libels and libellous matters, touching, appertaining to, and concerning the good name, fame and reputation of Judge Strange. While this matter was hanging up for investigation, I had no inclination to make it a subject of newspaper paragraphs. I could have no inducement to raise a *canting whine* for the purpose of exciting public *sympathy*. I desire not the *commiseration* of any individual in the community. All I ask is justice, stern — inflexible — unbiased — unbought Jus-TICE; and this I have a right to *demand!*

"But I have learned, within the last two weeks, that this prosecution, which is itself a 'libel,' has been the teeming source of a thousand slanderous misrepresentations; and I have determined that no man, although the legislature may have been prevailed upon, by his *tears* and *entreaties,* to pronounce him, by their vote, as *fully competent* to *prosecute* offenders and *guard* the interests of the state in her courts of justice, even if the whole *bar* and *bench* of the state could be brought up to his *influence,* shall throttle me with the strong arm of the *law,* and hold a *bill of indictment* over my head, as a kind of *scare crow;* while imputations dark as sin, and slanders black as hell, are *conjured up,* and sent abroad against me. My situation compels me to speak.

"Some time after the last March term of the superior court for the county of Orange," Swaim continued, "I was asked by one of those gentry, who earn their bread by the 'arts and frauds' of the 'legal profession,' if I had 'heard that Scott' — meaning the solicitor general, had got me *harnassed* in Orange as well as Guilford?' [Swaim was referring to the Emery case in Guilford.] I answered in the negative, and was then informed by the same gentleman, that such was the fact. My answer was, that I had been struggling against wind and tide for several years, for the purpose of forcing myself into public notice; but thus far, I had found myself unable to succeed; and that I was certainly under *infinite obligations* to Mr. Scott for the aid he was about to afford me in my struggles to become *conspicuous;* because certain *ambitious* men would rather be *infamously* FAMOUS, than not famous at all!

"The next intelligence I received on this subject came through Col. Logan, a very worthy man of this place. He showed me a capias which he had just received from John A. Mebane, with the information that it had just been sent to him by the solicitor general, from Lexington. I never took pains to ascertain whether the postage

317

was paid on this capias, by the solicitor general; or whether he sent it *through* Dr. Mebane, by *virtue of his office* as postmaster — thus bringing the 'patronage of the general government into conflict with the freedom of' — *the press!*

"I entered into bond with Col. Logan for my personal appearance at the next superior court, to be begun and held for the county of Orange, on the sceond Monday in September, 1833. That great and notable day of accounts rolled aruond, and found me in Hillsborough, *ready for trial.* A good deal of *back-door* business was carried on during the first three days of court, among the *black-coated* and *sheep-skin* gentry, in consulting whether it would not better subserve the purpose for which the prosecution was commenced; to procure a *nolle prosequi* to be entered by the solicitor general than to risk an *investigation* of it before a court of justice. and before the public. The 'aristocracy' who have the *full credit* of *originating* this indictment, found themselves in a *tight place.* They knew that if light could be let in upon the minds of the people, their craft was in danger of being overthrown; and they were awfully affraid that if the prosecution were allowed to go on, their deep and dark plans to restrain the liberty of the press, and curtail the freedom of discussion, would be *ript up* and blown beyond the verge of the world. What then could they do? If they *backed out,* they would exhibit to the community, their want of *strength* and *courage,* longer to maintain their hold upon the *pockets* and *throats* of the people! They knew that in the midst of *free,* and *bold,* and *unrestrained* discussion, the scales would ultimately fall from the eyes of the people, and *nabob power* would be shaken from its silken thrones!

"Here was the dilemma: if the prosecution was *carried on,* discussion would be *inevitable:* and if they *withdrew* it, discussion would as certainly follow through another channel, as the flitting shades of night retreat before the beams of morning — that they would be driven in confusion, before the *light of truth,* as *owls and bats* are chased to their dens before the *penetrating blaze of the*

318

*God of day!* After all these difficulties were duly *deliberated* and *debated* upon, until Thursday morning of court, it was proposed to let the trial come on; and to *over awe*, if possible, by their *august presence*, the *voice of truth!*

"Court was called at 10 o'clock; and Mr. Potter, having been released from prison for the purpose, appeared at the bar. It was agreed that he and myself should *sever* in the indictment and have *separate* trials. The indictment was read by the solicitor general. Mr. Potter admitted the authorship and publication of the pamphlet, containing the matter alleged in the indictment to be libellous, and plead the *truth* in *justification.* John Scott, Esquire, Solicitor General, and so forth, of the state of North Carolina, appeared for the prosecution; and Mr. Potter appeared for himself without the assistance of any other counsel. The examination of the witnesses, which lasted about three hours, *opened up* a conspiracy, on the part of the *bench*, the bar, and the bank aristocracy, which never could have been entered into by *honest* and *honourable* men.

"Here let it be understood, however, that in this *foul, corrupt, dishonest,* and *dishonourable* CONSPIRACY, I wish not to be understood as including *all* the members, either of the *bench* or the *bar;* nor do I design to implicate those honest men who have unwarily been found in *bad company,* in the management of the banks. I know many honourable exceptions in each of the classes here enumerated. Judge Donnell, for instance, who presided on this occasion, let him be what he may in other respects, certainly acquitted himself with great credit. He gave a latitude in the examination of witnesses and the argument of the case, which I think would have been denied by judges less liberal; but he certainly would have rendered himself culpable to his own conscience, and before the bar of public opinion, if he had cramped a discussion involving so many important considerations: But not to be tedious.

"When the examination of testimony was concluded, Mr. Solicitor Scott proposed to submit the case to the jury, under the charge of his honour. To this, Mr. Potter objected; and on objecting, rose

319

to his feet and commenced his defence. I have heard speeches, and not a few of them too, containing more *logic*, as well as more *sophistry;* but it was graceful — respectful — dignified — eloquent — bold — irresistable. The effect was *enthusiastic!*

"But he was replied to by Mr. Scott, whose *talents* as a *lawyer* and an *orator*, are too well known to require any *tribute* from me. Suffice to say, that as far as I could observe, he neither *fired* the *courthouse*, nor the *hearts* of the *jury* — nor did he, so far as I was able to learn, *beat the soul of the Judge into a tempest!*

"The jury, under charge of his honour, retired in the evening; and after deliberating two or three hours, returned into the courthouse, *hung*, and were discharged. Thus the storm had been spent in its rage, — *for a time!* This case now stands over for trial again, at the next court....

"On Friday morning the other part of the case come up — *State against William Swaim* charged as above stated. I evinced my readiness for trial; but the state declined meeting me on the *alleged* ground that a material witness was absent. I was then held to bail for my appearance at the next superior court, in the sum of *five hundred pounds!* Thus stands the case with me at this time.

"I wish not to impugn the *motives* of public officers, in the discharge of their *official* and *sworn* duty; but the difficulty presents itself, which I wish somebody would solve," Swaim wrote in conclusion. "In every section of the Union, the press te[e]ms with abuse of the greatest men known to our government, from the president down, — *down,* — DOWN — to the most contemptible recipient of power; and yet no *prosecution* ever *dreamed* of! But when I may happen to subject myself to the suspicion of having libelled a counter hopper, who came from a dry-goods store in Virginia, and *hopped* upon the *bench* of a *petty court* in this state, I must be dragged from my business, and from domestic quiet, to a distant county, to meet my betters — if I ever had any — and answer for a *violation of the law!*

"If no other end is proposed to be answered by the officers of *justice,* in thus pursuing me, than to see that no violation of the law is allowed to pass with impunity, why not lay their *official hands* upon *all offenders,* and not *single me* out as the only victim worthy of such pursuit? If I am to be indicted, denounced and proscribed, because some fog-headed fool had dreamed that I had been suspected of printing the truth for another man, why not arraign those who are known, by the prosecuting officers themselves, to earn their daily bread by violations of the law? Could these men persuade themselves to be honest for a moment they would answer me somewhat on the following key. 'Because, Swaim, we are mighty in the earth, — we are rich, and great and powerful, — we live in *ease* by keeping the people in *ignorance,* that they may not detect our swindling — we belong to the same craft, and with the connivance of the judges, we can protect it from harm — But thou art a poor printer — thou art friendless and a stranger, and therefore we can bring our discipline to bear upon thee with impunity — and moreover thy soul has indued thee with courage to speak evil concerning us, whereby our craft has been endangered — now therefore speak well of us, and print the things that we desire, and we will cease to persecute the[e]!!!' "[30]

Six months passed and no decision was announced. Then in March, 1834, the *Greensborough Patriot* carried the final reckoning of this highly dramatic chapter in Swaim's life. It ran as follows: "LIBEL SUIT, — for the last time. From a short paragraph in our last paper, the reader may be led to expect a notice of more detail, of the prosecution against us in Orange superior court, but on reflection, we do not deem it reputable to triumph over a prostrate foe! We shall therefore be brief and moderate, entertaining, as we do, a proper regard for the *feelings* of the solicitor general. . . .

"We attended the first court [in Orange] after the bill was found against us; and it is not too much to say, that we went to that court with a fixed and solemn determination, that if they did manage to get us in jail, we would rent a house, and have our printing establishment moved to that place, and thereafter, during our con-

321

finement, issue the Greensborough Patriot 'from the prison in Hillsborough!' We would have been able to frustrate the main object of the prosecution; which was, to silence, or subdue the tone of our press, because we scorn to ask those in *authority*, what we may publish! But they have thus far failed, and they will forever fail: We now, once and for all, bid them an eternal *defiance!* We ask not their *sympathy* — we scorn their *power* — and defy their *malignity*.

"Finding that *legal oppression* had no tendency to limber or subdue us; and learning that, to stifle the voice of freemen, and block up the only channel through which they can speak efficiently, was not likely to be as profitable as [Solicitor John Scott] at first expected, he began to call off the dogs with a view of quitting the drive before the Orange suit came on! When he reached it, however, he could not get his consent to let us 'ramble unconfined,' so he put off the trial for want of a witness which he *said* was material; and had us bound over in the sum of *five hundred pounds*, to appear in the borough of Hills again. During the six months which followed, he had time to converse with his feelings and friends, and very *wisely* damned himself if he would ever risk a trial of the [case] at all. He accordingly wrote Carbry [Swaim's brother-in-law] and Hanner [clerk of the Guilford County Court], discharging them as states witnesses; and also as our bail, and directing them to inform us, that a [*nolle*] *prosequi* would be entered; and that we need not attend, as he would not have us called: and so here ends the last chapter of the chronicles of John Scott. We would wind up with a few verses in relation to his *real character;* but we have had enough fun out of the *poor fellow*, and we have concluded *to let him off!* GOOD BYE!"[31]

About the time this case was dismissed, a purely local matter took the stage. Alfred E. Hanner and Watson W. Woodburn were in a controversy about which one was to serve as clerk of the county court of Guilford. In connection with the case, Swaim was accused of publishing materials favorable to Hanner because the *Greensborough Patriot* office was located in Hanner's building. Although

Swaim wrote that "town dignitaries had beat themselves into a foam" over the matter, he solemnly affirmed that he had released the evidence exactly as it came out in court, with no thought of favoring anyone. The patience and effort he made in trying to give a fair and clear understanding of the case was almost tedious. After a long explanation of the facts involved, and asserting that he did not care a "dried apple" for Hanner, and that he did not have to play up to him, he again reiterated his stand. "We are disposed to do our duty, regardless of consequences. We are neither the slave, the dupe nor the tool of any man. We ask no man what kind of opinions we shall form, and we thank no man for his advice in relation to the course we shall pursue. And before any man, either by advice, persuasion or threats shall exert the slightest influence over our opinions, or our manner and time of expressing them, we will clothe ourself in other habiliments, and no longer pretend to be a man, or any part of one. A person who will not think, speak and act for himself, is no man at all and ought to be rigged out in a bib and petticoat, and sent to the kitchen."[32]

These honest and daring procedures brought Swaim to at least six attempted or actual court trials, usually instigated by those who felt mortified by his exposure of their dishonest actions; but he fearlessly pursued his straightforward course without ever weakening. "He waged almost a one-man fight against the laws opposed to incendiary publications, championing freedom of speech and of the press," wrote Daniel M. McFarland in *The North Carolina Historical Review*.[33] It is a commentary upon the power of his pen that no suit entered against Swaim in connection with freedom of expression was ever brought to a final trial. Usually such cases were indefinitely postponed.

The years 1830-1835, when he was undergoing these various legal tests in defense of freedom of the press, brought conflicting reactions to him and his paper. The *Milton Spectator* alluded to the *Greensborough Patriot* as an 'infamous and incendiary publication."[34] An unsigned letter labeled it as "the most corrupt sheet I know of."[35] The *Fayetteville Journal*, speaking of the editor, declared, "We have carefully abstained from defiling our hands in any sort of contact with this common libeller, slanderer, and plagarist."[36]

From a sympathetic reader come a prepaid subscription and a letter which stated that "I pay already, a heavy tax for newspapers— being a subscriber to three, and a monthly periodical besides. But the manly, independent and honest course which you have pursued as the conductor of a public Journal, demands of *me*, that the feeble aid which I can render, shall be given to the support of your paper.

"There is so little true independence — so much cringing sycophancy; and so much corruption in the public press, generally, of our country, that I have almost lost sight of the stability of our free institutions. And when I find a man who acts, without the expectation of approbation, or the fear of censure; and who is honest in what he says and does, I feel myself called upon by every feeling of duty, to help and save him, if possible, from the hands of a merciless and villianous world."[37]

Stating that he was more accustomed to rceeiving "kicks than PUFFS and COPPERS," and saying if he did receive compliments he seldom included them in his cclumns, Swaim printed an excerpt from another letter which also contained a prepaid subscription to the *Greensborough Patriot*. The new subscriber said "I take the Raleigh Register, which gives me the same foreign and domestic news which yours will give; but I have been much pleased with that spirit of independence which flows from the Patriot; and by way of encouragement to a new beginner, who appears disposed to speak plainly of men and measures, independently of their grade or standing, I am desirous to encourage its circulation in this neighborhood."[38]

The nationally famous journalist, Mrs. Anne Royall, whose husband was a commanding officer in the Battle of Guilford Courthouse, visited Greensboro in February, 1830. And she observed that "Mr. Swaim, the editor of the Greensborough Patriot, is a free, generous, liberal man, I believe a Clay man, but I underrate no man for his opinions — he might underrate me for the same reason. [He] is a . . . young man, friendly and genteel. He is a spirited and independent Editor."[39]

And the editor of the *Danville Reporter*, Virginia, in February, 1835, when publishing a general survey of the newspapers in Virginia and North Carolina, drew the following conclusion: " 'But to the editor of the Greensboro Patriot a deeper, holier debt is owed, and we will discharge it at every hazard. Animated by "a mind as pure as aether," and a heart, "pregnant with celestial fire," his press is revolutionizing the moral condition of the contiguous country. With an eye that never winks, and a wing that never tires, he pounces upon the guilty and drags them to exemplary punishment.

" 'The editors of the Reporter accept "the ungloved hand of friendship" tendered to them by Mr. Swaim, as freely as "tis nobly given," and return that of proffered brotherhood with like cheerfulness.' "[40]

The spirit of John Peter Zenger must have looked with approval upon William Swaim, fighting editor.

# XIII

## FINANCING A FAMILY AND A NEWSPAPER

*"We have no disposition to whine for 'more,' after we shall have received 'enough.'"*[1]

Swaim did not amass a fortune through the *Greensborough Patriot;* but he kept his enterprise solvent, and that was no mean accomplishment. In fact, up to 1963, over a century and a quarter after it was first published, it held the record for any newspaper consecutively published in the state.

Greensboro's first newspaper, the *Carolina Patriot,* was undertaken in 1821, but only a few issues of it were released. It was succeeded by *The Patriot* (later changed to *The Patriot and Greensborough Palladium*) which was published regularly from April 24, 1826, until Swaim purchased it in 1829 and continued it under the name of *Greensborough Patriot.* With a few short-lived changes of name, but always coming back to *Greensborough Patriot,* it continued to be profitably published. In 1941 it was taken over by the Greensboro News Company and thereafter was issued as a state farm weekly. In 1950, retaining the ownership of the name *Greensboro Patriot,* the Greensboro News Company sold the good will and subscription list to the *Southern Agriculturalist.*

The first number of the *Greensborough Patriot* appeared on May 23, 1829, practically unannounced. Swaim's Prospectus of his forthcoming journal was almost totally ignored by the editors of other publications. Bearing the date of March 4, 1829, this announcement was first released on April 4, 1829, in the Greensboro

326

paper he had just purchased. Referring to it later, Swaim wrote: "We issued a prospectus, and asked our brethren of the type to aid us in forming acquaintances, by giving it a place in their respective papers, . . . [but] the only editor in the state who has yet been kind enough to publish [it is John I. Pasteur] of the *Newbern Specta-tor*. . . . When we found ourself so flatteringly noticed by one whose good opinions we esteem so highly, we were considerably in-spired. . . . [but] business at that time, compelled us to bring down our fancy from her stupendous flights, . . . a good looking kind of a man — who on any other business would have been perfectly welcome — stepped into our office, and in less time than a . . . hungry beggar [could] say grace, he plucked a patch that had some how come 'on-ript' from the sleeve of the best coat we have, and, after leading us into a corner of our office, where the Devil had deposited a bountiful chance of *pi*, he *whispered aloud*, that certain bonds had become due; he then went on to say such things as creditors generally say on such occasions: shortly after this we sold a quire of *warrants* and *executions*, to a constable, on credit! Now we are willing to submit the case to any *printer* in the United States, whether such a striking concatination of unpropitious cir-cumstances is not enough to freeze into adamant any thing but the soul of a poet, or the heart of a lover!"[2]

The *Genius of Universal Emancipation* of Baltimore, Maryland, and the *People's Free Press* of Norfolk, Virginia, were his only out of state promoters. Consequently, he continued, "We commenced business last spring, with a patronage so limited that we had no means of extending a knowledge of our existence to distant parts of the state."[3]

Having undertaken the publishing of a newspaper with such high hopes, Swaim had to swallow his pride at such a meager response from his fellow editors regarding his Prospectus. Four months later he lamented that "The truth shall not be concealed. The circulation of our paper *must be extended;* or we must procure a *sack and a walking staff!* It now rests with the friends of a paper devoted to *free* and to *fearless* enquiry, to say whether our humble pretensions shall meet with encouragement; or whether the prospects of approaching starvation shall compel us to *lay our prospects upon the shelf!*"[4]

This appeal was only partly serious, for Swaim had no idea of giving up. He said as much — before he closed this plea for support: "We are not *near* ready to fold our establishment in its *winding sheet,* and bury it in 'mute inglorious repose:'" he declared, "but we indeed have much to ask of the people for whom we spend our *days* and *nights* and *funds.*"[5]

This situation was not improved by what Swaim finally recognized to be a sort of "co-operative subscription" plan, by which one copy of the paper made the rounds of an entire community! He deduced that this was the case, when he noticed that wherever he went people would congregate around him and talk about having read this or that in his paper, and yet he had few of their names on his subscription list. When one fellow announced, "I take your paper, sir, . . . and I'll never deny it the longest day I live," as though it might be something to be ashamed of, Swaim began a little investigation. "'Very well, sir,'" said the editor, "'and how do you get my paper? I do not recollect seeing your name on my book.' 'How do I get it? . . . Why to be sure, I *borrow* it from neighbor Banks,'" Swaim was told.[6]

A few weeks later another man approached Swaim. "'*I like your paper very well,*' he volunteered, '*and should have subscribed for it before this time, but neighbor* (Blank,—) *who lives close by me is a subscriber, and I can always borrow his paper when I want to read it.*'"[7] Swaim must have winced as the man talked, for later he wrote: "We can safely say that fifty men have sung this song in our distracted organs of hearing, since the 23rd day of last May."[8]

Finally his pen found its way into the vitriol; and under the title of "BORROWING NEWSPAPERS — YET!" he let such readers know how he felt about it in no uncertain terms: "We have more than once alluded to this soul-tormenting sin. . . . We have all along remonstrated in vain; but we are now resolved that signal vengeance shall be visited upon those who persist in such wicked and downright abominable practices. . . . One man subscribes for a paper, and *sometimes* even *pays* for it, which serves for himself and four of his neighbors to read. These five men are furnished with the weekly news for the paltry sum of *two dollars* [per year], and that, too, in many, very *many* cases, *never paid!* . . . Any man who will read eight hundred and thirty-two columns of closely printed matter, every year, without contributing one cent toward remunerating the *toils* and defraying the *expenses* of him who had employed his hands and his thoughts, incessantly, day and night, to write, select, arrange, and print these columns for the express benefit of him, his family and country, deserves to be 'lashed round Heaven's vast expanse' with a whip-thong composed of twisted scorpions."[9]

It was now October, following the publication date of May, and Swaim decided to press his case a little farther. His first approach was through a combination of seriousness and levity. "We have been studying about an hour and three quarters," he wrote, "to find out some funny thing that would make people laugh, and get them to subscribe for our paper; but we have lately encountered two or three duns! and besides that, we are nearly out of paper; and if this a'nt enough to blunt the wit of a *young* fellow, who has neither *wife* nor *money* to *comfort* him, and whose creditors live in more places than one — with two constables now in town, and a Jail within three hundred yards, — we are at a loss to conjecture what would . . . But we have a newspaper story to tell, and we have come to the unconquerable determination to tell it while we are *foot-loose*. Now listen!

"An honest farmer, not five miles from this place, was asked why he did not take a newspaper. 'Because,' said he, 'my father, when he died — heaven rest his soul — left me a good many papers, and I ha'nt read 'em all through yet.' "[10]

Meanwhile Swaim resorted to the practical method of asking each subscriber to furnish an additional one, with the result that he gained a considerable number to add to his list. By December 5, 1829, he was able to announce: "We have more than doubled

the amount of subscribers to the *Patriot* within the past six months."
A few weeks later he reported, "Our list of patrons continues to
increase as fast as we have any right to expect; & we have no disposition to whine for 'more,' after we shall have received 'enough.'
But those who are unacquainted with our business, can form no
idea of the risks and expense we have incurred — nor of the difficulties which yet lift their bold front to oppose our progress."[11]
Commenting that there was still room for more circulation, and
that he had appointed twenty-six agents in North Carolina, Virginia, Maryland, and Indiana, he proudly announced: "Since our
last we have received three subscribers from among the first ladies
in this section of the country. If any body but a printer should think
himself capable of forming a conception of the pleasure we derive
from an opportunity of making this acknowledgement, we can
safely tell him that he knows nothing about it!"[12]

Swaim had been in Greensboro only a little over a year when
he announced that "the office of the *Greensborough Patriot* is removed to the editor's new building, on the right side of West Street
[West Market], seven doors from the Court-House [center of
town], where he will at all times be proud to see and converse with
his friends, but particularly so, with those who call to subscribe for
the Patriot, or to pay off their bills."[13] The building belonged to
Alfred E. Hanner, but it was from this location that Swaim's various businesses made their most progress.

By the time the *Greensborough Patriot* had been circulating
for about eighteen months, enough subscriptions had been added
to its list to permit its owner to buy a horse and a gig; and thereafter to travel in the manner of such dignitaries as lawyers,
physicians, and successful planters. This was a necessity not only
for professional use but for social appearances, since editors
occupied an elevated station in society. Swaim planned to travel
throughout the state in search of materials, and thus to make his
paper a fine and influential one. The plan definitely worked to his
advantage, for personal appearances in public places offered an

opportunity for extending the range of his publication as well as for gathering information for it.

Business success was also apparent in the quality of household furnishings Swaim bought for his bride. When he and Abiah Shirley were married, among other things he gave her a dining room suite of the finest mahogany—massive and splendid in design and workmanship. It was a suitable complement for the silver punch bowl which Abiah had inherited from one of her Stuart relatives. (The sideboard of the suite is now owned by Mrs. Edward P. Wharton who has it featured in her Greensboro home.)

An indication of continued progress comes from his announcement on May 30, 1832, that repairs were being made in the *Greensborough Patriot* office "to insure a better appearance of our paper for time to come."

Just how many subscribers the *Greensborough Patriot* eventually acquired during Swaim's editorship is not known; but after the first two years, subscriptions seem to have reached a "satisfactory number." The only reference to numbers in this connection was made in a playful mood, when the paper was about a year old. "One thousand subscribers added to the present list would make it doubly productive," Swaim wrote in the issue for September 1, 1830. Somewhat later he assured that subscriptions were in no way retarded.[14] A communication published by him on October 3, 1832, began, "Mr. Swaim, as your paper is so extensively circulated..." And on August 27, 1834, another contributor began, "Friend Swaim — Knowing you to be an independent and fearless editor, at all times willing to give your opinion upon all important subjects — and knowing the extensive circulation of your valuable paper..."

By way of seeing this in relation to other papers of his day, it should be remembered that no publication had a tremendous circulation in the 1830's. The *Morning Courier and New York Enquirer* had only four thousand subscribers in 1829.[15] In November, 1831, the *Carolina Watchman* had announced the intention of publishing its first issue when it had one thousand subscribers. On

January 23, 1833, the *Greensborough Patriot* carried a notice that the *Saturday Evening Post* (1728) which had been established over a hundred years had united with the *Saturday Bulletin* — "two large and ably conducted periodicals in Philadelphia" — and that the combined list of subscribers was less than twenty thousand.

In June, 1833, Swaim announced that he was about to begin his fifth volume with the most encouragement and support he had ever experienced, and that future prospects continued to grow brighter.[16] The fact that he was planning a great enlargement of his paper when he died in 1835 is evidence that he considered his following sufficient to warrant the venture. And the fact that *Godey's Lady's Book* of Philadelphia and *The New York Mirror*, a weekly journal featuring "fine arts and belle-lettres," were advertised in the *Greensborough Patriot* is evidence that the newspaper was known beyond the bounds of North Carolina.

Although the subscription price was only two dollars per year, the problem of collecting from subscribers beset Swaim for a while. To be sure collecting debts appears to have been a particularly difficult problem for other creditors as well as for Swaim. Sometimes private debtors were enjoined by name, and in the local press, to pay specified private debts. Examples of these advertised debts include those of both public and private nature. For example, *The Patriot and Greensborough Palladium,* in April before Swaim took it over in May, had thirteen advertisements, of which four were notices of private businesses asking their clients to pay their debts.[17]

The Town of Greensboro whose first tax assessment (1829) was $160, had collected only $86.25 before the end of a year; and town commissioners were threatening their brethren with the sheriff if they did not come across promptly with the unpaid balance of $73.75.[18]

The court records of Guilford County, containing practically every name of importance in the county in connection with debts ranging from $11 with interest to $300, or more, include such names as Archibald Murphey, Jonathan Parker, John M. Morehead, John A. Gilmer, Dr. David Worth, the Reverend William Paisley, John M. Logan, Henry Humphreys, the Reverend Amos Weaver, and many others.[19] It need not be surprising, then, that Swaim about once each year urged his clients to spank the "majigany down upon the nail-head."[20]

And it need not be surprising that he wrote the following little essay on the subject, in January, 1833: "This is the most *billious* month in the year; it is the season of duns and tipstaffs; and we can compare our citizens in these hard times, to a row of brick-bats which boys place erect along the pavement; push number one, and away go all the rest. The rich landlord begins to cry, and his clerk duns the merchant for rent; the merchant then pops a long bill into the face of the retailer — the retailer, as in duty bound, comes down upon the mechanic — the mechanic duns his customers — the customers dun *their patrons*, and thus the torrent swells from the nobility down to the boot black. Tailors, hatters and shoe-makers are all agog — 'pony up' is the cry — bills are due, and the *ready* must follow. Alas! what a mal-appropos salutation is 'a happy new year to you!' a new year is but the beginning of new troubles— which are always coming and never ending. Printers are no better off than other folks, and as we cannot be out of fashion we must echo the call, — 'Thank you for that small trifle — sir.' "[21]

Swaim at one time played with the idea of publishing occasion-ally a list of delinquent subscribers, and even asked some of his fellow editors about the advisability of such a move; but they disapproved. While he was in this mood, however, the *Saturday Evening Post* came out with the same thought and Swaim quoted it in his paper. " 'We are convinced,' " the *Post* said, " 'that it would would be a wholesome and sound principle for all Publishers, to insert once a month in their respective sheets, a list of their rogueish *patrons*, as a caution to the public and particularly to their brethren of the press, against similar deception. The practice would be universally beneficial, and no *honest* person, it is presumed, would object to this system.' "[22]

Such encouragement was all Swaim needed. First off, he published the suggestion as a forewarning, and soon followed with a reminder to the offenders, by name:

STOP THE RUNAWAYS! The following is a list of *gentlemen* who, after reading our paper for a time, have politely disappeared, and left us the "bag to hold." We give the name of each, together with the amount due, and the place of his residence at the time he *patronised* us! Should this publication meet the eye of any of these delinquents; and should they conclude yet to forward to us the amount due, we will publickly acknowledge the receipt, and *restore* him who sends it, to better credit than an act of the legislature could possibly give. Any person who will favor us with information of the residence of any one or all of these *absentees*, shall have a right to claim the homage of our 'sincere thanks!'

Joseph Aydelotte, Esq. Guilford County, North Carolina. Twelve dollars.
John Lackey, Tarborough, N. C. Nine dollars.
James Hiatt not recollected. Nine dollars.
William Atkinson, unknown. Nine dollars.
Jacob Miller, not recollected. Nine dollars.
Joseph Bryan, whipt anyhow and may be hung. Six dollars.
Job Hiatt, not findable. Nine dollars.[23]

It was characteristic of Swaim rather to enjoy teasing and cajoling his readers to keep their subscriptions paid up. He would write little articles in which he seemed to be entirely serious along some other line, then suddenly spring a surprise ending about dues. For example, an article entitled "WHO IS A GENTLEMAN?" he concluded thus: "But it would be endless to enumerate the different opinions, which go to make up a gentleman. And we may as well conclude at once, by saying, that with us he is a GENTLEMAN in large letters, who subscribes for the [*Greensborough Patriot*] and pays *in advance*."[24]

At another time he related a death bed scene to move the hard of heart. "A person being dangerously ill," he wrote, "was visited by a clergyman, who perceiving the poor fellow gave way to despondency, kindly inquired if any grievous sin lay heavy on his heart. The sick man replied with a sigh, that he had been guilty of a grievous sin, but its magnitude was so great he was almost afraid to name it. The clergyman asked him if he had been an unkind husband? No.

A tyrannical father? No. A treacherous friend? No, but I have done a great deal worse than either. 'Have you violated any of the commandments?' 'No, I believe not, but alas!' blubbered out the despairing invalid, '*I have taken a newspaper two years and neglected to pay for it.*'"[25]

Sometimes Editor Swaim was placed in an embarrassing financial position by delinquent subscribers. The records show that several times he was forced to borrow money; and at one time, the amount ($400) involved was great enough that he had to give as collateral for a loan all his printing materials plus a Negro woman and her two female Negro children who were his wife's slaves.[26] His hard work on collections, however, must have been successful since all mortgages were properly paid off at the appointed time.

In addition to subscription fees, advertisements constituted an important source of income. Swaim always took great pride in presenting them attractively, using his newest boldface type to make them stand out, and giving them a specific place on the last page of the paper. Conspicuous among a number of such advertisements were those of John M. Morehead and Henry Humphreys. Ten years before Morehead was elected governor of North Carolina, he boldly promoted his business in Swaim's newspaper (see page 236):

Humphrey's entry was equally arresting. After an announcement of the opening of his new Brick Store — which building still stands at the southwest corner of Elm and Market Streets in Greensboro — his advertisement filled three fourths of a column with almost unbelievable fabric offerings, including cassimeres, cassenets, bombazets, lastings, drillings, bang up cords, Denmark satteens, flannels, vestings, satins, sinchews, sarsonets, batices, ginghams, barages, calicoes, cambricks, and muslins. Moreover, since readers of that day were willing to read, and did not require pictures with captions only, his printed advertisement was irresistible: "[Mr. Humphreys] has no disposition to say he will sell at the Northern wholesale prices — because he wishes to support stronger claims to common sense than

# STILLS! STILLS!
# AND
# TIN WARE

I shall keep on hand at my new COPPER and TIN SHOP in Greensborough, a full supply of New

## STILLS

### HATTER'S DYE, AND COPPER

## KETTLES

### of every description.

Having purchased the patent Machinery for the manufacture of

## TIN

I shall keep on hand a very large supply of

## TIN WARE

Which shall be sold very low at WHOLE-SALE OR RETAIL.

Also on hand a supply of SHEET IRON for the manufacture of

## STOVES, STOVE PIPES, &c.

The above articles for sale for cash or on credit, at such prices as shall suit the purchaser.

Persons wishing to peddle in Tin Ware will give me a call.

# WHISKEY

Wanted, within two weeks, one or two loads of Good Whiskey.

JOHN M. MOREHEAD.[27]

*A Greensborough Patriot advertisement*

to suppose that any person would believe such a tale; neither does he say he will sell *'twenty-five per cent'* lower than any merchant in this vicinity. Such puffing as this, may, in a small degree, answer the purpose of those who are encumbered with an old and unsalable stock of goods, which have been old housekeepers this ten years in different villages in the adjacent counties, and which they would be glad to get rid of at any price; but it will not answer the purpose of an honest and impartial dealer.... [He invites customers] to call and examine his goods and hear his prices; ... he assures that they shall at all times be supplied with such articles as may suit their fancy, upon terms as *low,* if not generally *lower,* than those who make such high pretensions. At any rate, he will not sell [them] *one* article at cost, and *cheat* them out of *double price* for the *next.*"[28]

Some of the advertisements in Swaim's *Greensborough Patriot* are interesting to twentieth century readers for the information included as well as for the variety of advertising forms achieved through the skillful use of type. In one advertisement, headed by "TASTE AND TRY BEFORE YOU BUY," Humphreys explained that his stock was inferior to none in the southern states, but that he was able to offer lower prices than others because he purchased *"at the same time* for *four large retail Stores* of his own, one at Statesville, one at Lexington, and two in this place. The reduction in price to be derived from such extensive purchases, cannot be overlooked in these *pinching times.'* "[29] Humphreys' practice of making "extensive purchases" for several stores was similar to that later employed in developing the highly popular "chain stores."

Another advertisement, as interesting in the twentieth century as it was in the nineteenth, was that of King's Washer which Swaim presented in very large and impressive type. This washer was said to be so simple to use that a small girl could "do as much washing as several common washerwomen could accomplish in the same length of time."[30] The advertisement must have been quite as appealing to women of the 1830's as an advertisement for an electric automatic washing machine was to women of the 1960's.

As in the case of subscriptions, advertising also brought collection problems. Newspapers and court records bear evidence that Swaim made no effort to cover up his business difficulties. When he became unpleasantly involved with someone who owed him money, he soon learned that if he did not publish the whole truth about the matter, his irresponsible debtors would twist reports to his disadvantage. Although the following example is rather unusual, it illustrates how plainly he could say what he meant when someone was trying to swindle him: "Some time past, we done some advertising for a brace of puppies in Danville, calling themselves 'Jones and Palmer,' whose business, in part seems to have been, the vending of lottery tickets. They have paid us some money, and something in lottery tickets, but they are yet in our debt. As we wish to close our accounts during the present year, we respectfully wrote them for the amount due, and we received for answer, precisely the following words: *'Buss where we cannot. We have your receipt in full.'* Now, aside from the foul-mouthed vulgarity of this answer, it speaks an abominable lie! Let them have what 'receipts' they may, they are in our debt, and they know it! The sum is small, but the answer of the filthy whelps who owe it are *smaller!* If they are as scarce of *money* as they are of *decency,* they are *bankrupt* in both! We shall, therefore strike a balance, and blot the dirty blackguards from our book! With *honest* men we seldom have any difficulty."[31]

The last page of the *Greensborough Patriot,* however, was not Swaim's favorite. His main goal was to publish a well-balanced, informative newspaper; and business was a necessary side line. When advertising was heavy he apologized for it. "Our paper has been so crowded with advertisement &s.," he wrote, "that much interesting matter selected for our columns, has been deferred for want of room. Our readers are exhorted to bear this privation with becoming fortitude. We shall soon get through with this kind of *stuffing* and make room for *weighty matters!*"[32]

In addition to publishing the *Greensborough Patriot,* it will be remembered, Swaim had a printing establishment. In fact, from the beginning to the end of his editorship, he kept the people aware that he was well equipped for this work by printing in his paper such notices as this:

## JOB PRINTING

The subscriber has just received several Founts of New, Large, and Ornamental Type for Job printing of every description.

He solicits a share of the public encouragement, and pledges himself to execute his work with neatness and dispatch, and upon terms suited to the pressure of the times.

WILLIAM SWAIM[33]

He also ran a book shop, and frequently published a long impressive list of books which he had for sale. Among them were school books, histories, classics, novels, biographies, hymn books, ledgers, day-books, copy books, and others. He offered to order any wanted book and get it within a few days. And he forewarned that "The people may not adopt the conclusion that, because we have ceased to inflict a catalogue of books upon the public as long as a Congress speech, we have no more books to sell. We shall keep on hand constantly such books as are in common demand in this section of the country."[34] Furthermore, he had for sale blanks of various kinds, court necessities, souvenir pictures, steel engravings, almanacs, and Christmas cards.

Moreover, he used his establishment as an agency for placing students in suitable homes while they attended the local academies. Under the conspicuous heading of "BOARDING" he made life in Greensboro sound attractive. "We have three excellent schools in successful operation (1832), in our village, at this time. Health and good order prevail amongst us; and boarding in good families, may be had on very reduced terms. In short, every inducement is held out to parents and guardians in the surrounding country, who would give to those they have in charge a good education, to board them in this place at this time.

"The subscriber will soon be prepared to accommodate any number of boarders, in any style they may choose, on terms much lower than the common custom of the place. For particulars apply at the printing office."[35]

One attempt at increasing his income, however, was unsuccessful. On May 8 and 22, 1833, William Swaim, Thomas Caldwell, and John Draughan announced themselves as candidates for Clerk of the Superior Court of Guilford County. It will be remembered that in this year Swaim was a member of the Board of Commissioners of the Town of Greensboro, sometimes acting as constable and sometimes as secretary, and he reported its actions in the *Greensborough Patriot*. Having found this a satisfactory arrangement, he therefore explained that since he attended all the court sessions in order to be able to write them up firsthand for his paper, the office of Clerk of the Court would also fit very conveniently into his job of reporter. Thomas Caldwell on the other hand had held that office since the court had been first established in 1807; and his priority was left undisturbed. Thus Swaim suffered his only known outright defeat.

In addition to the successful sources of income, Swaim had acquired considerable real estate, which he could use as collateral when necessary. He was administrator of his father's estate which included altogether eight or more farms with a total of at least 1,706 acres of land, debt free.[36] His father left no will, and a plot of one hundred and thirty-five acres on which stood the "mansion house and all necessary outhouses thereto attached" was set aside for William's mother.[37] The remainder was divided among Marmaduke and Sarah Fanning Swaim's eight children. When any of the brothers or sisters wished to sell his or her part, William often purchased it. Eventually his purchases plus his inherited share totalled 533 acres of fine land, lying along Polecat Creek in Guilford and Randolph Counties.[38]

On May 24, 1833, Swaim purchased a house and lot in Greensboro, "for cash in hand."[39] As fantastic as it may sound to anyone who knew Greensboro in the mid-twentieth century, it is a fact that with this acquisition of a house and lot in 1833, Swaim owned (according to the Register of Deeds) the entire west frontage of the northwest center block of the town, with his property facing what was North Greene Street in the 1960's, and extending from West Market Street to Gaston Street. And he paid $1,200 for "a lot of ground with all improvements," which amounted to one half of one of Greensboro's centermost squares! Will L. Scott, who would have been able to get information firsthand, was unquestionably right when he wrote that Swaim did a "good business with his paper and job office and was able of his own means, to live full-handed and comfortably."[40]

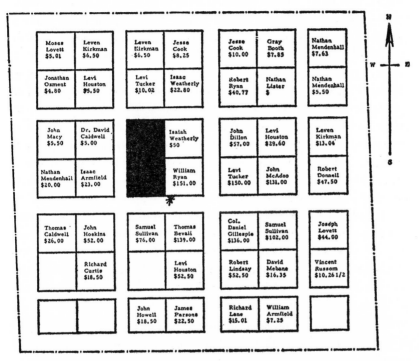

| Moses Lovett $5.01 | Leven Kirkman $6.50 | Leven Kirkman $6.50 | Jesse Cook $8.25 | Jesse Cook $10.00 | Gray Booth $7.85 | Nathan Mendenhall $7.63 |

Plat (1833) of the Town of Greensboro, showing (in black) the location and extent of Swaim's property and the *Greensborough Patriot office.**

The pressure of many interests, time out for libel suits, and more particularly his dominant desire to produce a creditable newspaper, often caused him to neglect the collection of fees from his various enterprises. In truth, in October, 1834, when he stopped to take notice, he found that he carried on his books the sum of between four and five thousand dollars — near five thousand by October,

1835 — of uncollected accounts.[41] This was a large amount when weighed against the fact that in 1829 the richest man in Greensboro listed his taxable property at $12,000, that the runner-up listed his taxable property at $4,200, and that wages were fifty cents per day from sunup until sundown. When he asked those indebted to him to pay promptly, he chided himself in his paper for failing to collect the money, and expressed fear that he might lose a large portion of it for doing such a loose business. This did not, however, prove to be true, for practically all of it was paid, and he was completely solvent.[42]

Although Swaim found time for a number of side interests, his main concern was for his *Greensborough Patriot*. One criterion by which the steadily expanding success of this newspaper may be measured was his call for apprentices. At first he advertised for one; a little later, two; and still later, three additional ones to be employed at one time. He promised them the best of working conditions, saying, "We already have the most conveniently arranged office for the business, to be found in the state; and we intend shortly to supply it with a new press, new type, & new everything." Sometimes this advertisement would be concluded thus: "We can safely promise facilities to the apprentice which can be found no where else in the south!"[43]

Two of these apprentices — Lyndon and John Swaim — merit special mention. Lyndon, who was a distant cousin, received most, if not all, of his journalist training under William. After the latter's death, Lyndon worked at a printing establishment in New Salem, North Carolina, until he was called back to Greensboro in 1839 to edit the *Greensborough Patriot*. Although lacking William's fiery and blasting editorial policy, the newspaper under Lyndon was very highly esteemed for its balanced judgment and constructive opinions. About the end of Lyndon's editorship in the mid-1850's the Oxford *Leisure Hour* said that the *Greensborough Patriot* "is really one of the largest and most admirably 'gotten up' Journals in this or any State. It is conducted with spirit and ability, and is an ornament to the typographical skill of North Carolina."[44]

John Swaim was William's youngest brother. In the summer of 1829, John had come to Greensboro to work and live with William. When he was at the point of experience where he would have been of great assistance, in August, 1832, he died. The only time William ever publicly referred to his family or relatives in his newspaper, was when he wrote for John a deeply moving obituary and placed it in his editorial column.[45] In this, William's reserve fell off, revealing his depth of affection:

## JOHN SWAIM

"the subject of this article, was born in Guilford county on the third day of June, 1812. He received the rudiments of his education, at an old field school, kept by his uncle, Michael Swaim, under whose tuition he was placed for about three months. During this time he passed from his alphabet to the New Testament, in which he could read, with ease and facility. He continued to labour on the farm, with his father and brothers, until the winter of 1822. . . .

"During the period last mentioned, I had him at school myself for a few months, where his application to study, and his progress in learning, had no parallel. The contents of every book that came in his way were devoured with eagerness. And while other boys were wandering in the paths of vice, and contracting those habits which have since covered their names with shame and disgrace, he was seeking a retreat from the temptations around him, storing his mind with useful knowledge, and bracing his youthful soul with the rigid heroism of virtue.

"He thus pursued the even tenor of his way until the summer of 1829. His father had paid the debt of nature, and obeyed the summons of death. He was left without a paternal hand to guide his youthful footsteps through an unfriendly, perverse, and unfeeling world! Given up entirely to the government of his own will, he left the roof under which he was born, and by which he had been 'sheltered from a thousand storms;' and commenced learning the art of printing, with me, about the first of August 1829. His progress far exceeded my expectations; and his industry and application to business soon became proverbial throughout the village.

"His modest, consistent, correct, and unobtrusive deportment, secured for him the abiding confidence of all who knew him. It may not be too much for me to say, that, during the three years he was permitted by Providence to live and to labour with me, I never detected in him a single action that would justify the slightest reproof. My *directions* to him never assumed the tone of *command*: it was only necessary to let him *know* his duty, and it was cheerfully *performed*. He never *disobeyed* and was never *rebuked!* ...

"During the summer of 1831, he became deeply impressed with the concerns of eternity. He at length experienced re-generation, and professed that his sins were blotted out from the book of remembrance. And those who knew him best, will not doubt the sincerity of his professions.

"About four weeks previous to his death, he was taken ill of a billious fever. He refused to have a physician sent for at an early stage of the disease, believing, as he said that he should recover without such aid.... About ten days before his departure, he was prostrated on the bed from which his soul took its flight. Medical assistance was then called; but death had singled out her victim, and refused to let go her unrelenting grasp. He lingered, and wasted away apparently without pain, until the morning of the 21st. inst. He then, surrounded by his friends, breathed his last, without a struggle — without a groan! ...

"A few days previous to his exit from time, he said, if it was the will of providence to restore him to health, for a time, he should feel thankful to remain yet longer in this 'vale of tears;' but if he were called hence, he felt fully prepared to meet his God in peace.

"What a solemn warning to the youths of our country? Four weeks ago, and he was flushed with life, spirit and activity — *now* his soul is gathered to the bosom of his father.... Those sprightly fingers which once picked the letters from the cases, to record the death of mortals, and the downfall of kingdoms, ... and those eyes which once flashed a wakeful intelligence around the midnight candle, are forever sealed in the midnight darkness of the tomb! These things call to each of us, in the stillness of meditation — 'Child of mortality — PREPARE TO MEET THY GOD!'"

It appears that John's death was the most serious loss that William experienced while he was editor of the *Greensborough Patriot*.

Despite handicaps and losses, in 1833, when Swaim came to the beginning of Volume V he paused to glance at the past and to look toward the future. "Four years we have laboured, successfully, and when we arrive at the threshold of the fifth we hold not back," he assured. "Our first volume was commenced with prospects as flattering as we had any right to expect, but not so much so as we could have wished. At the beginning of our second, the fogs of despondency were thicker around our path than we could have any inclination to desire. When we arrived to the third we felt as if we might, at some time, be called upon to relinquish our enterprise — not that our subscription had diminished, or that our business in any shape had declined; but that embarrassments from *another source* had increased [meaning the libel suits]. But when we came to the fourth, we began to see our way through the woods to cleared ground. And we are happy to assure our readers, — and we know they will participate in that happiness — that we have commenced the fifth volume with brighter prospects than ever beamed upon us, at any former period of our existence."[46]

By 1834 the prosperity of the *Greensborough Patriot* enabled Swaim to embark on a much larger enterprise. In the fall of that year he began to prepare the public for what was to come. Giving a hint of his future plans, he promised to publish the *Southern Citizen* which would be the "commencement of the largest and most useful family newspaper in the United States. This publication will be devoted *Generally*, to the interest, amusement and edification of the American people; but *particularly* to those of the Southern States, and *more especially*, to the people of North Carolina."[47]

345

His reasons for such an undertaking had grown out of the apparent need and market for such a journal. He had observed that several North Carolina publications were on the verge of collapse and that people were not only sending to the North for hats, shoes, and calicoes, but even for their newspapers. And many were under the honest impression that they could get better news in this way than they could get at home. As one old man told Swaim, "When he subscribed for a *nusepaper* he was going to take a *furren* paper, so's he could hear the *furren nuse* — *becase* he could hear all the nuse the home papers published without reading them; and besides that he was not going to pay any body for thinking for him!"[48] Swaim contended, however, that Northern papers did not give full coverage to news of North Carolina, for they printed largely happenings in the states where they were published, unless the news was of national or international interest. And he felt that local news was as important in many instances as wider coverages. It was his intention, therefore, to supply what seemed most important both at home and abroad, and thus to make the *Southern Citizen* an advance in newspaper publishing in harmony with other reforms which he had promoted and which he felt would be undertaken by the Whig party.

Before he proceeded very far with his prospects, he characterized and paid his respects to other newspapers of the state which he said were "on our side." The *Raleigh Register* he described as "venerable for its age and consistency." The Raleigh *Star* was "once in bad company, but now on the side of the people and the constitution." The *Carolina Observer* is "an untrammeled asserter of truth and correct principles." The *Western Carolinian*, "once tainted with the heresy of nullification, [is] now threatening death and desolation to the usurpers of imperial power." The *Carolina Watchman*, "like a faithful sentinel, [sounds] the alarm at any approach of danger." And last, though not least, the *Newbern Spectator*, "scoring the trammels of party discipline, and soaring high above temptations . . . stands like an everlasting pillar of truth in the midst of a wicked and perverse generation."[49]

Notwithstanding all these worthy qualifications of state newspapers, Swaim felt there was room for improvement and it was time to try a new experiment. He could see the need for reform in the press in proportion to the need for reform in all the other subjects he was promoting. "The people are nearly ripe for an improvement of the kind we purpose;" he wrote, then questioned, "and does anyone doubt our capacity to accomplish it?"[50] On October 8, 1834, he therefore began to issue specific plans "To Our Subscribers." In that communication he came straight to the point by announcing: "Our design is, at the end of the present Volume, to enlarge our paper so as to contain about three times the matter it now does, and print it on new type, with a new press, and on paper of the finest texture and most white and beautiful quality."

"Our object is," he explained, "if we can meet with sufficient encouragement, to issue about the fourth of July next, the most splendid sheet, by at least three hundred and fifty per cent, that ever escaped from a North Carolina press ... Our prospectus, with an address on the subject, shall soon be before the public .... 'Be ye therefore ready!' "[51]

This herald of something bigger yet to come was accompanied by a positive reminder that the first form of encouragement would be for all overdue subscriptions to be paid at once. Collections had been bad for three years, and between four and five thousand dollars of amounts then due were being solicited. Prompt payment was requested as soon as the statements arrived. With these thoughts he let the matter rest for almost six weeks.

And then, on November 19, 1834, he released the promised Prospectus, stretching it impressively across two first-page columns of his paper:

# SOUTHERN CITIZEN

"The subscriber proposes to publish, in the town of Greensborough, North-Carolina, a splendid, superfine imperial newspaper bearing the above title. Thousands of dollars are annually sent to the north to purchase periodical intelligence and literature; because the wants of the people, in this respect, are not supplied at home.

"It is the purpose of the 'Citizen' to fill this vacuum. It will contain everything of interest, in literature, politics, religion and morality, that can be found in the northern publications, or in the high-toned literary journals of Europe; — to which we shall add a rich fund of domestic and local information no where else to be met with.

"The southern press stands low in public estimation. In most cases the paper is bad, the mechanical execution slovenly, and the matter erroneous in principle, false in fact, and vulgar in sentiment. We aim at nothing less than a radical and thorough reformation in these respects; and the elevation of our periodical press to a standard of becoming dignity and decency. The 'Citizen' will contain about twice as much reading matter as any other paper in the state; and will be chiefly devoted to the following subjects:

"1. *Agriculture.* It shall be our business to glean from the floating mass, all such experiments and suggestions as may serve to enlighten our citizens on this practical science. Let them be inspired with *thought* and *action;* and then spread before them the broad page of intelligence — and our southern country, rich in resources, will bloom as the Eden of a new world, the bountiful productions of nature will crown the efforts of industry, commerce will flow at our bidding, and 'cattle will leap upon a thousand hills.'

"2. *Internal Improvement.* In regard to commercial facilities by water, nature seems to have frowned upon us; but she has left us rich in the means of internal communication, by rail roads and locomotives. Art is fully competent to overcome the deficiencies of nature *in* this respect. We shall strip the subject of all the false trappings that have been hung around it for sinister purposes, and lay it before the people as a plain matter-of-fact business. Instead of chasing butter-flies, we shall give practical results.

"3. *Education.* The maxim in all despotic governments, is, 'The more ignorance the more peace.' But with us, intelligence and virtue are the very pillars on which our institutions are based. In fact, our government, so far as it is a government of laws, is but the legitimate action of the popular will; and to enable this will to operate for the universal good of mankind, it should be *enlightened*.

"4. *General Politics*.  In regard to the constitutional powers of the general government, we are neither a strict constructionist, nor a latitudinarian. It is true that there are constructive powers to be exercised under the constitution; but death and desolation to that policy which would add anything to it, or take ought from it by *construction!* As soon would we pluck the sun from heaven, as to touch that model of human wisdom with a rude or unskilful hand. If it is defective, let it be amended — but let it never be violated. We believe, further, that the clearly ascertained will of the people should be a rule of conduct for all public officers, where that conduct is not checked and regulated by written constitution. All public servants, 'knowing the will of their master' — the public — 'and doing it not,' shall be 'beaten with many stripes!'

"5. *Law*.  As every man in the community should make himself familiar with those rules of civil conduct by which his actions are to be regulated, we shall appropriate a department of our paper to the discussion of such legal subjects as may be of general interest. Under this head we shall arrange all such legal decisions, acts of congress, and statutes of the state legislatures, as may be of service to *all* our citizens in the ordinary transactions of life.

"6. *Literature*.  Here is an immense field open before us, in which our readers shall ramble unconfined. We shall exchange for the richest gems of literature, wit and sentiment, both in Europe and America; and with the assistance of a few literary correspondents of the first order, we intend to place the 'Citizen' above any other family newspaper in the United States. It has become popular to speak of our journey through this world, as strowed with thorns, and overshadowed with gloom; but we intend to roll away the slander, and make it manifest to all our patrons, that most of their troubles are unsubstantial and visionary. Flowers may be plucked even from the thorns which beset our paths.

"7. *News*.  The world is at this time, in awful commotion. Tyrants look upon the march of liberty and tremble: The accumulated gloom of centuries is rapidly retreating before the stately steppings of truth. Millions of people who once licked the dust from the feet of their sovereigns, are now tramping crowns under their feet — and thrones are tottering to prostration! It will be wisdom in us to profit by the experience of others. We shall have the earliest access to means of information, from each state in the union, and from every kingdom and country in the world. And all the intelligence, both legislative, judicial, moral, religious, political and miscellaneous, that may serve to guide our footsteps, as a people, in the ways of prosperity and peace, shall be carefully collected, condensed and spread before our readers. In short, nothing shall pass unnoticed, that may serve to inform the mind, improve the manners, or mend the heart.

"8. *Variety*. The above subjects will be suitably interspersed with biographical sketches, humorous anecdotes, interesting tales, poetical selections, &c. We would also set apart a separate *head* in our paper for the ladies, but they would insist on having a *tongue* in it, and to this we would by no means consent, as such an *appendage* would render our paper entirely useless, so far as *news* is concerned! They shall, however, receive that attention to which the proud station they occupy in society so justly entitles them: — We shall give them all the praise their pre-eminent virtues demand; but, with due deference to their charms, we shall blame where we *must!*

"These are perilous times; and a responsibility, awful as the tomb and extensive as eternity, hangs over every man who shall take upon himself the management of a newspaper; because *public opinion* is measurably formed from the tone of the press — the *action* of the people depends upon *opinions previously formed* — and upon their *action* is suspended the *destinies of the republic.* An abiding reverence for the constitutional laws of the land, should be continually cherished and deeply inculcated; because upon their *acknowledged supremacy,* depend the happiness of man, the peace of society, the security of our institutions, the prosperity of our flourishing union, and the durability of our happy form of government.

"But aside from this secret, silent and irresistible power, before our hands shall be tied they shall be severed from our body and thrown to the dogs in the street — before our mind shall submit to shackles of any description, it shall be given up to despair, and frozen into a barrenness more gloomy than the deserts of Africa — before our soul shall be conquered by the 'hope of reward,' or the 'fear of punishment,' it shall be redeemed from the 'shackles of mortality,' and sent to receive its doom in the courts of eternity!"

In order to reaffirm his stand on freedom of speech, he repeated a statement he had made earlier:

"Before we will relinquish our right to think, speak, print and publish our own *deliberate opinions*, in relation to *public men* and *public measures*, we will *renounce existence itself*. Take away our rights as a *free man* and *life has no charm for us!* We shall *deal plainly* with the people; not caring who may be affected by our course. We would rather bask for *one hour* in the approving smiles of an *intelligent* and *undeceived people*, than to spend a *whole eternity*, amidst the *damning grins* of a *motly crew* of office-hunters, despots, demagogues, tyrants, fools and hypocrites.

"We shall watch with a lynx-eyed vigilence, the conduct of men in power; and in every case of political transgression, we shall apply the rod without distinction or mercy. Our pen will be dipped in *rose-water* or *gall*, as occasion may seem to require. *Private* friendship shall not protect *public* men from the severest scrutiny nor shall personal dislike turn away our support from a political benefactor to the country. In short: The 'Citizen' *shall be what it ought to be*— and just what every *good and great man wants it to be!*" Another printing *ended*: "*shall be just such a paper as the wants of the people imperiously demand.*"

In the same issue of the *Greensborough Patriot*, immediately following the Prospectus for the *Southern Citizen*, Swaim clearly stated his plans for his proposed journal. It would be published once a week, on a large imperial sheet, with a new press and new type.

The price would be three dollars and fifty cents per year, with an additional fifty cents for every three months that payment was delayed. No subscription would be taken for a period of less than twelve months; and no paper would be sent out of the state without payment of subscription money in advance.

On the same page with the Prospectus and terms, Swaim appealed to interested persons for co-operation in securing patrons in this manner:

"AGENCIES — We are making arrangement for the largest and most useful family newspaper in the United States. . . . We want five thousand subscribers, and *must have* two thousand, before we can hazard the expense of fitting up an office for the purpose. And in order to aid us in procuring these subscribers, we wish to employ an agent in each county in this state."

The editor offered to pay fifty cents for each subscription secured; and since postmasters in those days would often make up subscription lists, he later appealed through a notice in the *Greensborough Patriot* to every postmaster in the United States to solicit customers. Again he stated his plan to issue a publication that would interest, amuse, and edify North Carolinians, inhabitants of the South, and American people in all sections of the country.

As soon as the announcement appeared, the reaction was immediate. Into the *Greensborough Patriot* office poured storms of abuse and expressions of good wishes. An unsigned letter from the eastern part of the state bore the first postmark. It ran: " 'Sir, [in the last] number of your paper, (which by the bye is the most corrupt sheet I know of) I perceive a "notice to subscribers" in which you give notice of your determination to *enlarge* the "Patriot." This, sir, cannot be done; for a paper larger than the one now printed, by William Swaim would not receive sufficient patronage. The small sheet now printed is large enough to do much injury — and how much more would three times the size do? What would it contain? Why, exactly what it now contains — *Abuse!* . . . You stated that [North Carolina needs a new newspaper. I deny that statement, but were it true] *"God save the state"* if William Swaim is the man that is to draw us from our sloth!' " [52]

Personal criticism never deterred Swaim in his ambitions, but he seldom left it unanswered; and this he resented as a stab in the back. Usually he would not print communications without a signature, but he made this an exception because of his honest desire to present various reactions to his proposed paper, as well as to publish his opinion of this critic. Branding the correspondent as an "ill-bred, low priced lickspittle" for attacking without having the manhood to sign his name, he dismissed the matter.

The editor of the *Franklin* [*Weekly*] *Review,* Tennessee, chided Swaim quite roundly for his pompous attitude. He said that the Prospectus for the *Southern Citizen* had been read, and in it there appeared " 'the following sounding sentence. — "These are perilous times; and a responsibility, *awful as the tomb, & extensive as eternity,* hangs over every man who shall take upon himself the management of a *newspaper."* ☞Avast there brother Swaim, — hadn't you better roll up a range or two of the Apennines or the Alleghenies, to keep you from slipping while in the editorial chair? If you venture to "assume the responsibility" after uttering such a "parable," our head for it, you will need them.' "[53]

Swaim, taking this in good stride, topped the Tennessee editor by saying that he had "most egregiously misconceived 'the length, & breadth, and height, and depth,' of our *stability* or he never would have made such a *slip* as to suppose it necessary to brace ourself with such *moderate* things as a 'range of mountains rolled up!' Now for the publisher of the 'Weakly Review,' to need a *prop* is not at all wonderful, and he may naturally suppose others to be as *slippery* as himself; but, shielded by the panoply of truth, we shall go forth 'conquering and to conquer!' "[54]

Dennis Heartt, editor of the *Hillsborough Recorder,* surprised at such an ambitious undertaking, remarked that " 'a revolution surely will have been accomplished when the editor of the *Greensborough Patriot* becomes the fountain of literature for the South and the standard of "dignity and decency" for the periodical press.' " Swaim assured Heartt that "we have made our calculations in solemn sincerity, and we hereby renew our pledge to perform everything, to the letter, that we have promised in our prospectus, or we will never ask a cent from those who may subscribe for it. . . . Our list is rapidly increasing, and we shall steadily pursue our purpose."[55]

And John Pasteur, editor of the *Newbern Spectator,* thought Swaim was joking. He wrote in his paper that "'The editor of the Greensborough Patriot has issued proposals for a new paper which he intends to commence as soon as two thousand (!) subscribers shall have been obtained. [A subscription list of two thousand subscribers appeared to have been unheard of in New Bern.] . . . If one half be performed, the new paper will be a pand[ect], not of one art or science only, but of all; a complete cyclopædia of wit, of literature, general and particular, of law, physic[s], agriculture and cookery . . . its editor, William Swaim, Esq. our particular friend. — To be serious, however, we know not whether the Patriot is in earnest in this matter, or in its usual joking mood.'" If serious, the New Bern editor promised "'to add a few names to the two thousand.'"[56]

Swaim having replied that "We now give the Spectator the most solemn assuration of our sincerity,"[57] the New Bern editor, in a friendly gesture to help Swaim with his mammoth prospect, summarized the Greensboro editor's faults and virtues. First, we "'will tell him of his faults, for faults he has. He is somewhat too regardless of the feelings of those who err, either in politics or morality, and he handles them with so little ceremony that he renders them callous and incorrigible. He should know from experience that the Sangrado practice will sometimes effect a cure when the cauterization of the veterinary school would kill; and although it sometimes seems as if our friend had taken his degrees in the latter, and practices with considerable success, we would respectfully suggest that a blending of the two modes might succeed better than either singly. . . . The next is, that he too frequently drags private transgressors before the public, and, without the slightest prospects of reclaiming the faulty or guilty, makes innumerable enemies.

"'Fault third is, that he carries independence to recklessness, and sometimes meddles where he has no business, as we, perhaps, are doing now.

354

" 'On the other hand, a more vigilant sentinel on the watchtower of our country's liberties than WM. SWAIM cannot be found within the bounds of the State. We have full faith in his honesty of purpose, and ample evidence of his ability to be useful. Witty, searching and satirical, his paragraphs act not on the cachinnatory muscles alone, but on the whole system; and their effect is both edifying and pleasing to all but "the subject" dissected. To cut the matter short, however, and as a proof of our sincerity in recommending the forthcoming paper, we agree to pay a year's subscription for all such of our acquaintances as shall be dissatisfied with [the *Southern Citizen*].' "58

On the whole, response was encouraging and Swaim said "we are proud to possess the good opinion of many of our contemporaries." Within less than two months he announced that there were already over five hundred subscribers. And he felt so confident that he could command the approval of the public with his proposed publication he was tempted to say, "Give us a trial the first year, and then if we disappoint you, *withdraw yourselves at once and forever from us!*"59 Four months after the Prospectus appeared, Swaim wrote: "SOUTHERN CITIZEN. We are truly rejoiced at the rapid accession to our list of subscribers for this publication. Gentlemen in distant parts of the state, of whom we never even heard until lately, are exerting themselves to increase our list to the desired number.... Our prospects are so truly flattering, that if we could command the means, we would not hesitate to purchase the necessary apparatus, such as press, type, &c., and commence immediately: — But as it is, our list of two thousand must be made out before we can venture a dollar.... We have no inclination to *brag;* but we have an itching desire to show what it is to do things as they should be done! *We ask nothing but a fair trial!*"60

There appeared further evidence that Swaim had reason to feel confidence in the promise of his projected *Southern Citizen,* for his idea for that paper was in line with advanced thinking in northern urban areas. In April, 1835, the *Greensborough Patriot* carried a Prospectus of the *New Yorker,* a proposed publication to be undertaken by Horace Greeley & Company. This journal was to have three divisions — Literature Department, Political Intelligence, and General Intelligence — and was to be established along lines similar to those promised for the *Southern Citizen*. Editors practiced reciprocal exchanges of their papers, and it therefore appears that the *Southern Citizen* and the *New Yorker* had already entered a sphere of relationship.[61]

Deep tragedy unhappily attended the *Southern Citizen*. William Swaim died in the midst of preparations to launch this promising publication. It is evident that all the requirements had been met before his death, for one month afterward his cousin, Benjamin Swaim, took over the project and in February, 1836, began publishing the *Southern Citizen* from New Salem, North Carolina, and later from the near-by town of Asheboro.[62] Benjamin, however, did not have the editorial ability and public appeal that William had had, and the much anticipated journal, under Benjamin, fell short of William's goal.

Other than providing a livelihood for his family, William Swaim's chief ambition was to publish a creditable newspaper. Unquestionably, he published such a newspaper, and he was rewarded in material ways even beyond his expectations.

# XIV

## " 'TIS DEATH IS DEAD, NOT HE"

*"Lively, talented, incorruptible and fearless, though occasionally rough and imprudent, Mr. Swaim threw a charm around his writings — the charm of evidently honest patriotism — which attached his readers, not only to his labours, but to the man himself."*[1]

On December 31, 1835, William Swaim died at the age of thirty-three. For two months North Carolina newspapers, one after another, carried notices of his death, but none of those still in existence give the attendant circumstances. Issues of the *Greensborough Patriot*, which probably gave details, are missing. Thirty years later when Greensboro was under the control of Union forces after the Civil War, Will L. Scott, mayor of the town, recalled Swaim's warning against the South's policies which were leading toward such a catastrophe. In order that future generations might know of this southern editor who issued this warning a quarter of a century before it happened, Scott gathered, from Swaim's contemporaries, materials for a short biography.[2]

According to Scott, in the fall of 1835, Swaim hitched his horse to his gig and drove down to Fayetteville, North Carolina, apparently on one of his news gathering journeys at a session of the county court. While there, he had an accident which appeared to be of little consequence. In fact he thought it so insignificant that he finished his work before driving back to Greensboro.

For several weeks thereafter Swaim was in fine spirits, enjoying his business which was progressing "with brighter prospects than ever beamed upon us, at any former period of our existence."[3] He

357

was looking forward to launching his *Southern Citizen,* to reporting reform measures being undertaken by the Whig party, and to witnessing the advent of an era in which he was a leader.

Then came tragedy. The Fayetteville wound, which had appeared to heal completely, developed alarming complications. Said Scott, "Swaim became afflicted with a disease which the power of medicine could not arrest in its ravages upon his life." Scott was no more specific than that.

William Swaim's life ended with the year. According to his contemporaries, he was cheerful in spirits and inspiring in conversation until the very last moment of his existence. His last act was to call to his bedside his little daughter, Mary Jane Virginia, then in her third year, and as he spoke softly and privately to her, to place in her tiny hands two shining pieces of silver money. These coins were kept and cherished as long as she lived by Mary Jane Virginia Swaim Porter,[4] mother of William Sydney Porter (O. Henry).

William Swaim, "fiery crusader for freedom and humanity," lies buried in an unmarked grave in the First Presbyterian Church Cemetery in Greensboro.[5] Several of the gravestones in the cemetery have been broken and thrown away. It is thought that Swaim's tombstone was among those thus desecrated.

In the period immediately following his death, there are very few preserved copies of North Carolina newspapers; but in those which are available his brethren of the craft paid him tributes which have placed him in an enviable position in the newspaper world.

The editor of the *Charlotte Journal* wrote that "WILLIAM SWAIM, Esq., Editor of the 'Greensborough Patriot,'... has left an affectionate wife and an infant daughter, with whom a large circle of friends join in deeply deploring his early departure from their midst. *Requiescat in pace!*"[6]

From the *Raleigh Register* and Raleigh *Star* came similar references, lamenting the death of William Swaim, "the witty, talented and independent editor of the 'Greensborough Patriot.'"[7]

The *Carolina Observer* reported that "MR. WILLIAM SWAIM, Editor of the Greensborough Patriot, died in that place on the . . .

31st., ult. . . . Under his management the Patriot had acquired a reputation for wit, and for unsparing severity upon political opponents, and offenders of every degree, never equalled by any paper in the Southern States, and perhaps in no other quarter, except the celebrated 'Tickler,' published many years ago in Philadelphia."[8]

And the *Newbern Spectator* placed at the head of its editorial column, in a box with deep mourning lines, this sentiment: "WILLIAM SWAIM, Esq., Editor of the Greensborough Patriot, is no more! He departed this life on the 31st. day of December, . . . — No announcement of a similar nature has ever affected us more, or called forth more sincere regret, although our whole knowledge of the deceased was derived from the spirited and entertaining columns of the Patriot. Lively, talented, incorruptible and fearless, though occasionally rough and imprudent, Mr. Swaim threw a charm around his writings — the charm of evidently honest patriotism — which attached his readers, not only to his labours, but to the man himself; and his faults were far more than atoned for by his brilliant good humor and honesty of purpose."[9]

Three weeks later the *Newbern Spectator* carried this paragraph: "The *Greensborough Patriot* comes to us as usual, but we honestly confess — without intending any disrespect to the present editor, — that we have never before today had the heart to open a number of it since that which announced the death of the lamented SWAIM. We had a warm and friendly affection for poor Swaim, created and fostered solely by the wit, vigor, honesty and talents which enlivened the columns of the Patriot, and we are not of the number of those who can immediately bury the affections of the understanding in the grave of him who called them forth and deserved them."[10]

Perhaps more significant than a gravestone, or words of praise, or even stately memorials, is the legend on a bookmark of cross-stitched canvas, mounted on satin ribbon, which was found a century later in Abiah Swaim's Bible.[11] On it, hand-embroidered in tiny gold beads, is her tribute to her husband:

> *I've loved thee on earth,*
> *I'll meet thee in heaven.*

# NOTES

# MAJOR BIBLIOGRAPHICAL
# REFERENCES

# INDEX

# NOTES

## I. CENTRE COMMUNITY

1. Will L. Scott, *The Life of William Swaim, Former Editor of the Greensboro Patriot.* This brief biography was published only in the weekly installments of the *Greensboro Patriot,* beginning May 18, 1866, and continuing through June 22, 1866. It seems never to have been mentioned thereafter. *Non multa, sed multum* — not a few outstanding virtues, but many — is written at the head of each of its nine chapters. The first seven chapters are in the Greensboro Public Library, and the last two are in the Library of the University of North Carolina at Chapel Hill. This biography had been buried in old *Greensborough Patriot* files for almost a hundred years when it was recently found. (*Greensboro* after the Civil War.)

   William Swaim had kept a *Diary,* and much of Scott's writing was based on this record from which he frequently quoted. The original *Diary* has been lost, therefore quotations from it are taken from Scott's biography of Swaim, and are cited hereafter as William Swaim, *Diary.*

   Scott, a native of Guilford County, was born in 1828, and was therefore able to get firsthand information from contemporaries of Swaim, whose wife, his cousin Lyndon, and friends were still living in Scott's time. The author was an intelligent man — an honor graduate of the University of North Carolina, and valedictorian of the class of 1854. During the last days of the Civil War, under the provisional Union government, he was appointed Mayor of Greensboro. It was about the end of his mayoralty when he released *The Life of William Swaim, Former Editor of the Greensboro Patriot.* (Cited hereafter as Scott, *The Life.*)

2. Archibald Henderson, *North Carolina, The Old North State and The New,* II, 727.

3. John Spencer Bassett, *Anti-Slavery Leaders of North Carolina,* 51; Stephen B. Weeks, *Southern Quakers and Slavery,* 240; *Raleigh Register,* January 12, 1836; *Newbern Spectator,* January 15, 1836; *Greensborough Patriot,* December 24, 1834; January 21, 1835; Lyndon Swaim, "The Greensboro Patriot," in newspaper clippings file, Greensboro Public Library.

4. *The Greensborough Patriot,* extant consecutive issues in Greensboro Public Library, from May 23, 1829, to May 19, 1830; from May

30, 1832, to May 29, 1833; from July 14, 1834, to July 8, 1835; irregular numbers during Swaim's entire editorship in the Library of Duke University at Durham, N. C.; and a few odd editions in the North Carolina State Library at Raleigh, the Library of the University of North Carolina in Chapel Hill, and in the Library of Congress.

5. *Greensborough Patriot*, November 21, 1829; May 9, 1832; May 8, 1833.

6. Joshua E. Murrow, a native, a lifetime resident, and a reliable historian of Centre Community, in personal interviews furnished much of the early history of his community as it appears in this book. (Cited hereafter as Murrow, interview.)

7. Scott, *The Life.*

8. State Records, Office of the Secretary of State.

9. Marmaduke and Sarah Fanning Swaim's Family Bible, now in the possession of their great-great-granddaughter, Massa E. Lambert, Asheboro, North Carolina; unpublished Genealogical Records of many North Carolina families, compiled by Mrs. Elvira E. Moffitt, daughter of Governor Jonathan Worth. The original of this valuable collection is owned by Mrs. Moffitt's granddaughter, Evelyn H. Jackson, Richmond, Virginia. (Cited hereafter as Moffitt, Genealogical Records.)

10. *The Colonial Records of North Carolina*, collected and edited by William L. Saunders, V, 1223.

11. Calvin H. Wiley, *Alamance Church, A Historical Address*, 8n.

12. J. Hector St. John DeCrevecoeur, *Letters from an American Farmer*, 133-135.

13. Marmaduke and Sarah Fanning Swaim's Family Bible; Guilford County Register of Deeds, Book 21, 335.

14. *O. Henry from Polecat Creek*, by Ethel Stephens Arnett, 1, also note 1.

15. Hugh T. Lefler and Albert R. Newsome, *North Carolina, The History of a Southern State*, 314. (Cited hereafter as Lefler, *North Carolina.*)

16. Murrow, quoting from "Peter Dick's Diary."

17. Scott, *The Life*. Sulkies, now associated with harness races, were used for transportation as early as 1767; and gigs were used after 1806. See *Dictionary of American English.*

18. Murrow, interview; Kathryn Worth, *They Loved to Laugh*, 98. This book was written by a great-great-granddaughter of Doctors David and Eunice Worth. Although it is presented as fiction, Mrs. Nellie Rowe Jones, former librarian of the Greensboro Public Library, assisted the author in collecting the bona fide facts upon which it is based.

19. Murrow, quoting from "Peter Dick's Diary."

20. Sallie W. Stockard, *The History of Guilford County, North Carolina,* 57.

21. Murrow, interview.

22. Kathryn Worth, *They Loved to Laugh,* 110-114.

23. Hiram B. Worth, whose ancestors date back to the origin of the Festival, interview.

24. William K. Boyd, *History of North Carolina,* II, 88. (Cited hereafter as Boyd, *North Carolina,* II.)

25. Moffitt, Genealogical Records.

26. Mrs. Sarah Trogdon Lambert, Family Records, now in the possession of her daughter, Massa E. Lambert, Asheboro, North Carolina. (Cited hereafter as Lambert, Family Records.)

27. Murrow, interview.

28. Kathryn Worth, *They Loved to Laugh,* 190-193; Samuel A. Ashe, *History of North Carolina,* II, 387. (Cited hereafter as Ashe, *North Carolina,* II.)

29. *History of Centre Friends Meeting,* compiled by members of the Meeting.

30. Murrow, interview.

31. Scott, *The Life.*

32. Joseph Addison Blair, *Reminiscences of Randolph County,* included in *The History of Naomi Wise,* reprinted by the Randleman Rotary Club, 56.

33. Levi Coffin, *Reminiscences of Levi Coffin,* 72.

34. William Swaim, *Diary.*

35. Ethel Stephens Arnett, *Greensboro, North Carolina: The County Seat of Guilford,* 359-361.

36. Scott, *The Life.*

37. *Ibid.*

38. William Swaim, *Diary.*

39. Murrow, interview.

40. Jerome Dowd, *Life of Braxton Craven, D.D., L.L.D.,* 211-246; *The Story of Naomi Wise,* reprinted by the Randleman Rotary Club, 7-31.

41. William Swaim, *Diary.*

42. Moffitt, Genealogical Records; "Dr. David and Dr. Eunice Worth," by May McAlister, an unpublished manuscript now held by Hope Hubbard of Farmer, N. C.

43. Murrow, Hope Hubbard, and Mrs. Dorothy Hubbard Kearns, interviews; May McAlister, "Dr. David and Dr. Eunice Worth;" Guion Johnson, *Ante-Bellum North Carolina*, 744; Dorothy Long, Reference Librarian, North Carolina Memorial Hospital, Division of Health Affairs, The University of North Carolina. Miss Long wrote to Ethel Stephens Arnett on July 5, 1958, "I had checked as far as I could the records prior to 1820, and had found no record of any real general hospital up to that time." Research on general hospital plans for Winston-Salem and Beaufort show that they did not materialize. Dr. Worth's hospital was built soon after 1820, and thus became the first known general hospital in North Carolina.

44. May McAlister, "Dr. David and Dr. Eunice Worth."

45. Fernando G. Cartland, *Southern Heroes, The Friends in War Time*, 41-43.

46. Guion G. Johnson, *Ante-Bellum North Carolina*, 560.

47. Clement Eaton, *Henry Clay and the Art of American Politics*, 132.

48. Charles A. & Mary R. Beard, *The Beards' Basic History of the United States*, 176.

49. Levi Coffin, *Reminiscences of Levi Coffin*, 74.

50. *Ibid.*, 75.

51. *Minutes of the N. C. Manumission Society, 1816-1834*, edited by H. M. Wagstaff, 87. (Cited hereafter as *Minutes of the N. C. Manumission Society.*)

52. Benjamin Lundy, *The Life, Travels and Opinions of Benjamin Lundy*, 218.

53. Scott, *The Life*.

54. William Swaim, *Diary*.

55. Scott, *The Life*.

56. *Minutes of the N. C. Manumission Society*, 105.

57. Scott, *The Life;* Addison Coffin, "Early Settlements of Friends in North Carolina," a book-length unpublished manuscript in the Guilford College Library.

58. *Greensborough Patriot*, July 25, 1829; Scott, *The Life*.

59. C. C. Weaver, "The North Carolina Manumission Society," *Historical Papers, Historical Society of Trinity College*, 75.

60. *Minutes of the N. C. Manumission Society*, 138, 204.

## II.   A REFORMER IN THE MAKING

1. William Swaim, *Diary*.

2. Scott, *The Life*.

3. *Greensborough Patriot,* August 29, 1832.

4. Scott, *The Life.*

5. *Records of the Moravians in North Carolina, 1752-1775,* II, edited by Adelaide L. Fries, "John Swaim," 791; Lambert, Family Records.

6. Scott, *The Life.*

7. *Ibid.*

8. Register of Deeds, Guilford County, showing ownership of eight farms, which aggregated at least 1,706 acres of land; Scott, *The Life;* Swaim's Family Bible, for birth.

9. Lambert, Family Records.

10. Henry M. Robins, a grandnephew of William Swaim, got the name of Peggy from an aunt who was a great-great-granddaughter of Peggy. This aunt was well versed on the Swaim family, being a descendent therefrom. Henry Robins' brother, Dr. Sidney S. Robins, Carolina Inn, Chapel Hill, N. C., held this record in 1959.

11. Scott, *The Life.*

12. The family records of the Swaims do not always give the maiden surname of the wife, but instead combine her maiden given name with her surname by marriage.

13. The Anson County Register of Deeds shows Thomas Fanning to have been a landowner in that county.

14. Scott, *The Life.*

15. *The Colonial Records of North Carolina,* collected and edited by by William L. Saunders, VII, 806-810, showing the two Fannings as signers of a petition from Anson County to North Carolina's Governor William Tryon for redress of grievances, and Governor Tryon's reply.

16. *Ibid.,* VIII, 256; Hugh T. Lefler, "Orange County and the War of the Regulation," *Orange County—1752-1952,* Chapter IV; Lefler, *North Carolina,* 173.

17. *The Colonial Records of North Carolina,* VII, 806-810.

18. Lambert, Family Records.

19. *Ibid.;* also Henry M. Robins' Records; and Scott, *The Life.*

20. Anson County Records, State Department of Archives and History, Raleigh.

21. Lambert, Family Records.

22. *Ibid.*

23. *Ibid.*

24. Scott, *The Life.*

25. *Ibid.*

26. Lambert, Family Records.

27. Scott, *The Life.*

28. *Greensborough Patriot,* August 29, 1832.

29. Scott, *The Life.*

30. *Ibid.*

31. *Ibid.*

32. *Ibid.;* William Swaim, *Diary.*

33. Minute Book of the organized Town of Greensboro, 1829-1843, in the vault of the Greensboro Public Library.

34. William Swaim, *Diary.*

35. Martin F. Douglas, quoted by Ethel Stephens Arnett, in *Greensboro. North Carolina: The County Seat of Guilford,* 59.

36. William Swaim, *Diary.*

37. Scott, *The Life.*

38. William Swaim, *Diary.*

39. *Ibid.*

40. Scott, *The Life.*

41. *History of Centre Friends Meeting,* compiled by members of the Meeting.

42. *The Patriot,* April 24, 1826, was the first newspaper to be continuously published in Guilford County. Its predecessor, *Carolina Patriot,* lived through only a few issues.

43. Scott, *The Life.*

44. William Swaim, *Diary.*

45. Scott, *The Life.*

46. William Swaim, *Diary.*

47. *Ibid.*

48. *Greensborough Patriot,* November 21, 1829; May 9, 1832; May 8, 1833; Scott, *The Life.*

49. Levi Coffin, *Reminiscences of Levi Coffin,* 72.

50. Scott, *The Life.*

51. *Ibid.*

52. *Ibid.*

53. William Swaim, *Diary.*

54. Scott, *The Life.*

55. Joseph M. Rogers, *The True Henry Clay,* 29.

56. William Swaim, *Diary*.

57. Lefler, *North Carolina,* 334.

58. Boyd, *North Carolina,* II, 151-152.

59. State Records, Offiice of the Secretary of State.

60. Scott, *The Life*.

61. William Swaim, *Diary*.

62. Scott, *The Life*.

63. *Ibid*.

64. *Ibid*.

65. *Ibid*.

### III.   A BONA FIDE MEMBER OF THE FOURTH ESTATE

1. *Greensborough Patriot,* June 6, 1832; November 19, 1834.

2. Scott, *The Life*.

3. Benjamin Lundy, *The Life, Travels and Opinions of Benjamin Lundy,* 25.

4. *Ibid*.

5. *Ibid.,* 22.

6. *Ibid.,* 25.

7. *Ibid.,* 21n, 199.

8. *Ibid.,* 13-20, 26-28n.

9. *Ibid.,* 238, 244, 263, 266.

10. *Ibid.,* 25.

11. *Ibid.,* 26-28n, 27-28.

12. *Ibid.,* 306.

13. Scott, *The Life*.

14. *Ibid*.

15. Benjamin Lundy, *The Life, Travels and Opinions of Benjamin Lundy,* 27-28.

16. Scott, *The Life*.

17. *Ibid*.

18. William Swaim, *Diary*.

19. Scott, *The Life*.

20. Nettie Fleming, "The Press of Guilford County," unpublished manuscript in the Library of Woman's College of the University of North Carolina.

21. Scott, *The Life*.

22. Lyndon Swaim, "The Greensboro Patriot," published in the *Greensboro Patriot* about 1880. Filed under newspaper clippings, Greensboro Public Library.

23. *The Patriot*, April 24, 1826.

24. T. Early Strange, quoted in Scott, *The Life*.

25. *Greensborough Patriot*, May 23, 1829.

26. Scott, *The Life*.

27. The *Carolina Observer and Fayetteville Gazette* (*Carolina Observer*, 1834-1865) was started earlier, but it had a period of suspension after the Civil War, and was reissued in 1883. The Greensboro paper was published until 1950.

28. Stephen B. Weeks, in *Publications of the Guilford County Literary and Historical Association*, I, 17.

29. Guion G. Johnson, *Ante-Bellum North Carolina*, 768.

30. *Ibid.*, 770.

31. Boyd, *North Carolina*, II, 376.

32. *Ibid.*

33. Harriett Martineau, *Society in America*, I, "Newspapers," 147-148.

## IV.   A UNIQUE NEWSPAPER

1. *Greensborough Patriot*, Prospectus, May 23, 1829.

2. Library of Congress, Annex Building, Room 5010, review of old newspapers, 1828-1829.

3. *Greensborough Patriot*, May 30, 1832.

4. *Ibid.*, May 30, 1829.

5. Comparison of old newspapers, 1828-1829, Library of Congress, North Carolina State Library at Raleigh, Library of the University of North Carolina at Chapel Hill, and Library of Duke University in Durham, N. C.

6. *Greensborough Patriot*, August 29, 1829.

7. *Ibid.*, September 5, 1829.

8. Comparison of old newspapers, 1828-1829, Library of Congress, North Carolina State Library at Raleigh, Library of the University of North Carolina at Chapel Hill, and Library of Duke University in Durham, N. C.

9. Daniel M. McFarland, "North Carolina Newspapers, Editors, and Journalistic Politics, 1815-1835," *The North Carolina Historical Review*, July, 1953, 387.

## V. FOR AN EDUCATED CITIZENRY

1. *Greensborough Patriot,* February 24, 1830; March 17, 1830.
2. Scott, *The Life;* marriage record, Greensboro Public Library. Scott and other records give 1831 as the marriage date, but the state contract seems more authentic.
3. Photostat of the Swaims' marriage bond, Greensboro Public Library; Guion G. Johnson, *Ante-Bellum North Carolina,* 203.
4. Scott, *The Life.*
5. Register of Deeds, Book 19, 490-491, February 17, 1832; Abiah Shirley Swaim's Bible, on the inside back cover of which she had written the birth dates of her slaves.
6. Scott, *The Life.*
7. Evelyn P. Shirley, *Stemmata Shirleiana.*
8. Scott, *The Life.*
9. *Ibid.*
10. Mrs. Thomas Sherwood, interview with Mrs. Nellie Rowe Jones, Librarian, Greensboro Public Library; Scott, *The Life.*
11. Lefler, *North Carolina,* 312.
12. *Ibid.,* Chapter 21, "The Murphey Program for State Development."
13. *Ibid.*
14. *Greensborough Patriot,* May 23, 1829, to December 31, 1835.
15. Lefler, *North Carolina,* 304.
16. Ashe, *North Carolina,* II, 283; Boyd, *North Carolina,* II, 102-104.
17. Lefler, *North Carolina,* 304.
18. *Greensborough Patriot,* "Address to Our Patrons," May 23, 1829.
19. *Ibid.*
20. *Ibid.,* February 11, 1835.
21. *Ibid.,* October 24, 1829.
22. *Ibid.,* May 30, 1829.
23. *Ibid.,* September 5, 1829.
24. *Ibid.,* June 13, 1829.
25. *Ibid.,* March 31, 1830.
26. *Ibid.,* October 10, 1835.
27. *Ibid.,* January 1, 1831.
28. *Ibid.,* June 12, 1833.
29. *Ibid.,* March 27, 1833; April 10, 1833.

30. *Ibid.*, October 30, 1833; February 22, 1834; Guion G. Johnson, *Ante-Bellum North Carolina*, 795 and 795n.

31. *Greensborough Patriot*, September 12, 1829.

32. *Ibid.*, September 25, 1833; September 12, 1829; April 11, 1832.

33. *Ibid.*, February 17, 1830.

34. *Ibid.*, September 26, 1829.

35. Ethel Stephens Arnett, *Greensboro, North Carolina: The County Seat of Guilford*, 82.

36. *Greensborough Patriot*, November 28, 1829.

37. *Ibid.*, December 12, 1829.

38. *Ibid.*, January 27, 1830.

39. *Ibid.*, March 17, 1830.

40. Charles L. Coon, *The Beginnings of Public Education in North Carolina*, II, 546-548, 555, 556, quoting *Letters on Popular Education, Addressed to the People of North Carolina*, by Dr. Joseph Caldwell.

41. *Greensborough Patriot*, January 6, 1830.

42. *Ibid.*, November 19, 1834.

43. Lefler, *North Carolina*, 334.

## VI.     FOR SCIENTIFIC AGRICULTURE

1. *Greensborough Patriot*, July 19, 1834.

2. Lefler, *North Carolina*, 300.

3. Ashe, *North Carolina*, II, 305-306; Boyd, *North Carolina, II*, 100-101.

4. Lefler, *North Carolina*, 305.

5. Boyd, *North Carolina*, II, 83.

6. *Greensborough Patriot*, May 13, 1835.

7. *Ibid.*, 'Address to Our Patrons," May 23, 1829.

8. *Ibid.*, October 8, 1834.

9. *Ibid.*, March 4, 1835.

10. *Ibid.*, April 11, 1835.

11. *Ibid.*, November 28, 1832.

12. *Ibid.*, October 3, 1829.

13. *Ibid.*, July 18, 1832.

14. *Ibid.*, June 17, 1835.

15. Boyd, *North Carolina*, II, 332.

16. *Greensborough Patriot*, May 13, 1835.
17. *Ibid.*, October 31, 1832.
18. *Ibid.*, November 30, 1831.
19. *Ibid.*, October 17, 1829.
20. *Ibid.*, November 7, 1832.
21. *Ibid.*, November 28, 1832.
22. *Ibid.*, March 3, 1830.
23. *Ibid.*, December 12, 1832.
24. *Ibid.*, November 30, 1831.
25. *Ibid.*, July 4, 1829.
26. *Ibid.*, July 19, 1834.
27. Ashe, *North Carolina*, II, 387.
28. *Greensborough Patriot*, July 25, 1829.
29. *Ibid.*, June 20, 1829.
30. Lefler, *North Carolina*, 371.
31. *Greensborough Patriot*, May 23, 1829.
32. *Ibid.*, June 13, 1829.
33. Boyd, *North Carolina*, II, 341.
34. Lefler, *North Carolina*, 372; *Greensborough Patriot*, March 17, 1830.
35. *Greensborough Patriot*, May 12, 1830.
36. *Ibid.*, August 8, 1829.
37. *Ibid.*, July 28, 1830.

## VII.    FOR INDUSTRIAL DEVELOPMENT

1. *Greensborough Patriot*, October 17, 1829.
2. *Ibid.*, June 13, 1835.
3. Tench Coxe, *A View of the United States of America*, 298.
4. *Ibid.*, 274.
5. Tench Coxe, *A Statement of the Arts and Manufactures of the United States for the Year 1810*, 4, 130.
6. Boyd, *North Carolina*, II, 84.
7. Lefler, *North Carolina*, 301.
8. *Greensborough Patriot*, June 30, 1830.
9. *Laws of the State of North Carolina, 1823-1824*, 11; 1828-1829, 24.
10. Diffee W. Standard and Richard W. Griffin, "The Cotton Textile

Industry in Ante-Bellum North Carolina," *The North Carolina Historical Review*, January, 1957, 29.

11. *Ibid.*, April, 1957, 133.

12. Ethel Stephens Arnett, *Greensboro, North Carolina: The County Seat of Guilford*, 165-167.

13. Diffee W. Standard and Richard W. Griffin, 'The Cotton Textile Industry in Ante-Bellum North Carolina," *The North Carolina Historical Review*, January, 1957, 33.

14. *Greensborough Patriot*, May 30, 1829.

15. Henry W. Grady, "The South and Her Problems," *The Complete Orations and Speeches of Henry W. Grady*, edited by Edwin D. Shurter, 50-52, 63-64.

16. *Greensborough Patriot*, June 1, 1831.

17. *Ibid.*, October 10, 1829.

18. *Ibid.*

19. Charles A. & Mary R. Beard, *The Beards' Basic History of the United States*, 252.

20. Harry J. Carman and Samuel McKee, Jr., *A History of the United States*, I, 530-531.

21. *Greensborough Patriot*, May 23, 1829; May 30, 1829; September 12, 1829; October 10, 1829. Although Swaim expressed views at various times in keeping with the American system, he did not mention all of that plan in a single issue. For a clear outline of the American system, see Clement Eaton, *Henry Clay and the Art of American Politics*, 46.

22. *Greensborough Patriot*, May 30, 1829; Harry J. Carman and Samuel McKee, Jr., *A History of the United States*, I, 528, 532.

23. *Greensborough Patriot*, May 30, 1829.

24. *Ibid.*

25. *Ibid.*, July 4, 1829.

26. *Ibid.*, October 17, 1829.

27. *Ibid.*

28. *Ibid.*, May 15, 1833.

29. *Ibid.*

30. *Ibid.*, August 22, 1832.

31. *Ibid.*

32. *Enclopædia Britannica*, Fourteenth Edition, Vol. 22, 491.

33. *Greensborough Patriot*, October 17, 1832.

34. *Ibid.*, November 21, 1832.

35. *Ibid.*, December 12, 1832; January 30, 1833.

36. *Ibid.*, December 26, 1832.

37. *Ibid.*, December 26, 1832; January 9, 1833.

38. *Ibid.*, July 7, 1830.

39. *Ibid.*

40. *Ibid.*

41. *Ibid.*, February 28, 1833.

42. *Ibid.*

43. *Ibid.*

44. Diffee W. Standard and Richard W. Griffin, "The Cotton Textile Industry in Ante-Bellum North Carolina," *The North Carolina Historical Review*, January, 1957, 27.

45. Sallie W. Stockard, *The History of Guilford County, North Carolina,* 64.

46. *Greensborough Patriot,* December 5, 1832.

47. *Ibid.*, December 12, 1832.

48. *Ibid.*, May 15, 1833.

49. Addison Coffin, "Early Settlements of Friends in North Carolina," Guilford College Library.

50. Murrow, interview.

51. *Greensborough Patriot,* July 11, 1829.

52. *Ibid,* December 19, 1829.

53. *Ibid.*, April 18, 1835.

54. *Ibid.*, October 17, 1829.

55. *Ibid.*, January 6, 1830.

56. *Ibid.*, October 17, 1829.

57. *Ibid.*, August 2, 1834.

58. *Ibid.*, February 23, 1831; May 29, 1833; April 22, 1835; April 11, 1835; July 26, 1834.

59. *Ibid.*, June 6, 1832.

60. Ethel Stephens Arnett, *Greensboro, North Carolina: The County Seat of Guilford,* Chapters 4, 5, 6, 7, 8, and 9.

61. *Ibid.*, 20.

62. *Greensborough Patriot,* February 2, 1831.

63. Mrs. Thomas Sherwood, granddaughter-in-law of the original owner M. S. Sherwood, as told to Mrs. Nellie Rowe Jones, Librarian (1920-1949), Greensboro Public Library.

64. Scott, *The Life.*

65. *Ibid.*

66. Minutes of the Town of Greensboro, 1829-1843, in the vault of the Greensboro Public Library.

67. *Ibid.*

68. *Greensborough Patriot,* beginning March 10, 1830.

69. *Ibid.,* February 13, 1833; Minutes of the Town of Greensboro, 1829-1843, vault of Greensboro Public Library.

70. Ethel Stephens Arnett, *Greensboro, North Carolina: The County Seat of Guilford,* 29.

71. Minutes of The Town of Greensboro, 1829-1843.

72. *Ibid.*

73. *Ibid.*

74. *Ibid.*

75. *Greensborough Patriot,* December 26, 1832.

76. *Ibid.,* May 29, 1833.

77. Thomas J. Shaw, Jr., "Greensboro Visitor 100 Years Ago was Impressed with Climate, Some People," *Greensboro Daily News,* February 19, 1939, in which he quoted a report of Anne Royall to the *Washington Post,* February 21, 1830.

## VIII.   FOR IMPROVED TRANSPORTATION

1. *Greensborough Patriot,* August 15, 1832.

2. Lefler, *North Carolina,* 314.

3. Boyd, *North Carolina,* II, 92n.

4. Lefler, *North Carolina,* 316.

5. Boyd, *North Carolina,* II, 93-94.

6. *Ibid.,* 94-95.

7. *Ibid.,* 97; and Lefler, *North Carolina,* 317.

8. *Ibid.,* 98.

9. Lefler, *North Carolina,* 319.

10. *Greensborough Patriot,* November 7, 1829.

11. *Greensborough Patriot,* July 25, 1829; September 19, 1829.

12. *Ibid.,* July 18, 1829.

13. *Ibid.,* November 28, 1829.

14. *Ibid.*

15. *Ibid.,* December 30, 1829.

16. *Ibid.*, January 23, 1833.

17. *Ibid.*, February 13, 1833.

18. Dr. Joseph Caldwell, *The Numbers of Carlton, Addressed to the People of North Carolina, on a Central Railroad thru the State,* Chapter IV.

19. *Greensborough Patriot,* July 25, 1829.

20. *Ibid.*, October 1, 1834.

21. *Ibid.*

22. *Ibid.*, April 24, 1833.

23. *Ibid.*, April 10, 1833.

24. *Ibid.*, July 8, 1835.

25. *Ibid.*, December 15, 1830. Jesse A. Bynum of Halifax County was a member of the House of Commons in 1829 and 1830.

26. *Ibid.*, January 27, 1830.

27. Scott, *The Life,* quoting from the *Greensborough Patriot.*

28. Scott, *The Life.*

29. *Greensborough Patriot,* January 12, 1831.

30. *Ibid.*

31. *Ibid.*

32. *Ibid.*, August 15, 1832.

33. *People's Press,* quoted in *Greensborough Patriot,* May 15, 1833.

34. *Greensborough Patriot,* May 15, 1833.

35. *Ibid.*, August 13, 1834.

36. *Ibid.*, July 14, 1834.

37. Boyd, *North Carolina,* II, 99.

38. *Greensborough Patriot,* October 8, 1834.

39. *Ibid.*, August 20, 1834.

40. *Ibid.*, November 26, 1834.

41. *Ibid.*, August 13, 1834; September 3, 1834.

42. Lyndon Swaim, "The Greensboro Patriot," *Greensboro Patriot,* about 1880; Scott, *The Life.*

43. *Ibid.*, October 8, 1834.

## IX.   FOR SOUND BANKING AND CURRENCY

1. *Greensborough Patriot,* November 14, 1829.

2. Broadus Mitchell and Louise Pearson Mitchell, *American Economic History,* 376.

3. *Greensborough Patriot*, August 1, 8, 1832.

4. *Ibid.*, May 23, 1829.

5. Joseph B. Cheshire, *Nonnulla*, 72.

6. *The Patriot and Greensborough Palladium*, January 17, 1829.

7. *Ibid.*

8. *Ibid.*

9. *Ibid;* also see Boyd, *North Carolina*, II, 122-128.

10. *The Patriot and Greensborough Palladium*, January 17, 1829.

11. *Journals of the Senate and House of Commons of the General Assembly, 1828-1829.*

12. Jonathan Parker, "Address to the Freemen of Guilford County," *Greensborough Patriot*, May 23, 1829.

13. *Greensborough Patriot*, February 3, 1830.

14. *Ibid.*, November 14, 1829.

15. *Ibid.*

16. *Ibid.*

17. *Ibid.*

18. *Ibid.*

19. *Ibid.*, January 6, 1830.

20. *Ibid.*, May 19, 1830.

21. *Ibid.*, January 20, 1830.

22. *Ibid.*, May 23, 1829; December 5, 1832; February 13, 1833; *Raleigh Register*, December 30, 1830.

23. *Ibid.*, August 2, 1834.

24. *Ibid.*, November 21, 1832.

25. *Ibid.*, December 5, 1832.

26. *Ibid.*, February 28, 1833.

27. *Ibid.*, May 22, 1833.

28. *Laws of the State of North Carolina, 1833-1834;* Ashe, *North Carolina*, II, 359.

29. *Greensborough Patriot*, February 22, 1834.

30. Charles A. & Mary R. Beard, *The Beards' Basic History of the United States*, 254.

31. *Greensborough Patriot*, January 20, 1830.

32. *Ibid.*, November 26, 1831.

33. *Raleigh Register*, quoted in the *Greensborough Patriot*, March 13, 1833.

34. *Greensborough Patriot,* August 8, 1832.

35. *Ibid.,* December 26, 1832.

36. *Ibid.,* July 25, 1832.

37. *Ibid.,* August 1, 1832.

38. *Ibid.,* September 5, 1832.

39. *Ibid.,* August 22, 1832.

40. *Ibid.,* April 3, 1833.

41. *Ibid.,* October 30, 1833.

42. *Ibid.,* December 12, 1832; March 26, 1834.

## X.  FOR SOCIAL JUSTICE

1. Thomas Jefferson, quoted in the *Greensborough Patriot,* February 24, 1830.

2. *Greensborough Patriot,* May 23, 1829.

3. *Minutes of the N. C. Manumission Society,* 18.

4. John Spencer Bassett, *Slavery in the State of North Carolina,* 104-105.

5. Stephen B. Weeks, *Southern Quakers and Slavery,* 240.

6. *Greensborough Patriot,* July 25, 1829.

7. R. D. W. Connor, *North Carolina, Rebuilding an Ancient Commonwealth,1584-1925,* I, 607.

8. Boyd, *North Carolina,* II, 207.

9. Scott, *The Life.*

10. *Greensborough Patriot,* September 12, 1829, POLYDORE, "North Carolina, No. III"

11. *Ibid.,* May 30, 1829.

12. *Ibid.*

13. *Ibid.,* July 18, 1829.

14. *Ibid.*

15. *Ibid.,* August 1, 1829.

16. *Ibid.,* January 27, 1830.

17. Levi Coffin, *Reminiscences of Levi Coffin,* 73-74.

18. *Greensborough Patriot,* April 25, 1835.

19. *Ibid.,* September 5, 1829; November 19, 1834.

20. *Ibid.,* January 6, 1830; January 2, 1833.

21. *Ibid.,* January 20, 1830; January 19, 1831; June 1, 1831; September 5, 1832.

22. *Ibid.,* October 31, 1829.

23. *Washington City Chronicle,* quoted in *Greensborough Patriot,* January 27, 1830.

24. *Greensborough Patriot,* June 12, 1833.

25. John Spencer Bassett, *Anti-Slavery Leaders of North Carolina,* 51.

26. *Minutes of the N. C. Manumission Society,* 97-98, 113, 138, 204.

27. *Greensborough Patriot,* August 22, 1829.

28. *Minutes of the N. C. Manumission Society,* 78, 150, 175-179, 205.

29. *Greensborough Patriot,* August 22, 1829.

30. Benjamin Lundy, *The Life, Travels and Opinions of Benjamin Lundy,* 306-307.

31. *Ibid.,* 266.

32. *Greensborough Patriot,* May 30, 1829; June 17, 1835.

33. *Ibid.,* May 5, 1830.

34. *Minutes of the N. C. Manumission Society,* 179.

35. *Ibid.,* 180.

36. *Ibid.,* and report received, 188.

37. C. Alphonso Smith, *O. Henry Biography,* 21; John Spencer Bassett, *Anti-Slavery Leaders of North Carolina,* 51.

38. C. Alphonso Smith, *O. Henry Biography,* 22.

39. William Swaim, *An Address to the People of North Carolina, on the Evils of Slavery.* Copies of both the first and second editions are in the Library of the University of North Carolina.

40. *Minutes of the N. C. Manumission Society,* 193-195.

41. *Laws of the State of North Carolina,* Session of 1830-1831.

42. Boyd, *North Carolina,* II, 218.

43. Levi Coffin, *Reminiscences of Levi Coffin,* 69-70.

44. Sallie W. Stockard, *The History of Guilford County, North Carolina,* 58-60.

45. *Greensborough Patriot,* February 16, 1831.

46. *Ibid.*

47. *Ibid.,* February 23, 1831.

48. *Western Carolinian,* January 25, 1831.

49. *Laws of the State of North Carolina,* 1830-1831..

50. Boyd, *North Carolina,* II, 218-220.

51. *Boston Courier,* quoted in *Greensborough Patriot,* November 5, 1831.

52. *Greensborough Patriot,* April 11, 1832; Arthur M. Schlesinger, Jr., *The Age of Jackson,* 190.

53. *Ibid.,* December 12, 1832; *Laws of the State of North Caroolina, 1831-1832,* 7.

54. *Minutes of the N. C. Manumission Society,* 207.

55. *Greensborough Patriot,* March 20, 1833.

56. *Ibid.,* June 17, 1835.

57. *Minutes of the N. C. Manumission Society,* 101, 168; Murrow, interview; *Greensborough Patriot,* August 1, 1829

58. John Spencer Bassett, *Anti-Slavery Leaders of North Carolina,* 9-10.

59. *Greensborough Patriot,* May 23, 1829.

60. *Ibid.,* August 15, 1829.

61. *Ibid.,* March 31, 1830.

62. *Ibid.,* January 6, 1830.

63. *Greensborough Patriot,* March 24, 1830.

64. R. D. W. Connor, *North Carolina, Rebuilding an Ancient Commonwealth, 1584-1925,* II, 16.

65. *Greensborough Patriot,* March 17, 1830.

66. *Ibid.,* October 31, 1829.

67. Guion G. Johnson, *Ante-Bellum North Carolina,* 645, 651, 652.

68. *Greensborough Patriot,* November 14, 1829.

69. *Ibid.,* December 5, 1829; January 13, 1830.

## XI.  FOR CLEAN POLITICS

1. *Greensborough Patriot,* July 4, 1829.

2. Lefler, *North Carolina,* 336.

3. Lyndon Swaim, "The Greensboro Patriot," in the *Greensboro Patriot* about 1880, clipping file of Greensboro Public Library.

4. Lefler, *North Carolina,* 342.

5. *Ibid.,* 355.

6. *Ibid.,* 342-355, 606.

7. *Ibid.,* 358-359, 361.

8. *Greensborough Patriot,* November 12, 1834.

9. *Ibid.,* March 9, 1831.

10. *Ibid.,* December 5, 1832.

11. *Ibid.,* January 9, 1833.

12. *Ibid.*, October 30, 1833.

13. *Ibid.*

14. *Ibid.*, January 1, 1834.

15. *Ibid.*, January 16, 1833.

16. *Ibid.*, November 19, 1834.

17. *Ibid.*, August 29, 1832.

18. *Ibid.*, March 26, 1834.

19. *Ibid.*, July 14, 1834.

20. *Ibid.*, May 12, 1830.

21. *Ibid.*, May 5, 1830.

22. *Ibid.*, May 12, 1830.

23. *Ibid.*, July 7, 1830.

24. *Ibid.*, August 1, 1832; December 29, 1834; May 6, 1835.

25. *Ibid.*, November 26, 1834.

26. *Ibid.*, quoted in Scott, *The Life*.

27. *Ibid.*, January 7, 1835.

28. *Ibid.*, January 14, 1835.

29. *Ibid.*

30. *Ibid.*, January 7, 1835.

31. Boyd, *North Carolina*, II, 151-153.

32. State newspapers of this time reviewed, North Carolina State Library in Raleigh; Library of the University of North Carolina in Chapel Hill; Library of Duke University at Durham.

33. *Greensborough Patriot*, June 6, 1832; June 27, 1832; July 18, 1832; May 15, 1833.

34. *Ibid.*, July 18, 1832.

35. *Ibid.*

36. *Ibid.*, August 1, 1832.

37. *Raleigh Register*, November 10, 1831.

38. *Greensborough Patriot*, December 5, 1832.

39. *Ibid.*, January 23, 1833; Boyd, *North Carolina*, II, 155.

40. *Ibid.*, June 12, 1833.

41. Boyd, *North Carolina*, II, 155. Thirty-one western counties voted on it.

42. *Greensborough Patriot*, August 13, 1834.

43. *Ibid.*, September 3, 1834, quoting the *Carolina Watchman*.

44. *Ibid.,* December 3, 1834.

45. North Carolina *Journals of the Senate and House of Commons, Sessions 1834-35,* 99-100; *Greensborough Patriot,* January 7, 1835.

46. *Greensborough Patriot,* January 14, 1835.

47. Boyd, *North Carolina,* II, 157.

48. Burton A. Konkle, *John Motley Morehead and the Development of North Carolina, 1796-1866,* 170.

49. Lefler, *North Carolina,* 336.

50. North Carolina *Journals of the Senate and House of Commons, Session 1834-35,* 99-100, 102-104, 123, 242-244, 252-253; Ashe, *North Carolina,* II, 366-367.

51. *Greensborough Patriot,* January, February, March, 1835.

52. *Greensborough Patriot,* January 14, 1835.

53. *Ibid.,* February 4, 1835.

54. *Ibid.*

55. *Ibid.,* February 18, 1835; March 25, 1835.

56. *Ibid.,* February 4, 1835.

57. *Ibid.,* February 18, 1835.

58. *Ibid.,* February 25, 1835.

59. *Ibid.,* February 11, 1835.

60. *Ibid.*

61. *Ibid.,* April 22, 1835.

62. *Ibid.,* February 18, 1835.

63. *Ibid.,* February 11, 25, 1835; March 4, 1835.

64. *Ibid.*

65. *Ibid.,* May 13, 1835.

66. Lefler, *North Carolina,* 338.

67. *Ibid.,* 337-338.

68. *Greensborough Patriot,* March 10, 1830.

69. *Ibid.,* April 7, 1830.

70. *The Autobiography of Sam Houston,* edited by Donald Day and Harry H. Ullom, 66-71.

71. *Ibid.,* 71.

72. *Greensborough Patriot,* May 30, 1832; June 6, 1832; July 18, 1832.

73. *Ibid.,* September 12, 1832.

74. *Ibid.,* May 5, 1830.

75. *Ibid.*, August 1, 1829.

76. *Ibid.*, December 19, 1829.

77. *Ibid.*, May 30, 1829; June 6, 1829; December 19, 1829.

78. *Ibid.*, August 22, 1829.

79. *Ibid.*, June 6, 1829.

80. *Ibid.*, September 12, 1832. This announcement had probably appeared earlier, for the committee had met before this time.

81. *Ibid.*, June 13, 1832.

82. *Ibid.*, December 26, 1832.

83. *Ibid.*, September 19, 1829; April 6, 1831.

84. *Ibid.*, September 5, 1829; Ashe, North Carolina, II, 364-365.

85. *Ibid.*, August 25, 1830.

86. *Ibid.*

87. *Ibid.*, August 22, 1829.

88. *Ibid.*, August 25, 1830.

89. *Ibid.*

90. *Ibid.*

91. *Ibid.*

92. *Ibid.*

93. *Ibid.*, June 13, 1835.

94. *Ibid.*, May 23, 1829.

## XII.     FOR FREEDOM OF THE PRESS

1. *Greensborough Patriot,* April 6 and June 1, 1831; June 6, 1832.

2. *Ibid.*, April 6, 1831.

3. Gerald W. Johnson, *Peril and Promise,* 28.

4. *Greensborough Patriot,* July 4, 1829; August 25, 1830; June 5, 1833.

5. *Ibid.*, November 30, 1831.

6. *Ibid.*, March 2, 1831.

7. *Ibid.*, June 6, 1829.

8. *Ibid.*

9. *Ibid.*, June 27, 1829.

10. *Ibid.*, February 3, 1830; Scott, *The Life.*

11. *Minutes of the N. C. Manumission Society,* 196; Scott, *The Life.*

12. *Greensborough Patriot,* March 17, 1830.

13. *Ibid.*

14. *Ibid.,* May 6, 1835.

15. *Ibid.,* November 11, 1835.

16. *Ibid.,* July 7, 1830.

17. *Raleigh Register,* November 10, 1831.

18. *Greensborough Patriot,* March 26, 1834.

19. Dillard S. Gardner, Marshal-Librarian, State of North Carolina, Supreme Court Library, letter to Mrs. Ethel S. Arnett, January 26, 1959.

20. *Greensborough Patriot,* December 15, 1830.

21. *Ibid.*

22. *Ibid.*

23. *Greensborough Patriot,* September 19, 1829.

24. *Journals of the Senate and House of Commons, Session 1830-1831.*

25. *Greensborough Patriot,* January 12, 1831.

26. *Ibid.,* January 19, 1831.

27. Benjamin Lundy, *The Life, Travels and Opinions of Benjamin Lundy,* 256.

28. Joseph B. Cheshire, *Nonnulla,* 75-76.

29. *Ibid.,* 76.

30. *Greensborough Patriot,* September 25, 1833.

31. *Ibid.,* March 26, 1834.

32. *Ibid.,* May 28, 1834.

33. Daniel M. McFarland, "North Carolina Newspapers, Editors and Journalistic Politics, 1815-1835," *The North Carolina Historical Review,* July, 1953, 388.

34. *Greensborough Patriot,* November 12, 1834.

35. *Ibid.,* December 24, 1834.

36. *Ibid.,* October 1, 1834.

37. *Ibid.,* July 26, 1834.

38. *Ibid.,* January 23, 1833.

39. Thomas J. Shaw, Jr., "Greensboro Visitor 100 Years Ago Was Impressed With Climate, Some People," *Greensboro Daily News,* February 19, 1939.

40. *Danville Reporter,* quoted in *Greensborough Patriot,* February 4, 1835.

## XIII.  FINANCING A FAMILY AND A NEWSPAPER

1. *Greensborough Patriot*, January 27, 1830.

2. *Ibid.*, January 13, 1830.

3. *Ibid.*

4. *Ibid.*, September 26, 1829.

5. *Ibid.*

6. *Ibid.*, June 6, 1829.

7. *Ibid.*, July 18, 1829.

8. *Ibid.*

9. *Ibid.*, April 28, 1830.

10. *Ibid.*, October 10, 1829.

11. *Ibid.*, December 5, 1829; January 27, 1830.

12. *Ibid.*, January 27, 1830.

13. *Ibid.*, September 29, 1830.

14. *Ibid.*, *June* 5, 1833. In connection with the growth of Swaim's business which enabled him to buy a horse and a gig, perhaps it should be noted that Scott referred to the gig as a "sulky," but sulky seems to have been the local name used for all two-wheeled vehicles.

15. New York *Morning Courier and New York Enquirer*, May 25, 1829.

16. *Greensborough Patriot*, June 5, 1833.

17. *The Patriot and Greensborough Palladium*, April 4, 1829.

18. Minutes of the Town of Greensborough, 1829-1843, vault of the Greensboro Public Library.

19. Court Records, Guilford County, 1830's.

20. *Greensborough Patriot*, April 28, 1830.

21. *Ibid.*, January 30, 1833.

22. *Ibid.*, March 6, 1833.

23. *Ibid.*, March 13, 1833.

24. *Ibid.*, May 5, 1830.

25. *Ibid.*, September 19, 1832.

26. Register of Deeds, Guilford County, Book 19, 490-491.

27. *Greensborough Patriot*, June 30, 1830.

28. *Ibid.*, June 13, 1829.

29. *Ibid.*, April 14, 1830.

30. *Ibid.*, August 29, 1832.

31. *Ibid.*, November 12, 1834; December 10, 1834.

32. *Ibid.*, October 3, 1832.

33. *Ibid.*, April 28, 1830.

34. *Ibid.*, October 17, 1829; April 14, 1830.

35. *Ibid.*, August 29, 1832.

36. Register of Deeds, Guilford County, Book 19, 254, Book 21, 178, 300, 335, 368; Minutes of Guilford County Court, 1832-1837, August term, 1834.

37. *Ibid.*, Book 21, 335.

38. *Ibid.*, see note 36 above.

39. *Ibid.*, Book 20, 138.

40. Scott, *The Life.*

41. *Greensborough Patriot*, October 8, 1834; October 10, 1835.

42. Minutes of the Town of Greensborough, 1829-1843; Guilford County Records, Division of Wills, showing Swaim owed about $500 and about $500 was owed to him at death. His administrator was able to collect enough to strike a balance.

43. *Greensborough Patriot*, August 29, 1832; September 5, 1832; November 5, 1834, and several issues thereafter.

44. Guion G. Johnson, *Ante-Bellum North Carolina*, 769.

45. *Greensborough Patriot*, August 29, 1832.

46. *Ibid.*, June 5, 1833.

47. *Ibid.*, November 19, 1834.

48. *Ibid.*, March 18, 1835.

49. *Ibid.*, December 24, 1834.

50. *Ibid.*

51. *Ibid.*, October 8, 1834.

52. *Ibid.*, December 24, 1834.

53. *Ibid.*, February 11, 1835.

54. *Ibid.*

55. *Ibid.*, April 4, 1835.

56. *Ibid.*, December 24, 1834.

57. *Ibid.*

58. *Ibid.*, January 21, 1835.

59. *Ibid.*, February 25, 1835.

60. *Ibid.*, March 18, 1835.

61. *Ibid.*, April 1 and 4, 1835.

62. Guion G. Johnson, *Ante-Bellum North Carolina*, 795, 795n; *The North Carolina Historical Review*, July, 1953, 389; *Raleigh Register & North Carolina Gazette*, February 16, 1836.

## XIV. "'TIS DEATH IS DEAD, NOT HE"

1. Chapter title, "Adonais," by Percy Bysshe Shelley, line 361; quotation, *Newbern Spectator*, January 15, 1836.

2. Will L. Scott, *The Life of William Swaim, Former Editor of the Greensboro Patriot*, *Greensboro Patriot*, May 18-June 22, 1866.

3. *Greensborough Patriot*, June 5, 1833; July 8, 1835.

4. Scott, *The Life*.

5. *Ibid.*

6. *Charlotte Journal*, January 15, 1836.

7. *Raleigh Register*, January 12, 1836; Raleigh *Star*, January 14, 1836.

8. Fayetteville *Carolina Observer*, January 14, 1836.

9. *Newbern Spectator*, January 15, 1836.

10. *Ibid.*, February 5, 1836.

11. Abiah Swaim's Bible, locked case, O. Henry Room, Greensboro Public Library.

# BIBLIOGRAPHY

## BOOKS

Arnett, Ethel Stephens, *Greensboro, North Carolina: The County Seat of Guilford*, written under the direction of Walter Clinton Jackson. Chapel Hill, The University of North Carolina Press, 1955.
——————————, *O. Henry from Polecat Creek*. Greensboro, Piedmont Press, 1962.
Ashe, Samuel A., *History of North Carolina*, II. Raleigh, Edwards & Broughton, 1925.

Bassett, John Spencer, *Slavery and Servitude in the Colony of North Carolina*. Baltimore, The Johns Hopkins Press, 1896.
——————————, *Anti-Slavery leaders of North Carolina*. Baltimore, The Johns Hopkins Press, 1898.
——————————, *Slavery in the State of North Carolina*. Baltimore, The Johns Hopkins Press, 1899.
Beard, Charles A. & Mary R., *The Beards' Basic History of the United States*. Philadelphia, The Blakiston Company, 1944.
Blair, Joseph Addison, *Reminiscences of Randolph County*. Greensboro, Reece & Elam, Book and Job Printers, 1890.
Boyd, William K., *History of North Carolina*, II. Chicago, The Lewis Publishing Co., 1919.

Caldwell, Dr. Joseph, *The Numbers of Carlton, Addressed to the People of North Carolina, on a Central Railroad thru the State*. New York, G. Long, 1828.
——————————, *Letters on Popular Education, Addressed to the People of North Carolina*. Hillsborough, Printed by Dennis Heartt, 1832.
Carman, Harry J. and McKee, Samuel, Jr., *A History of the United States*, I. Boston, D. C. Health and Company, 1931.
Cartland, Fernando G., *Southern Heroes, The Friends in War Times*. Cambridge, Riverside Press, 1895.
Cheshire, Joseph B., *Nonnulla*. Chapel Hill, The University of North Carolina Press, 1930.
Coffin, Levi, *Reminiscences of Levi Coffin*. Cincinnati, Western Tract Company, 1876.
Coit, Margaret L., *John C. Calhoun, American Patriot*. Boston, Houghton Mifflin, 1950.
Connor, R. D. W., *North Carolina, Rebuilding an Ancient Commonwealth, 1584-1925*, I, II, VI, VII. Chicago, The American Historical Society, Inc., 1929.

388

Coon, Charles L., *The Beginnings of Public Education in North Carolina*, I, II. Raleigh, Edwards & Broughton, 1908.

Coxe, Tench, Editor, *A View of the United States of America*. Philadelphia, 1794.

————————————, Editor, *A Statement of the Arts and Manufacturers of the United States of America for the Year 1810*. Philadelphia, 1814.

Day, Donald & Ullom, Harry H., Editors, *The Autobiography of Sam Houston*. Norman, University of Oklahoma Press, 1947.

De Crevecoeur, J. Hector St. John, *Letters from an American Farmer*, written in 1782. New York, E. P. Dutton, 1912.

Dowd, Jerome, *Life of Braxton Craven, D.D., L.L.D.* Raleigh, Edwards & Broughton, 1896.

Eaton, Clement, *Freedom of Thought in the Old South*. Durham, Duke University Press, 1940.

————————————, *Henry Clay and the Art of American Politics*. Boston Little Brown, 1957.

*Encyclopædia Britannica*, Fourteenth Edition. New York, Encyclopædia Britannica, Incorporated, 1929.

Fries, Adelaide L., Editor, *Records of the Moravians in North Carolina, 1752-1775*, II. Raleigh, Edwards & Broughton Printing Company, 1925.

Grady, Henry W., *The Complete Orations and Speeches of Henry W. Grady*, edited by Edwin D. Shurter. New York, Hinds, Noble & Eldridge, 1910.

Gabriel, Ralph Henry, *The Course of American Democratic Thought*. New York, The Ronald Press Company, 1940.

Hamilton, J. G. DeRoulhac, Editor, *The Correspondence of Jonathan Worth*. Raleigh, Edwards & Broughton Printing Company, 1909.

Henderson, Archibald, *North Carolina, The Old North State and the New*, II. Chicago, The Lewis Publishing Company, 1941.

Hinshaw, William Wade, *Encyclopedia of American Quaker Genealogy*, I. Ann Arbor, Edwards Brothers, Inc., 1936.

*History of Centre Friends Meeting*, compiled and published by members of the Meeting.

Hoyt, William H., Editor, *The Papers of Archibald D. Murphey*. Raleigh, E. M. Uzzell & Co., State Printers, 1914.

Johnson, Gerald W., *Peril and Promise*. New York, Harper & Brothers, 1957.

Johnson, Guion Griffin, *Ante-Bellum North Carolina*. Chapel Hill, The University of North Carolina Press, 1937.

*Journals of the Senate & House of Commons, Session of 1830-1831*. Raleigh, Lawrence & Lemay, Printers to the State, 1831.

————————————, *Session of 1834-1835*. Raleigh, Philo White, Printer to the State, 1835.

389

BIBLIOGRAPHY

Konkle, Burton A., *John Motley Morehead and the Development of North Carolina, 1796-1866*. Philadelphia, William J. Campbell. 1922.

*Laws of the State of North Carolina*, 1823-1824. Raleigh, J. Gales & Son, State Printers, 1824.

————————————, 1828-1829. Raleigh, Lawrence & Lemay, Printers to the State, 1829.

————————————, 1830-1831. Raleigh, Lawrence & Lemay, Printers to the State, 1831.

————————————, 1831-1832. Raleigh, Lawrence & Lemay, Printers to the State, 1832.

————————————, 1834-1835. Raleigh, Philo White, Printer to the State, 1835.

Lefler, Hugh and Wagner, Paul, Editors, *Orange County 1752-1952*. Chapel Hill, 1953.

Lefler, Hugh T. and Newsome, Albert R., *North Carolina, the History of a Southern State*. Chapel Hill, University of North Carolina Press, 1954.

Lundy, Benjamin, *The Life, Travels and Opinions of Benjamin Lundy*, compiled under the direction, and on behalf of his children. Philadelphia, Published by William D. Parrish, 1847.

Martineau, Harriet, *Society in America*, I. London, Saunders and Otley, 1837.

Mitchell, Broadus and Louise Pearson, *American Economic History*. Boston, Houghton Mifflin, 1947.

*North Carolina Supreme Court Reports*, 1830-1836.

*Publications of the Guilford County Literary and Historical Association*, I Greensboro, Jos. J. Stone & Co., 1908.

Robins, Dr. Sidney Swaim, *A Letter on Robins Family History*. Asheboro, Durham Printing Company, nd.

Rogers, Joseph M., *The True Henry Clay*. Philadelphia, J. B. Lippincott, 1904.

Saunders, William L., Collector and Editor, *The Colonial Records of North Carolina*, I-X. Raleigh, Josephus Daniels, Printer to the State, 1887-1890.

Schlesinger, Arthur M., Jr., *The Age of Jackson*. Boston, Little, Brown and Company, 1945.

Scott, Will L., *The Life of William Swaim, Former Editor of The Greensboro Patriot*. Greensboro, Greensboro Patriot, 1866.

Shirley, Evelyn P., *Stemmata Shirleiana*. Westminster, Nichols and Sons, 1873.

Smith, C. Alphonso, *O. Henry Biography*. New York, Doubleday, Page & Company, 1918.

Stockard, Sallie W., *The History of Guilford County, North Carolina*. Knoxville, Gaut-Ogden Co., 1902.

*Story of Naomi Wise, The*, published by the Rotary Club, Randleman, North Carolina, 1944.

Swaim, William, *An Address to the People of North Carolina, on the Evils of Slavery.* Greensborough, William Swaim, Printer, 1830.

———————, *Diary.* Excerpts included in *The Life of William Swaim,* by Will L. Scott, *Greensboro Patriot,* May-June, 1866.

Wagstaff, H. M., Editor, *Minutes of the N. C. Manumission Society. 1816-1834.* Chapel Hill, The University of North Carolina Press, 1934.

Weeks, Stephen B., *Southern Quakers and Slavery.* Baltimore, The Johns Hopkins Press, 1896.

Wheeler, John H., *Historical Sketches of North Carolina.* Philadelphia, Lippincott, Grambo and Co., 1851.

Wiley, Calvin H., *Alamance Church, A Historical Address.*

Worth, Kathryn, *They Loved to Laugh.* Garden City, N. Y., Doubleday, Doran & Co., 1944.

## ARTICLES

McFarland, Daniel Miles, "North Carolina Newspapers, Editors, and Journalistic Politics, 1815-1835." *The North Carolina Historical Review,* July, 1953.

Shaw, Thomas J., Jr., "Greensboro Visitor 100 Years Ago Was Impressed with Climate, Some People." *Greensboro Daily News,* February 19, 1939.

Sherrill, P. M., "The Quakers and the North Carolina Manumission Society." *Historical Papers, Trinity College Historical Society,* Series X, 1914.

Standard, Diffee W. and Griffin, Richard W., "The Cotton Textile Industry in Ante-Bellum North Carolina." *The North Carolina Historical Review,* January 1957, April 1957.

Swaim, Lyndon, "The Greensboro Patriot." *Greensboro Patriot,* about 1880.

Weaver, C. C., "The North Carolina Manumission Society." *Historical Papers, The Historical Society of Trinity College,* Series I, 1897.

## UNPUBLISHED SOURCES

Anson County Register of Deeds, on microfilm in the North Carolina State Department of Archives and History.

Coffin, Addison, "Early Settlements of Friends in North Carolina," 1890.

Fleming, Nettie, "The Press of Guilford County," 1911.

Gardner, Dillard S., Marshal-Librarian, State of North Carolina Supreme Court Library, letter to Mrs. Ethel S. Arnett, 1959.

Guilford County Register of Deeds.

Lambert, Mrs. Sarah Trogden, Family Records.

McAlister, May, "Dr. David and Dr. Eunice Worth."

Minute Book of the Organized Town of Greensboro, 1829-1843.

Moffitt, Mrs. Elvira E., Genealogical Records.

Register of Deeds, Guilford County Courthouse.

Robins, Henry M., Robins Family Records.

State Records, Office of the North Carolina Secretary of State.

BIBLIOGRAPHY

# NEWSPAPERS AND PERIODICALS

Publications used only for various comparisons are not included in this list.

*Carolina Watchman*
*Charlotte Journal*
*Danville (Virginia) Reporter*
Fayetteville *Carolina Observer*
*Genius of Universal Emancipation, The*
*Greensboro Daily News*
*Greensborough Patriot*
*Hillsborough Recorder*
*Historical Papers, Historical Society of Trinity College*
*National Intelligencer*
*Newbern Spectator*
New York *Morning Courier and New York Enquirer*
*Niles' Weekly Register*
*North Carolina Historical Review, The*
*North Carolina Journal*
*Patriot and Greensborough Palladium, The*
*Raleigh Register*
Raleigh *Star*
*Roanoke Advocate*
Tarborough *North Carolina Free Press*
*Weekly Gleaner*
*Western Carolinian*

# INDEX